WOMEN IN ISLAMIC CULTURE AND SOCIETY
A Study of Family, Feminism and Franchise

WOMEN IN ISLAMIC CULTURE AND SOCIETY

A Study of Family, Feminism and Franchise

REHANA SIKRI

KANISHKA PUBLISHERS, DISTRIBUTORS
New Delhi–110 002

KANISHKA PUBLISHERS, DISTRIBUTORS
4697/5-21 A, Ansari Road, Daryaganj
New Delhi–110 002.
Phones: 327 0497, 328 8285
Fax: 91-328 8285 (Kanishka)

First Published 1999

ISBN 81-7391-268-8

PRINTED IN INDIA

Published by Madan Sachdeva for Kanishka Publishers, Distributors, 4697/5-21 A, Ansari Road, Daryaganj, New Delhi-110 002; Typeset by Baba DTP Services, Delhi, and Printed at Tarun Offset Printers Delhi.

Preface

The teachings and tenets of Islam and the Islamic way of life have had a purposive and definitional influence on most world cultures. The way of Islam being the way and path of purity, sacrifice and endeavour, the position and power of women in Islamic culture and society have been the subject of prolific amounts of analytical literature by both occidental and oriental sources of learning and research.

The present publication represents a modest attempt to profile the various critical issues that engender widespread debate and discussion in the context of women in Islamic culture and society: the subjects of marriage, divorce, succession, dower and custody of children. Particular focus is on women in non-Islamic society, with ample references drawn from Israel and environs. While the text provides illuminating reading and enlightenment for both student and scholar, the copious endnotes and references to various religious and legal or theological texts make the compilation focused and articulate. Of particular interest are the profile papers on women's participation in feminist and political activism in selected Islamic nations—Egypt, Turkey and Iran—and also the illuminating note on the mystic and *sufi* tradition among Muslim women. The present publication would hopefully be a welcome addition to the rather meagre literature in this vital area.

REHANA SIKRI

Contents

Contents

1

Status of Women: Asian Context

Sub-Regional Variation

In any study of women and their status in society, it is expected that certain clear-cut patterns would emerge, with traditions which could be attributed to patterns of subsistence and economic production from the land, settled, irrigated or swidden, and to the major religions and ethnic cultures. Studies have shown that Asia may be divided into 3 main regions in relation to the status of women, south Asia, southeast Asia and east Asia. In south Asia up to the border of Burma, women originally were respected by their husbands and by their society. They were educated before marriage, which occurred only after physical maturity. In early China too, women enjoyed an egalitarian position. But in south Asia and China, around 500 B.C. the position of women gradually deteriorated. Their subservient role to men became enshrined in India in the *Laws of Manu,* which took final form around the third to second centuries B.C., and in China in the tenets of Confucius which took shape progressively in the centuries after Confucius' death. Around the same time Buddhism arose, absorbing the prevalent atmosphere. It must be left to China scholars to determine to what extent women's position was already deemed to be inferior in Chinese civilization at that period, and how far the acceptance of Buddhism influenced Chinese norms.

Among the patrilineal majority in western and eastern monsoon Asia women had no rights to land or property; remarriage of widows was proscribed, and a woman who divorced lost access to her children. These customs remained so deeply entreached in society that more liberal faiths and modern legislation have done little to improve the lot of rural women. In southeast Asia, among tribal groups of south Asia and among some non-Han groups in China, woman have always enjoyed higher status in society, have been able in divorce and remarry, have retained rights to property and the right to raise their children.

The status of women has been attributed by many specialists, most notably Boserup (1970), to environmental conditions and the forms of agriculture that these permit. Undoubtedly, environment has played a part in determining the status of women in Asia.

Most of the forests which formerly covered the countries of the south Asian subcontinent and eastern China have been progressively cleared to provide land for settled crop cultivation, dryland or irrigated, leading to characteristic types of agrarian structure. Outside those parts of the region which were formerly covered by tropical or subtropical rapidly regenerating vegetation under high rainfall, it is difficult to conceive that even the most primitive forms of agriculture began on the basis of shifting cultivation, fertilized by ash from burnt tree cover. This applies to the north and northwest of south Asia, and to the non-monsoonal lands of northwest China, including the area until recently accepted as the nuclear zone of Chinese civilization. Women worked in the fields in these regions until the invention of the plough.

It is only relatively recently, within the last 100 or 200 years, that the forest cover of most of southeast Asia has been cleared, first for the establishment of plantations but more recently for widespread cultivation of padi. Up until then, there were small groups of hunters and gatherers, and early cultivators who practised swidden agriculture with mixtures of upland grain and other crops on limited areas of the vast forested lands; irrigated rice was grown only around larger centres of population in favourable areas of valley or lowland.

We have seen that it is in swidden groups that the status of women is high in both family and sometimes community matters. It is suggested, therefore, that the position of women in Asia has been largely ecologically determined (Table 1.1). The swiden way of life, with its respect for women in family, economic, community and religious affairs, her independence and freedom of action, is a comparatively recent cultural memory in equatorial and tropical Asia. If these favourable characteristics had existed under other primitive agrarian systems, they have long since been obliterated by centuries of settled agriculture, male ownership of land, patrilineal kinship and female subservience in south and east Asia.

Beyond this broad level of generalization, regarding the position of Asian women, it would be unwise to proceed. There is great variation of custom within country, culture and limited geographical areas. The choice of marriage partners traditional in one set of villages may be quite different from that adopted only a few miles away where mode of subsistence, ethnicity and culture are almost identical. Conflicting reports of behaviour are common, further complicated by class or caste differences. An educated observer from a capital city may have quite different conceptions of the norms of society from those of a foreigner who has lived for some time in a remote village. Observers in Malaysia have noted the importance of women in family decisions (see related section), but Hashimah Roose (1963) observed that women had no power over matters affecting the family as a whole.

The human geneticist, considering the prevalence of exogamy in north India and China, and of endogamy and cousin-marriage in south India and southeast Asia, will undoubtedly express concern at the degree of inbreeding which must occur in the 2 regions. There is a cumulative risk of mental and physical abnormalities and reduced resistance to disease among the progeny of succeeding generations. Anthropologists familiar with India often counter such arguments by claiming that cousin-marriage may be the preferred form, but it is in fact adopted less frequently than might be anticipated. Conclusions can be reached only by comparative study of the incidence of abnormalities and of disease in communities which have traditionally been exogamous

TABLE 1.1
Status of Women and Associated Ecological and Cultural Practices

Ecosystem	Predominant Method of Subsistence/ Cultivation	Role in Production	Kinship	Land Ownership	Choice of Partner	Status in	
						Family	Community
A. Tropical rain forest	Hunting and gathering	Equal importance	Bilateral	—	Free	High	High
B. Tropical rain forest	Swidden	Equal importance	Bilateral/ matrilineal	Customary usage rights	Free	High	High
C. Dry thorn forest or scrub, and dry deciduous forest	Hoe agriculture with long fallow	Equal importance	Patrilineal?/ matrilineal?	?	Free	High	High
D. Tropical rain forest, cleared	Padi cultivation: plough, broadcast/ transplanting	Equal importance	Bilateral/ matrilineal	Male and female owner-ship	Women have say	High	Lower
E. Tropical rain forest to monsoon forest, cleared	Padi cultivation: plough, transpla-nting/sowing	Equal importance	Patrilineal	Male	No say	Lower	Low
F. Tropical monsoon or subtemperate forest, cleared	Wheat/millets on dry or irrigated land. Plough and drill seeding.	Lesser role	Patrilineal	Male	No say	Lower	Low
G. As F.	As F.	Restricted by purdah to processing of crop	Patrilineal	Male	No say	Low	Low

Note: Density of population increases from ecosystem A to E and into F and G if crops are irrigated. Cereal cultivation on dryland with low rainfall is characterised by low population density.

and those which have long practised endogamy and marriage with close kin. This would involve investigations by a geneticist, a medical practitioner and an anthropologist.

A major factor of change in rural Asia is the reduction of available land for cultivation, bringing about constant modification of social relations within the group of kin with which a family relates, based upon what can be contributed in exchange of land and labour. Changes in cropping systems, whether from swidden to settled agriculture, dryland to irrigated cropping or the adoption of new cash crops or high-yielding, crop varieties, cause changes in social relations and often in the position of women within their families and in their communities. The family itself may disintegrate under the strains of extreme poverty, as revealed by higher proportions of female heads of household among lower socio-economic groups.

Some Measures of Improvement

It may be asked whether the lot of women has in fact improved at all over recent decades. Undoubtedly, life has improved for large numbers of women. Even if preference is still expressed among Chinese, Indian, Pakistani and Korean families for sons, for both religious and economic reasons, there is no longer female infanticide, nor the giving away of girls during times of acute distress. The adoption of daughters, to be brought up as future brides for sons among lower socio-economic groups unable to afford the cost of major marriage in Taiwan and China is no longer practised (Wolf, A., 1975; Wolf, M., 1975; Smith, 1899/1970). The mortality rate among girl infants and children in Taiwan was higher than that for boys, largely accounted for by deaths of adopted girls (Wolf, M., *loc. cit.*).

Costly medical care may still be sought more swiftly for a sick boy than for his sister, as neonatal death rates in India show—74 male, 76 female deaths per 1,000; in the 0 to 4 age group, 58 male and 70 female deaths (ICSSR, 1975). A study in Punjab showed the growth curves of female children were consistently below those of males, and morbidity was 2:1 female to male (Neumann, 1969). An Expert Committee of the Indian Council of Social Science Research has noted in a special memorandum to the government that the mortality rate for girls is from 30 to 60 per cent higher than that for boys. However, prosperity gained under the green revolution in a Rajput village in Uttar Pradesh has improved the quality of medical care for girls, and the sex ratio has improved from 66 per cent male/33 per cent female in 1954 to 55 per cent male/45 per cent female in the 1970's (Minturn, 1976). It seems likely that a study of the health of Asian females would provide a valuable indicator of their status within their families and socio-economic groups, but no systematic investigation has yet been undertaken.

Levels of literacy are slowly rising, especially in the countries of southeast Asia and eastern Asia where girls are likely to attend at least some years of primary school. In these same countries the age of marriage is also rising. In east Asia where a woman who left or was cast out from her husband's home lost access to her children and was often left destitute, she is today given protection, if she knows how to seek it. This is true also for the south Asian subcontinent, though the numbers involved are still very small. The situation of women in southeast Asia in these respects has never been so disadvantaged; they have commonly held property independently, have been able to divorce and take their children with them. In the People's Republic of China, women's rights were protected in the Marriage Act of 1950, but while divorce and remarriage are sanctioned, a woman still receives no share of the property for which she worked during the marriage, and still loses her sons to her husband's family (Parish and Whyte, 1978).

Superficially, it is easy to discern the continuity of tradition in rural Asia, since change is slower and less dramatic than in urban areas. Yet even where custom seems most entrenched, changes in women's attitudes over the past hundred years have been profound. A Bangladeshi woman whose husband was unable to work was able to overcome her fear of the stigma of abandoning purdah to work then financial problems had become overwhelming:

> I decided that I would take the only recourse left to me. I would find work and support my family. And so

> I did. I accepted any kind of work I could find just so long as it helped us to survive. I have not been able to send my children to school as before but there was nothing I could do about that . . . Perhaps some day . . . When I first heard of earthwork I was hesitant about going for it. I was not sure I would be able to do those long hours of arduous work. Look at me today. I cannot only do it but do it well. I earn enough wheat for my family's consumption. I even manage to save a little. It is not work that I am afraid of, but the lack of it (quoted by Chen and Chuznavi, 1977).

This is a far cry from the helplessness of a Chinese woman nearly a hundred years ago, who told Ida Pruitt (1945):

> Day after day I sat at home. Hunger gnawed. What could I do? My mother was dead. My brother had gone away. When my husband brought home food I ate it and my children ate with me. A woman could not go out of the court. If a woman went out to service the neighbours all laughed. They said "So and so's wife has gone out to service" . . . I did not know enough even to beg. So I sat at home and starved . . . How could I know what to do? We women knew nothing but to comb our hair and bind our feet and, wait at home for our men. When my mother had been hungry she had sat at home and waited for my father to bring her food, so when I was hungry I waited at home for my husband to bring me food.

Few Asian women today would remain so ineffective in the protection of themselves and their children. The change has been imperceptible, but real in those societies which are modernizing by means of evolution. In those which are modernizing by means of revolution, change has been dramatic, but tradition still remains significant.

Major Future Needs

Several studies have tried to examine the position of women in

Asian societies and in their own families. It has not been part of the brief to suggest how their lives might be improved. This is best done by people sharing their own culture, even though it has been seen that there is a severe shortage of female professionals in most countries. Only women are able to penetrate female society and gain the confidence and trust of rural women.

Certain conclusions appear to indicate the directions in which special efforts are needed to improve the lives of women. Legislation is not lacking in most countries for the protection of women in the fields of personal rights and in the labour market. Tradition still strongly affects the operation of these legal rights within the family, and the supply of and demand of labour affects the enforcement of laws relating to employment and equality of pay. It is clear that an educational thrust aimed at changing attitudes towards the sexual division of labour, however slow it may be to take effect, would do much to relieve women of the exhaustion characteristic of the double role performed by most within and outside the home. Adequate facilities for child care are a matter of vital concern to rural women obliged to work outside the home, but so far only the Communist countries have given systematic attention to this need. The National Committee on the Status of Women in India recommended that laws be revised to ensure the provision of child care services wherever 20 or more women are employed (the present minimum is 50). Such provision should also be made for casual or contract labour. It is admitted that even in the organized sector to which these laws apply at present, this regulation is inadequately observed. Poor working women have said that though they would prefer child care to be free, they would be prepared to pay (INCCU, 1977).

In many Asian countries there are significant proportions of women who are heads of households; these are in an especially vulnerable position, since rates of pay for women so often fall well below those of men.

Techniques of family planning are probably adequate to meet national requirements for fertility control; what is needed above all in most countries is more effective coverage—more clinics, more vehicles, which can travel to villages in which women have no time to leave their daily tasks, and more trained staff. There is still much to be learned of the motivation for accepting and continuing to practise contraception.

Education

Educational developments have tended to respond to social demand rather than to strategies for equal education. It has been recognized that in order to meet some of the shortcomings in educational systems, particularly as they affect girls, a more innovative approach is necessary (UNESCO, 1978a). Poverty is the chief obstacle to female education. Asian countries have devised a variety of measures to assist some of their most underprivileged groups. Malayasia offers a textbook loan scheme; India pays stipends to children of Scheduled Castes and Tribes to cover costs of attending school. Girls in remote areas of Nepal are given preference in the distribution of textbooks. Hostel accommodation has been started in Rajasthan, India and Nepal, to overcome parental resistance to their daughters' attending school and to avoid the cost of transport from remote areas. Inadequate numbers of female teachers in the rural areas of countries practising segregation are a great obstacle to female enrolment; Bangladesh has started a scheme to recruit local female teachers, providing free clothing, books, food and medical care.

Many children are quite simply beyond the reach of primary schools. This applies particularly to nomadic groups, and while no special measures have been taken in monsoonal Asia, the teachers of Afghanistan who travelled with the nomads, or the schools which were provided along the main routes of migration in Iran, may serve as models of what might be done. Some children of cattle herdsmen in Nepal are taught informally in their fields, though boys are more likely than girls to benefit. Elementary boarding schools have been started for the hill tribes of Thailand; 3 grades of primary school are available at medical posts in jungle areas for some of the children of Malaysia's tribal (Orang Asli) groups.

Non-formal programmes have been devised to give at least part-time education to Asian children who are unable to attend school regularly; Indonesia, the Philippines, India and Pakistan all have schemes in progress, characterized by flexible time schedules and short hours for girls fully involved in household chores, with curricula suited to community needs. The use of modern media to supplement local education facilities is expected to expand in the future (UNESCO, 1978a).

Nepal, with its high, remote areas and difficulties of access, presents particular problems in raising levels of female education. An innovative programme aimed at increasing the number of female teachers in rural areas began in 1970, with the help of UNESCO, UNICEF and the U.N. Development Programme (UNDP). Rural girls who have not completed school are recruited, hepled to complete secondary education and provided with teacher training at high schools with special hostel accommodations. Stipends, travel allowance, medical care, books and clothing are provided, although it is acknowledged that financial incentives cannot be regarded as a permanent measure. It is hoped that attitudes will gradually change to a point where parents will be willing to cover costs. Teachers trained in this way are expected to return to their own areas to teach. A mid-term evaluation of this project showed that there had been an increase in enrolment of girls in primary schools in all 8 districts surveyed, with the proportion of girls in the 40 schools where teachers trained under the scheme ranging from 14.2 to 43.8 per cent of total enrolment. At the same time the ratio of women teachers has also increased somewhat; the national average is 4 per cent, while within the areas served by the project the ratio ranges from 5.2 to 8.8 per cent (UNESCO, 1978c).

Opportunities for Supplementing Family Income

Perhaps the most important conclusion reached from this study is that agriculture is no longer able to offer a satisfactory standard of living to vast numbers of rural families, particularly the landless and those with small holdings (Whyte, 1982). This trend will continue ineluctably as the cultivated land capable of sustaining high-yielding crop varieties is fully utilized, as monocrop regions reach production plateaux—many have already done so—and, above all, as population growth makes progressively less land available per head with each succeeding generation.

The availability of non-farm employment near farms in Taiwan has been responsible for increased rural incomes, particularly of households owning less than 0.5 hectares. This has been a means of off-setting disparities in income between larger and smaller landholdings. Moreover, employment has provided capital for farm investment, further increasing productivity (Chinn, 1979).

Unless there is, throughout Asia, widespread development of rural industry to provide opportunities to the rural young now increasingly being educated away from their family setting, these young people will flock to the primate cities. Urban opportunities for employment are scarce, and living conditions less favourable than in the villages, where friendly neighbours and kin help both in bridging family crises and providing trusted companionship for daily tasks and leisure. Paradoxically, the outward flow of rural youth can give rise to labour shortages at peak seasons in the agricultural cycle.

We have seen that unemployment and underemployment are greater for women than for men. Men move out of agricultural employment more easily than women (Devadas, 1978; Palmer, 1978). Moreover, increasing the efficiency of agriculture has been widely shown to have adverse effects on the employment of women, due to the realignment of tasks in the sexual division of labour. Only now is it beginning to be realized that plans for development must have components aimed specifically at women, if women are to benefit from them. An ILO seminar on the status and role of women in the organized sector (1978) recommended the adoption of innovative types of approaches to female education to reach those who never get a chance to break away from the village milieu. Such education should aim at providing women with skills, leading to employment. In the labour-surplus countries of Asia, policies have to be geared to promoting opportunities for self-employment without reducing efforts to increase openings for wage-employment. Skills imparted must be of high quality, so that they are marketable. Organizations at district or state levels should take over co-ordination of both marketing and training in accounting and business skills, and in management and the provision of credit so that women entrepreneurs can set up their own businesses.

The proportions of women engaged in traditional rural industries in India are given by Devadas (1978), while suitable activities designed to increase the employment of women in rural areas are discussed by Dixon (1980).

It has been suggested that the upgrading of women's productive activities by the provision of income-generating employment outside the home may intervene in the cycle of rural poverty and high fertility characteristic of economically stagnant rural economies (Dixon, 1978). Eight prerequisites are proposed for such employment: women should have control over the income generated; jobs should be in villages and small towns; they should be outside agriculture; they should focus on small-scale, labour intensive light industries; work should be centrally located away from the home; jobs should attract only or primarily women in early reproductive years; production should be organized on principles of economic and social co-operation; additional social services and incentives should be provided.

In 1977, a project designed by T. Scarlett Epstein of the University of Sussex and Ranjit Senaratne of Sri Lanka initiated 8 micro-studies of the role of women in rural development, 2 each in Bangladesh, India, Sri Lanka and Pakistan. Studies covering different socio-economic strata aim at the eventual formulation of measures to include women in rural development and the training of local personnel in the introduction of appropriate technologies to increase both agricultural and non-agricultural activities.

Until the considerable technological and administrative changes such recommendations imply can be brought about on an adequate scale, there is a pressing need for the creation of jobs that women can do near or in their homes, and the organization of advice and channels for providing raw materials for rural handicrafts and their sale, such as has been attempted in Malaysia. Rural embroidery schools have been established in Pakistan to meet this need, though on a small scale so far. Women are more anxious to learn marketable skills than to acquire literacy (Khan and Bilquees, 1976), and this has given rise to the concept of training for "functional literacy" in Bangladesh. Small amounts of credit and training could help the promotion of cottage industries in Java in which the landless engage, although it is acknowledged that methods for doing this successfully are nowhere well understood. "If village handicraft products were more competitive price-wise in the urban markets, it would be a catalyst to small-scale industrial development" (Collier, 1978). The difficulties involved in organizing cottage industries, and ensuring that proceeds go to workers and not to middlemen, have led many to discount handicrafts as a means of supplementing family income. Workers in Bangladesh regard cottage industries as they now operate as "essentially non-productive" (McCarthy, Sabbah and Akhter, 1978a). Sewing groups in Sri Lanka have failed to arouse enthusiasm because they are not income-generating (Wijeratne, 1978).

Women in Thailand said they wanted to know more about nutrition, health family planning, better agricultural practices, improved animal husbandry, crafts and literacy. If training were to be limited to only one area, however, 31 per cent selected sewing instruction, 20 per cent training in better crop management and 19 per cent improved animal care. Only 9 per cent chose literacy training. The low esteem accorded handicrafts is attributed to the lack of a market for such products (Nantanee *et al.*, 1977).

Plans and Activities: National

A series of seminars was held in the states of the Indian Union to prepare a national analysis of current women's needs for presentation at the regional meeting of the Economic and Social Council in New Delhi. It was noted from the composition of delegations to these meetings that women's leaders in India continue to come from higher socio-economic groups. While participation in politics and trade union activities, improvements in health services and education were considered important by each state, employment opportunities for women are the most vital concern throughout the country (Awasty, 1979).

The Government of India planned the removal to rural areas of the manufacture of all products of village consumption which can be cheaply produced without sophisticated technology or costly infrastructure. Agricultural produce was also to be processed in rural areas. This is similar to the commune self-sufficiency which has long been attempted in China. It gives rise to a two-tier industrial structure, with quality control of sophisticated products in the large industrial centres, requiring transportation networks to the regional, national or international markets, and the manufacture of products for local consumption in the rural areas. Here quality may not be high, but it is hoped to keep costs lower and, above all, to create employment.

An Expert Committee of the Indian Council of Social Science Research addressed a memorandum to the government expressing its disquiet at recent trends in women's employment, and the "erosion of women's productive roles (which) emphasizes women's position primarily as consumers and bearers of children." The Committee has recommended that at least 25 per cent of investment and promotional activities in the small scale and cottage industries sectors, and public works and services in the trading and commercial sector be earmarked to increase economic opportunities for women. Stress is laid on extension services aimed at women, and on the need to train rural women (ICSSR, 1978). There are 218 small-scale units throughout the country giving training to women in handicrafts, handlooms, agro-units, small-scale industries and ancillary units to larger industries (INCCU, 1977). The scale of such operations needs greatly to be increased.

It has been recognized in the *Draft Five Year Plan 1978-1983* (India: Planning Commission, 1978a) that women have lost employment because of changes which have transferred jobs from homes and cottages to factories and machines, while family and community power structure prevents their seeking adequate education and outside employment. A policy for female employment recognizes that the need of the majority of women is for part-time or seasonal employment. It is hoped to expand and diversify training for women, and to stimulate occupations preferred by women, especially in food processing—grain-milling, oil crushing and the manufacture of dairy products; the spinning and weaving of textiles, the manufacture of coir and *bidi* products and domestic, laundry and sanitation services. In the allocation of co-operative and commercial bank credit and other aid (training, technical assistance, marketing facilities and hire/ purchase of machinery) a reasonable share is to be made available for potential women entrepreneurs and women's co-operatives employing a majority of women workers. Manpower budgeting of the female labour force is to be a component of all area development schemes. A Working Group of the Planning Commission will study all aspects of female employment, and sub-groups will deal with: existing programmes for women; the development of self-employment and entrepreneurship among women; and the development of cadres for promoting the employment of women.

Individual states in the Indian Union undertake activities to help women. The state government of Uttar Pradesh is setting up a training-cum-shelter workshop for destitute women of some hill areas in the Himalayan foothills. Grants-in-aid are given to poor women to purchase sewing, knitting and weaving machines. *Nari Niketans* are being established in 5 tribal blocks where 250 women and girls will be trained in gainful trades (Uttar Pradesh State Planning Department, 1977).

Proposals have been made for reinforcing Pakistan's Rural Development Programme, stressing the training of suitable women for leadership and developing special skills, and increasing opportunities for rural women to raise their earning ability, especially in food processing and rural agro-industries, as well as in small businesses (Rashid, 1977).

Considerable work is necessary on refining the implements used by women in agriculture, in processing and within the home. The installation of tubewells in Bangladesh has been enthusiastically welcomed, although it is not known whether this is because they facilitate work, because of the water is pure, or because they make the observation of purdah easier. Similarly, water-sealed latrines from the Comilla project are welcomed because increased population pressure makes seclusion in the fields more and more difficult (Abdulla, 1976).

It is found in Bangladesh that, despite the restrictions of purdah, women are willing to come to some central place for functional education classes, for mothers' clubs and paramedical services. Women will work and harvest a plot collectively with other women, and are willing to work in family planning and on functional education both within their own and other villages. Women walk miles to attend classes they see as useful, and will even travel outside their locality for training (Abdulla, *loc. cit.*). Women can be encouraged to design and implement development activities. Urban women can be induced to work in rural areas. Even relatively inexperienced women, given sufficient training, can plan, design, implement and monitor a development programme. Social constraints can be overcome if females work in pairs or teams. Women will leave their homes to attend meetings and will voice opinions. Some activities do not succeed: programmes which address welfare needs without economic or tangible benefit; programmes which do not take account of felt needs; imported or imposed ready-made programmes which do not evolve from the participants themselves; and programmes which do not take into account problems of training, supervision, management, procurement and marketing. The Bangladesh Institute of Education and Research is developing functional educational materials for their programmes (Abdulla, *loc. cit.*).

The Rubber Smallholders Development Authority of Malaysia (RISDA) has so far concentrated on improving agricultural practices and marketing, but has now realized that women need help in running their families and managing households on a low budget. Twenty-five field workers, themselves mostly from smallholder families, have been trained to advise women on the best use of their budgets for improved family nutrition, and to make suggestions on what can be produced by the women themselves.

The Malaysian Farmers Organization Authority (FAMA) is drawing up a new system of group farming, with special courses for rural women to show them how they may increase their incomes through group activities. Between 2 and 10 farmers are to cultivate 2 or 3 crops together, as well as rearing poultry and livestock. In 1977, 222 units of farmers' co-operatives carried out 331 group schemes of this kind.

Tengku Maziedah Khaulah Ahmad, director of women's activities at the Farmers Organization Authority (FAMA), states that women's participation has been steadily increasing since the department was founded in 1975. Guidebooks are distributed describing typical projects, but women themselves must take the initiative; they may submit a proposal to the FAMA for capital to start the project, but it is then expected to become self-sustaining. There are 1,000 agro-based co-operatives in Malaysia with a combined membership of over 300,000. Wives of farmers and fishermen engage in poultry-rearing co-operatives, cottage industries, tailoring and the making of kerepok (fish and tapioca crisps).

A long scheme designed by the Johore State Economic Development Corporation is aimed specifically at young, single girls from families which depend mostly on rubber and coconut for income, over 80 per cent of which is spent on food, with 10 per cent spent on education and the remainder on transport and clothing. Most girls have been educated up to Standard Six, although some possess a lower Certificate of Education. The main crop on the land scheme is oil palm, and each participant receives an allowance of M.$ 30 per month, plus an additional average of M.$ 20, depending on the price received at the time of sale of the crop. Men assist in harvesting the fruits and weeding. Accommodation, recreational and sporting facilities and classes in domestic science and religion are provided; there is a small town 2 miles away, and a larger one 17 miles distant. It may be difficult to maintain the emphasis on employment of women, however, since girls leave upon marriage; separate accommodations for couples are being constructed to counteract this. It may be asked whether schemes which include divorced women, requiring special child care facilities, might not meet a great need in Islamic southeast Asia.

The U.N. Asian and Pacific Centre for Women and Development has embarked on a project with the government of Thailand to train "multi-purpose field workers who can undertake activities in agriculture, nutrition, health/disease and public health" (UNAPCWD, 1978). Nine groups, each composed of 450 women from rural areas, have received four-month training courses in community development regional centres under a scheme devised by the Thai Government to teach women how most productively to use their time, with training in special skills in cottage industries, agriculture and nutrition (Vichai, 1978).

The Institute of Philippine Culture sought to design a programme to improve the situation of rural women in the Philippines on the basis of careful analysis of their present economic status and outlook in a sample region in the Bicol River Basin (Illo, 1977). Three different projects have been evolved, relating respectively to women with a wholly traditional role, those who occupy a more transitional position and the few non-traditional, career women. The first project stresses home and family management and the improvement of community services; the second stresses adult education and the training of women in skills likely to generate income; the last stresses skills at a higher level, including tasks generally performed by men, involvement in leadership and the setting up of day care centres.

A woman's leadership training course has been planned by the Korean Women's Institute of Ewha University, and the first course on women's studies began in autumn, 1977 (Kim, 1977). Under the *Saemaul Undong* village development schemes, villagers elect 2 leaders, one male, one female, to organize activities (Kim, 1978).

The Home-Living Improvement Section of the Ministry of Agriculture and Forestry, Japan, has, since 1948, been advising farm women on improved technology relating to clothing, food, housing and home management. Today there are over 2,000 female home advisers. These receive instruction at a central institute in Tokyo, which also provides refresher courses and a forum for experiments designed to further improve techniques. The functioning of this institute would be of great interest to those in other Asian countries responsible for instructuring rural women on better practices in and around the home.

Japan has taken the lead, in attempting to incorporate into national policy measures decisions by the World Conference of International Women's Year, by setting up the Headquarters for the Planning and Promoting of Policies Relating to Women, headed by the Prime Minister (Japan, 1977). It is seeking to clarify targets and formulate a plan of action.

International Activities

The period of 1976-1985 has been designated the U.N. Decade

for Women: Equality, Development and Peace, with the subthemes: employment, education and health. A three-week meeting to review progress was held in Copenhagen in July, 1980, against a background of a world economic situation which had deteriorated since the first meeting in 1975. Delegates to the 1980 meeting agreed that the situation of women in employment had also deteriorated since 1975, and educational gains by middle-class women were not matched by increased opportunities for employment. A report presented to the meeting hoped that links could be established between women's advancement and the solution of major problems of recession and inflation. Many delegates signed a convention forbidding discrimination on the basis of sex; it is difficult to see how this convention can be enforced. In common with many international conferences, politics displaced the more substantive considerations for which the delegates had been convened. Various aspects of the practice side of women's lives were discussed at a non-governmental conference which took place in Copenhagen at the same time.

In 1977, the Economic and Social Council of the United Nations invited its regional commissions to consider ways of contributing effectively to the 1980 Copenhagen meeting; the Asian and Pacific Commission held a regional preparatory conference in November, 1979, in New Delhi, in which 26 member countries participated and presented national views. Methods for involving women in development were described, and critical issues, short-range strategies and long-term plans discussed. Four workshops concentrated on problems relating to: (1) employment; (2) health; (3) education; and (4) *(a)* equality, development and peace, and *(b)* policy, mechanisms, monitoring and appraisal. The conference concluded that equality must mean greater access to power over the allocation of resources, and stressed the importance of grass-roots organization of women in sustaining national political will help to them.

International Women's Year showed that the inclusion of women in schemes for development could not be taken for granted, but must be planned for. A set of criteria for evaluating development projects involving women has been prepared (American Council of Voluntary Agencies for Foreign Service,

1975). A programme of international action aimed at promoting the advancement of women and their integration in development has been suggested by FAO (FAO, 1973; FAO, Home Economics and Social Programmes Service, 1975). An inventory of FAO activities relating to women is available (FAO, 1977). A model for extension programmes in home economics aimed at rural women in southeast Asia has been proposed (Purvis, 1976). Above all, greater attention needs to be paid to agricultural extension aimed specifically at women, preferably conducted by women. This is especially true in the field of animal husbandry; it has been seen that women are, to a large extent, responsible for the care of domestic animals in Asia, yet extension is aimed usually only at men. The Applied Nutrition Program of FAO, WHO and UNICEF does stress poultry care production as an important component. Much more could be achieved if existing extension services giving advice on better husbandry of large and small farm animals were to reach women.

Planners have long placed much faith in the "trickle-down" theory, whereby improved techniques would slowly penetrate to the village from larger centres, such as small towns (Whyte, 1982). The U.N. Center for Regional Development considers that evidence shows the theory to be erroneous, and is now strongly in favour of greater emphasis on work at the village level. It must be admitted, however, that the number of people with some degree of training which would be required, and the logistics and organization involved, represent daunting obstacles. Moreover, as has been shown, there is abundant evidence that efforts even at the village level may not help women. It has been demonstrated, however, that there is a great potential for improving women's lot within the framework of current village life by means of trained village women and co-operative work done by women's clubs (for example, in Bangladesh and Korea).

Food aid has been shown to have considerable potential for improving women's status, providing a means of bringing in new ideas, particularly to rural areas, and offering possibilities to women for assuming new roles. Food for Work projects in Bangladesh have been one example (World Food Program, 1977).

The Protein Advisory Group of the United Nations, considering the vital role of women in food and nutrition, undertook a two-year study in Africa to assess "the adequacy of conceptual and methodological orientations of current research on women's role in food production, food handling and nutrition; indicating linkages between food and nutritional status and various aspects of women's role in food production; using information from research in both nutrition and the social sciences, and identifying new directions in research to provide a better basis for planning and implementation of practical programmes" (PAG Bulletin 7[3-4]: 40-49, 1977). Conclusions reached in this study are applicable to most parts of the developing world, and guidelines have been drawn up for examining women's activities (PAG, 1977).

A consultative group from the United Nations University is to study the role of women in post-harvest conservation, with special attention to the technologies used, as well as to the social background of village, market and district, the time women devote to such activities and the degree to which their families benefit, nutritionally and economically.

Participants at the Wingspread Workshop on Women and Development, convened by the Centre for Research and development of Wellesley College in 1976, formed working groups to assess current research, to identify research practices and new methodologies and to suggest ways of creating new research institutions and networks to advance knowledge in the following fields:

(1) labour force participation of women;
(2) education and training as they affect women;
(3) women and health;
(4) women and the family;
(5) ideology, values and religion;
(6) women and political participation; and
(7) women and the world economic order.

The working group on labour force participation recommended the establishment of regional centres to co-ordinate future research. In Asia, Dr. Vina Mazumdar of the Indian Council of Social Science Research, New Delhi, is regional co-ordinator (Casal *et al.*, 1976). An international directory of women's development organizations has been prepared to enable women in different parts of the world to establish contact (U.S. AID, 1977).

In 1977, the United Nations Asian and Pacific Centre for Women and Development was set up in Teheran, moving to Bangkok in 1979. It aims at working with women for a more equitable distribution of resources and opportunities for participation in decision-making and to achieve better understanding of the effect of development on women. An Expert Group Meeting on the Identification of Basic Needs of Women held in December, 1977, stressed the importance of changing the attitudes of society—of both men and women—towards women, and the need for redesigning the workforce to include opportunities for part-time work, more flexible hours and job sharing to benefit women. Women need to be trained in the making of consumer goods from locally available resources, for both rural and urban markets, to increase their incomes. There was a call for greater participation of women in community decisions, which would require training, and for the creation of pressure groups on specific aspects of importance to women.

The new Centre will concentrate initially on identifying priority needs, and will attempt to intervene at the planning stage of development projects likely to affect women. It will study the effect of mechanization on the displacement of women from the labour market. Training, technical and advisory activities will be carried on, and links created with women's organizations throughout the region. The meeting drew up guidelines for the activities of the Institute (UNAPCWD, 1977).

We have been able to give here examples of only some of the innumerable activities under way in Asia, aimed at a better understanding of the needs and goals of women, and at bringing about practical improvements to their ways of life.

Changing Attitudes

Other less tangible problems present greater difficulty, particularly those relating to status. The application of the new household economics to the present, and its concomitant integration of market and non-market activities into economic analyses, should enhance women's status among policy-makers by giving more value to non-wage earning activities in the home. Women's status at community levels will, however, not improve rapidly. It has long been held that progress is evolutionary, and modernization would, of itself, bring about female emancipation. In fact, modernization may well have an adverse rather than a salutary impact on the status of women (Youssef, 1977) (discussed later).

Much faith is placed in the effect of education on changing traditional attitudes, and it has been seen in India, Taiwan and Japan that the educated daughter-in-law has an edge over her conservative, sometimes tyrannical mother-in-law, which was undreamed of by her mother. Yet the education of girls continues to remain subsidiary to that of boys, and the need for their help in the rural home is not likely to change this situation in the foreseeable future. Even in Japan, where universal education has long been in force and the majority of girls receive some form of higher education, attitudes towards child-raising remain traditional. In a recent survey, 74.9 per cent of women thought boys should be trained to be "strong and courageous" and girls "tender and gentle." Only 19.4 per cent thought boys and girls should be trained in the same way (UNESCO, 1976).

It will take much time to eradicate the acceptance of a secondary, submissive role for females, which automatically assigns to males a greater right to education and prevents women from taking the initiative to improve their own lot, or that of the family, by activities at the village level or in leadership roles. The weak, passive, home-oriented woman, less intelligent and capable than men, is enshrined in mythology, symbolism and stereotypical ideals, and the picture is perpetuated in school textbooks, adult literature and all forms of visual entertainment. It will, above all, take time to change the unconscious assumption of preordained privilege which may be encountered among Asian men at every socio-economic level.

Yet in the short period since worldwide prominence was given to the needs of women during International Women's Year, 1975, much has been achieved. Some Asian governments have appointed female ministers, or at least advisers at cabinet level, on women's affairs. And, throughout the region, there are many individual educated women who are no longer willing to tolerate injustice in the treatment of their sex, nor are they content to be passive participants in national development.

The efforts of these leaders will receive support and understanding from rural women only when economic conditions give them adequate income and leisure to participate in community decisions. Then they may hope to gain recognition from men for their rights and abilities, without which equality in daily life will never be attained.

It must, however, be recognized that as long as total income in most of the rural communities of Asia is inadequate to maintain acceptable standards of living for the family as a whole, attempts to improve the position specifically of women are not likely to proceed far beyond the realm of good intentions. Increased prosperity for the family may improve the status of its women members, though this cannot be taken for granted. It will be very difficult to emphasize the needs of women in the socio-economic environment of poverty and under-employment in which most rural households live.

2

Islamic Society: Age of Marriage and Consent

Legal Background

Orthodox Islamic law imposes no age qualification whatever for marriage, and there is thus no bar to the marriage of minors. The provisions as to competence for marriage in the Ottoman Family Rights Law are based on the puberty rules of the *Mejelle*, the Ottoman civil code, which follows the Hanafi school of law, though with some material differences: the minimum age of puberty of the *Mejelle*—nine years for girls and 12 for boys (article 986)—has become the minimum age of marriage (article 7); a marriage below that age is considered irregular (*fāsid*) (article 52) and must therefore be terminated. The condition of competence that the groom should be at least 18 and the bride at least 17 (article 4) is an innovation as against the *Mejelle*, which provides that the maximum age of puberty for both sexes is 15 years completed (articles 986 and 987). At the same time, the Ottoman legislator left a wide loophole for circumvention of that condition by giving the *qāḍī* discretion to approve the marriage of a bride and groom below the said ages on the grounds of early physical maturity; in the case of the bride, the consent of the marriage guardian is also required (articles 5 and 6)—these provisions, too, being modeled on the *Mejelle* (articles 985, 988 and 989). The plea of physical maturity may thus be made in respect of boys between the ages of 12 and 18 and, until the repeal of this part of the provision, it might formerly have been made in respect of girls between the ages of nine and 17.[1]

Though trying to find warrant for these reforms in the Islamic legal heritage, the Ottoman legislator was guided by social considerations, and especially strove to improve the position of women. The fixing of a minimum age of marriage was prompted by abuse, for economic reasons, of the legal permission to marry off minors without limitation of age. The raising of the age of puberty from 15 to 17 and 18 was prompted by the heavy responsibility resting on the family as the basis of society, a responsibility immeasurably greater than that attaching to the capacity for owning property under the *Mejelle*. Especial concern was shown for the girl's physical and mental health, for fear of possible defects in the physical or mental health of the offspring.[2]

In regulating the marriage of minors within the framework of the Criminal Code Ordinance, the British Mandatory legislator followed the *Mejelle*. He fixed the minimum age of marriage at 15 years completed and prescribed a penalty of six months' imprisonment for marrying or solemnizing or assisting in the solemnization of the marriage of a girl under that age. At the same time, a good defense to such a charge was provided along the lines of the Ottoman Family Rights Law: physical maturity of the girl, a medical certificate that sexual intercourse would not damage her health, and the consent of her parents and guardians.[3]

The Knesset considered that a girl of 15 was not fit for marriage because physical maturity was not sufficient and psychological maturity and vocational training were also to be taken into account. Nor was the Knesset prepared to accept consent of the parents as a criterion of marriageability because parents frequently bore the chief responsibility for pressuring a girl into an early marriage against her will.[4] The Age of Marriage Law, 5710-1950, raised the minimum age of the bride from 15 to 17 years, as in the Ottoman Family Rights Law (which applies only to Muslims), but in addition—and this is the main point—the Knesset abolished the Mandatory good defense and thus eliminated the principal means of circumventing the provisions relating to the age of marriage. The penal sanction was made still more severe: a person who marries, or solemnizes, or assists in solemnizing marriage of a girl under 17 or who, being her father or guardian, marries off such a girl, is liable to imprisonment for up to two years, or to a fine of up to IL 600, or to both.[5] Where a girl has given birth or is pregnant, the district court (but not the religious court) may permit her to marry the father, and a marriage performed under these circumstances is not considered a criminal offense (section 5). In 1960, the district court was empowered to permit the marriage of a girl of 16 even if she had not given birth or become pregnant, provided that special circumstances existed which in the opinion of the judge justified the grant of such permission.[6]

TABLE 2.1
Age of Marriage of Women According to Religion (In Percentages)[a]

Age at time of (first) marriage	*Jewish*[b]	*Muslim*	*Christian*	*Druze*
Up to 15	2.9	21.6	11.4	22.2
16 to 17	6.4	21.1	15.4	20.3
Up to 17	9.3	42.7	26.8	40.5
Up to 21	60.5	77.6	62.5	76.7

(a) Census Publication No. 17, Table XVIII, p. XXXVIII.
(b) Provisional data.

Marriages of Minor Girls

The *sijills* of the *sharīa* courts reveal hundreds of offenses against the Age of Marriage Law, especially in the first years after its passage. Most of them became apparent in the immediate context of the performance of the marriage, others in proceedings concerning various matrimonial matters.[7] There is also evidence of girls being married off at a very early age.[8] Moreover, the offenses are reflected—though not fully—in the data of the Central Bureau of Statistics. The Population and Housing Census of 1961 indicates a relatively high percentage of Muslim women married at an early age, as shown in Table 2.1.

Twenty-two per cent of Muslim married women had been married by the age of 15, as against 11% of the Christians and 3% of the Jewesses. Forty-three per cent had been married by the age of 17, as against 27% of the Christians and 9% of the Jewesses. The percentage of Muslim women who married at an age up to 15 in the years 1951 to 1961, that is, in the first decade after the enactment of the Age of Marriage Law, was 7 as against 2.5 for Christians.[9] These data are underestimates; the rate of offenses against the Age of Marriage Law was undoubtedly higher than is reflected in the official statistics, since the Bureau's data are based on the marriage registers. They do not reflect marriages confirmed *ex post facto* by the courts (by declaratory judgment) nor, of course, marriages performed without restort to a court or its agents.[10]

The Age of Marriage Law was circumvented in various ways: for instance, through the mechanism provided by the Ottoman Family Rights Law: a girl under 17 would ask the *qāḍī* to permit her to marry on the grounds of physical maturity and consent of the marriage-guardian. The accepted criterion of physical maturity is menstruation. The girl sometimes supported her application with various documents, such as a *maḍbaṭa* (petition) signed by the village *mukhtār* (a functionary appointed by the Government from among local notables) and others, and a medical certificate attesting that she was able to have sexual inter-course and conceive without injury being caused to her, and with the testimony of persons who knew her. The court would grant the application if the applicant's submissions were proved to its satisfaction. This was the principal means, under the Mandate and in Israel,of circumventing the provisions of the Criminal Code Ordinance as to the age of marriage before the enactment of the Age of Marriage Law, and this method was also applied for a time to circumvent the latter. Thus, from the enactment to this law to the end of 1951, the *Sharī'a* Court of Tayyiba issued 80 marriage permits for women in reliance on article 6 of the Ottoman Family

Rights Law, including several dozen for girls under 17.[11] These offenses were probably committed in good faith since there was no attempt to conceal the fact that the girl was not yet 17. The loophole was stopped after less than a year, when the *qāḍīs* ceased to grant marriage permits under these circumstances.

Another means of circumventing the Age of Marriage Law, which likewise involved reliance on the Family Rights Law, does not seem to have always been adopted in good faith: the girl would declare in the court that she had completed her 17th year or was of marriageable age and that statements in various documents making her out to be younger were erroneous. She would apply for and obtain a marriage permit on the basis of article 6 of the Family Rights Law. If her claim that she was over 17 was correct, she did not have to prove physical maturity and did not need a permit. In the first year after the enactment of the Age of Marriage Law, 120 marriage permits for girls were issued under these circumstances in the *Sharī'a* Court of Nazareth and more than 20 in the *Sharī'a* Court of Ṭayyiba. Most of the women in these cases had no official birth certificates, and this was probably why the *ma'dhūn li uqūd al-ankiḥa al-shar'iyya* (authorized *shari'* marriage notary, hereinafter referred to as *ma'dhūn*) refused to solemnize and register the marriage and a permit from the *qāḍī* had to be sought.[12] To prove the allegation as to the women's ages, extensive use was made of the *maḍbaṭa* and the testimonies and medical certificates, in which the estimated ages were indicated.[13] It has happened that signatories to the *maḍbaṭa* "assumed responsibility toward the law in case a religious-legal or secular-legal impediment to the marriage was discovered."[14] Though it may be supposed that errors in indicating the date of birth in official documents did occur, this method of proving age was probably used deliberately to obtain marriage permits so as to avoid a criminal charge. This method, too, was no longer available once the Population Registry had advised the public, shortly after the enactment of the law, that the date of birth might only be corrected on the basis of an official birth certificate and a medical certificate from the Government Health Office, accompanied by a sworn declaration by the father or marriage guardian.[15]

A third method of circumventing the law was recourse to an official correction of the date of birth. From early in 1951 there are to be found dozens of cases in the Nazareth *sijills* where a marriage permit was issued after correction of the date of birth. The correction was made, without great formality, in a magistrates' court, whereupon the permit was obtained from the *Sharī'a* court. In one case, a girl, her father and her fiancé's father appeared in the *Sharī'a* court and declared that the girl wished to be married to her fiancé, that her father agreed to the marriage and that the fiancé had already prepared the prompt dower, but that they had all agreed to postpone the marriage until the girl's age had been corrected "in accordance with the truth."[16]

Also resorted to was solemnization of the marriage without a *ma'dhūn,* and, after the girl had reached the age of marriage, receipt of a declaratory judgment from the *Sharī'a* court as to the validity of the marriage, in other words, a confirmation of the marriage (*ithbāt al zawāj*) retroactively to the date of slemnization. The provisions of the Family Rights Law as to the solemnization of marriages are not of a substantive character, and a deviation from them does not affect the validity of the marriage so long as it is slemnized in accordance with the *shar'i* rules as to offer and acceptance (*ijāb waqabūl*) and the presence of witnesses.[17] The court is not debarred from granting relief under these circumstances.[18] It is indeed not always possible to prove intent to circumvent the law in this manner; the applicants may have acted in good faith, in ignorance of the need to register the marriage. But there can be no doubt that in many cases this method was used to circumvent the law. The more than 200 marriage confirmations issued by the *Sharī'a* Court of Jaffa up to the beginning of 1970 included 30 clear cases of marriages of girls under 17.[19] It has happened that a couple applied to the court several years after the marriage, when they already had children, to confirm the marriage and declare that the children were theirs.[20]

In dozens of other cases in Jaffa, there is suspicion that the marriage confirmation was obtained in circumstances involving an offense against the Age of Marriage Law. No definite proof is provided by the judicial findings because basic data, such as the wife's age, exact date of marriage, and age of the children, are lacking. The suspicion arises precisely from what appears to have been a systematic attempt to blur the evidence. Thus, some couples asserted in court in 1960 and 1961 that they had been married "for about ten years," but it is impossible to tell from this finding whether they were married before or after the enactment of the Age of Marriage Law.[21] In other cases, when a marriage was contracted before the Age of Marriage Law, but a suspicion might have arisen that an offense had been committed, the date of the marriage was exactly stated so as to remove all doubt.[22]

The *sijills* of Nazareth and Acre also record many dozens of marriage confirmations, but in these cases, too, it is almost impossible to trace offenses against the Age of Marriage Law owing to the lack of sufficient data in the judgments. The *Sharī'a* Court of Ṭayyiba issued five marriage confirmations, two of which indicated the clear intent to circumvent the Age of Marriage Law. In the first case, the couple alleged that the *ma'dhūn* had solemnized the marriage when the bride was "a few months" short of the legal age. The *ma'dhūn* denied this emphatically (the marriage had not been registered). An examination of the identity booklets revealed that the woman had married at the age of 15. In the second case, the couple admitted that they had married without having the marriage registered because the wife had been under 17 at the time; but they added that they had not known then of the legal prohibition. In another case, the couple said that they had cohabited (and had a child) without marriage because the woman had not reached the legal age at the time.[23]

The *sharī'a* courts issue certificates of marital status (*ithbāt ḥātā madaniyya*) which include certificates given to women for the purpose of establishing that the holder is single and that there is no religious-legal or secular-legal bar to her marrying. Certificates of the latter kind usually indicate that they were required for the purpose of marriage. Some such certificates were issued to girls under 17.[24]

At least in the first year after the enactment of the Age of Marriage Law, its circumvention was facilitated by the fact that *ma'dhūns* were not particularly strict about the bride's age. Though the *sijill* usually attests that the *ma'dhūn* refused to solemnize the marriage on the ground that the bride's competence with regard to age had not been proven to his satisfaction,[25] there is also evidence of several cases where a *ma'dhūn* lent his hand to the marriage of a girl below the legal age.[26] Incomplete and faulty entries in birth certificates and identity booklets provided favorable opportunities for such offenses. Until the end of 1950, many residents, especially Nagev Beduin, had no identity documents at all, and the provisional documents issued by the military authorities gave estimated dates of birth on the strength of the testimony of *mukhtārs,* shaykhs and local notables. In 1951, *ma'dhūns* were forbidden to regard the temporary documents as evidence of a woman's age; they were requested to rely on official birth certificates or, failing these, on identity booklets issued by the Ministry of the Interior.[27] The transtition period, of course, facilitated circumvention of the legal age of marriage. Commissions consisting of regional *qāḍīs* and representatives of the Muslim Division of the Ministry of Religious Affairs inspected the records of the *ma'dhūns* from time to time to try to discover to what extent religious and secular law was being complied with.[28] Especial care was taken to give guidance to *ma'dhūns* recruited from among Negev Beduin shaykhs and tribal chiefs.[29] The *Qāḍī* of the *Sharī'a* Court of Jaffa, in whose area of jurisdiction the Beduin were located, met with them from time to time for this purpose. Despite all these measures, the official statistics disclose offenses as to the age of marriage even in the most recent years. As these statistics are based on the marriage registers, the inescapable conclusion is that the offenses were committed with knowledge of the *ma'dhūns*.

Yet another method of circumvention consisted in the drawing up of the terms (*shurūṭ*) of the marriage of a girl under 17 by the *ma'dhūn* on the strength of an assurance that the wife would only take up residence with the husband after reaching the legal age. The Muslim Division made it clear to the *ma'dhūns* that the drawing up of the terms of a marriage was tantamount to a marriage within the meaning of the law and that it made no difference whether the couple established their joint residence immediately or after a lapse of time.[30]

The only lawful way of by-passing the restrictions as to the age of marriage in certain circumstances is, as stated, the receipt of a marriage permit from the district court, but the author found no indication that Muslims availed themselves of this opportunity, although in many cases it would not have been difficult to obtain this relief, especially where there were children born out of wedlock.[31] Muslims preferred in such circumstances to obtain a marriage confirmation[32] or at any rate not to have recourse to a civil court.

Offenses against the Age of Marriage Law are encountered especially in periods of transition from one political regime to another: in the first years after the establishment of the State of Israel and since the reunification of Jerusalem[33]—when people had not yet become acquainted with the law and learned to adjust to it or to circumvent it. Marriages of minor girls were widespread in all types of settlements, including the towns.[34] At the same time, they were particularly frequent among the Negev Beduin, as Shaykh Tawfiq 'Asaliyya confirmed: according to him "they unfortunately do not know the elementary rules concerning marriage although *ma'dhūns* are distributed among their encampments."[35] There is a great deal of evidence of Beduin girls getting married at the ages of 12 and 13.[36]

With a few exceptions, offenses and reasonably suspected offenses against the Age of Marriage Law involved completely illiterate women. This appears from the fact that instead of their signatures they affixed their thumbprints (*baṣma*) to the court judgments.[37] The type of marriage may also have something to do with the age at which women marry. Marriages between cousins or within the clan and exchange marriages (*tabādul al-zawjāt, shighār*) may create strong family pressures to circumvent the legal age of marriage. In one case, for example, the couple explicitly admitted that the reason for the wife's marrying below the legal age was their common family background (*ḥasab*).[38] Other cases involved a combination of exchange marriage and clan endogamy or cousin marriage.[39] This is perhaps the situation most conducive to the generation of structural pressure to circumvent the Age of Marriage Law, because of the combination of property and relationship considerations involved in these types of marriage. However, the rate of such marriages, in violation of the Age of Marriage Law, was not particularly high, whence it may be concluded that the type of marriage was not a decisive factor with regard to marriages of minor girls. The occurrence of such marriages was no doubt favoured by the fact that Islamic law knows no age qualification for marriage, as well as by the personal example of the Prophet Muhammad. Thus, in one case, a man contended that it was permissible to marry off a nine-year-old girl, adducing the marriage of Muḥammad and 'Ā'isha as evidence.[40]

Rise in the Age of Marriage

The rate of marriages of minor girls has dropped drastically in Israel as compared with the period of the Mandate as is clear from Table 2.2.

TABLE 2.2
Girls Marrying Up to the Age of 15 According to Time of Marriage and Religion (In Percentages)[a]

Religion	*Time of Marriage*			
	Up to 1930	*1931-40*	*1941-50*	*1951-61*
Muslim	33.4	31.1	27.0	6.8
Christian	22.0	16.9	8.2	2.5
Druze	33.8	34.6	21.0	4.0

(a) *Census Publication No. 17,* Table XIX, p. XXXIX.

Although a decrease was already noticeable during the Mandate, it is particularly striking in the first decade of the State. During that decade, the percentage of Muslim minor brides dropped to one-quarter of the figure of the preceding decade: from 27 to 7 (the same applies, more or less, to the other communities). In some years of the second decade of the State, the number of Muslim girls marrying below the legal age did not exceed a few dozen.[41] The data in Table 2.2 may tempt one to jump to the conclusion that the main cause of the steep decline in the number of marriages of minor girls was Israeli legislation, but it seems that this proposition must be considerably qualified in the light of a number of factors.

The registration of the marriages of minor girls after the enactment of the Age of Marriage Law is incomplete owing to a desire to avoid penal sanctions (as far as they have a deterrent effect). The deterrent effect of these sanctions was rather limited; they were seldom applied, and then only in the form of fines that were small in relation to the dower.[42] The rate of marriages of Muslim minor girls was already on the decrease in Mandatory times, when the age qualification of the Criminal Code Ordinance could be circumvented without great difficulty through the mechanism provided by the Ottoman Family Rights Law. Then again, in other communities in Israel as well, the rate of marriages of male minors has dropped drastically (as against a moderate decline under the Mandate) although the Age of Marriage Law does not apply to the groom.[43]

The decline in the rates of marriage of both male and female juveniles must therefore be attributed in part—perhaps even mainly—to factors other than penal legislation. The effect of these factors was particularly noticeable in the age-groups over 17-18, which were not affected by the Age of Marriage Law or the Criminal Code Ordinance. The median age of marriage of Muslim women rose from 19 in 1951-1955 to 20 years in 1968.[44]

The main factors tending to raise the age of marriage were economic, cultural and social[45]: changes in the occupational structure and women's increasing participation in economic life; the increase in the amounts of dower[46]; the spread of education (there was a distinct correlation between women's level of education and the age of marriage)[47]; the rapid disintegration of the extended family and transition to the nuclear family; the adoption of modern concepts of marriage, such as the right of a free choice of partner for marriage and the necessity of mutual maturity, under the influence of Israeli society; increased expectations as to the marriage partner, as well as economic requirements (a dwelling with all modern comforts) as a necessary condition for marriage. These factors are reflected in the statistics of women's ages of marriage according to type of settlement, as is shown in Table 2.3.

TABLE 2.3
Average Age of Marriage of Muslim Women According to Type of Settlement[a]

National Average	*Towns*			*Villages*			*Beduin*	
	Nazareth	*Shafā 'Amr*	*Mixed Towns*	*Northern District*	*Haifa District*	*Central District*	*Galilee*	*Negev*
20.5	20.0	19.7	21.2	20.3	20.5	20.4	19.9	20.8

(a) AI, vol. 8(1962), Nos. 1-2, p. 15. For explanatory note to table see English Summary, *ibid.*, p. 4.

The age of marriage was highest in mixed towns, owing to direct contact with Jewish society. The age of marriage in Arab towns was not materially different and might be earlier than that in the villages of the Haifa and Central Districts. The data concerning the Beduin are implausible. According to all the evidence, marriages of minor girls were more common among them than in any other ecological group. The explanatory note to these data states that the late age of marriage among the Beduin is due to "late registration of marriages concluded in earlier years."[48]

In sum, although the Age of Marriage Law undoubtedly contributed to the drop in the rate of marriages of minor girls,[49] the factors mentioned above were the main causes of this phenomenon and of the rise in the age of marriage of both bride and bridegroom.[50] If marriages of minor girls still occur in certain areas, it is not only because the authorities are unable to punish offenders wherever they are, but mainly because social and cultural conditions in those areas have not yet radically changed.

The *Qāḍīs* and the Age of Marriage

Since the Knesset's interference in the matter of the age of marriage was not of a substantive character, and did not *invalidate* the marriage of a girl under 17, the *qāḍīs* were put to no severe test, especially as the minimum age of marriage prescribed by the Ottoman Family Rights Law remained unchanged. At their first conference in 1950, the *qāḍīs* resolved that "the age of marriage shall be 17 years in accordance with the Family Rights Law and the law passed by the Knesset."[51] This vague resolution blurred the material differences between the two laws as regards both the possibility of circumventing their provisions and the criminal sanctions they impose. Shaykh Ṭāhir al-Ṭabarī and Shaykh Hasan Amīn al-Habash granted marriage permits to minor girls on grounds of physical maturity and consent of the marriage-guardian. The *qāḍīs* were no sticklers for documents but relied on witnesses and their own visual impressions. If the external appearance of the girl supported her plea of maturity, the *qāḍī* would declare that she was marriageable and that there was no religious-legal or secular-legal bar to her marriage, and would order the *ma'dhūn* to solemnize it. In several cases, Shaykh Ṭāhir al-Tabarī issued a marriage permit to a girl after it had been ascertained that she was "about the age of competence [for marriage]."[52] In other cases, when a girl had been married under 17, the *qāḍī* declared that the *ma'dhūn* should not have solemnized the marriage "without a *shar'i* permit"[53] (within the meaning of the Family Rights Law but not the Age of Marriage Law). But apart from a few exceptions, the *qāḍīs* ceased to issue marriage permits for minors after a transition period of less than one year.

Shaykh Ṭāhir Ḥamād and Shaykh Tawfīq 'Asaliyya issued marriage confirmations frequently and even in cases involving offenses against the Age of Marriage Law. Other *qāḍīs* did so to a varying extent. This method, as stated, has been and still is one of the principal means of circumventing the Age of Marriage Law, either deliberately or in good faith. In both cases, the *qāḍīs* validated the marriage retroactively insofar as it was valid according to the *sharī'a*. Shaykh Ṭāhir Ḥamād proposed at the first *qāḍīs'* conference that the marriage of a girl under 17 "should be brought before the *sharī'a* court, which should pronounce on its legality; it should be possible to impose punishment, but on no account should the marriage be terminated."[54] Already in one of his first judgements, this *qāḍī* held that "age does not affect the validity of the marital bond." The only impediment to the marriage of a minor girl was, in his opinion, her sexual immaturity.[55] This had indeed been his guiding principle in day-to-day practice. Neither he nor other *qāḍīs* had ever raised the question of the criminality of solemnizing the marriage of a minor or of the prosecution of offenders under the Age of Marriage Law. If, on the retroactive validation of a marriage it appeared that it had been solemnized in contravention of the law and constituted a criminal offense, the *qāḍīs*, apparently for fear of disrupting the couple's married life, did not bring this fact to their attention or to that of the competent civil authorities. This attitude of the *qāḍīs* was probably one of the reasons by Muslims did not apply to a civil court for a marriage permit.

Notes and References

1. See Anderson, *Contract of Marriage*, pp. 114, 116 *seq.*; Coulson, *History,* p. 194; Fyzee, p. 90; Levy, pp. 106-7, 140-2; Eisenman, p. 118; Qadrī, arts. 140-2; *FRL* arts. 75-7. No age qualification exists as to betrothal (*khuṭba*), since neither it nor the promise of marriage (*wa' d*) creates a marital bond (*FRI art.* 1).
2. *ENFRL.* See also Goitein and Ben-Shemesh, pp. 215-6.
3. Criminal Code Ordinance, sec. 182(a) and (b), sec. 183.
4. The immediate cause of the Knesset's interference in the matter of the age of marriage was the great number of marriages of minor girls among Oriental Jewish immigrants. See *KP*, vol. 5, p. 1703 col.1, p. 1704 col.2. See also *KP*, vol. 4, p. 638 col.2, p. 639 col.1.
5. Age of Marriage Law, secs. 1, 2, 6 (repeal of pars. *(b)* and *(c)* of sec. 182, and of sec. 183 of the Criminal Code Ordinance). See Criminal Code Ordinance (Amendment) Bill, 5710-1950, *Bills*, No. 31 of January 15, 1950, pp. 77-8.
6. Age of Marriage (Amendment) Law, 5720-1960, sec. 1. See Explanatory Note to Age of Marriage (Amendment) Bill, 5719-1959, *Bills*, No. 339, p. 415; *ha-Aretz* of July 21, 1960. For the reasons for this amendment see the remarks of the Minister of Justice in the Knesset, *KP,* vol. 28, p. 10, col.1.
7. See, e.g., *JfQ3*, p. 331: no. 472-f.8/67; *JfQ4,* p. 113: no. 126-f.82/68; *JFQ5,* p. 49: no. 85-f.89/69; *NzḤ20*, p. 10: no.4/105 and p. 11: no.5/106 (the *qāḍī* ordered the *tafriq* of the couple because they had not been married in accordance with the *sharī'a*, and on the same day the man applied for a marriage permit, alleging that the woman was "about marriageable age"): *AcT3*, p. 192: f.35/60.

8. See, e.g., *JfQ1*, p. 175: no.289-f.19/55 (a Beduin girl alleged that her father had married her to a relative "while still a little child"); *AcD4*, p. 69:f.114/65 (girl married off at 12).
9. See Table II. For further data see *SAI*, 1967, No. 18, p. 49; *AI*, vol.7 (1959), Nos.1-2, p. 34.
10. The *sijills* record hundreds of instances of marriages concluded according to local custom (not according to the rules of the *Sharī'a*), which mostly involved minor female partners. See Layish, *Custom*, pp. 380-3.
11. For instances of this kind of circumvention of age of marriage legislation under the Mandate see *NzḤ14*, pp. 1, 4, 5, 9,29, 30, 36, and in Israel (about a hundred cases) see *NzḤ14*, pp. 76-126; *NzḤ15*, pp. 4-104; *ṬbḤi*, p. 6: no. 3/11, p. 39: no. 23/69 p. 83: no.19/34, p. 95: no.11/57.
12. See, e.g., *NzḤ16*, p. 38: no. 263/62 (the woman alleged that she was over 16 and that the entry in the identity booklet giving her age as 12 was erroneous).
13. See, e.g., *NzḤ15*, p. 126: no.4/180; *NzḤ16*, p. 1: no. 11/212 (according to the identity booklet, the girl was 14; the medical certificate said she was 17); *ṬbḤ1*, p. 35:no.16/62 (the woman alleged that she was between 17 and 18 and produced a medical certificate to this effect; the *maḍbaṭa* said that according to an official birth certificate she was over 14; and according to the testimony of the *mukhtār* and others "her appearance shows conclusively" that she was over 16).
14. See, e.g., *ṬbḤ1*, p. 78: no.8/23.
15. *AI*, vol. 2 (1951), No. 2, p. 27.
16. *NzḤ17*, p. 134: no.34/285. See also *NzḤ16*, p. 97: no.53/35 (the girl alleged that she had completed her 17th year and that the entry in the identity booklet giving her age as 13 was erroneous; she and her mother went to the magistrates' court, where the mother swore to her true age), p. 120: no.14/85 (a medical certificate and a sworn declaration as to the girl's age made by her father in the magistrates' court, were submitted to the *sharī'a* court).
17. A *shar'i* marriage not solemnized by the *ma'dhūn* is popularly called a *barrāni*, (external) marriage. According to interviewee Su'ād Qaramān and others, it serves, *inter alia*, to circumvent the Age of Marriage Law.
18. As it is, e.g., in Egypt under modern legislation. See Anderson, *Islamic Law*, p. 48.
19. See. e.g., *JfQ2*, p. 310: no.480-f.23/58 and p. 315: no.490-f.27/58 (in the course of the proceedings, it was incidentally discovered that the wife had been 13 years old at the time of her marriage);

JfQ3, p. 145: no.231-f.125/64 (the father admitted marrying off his daughter at the age of 13, and witnesses stated that she had been "a minor below the legal age"), p. 204: no.336-f.12/66, p. 258: no.398-f.86/66 (the wife had been 15 at the time of the marriage).

20. See, e.g., *JfQ3*, p. 166: no.270-f.24/65, p. 204: no.12/66. p. 257: no.397-f.84/66, p. 258: no.398-f.86/66, p. 337: no.477-f.42/67 (the wife had been 12 at the time of the marriage; she received confirmation of the marriage 15 years later, when she had seven children).

21. *JfQ2*, p. 454: no. 461-f.34/60, p. 509: no.471-f.107/61, p. 510: no.472-f.108/61. See also *JfQ2*, p. 599: no. 642 (the couple alleged in 1963 that they had been married for 13 years; the husband's year of birth is given, but not the wife's), p. 289: no. 448-f.66/57 (the couple's years of birth are given, but the year of the marriage is not); *JfQ5*, p. 16: no.29-f.121/69 (the wife was born in 1952; the year of the marriage is not given, but the marriage was confirmed on June 8, 1969).

22. See. e.g., *JfQ1*, p. 224: no.347-f.8/52, p. 229: no.355-f.19/59, p. 328: no.515-f.67/58: *JfQ5*, p. 11: no.21-f.110/69, p. 13: no.23-f.113/69.

23. *ṬbḤ4*, p. 48: no. 5, p. 74: no.39, and p. 77: no. 42, respectively. The Knesset was told of hundreds of Israeli couples cohabiting without marriage until the girl reached the age of 17, *KP*, vol. 28, p. 24.

24. See. e.g., *JfQ4*, p. 10: no.10-f.106/67 (it expressly indicated that the certificate was for purposes of marriage), p. 81: no.77-f.36/68; *AcD8*, p. 15: f.15/68.

25. See, e.g., *NzḤ16*, p. 112: no.2/73 (the bride's date of birth was not indicated); *ṬbḤ1*, p. 16: no.50/31 (the bride was under 17): *JfQ3*, p. 194: no. 320-f.45/65 (the *ma'dhūn* saw from the identity booklet that the girl was a minor and not permitted for marriage).

26. See, e.g., *NzḤ15*, p. 124: no.2/178 (the *qāḍī* found that the *ma'dhūn* should not have performed the marriage because the bride had been under 17); *NzḤ16*, p. 6: no.18/219 (the marriage was performed by the *ma'dhūn* "regardless of the fact that according to the identity booklet the bride was under 17").

27. *AI*, vol. 1(1950), No. 7, p. 5; *AI*, vol. 2(1950), No. 1, pp. 6-7.

28. *Yedi'on*, vol. 1(1950), No. 1, pp. 1-2; *AI*, vol. 2(1951), No. 2, pp. 18-19.

29. For a list of their names see *AI*, vol. 2(1951), No. 2, p. 20.

30. *AI*, vol. 2(1951), No. 1, pp. 6-7.

31. This mode of circumventing the law was particularly common in Jewish society. In many cases, pregnancy was deliberately brought about so that it might be possible to obtain a marriage permit. Sometimes a fictitious medical certificate attesting pregnancy was submitted. See *KP*, vol. 28, p. 10, 24, 28; *KP*, vol. 29, p. 1929.
32. See, e.g., *ṬbḤ4*, p. 77: no. 42.
33. About a third of the approximately 100 marriage confirmations issued by the *Qāḍī* of Jaffa to residents of East Jerusalem (the city and the villages in its area of jurisdiction) were clear cases of offenses against the Age of Marriage Law or of reasonable suspicion of such offenses.
34. For the causes of early marriages of women in traditional society see Baer, p. 23; Rosenfeld, *Peasants*, pp. 65-6.
35. *AI*, vol. 11(1868), Nos.1-2, p. 12.
36. See, e.g., *JfQ2*, p. 310: no.480-f.23/58, p. 315: no.490-f.27/58; *JFQ3*, p. 6: no.10-f.90/63, p. 145: no.231-f.125/64 (the husband was from Arab al-Jawārīsh, Ramla), p. 156: no.253-f.160/64, p. 337: no.477-f.42/67; *JFQ5*, p. 22: no.39-f.135/69, p. 66: no.112-f.222/69. Cf. Marx, *Bedouin*, p. 103-6; *idem, Marriage Patterns*, p. 398.
37. See, e.g., *ṬbḤ1*, p. 25: no.1/47, p. 75: no.4/19. For rare instances of a woman's signature see, e.g., *NzḤ15*, p. 120: no.18/173; *NzḤ17*, p. 41: no.45/169 (in both cases the women were from Nazareth).
38. *ṬbḤ4*, p. 74: no.39. See also *ṬbḤ4*, p. 48: no.5 (marriage within the *hamūla*).
39. *ṬbḤ1*, p. 55: no.21/93 and p. 56: no.1/94, p. 90: no.1/47 and p. 91: no.2/48.
40. *JfQ1*, p. 41: no.70-f.39/51.
41. *AI*, vol. 8(1962), Nos. 1-2, p. 15; *ibid.*, Nos.3-4, p. 32; *AI*, vol. 9(1964), Nos.1-2, p. 51; *ibid.*, Nos.3-4, p. 23; *AI,* vol. 10(1966), Nos.1-2, p. 94; *AI*, vol. 11(1968), Nos.1-2, p. 93. As to the years 1968 and 1969, see unpublished data of the Central Bureau of Statistics.
42. See, e.g., *ha-Aretz* of July 14, 1970 (the husband and the father of a minor girl of the al-Huzayyil tribe were each sentenced to a fine of IL 500 or 60 days' imprisonment; in passing sentence, the judge had regard to the custom of minor girls' marriages among the Beduin). See also *ha-Boqer, Lamerḥav* and *The Jerusalem Post* of June 2, 1964.
43. See *Census Publication No. 17,* Table XIX, p. XXXIX.
44. *Ibid.*, pp. 39-40; *SAI,* 1970, No. 21, p. 69.

45. Where no other source is indicated, the analysis of the factors is based on Rosenfeld, *Peasants*, pp. 66-7, and *NzDS,* pp. 38-40.
46. See Marx, *Social Structure*, p. 4. See also the chapter "Dower," pp. 41 *seq.*
47. See *Census Publication* No. 32, p. 22. Cf. Woodsmall, p. 95.
48. *AI*, vol. 8(1962), Nos.1-2, p. 15; explanatory note in English see *ibid.*, p. 4. Cf. Muhsam, *Marriage Habits*, pp. 64-6; Marx, *Social Structure,* p. 3.
49. *AI*, vol. 5(1957), Nos.1-2, p. 25.
50. Rosenfeld, on the other hand, holds that despite the Knesset legislation the early age of marriage of women in rural areas has not materially changed. Rosenfeld, *Peasants*, pp. 29, 65.
51. *AI*, vol. 1(1950), No. 7, p. 4.
52. See, e.g., *NzḤ16,* p. 23: no.40/241. In one case, this *qāḍī* estimated the woman's age at her request and decided on the basis of her appearance that she had completed her 17th year. See *NzḤ15,* p. 41.
53. See, e.g., *NzḤ15,* p. 124: no. 2/178.
54. *Yedi'on,* vol. 1(1950), No. 7, p. 3.
55. *JfQ1*, p. 50: no.79-f.38/52 (the girl had married during the Mandate).

3

Practice of Polygamy: Sanction and Society in Non-Islamic State

Legal Background

Polygamy in Islam is a right reserved to men. It was adopted as part of the legacy of patriarchal Arab society. The Qur'ān does not unequivocally limit the number of wives a Muslim is permitted to have, but all the schools of law agree that no more than four legal wives may be kept at one time. The Qur'ānic verses relating to polygamy stress the need for equal and just treatment of the wives as a condition of polygamy, but orthodox interpretation confines equality to measurable technical criteria, such as the provision of maintenance (*nafaqa*) and the apportionment (*qasm*) of the husband's time among the wives; as for the "inclination of the heart" (*mayl al-qalb*), it is not treated as a condition with binding legal effects but as a matter of ethics, left to the individual conscience. The Ottoman legislator, who sought to improve the position of women in this sphere, did not dare to tackle polygamy by a substantive provision; he reaffirmed it by laying down that "it is forbidden for a man with four wives, married to him or in the waiting-period (*'idda*), to take an additional wife." On the other hand, he sought to circumvent it by the device of the stipulation in the marriage contract,[1] in reliance on Ḥanbali doctrine in this matter and on the fact that the Qur'ānic provision is permissive and not mandatory. Article 38 of the Ottoman Family Rights Law permits the wife to stipulate in the marriage contract that her husband may not take an additional wife and that if he does she or her rival shall be regarded as divorced. The legislator assumed that no wife would agree to her husband taking an additional wife and so the mechanism of the stipulation seemed sufficient to him. He was also careful to restate the husband's duty of treating his wives equally and justly, but this time, too, the injunction was without teeth.[2]

The Mandatory legislator, who regulated the question of polygamy in the Criminal Code Ordinance, gave a "good defense" to this charge to non-Jews whose personal law permitted polygamy.[3] This defense was, in fact, meant only for Muslims or, more exactly, for Muslim men because, as stated, Islamic law does not recognize polyandry. The intention was to exempt Muslims *qua* Muslims from the criminal sanction provided for polygamy by the Ordinance (five years' imprisonment).

In 1951, the Knesset abrogated the "good defense" available to Muslims against the charge of polygamy.[4] The intention was to adjust Muslims to the monogamous form of marriage accepted in Israeli society.[5] As a result, Muslim men were given the defense intended until then for non-Muslims: absence of the spouse for a consecutive period of seven years without her being known to be alive.[6] In 1959, Muslims were given an additional defense: inability of the spouse by the earlier marriage to agree to its dissolution or annulment owing to mental illness.[7] These two defenses are conditional on receipt of a judgment of the religious court permitting the new marriage.[8] In other words the *qāḍī* is empowered to permit polygamy on either of two grounds absence or mental illness. These two defenses are essential to the Muslim because the Knesset also forbade him to divorce his wife against her will without a court judgment.[9] The Knesset's intention, at any rate, was to give Muslims the same defenses as are available to Jews.[10]

From the point of view of the equality of Muslim women, the abrogation of the defense available to Muslim men under the Criminal Code Ordinance against the charge of polygamy did not remove the traditionally basic discrimination between men and women given religious sanction in the Qur'ān. True, both men and women are exempt from criminal responsibility in the event of their taking a spouse in addition to the one who is a absent or ill, but while the man's new marriage is valid according to religious law, the woman's is not, and the Israeli legislator was not prepared to interfere with any religious-legal prohibition or permission relating to marriage or divorce.[11]

In effect, the Knesset did not abolish polygamy but prohibited its practice. Islamic law, in this matter remains in force. If a man takes an additional wife, the additional marriage is valid as far as it is so under the *sharī'a*, but he is liable to the secular criminal sanction provided for that offense. At the same time, the Knesset made it possible to circumvent the prohibition in the above-mentioned cases. The same technique was used by countries such as Syria and Iraq: they, too, prohibited polygamy but did not abolish it, and infringers of the prohibition are liable to statutory sanctions; but Syrian and Iraqi *qāḍīs* have wider discretion than their Israeli colleagues to permit polygamous marriages.[12]

Contravention of the Ban on Polygamy

There are no official statistics of polygamy in Israel. The official data on marriages are indeed based on the registers of marriage contracts, but infringers of the ban on polygamy were not anxious to incriminate themselves, and in so far as they married with the participation of a *ma'dhūn*, they were careful, as far as possible, to conceal their true marital status in various ways, as will be seen below. The detection of polygamous marriages through the *sijills* is also difficult, because this type of marriage was not as such a subject-matter of court actions. Polygamous marriages are discovered incidentally, in the course of the hearing of other matters, especially actions for the confirmation of marriages (*ithbāt nikāḥ*) maintenance, obedience and divorce. In this way, the author came across more than 70 instances.[13] The number was undoubtedly greater than is reflected in the *sijills,* but this does not seem to alter the basic finding that polygamy was not widespread among Israeli Muslims. This finding is confirmed by field research in different regions.[14] The cases ascertained mostly involved two wives, but there were men who had three or even four.[15]

Polygamous marriages are found in all ecological groups. Particularly striking was their frequency among Beduin—about 40% of all cases discovered in the *sijills*. Another 40% occurred among the rural population, half of this in the Little Triangle villages. Polygamy was also still extant in urban areas, though on a smaller scale: some 16%[16] which included Beduin who had recently settled in towns such as Lod, Ramla and Jaffa.[17] Polygamy was thus a problem for urban women as well. In some cases, they tried to protect themselves against it by a stipulation in the marriage contract. In one case, the wife stipulated that the husband should not take an additional wife so long as she was able to fulfil her marital duties and that if he did he should pay her IL 5,000. In two other cases, the stipulations were respectively that the wife should be delegated by the husband the power to divorce herself if he took an additional wife, and, in the second case, that any additional wife, the husband might take should be regarded as divorced.[18]

In about 30% of the cases of polygamy discovered through the *sijills*, there is express evidence or a reasonable suspicion that the marriage was contracted in contravention of Israeli law.[19] There can be no doubt that the actual proportion of offenses was higher. Thirteen persons were convicted of polygamy in district courts in 1966 and nine in 1969.[20] These data indeed do not necessarily relate to offenses committed in those years, but on the other hand it may be supposed that not all offenders were caught and brought to trial. Two-thirds of the offenses discovered through the *sijills* were committed by Beduin, mostly in the Negev. Most of the offenses in rural areas were committed in the Little Triangle. Polygamy thus occurred in Israel despite its prohibition by law (and there were those who said that it was more frequent than divorce).[21] Three years after the passage of the law by the Knesset 13 tribal chiefs in the Negev sent a petition to the Prime Minister declaring that the ban on polygamy was a disaster the like of which had never befallen Muslims before and that the Beduin could not endure it.[22]

There were a number of different ways of circumventing the ban on polygamy. One of the commonest methods was the performance of polygamous marriages otherwise than by a *ma'dhūn*. In this way, the question of criminality did not arise. The Negev Beduin did not appear to be prompted by the wish to circumvent the law[23] and their polygamous, as well as their first, marriages were performed in good faith in accordance with tribal custom; only later, when some occasion arose for the updating of their identity booklets, did they apply to the *sharī'a* court for confirmation of the marriage.[24] But deliberate circumvention was practiced in other regions. Thus, for instance, a woman from a Little Triangle village alleged that her husband had left her and taken a second wife "without a legal tie."[25] Su'ād Qaramān, a well-known figure active in women's affairs, and social workers in the Haifa and northern regions, attested that the circumvention of the ban on polygamy by *barrāni* (external) marriages, i.e., marriages performed without the participation of a *ma'dhūn*, was a familiar feature in Muslim society.[26] This was confirmed to the author by Judge Muhammad Nimr ul-Hawwārī of the District Court of Nazareth. According to him there were *ma'dhūns* who charged twice as much for the performance of marriages without registration as for the regular procedure because of the risk of prosecution involved.[27]

A man might cohabit with an additional woman without a proper marriage having been performed, in a kind of common-law marriage. This phenomenon in Muslim society was probably a consequence of the ban on polygamy. It is true that cohabitation without a *shar'ī* marriage was widespread among Beduin and also among the recently settled rural population, which had not yet been fully absorbed into orthodox Islam but still adhered to their tribal customary law in matters of personal status. The occurrence of common-law marriages as deliberate means to circumvent the ban on polygamy was confirmed to the author by the Central Bureau of Statistics.[28] There are also some indications of it in the *sijills*. In one case, a wife alleged that she had been compelled to leave her husband's house because he had taken another wife. The husband admitted that the other woman was at his house, together with the first, but denied that he had married her.[29]

Obtaining the first wife's consent to the new marriage was another means of circumventing the ban on polygamy. Although this was not a "good defense" to a charge of polygamy it did afford some assurance that the party most interested in preventing that marriage would take no legal steps.[30] In one case, a wife alleged that her husband had told her to sign a document confirming that she agreed to the second marriage, and that when she refused, he began to ill-treat her and to lock her up in the house.[31] The husband may have honestly believed that, as in the case of divorce, the wife's consent released him from criminal responsibility, and it is easy to imagine that under certain circumstances the wife would prefer acceptance of the second marriage to divorce.

After the Six-Day War, some men resorted to importing a second wife from the Israel-administered areas.[32] Although the chief reason for marrying a Gaza Strip or West Bank woman seems to have been the smaller dower she commanded,[33] the possibility cannot be ruled out that the choice of such a woman as an additional wife was also prompted by a desire to evade the penal sanction. For polygamy's is not prohibited in the Israel-administered areas, where Israeli law does not apply. (In East Jerusalem Israeli law has applied since the reunification of the city in 1967). The law indeed says that an Israeli national or resident who marries an additional wife abroad is also liable to punishment,[34] but this provision was not known among the general public.[35]

Yet another device resorted to was to repudiate one's wife by revocable divorce (*talāq raf'ī*) and to take her back after marrying an additional wife. A revocable divorce does not undo the marital bond immediately, and the husband may take the divorced woman back during the waiting-period *(idda)* without need for a new union or a new dower. As far as secular law is concerned, the husband was in the clear on notifying the divorce and amending the marital status entry in the identity booklet. The reinstatement of the wife did not involve legal proceedings; a verbal utterance, or significant conduct, of the husband was sufficient. The divorced wife remained in the husband's house throughout the *idda*. It was very difficult to prove an offense of this kind because the husband could always say that he admitted his former wife into his house out of pity.[36] In one case, a man declared, after divorcing his wife, that he was free of wives, including wives in the *idda* following a revocable or other divorce, and there was no wife in his "protection" (*'iṣma*): he was seeking confirmation of the divorce for the purpose of changing the description of his marital status in the Population Register.[37] One *qāḍī* sometimes warned a man who had divorced his wife not to take her back so long as he had another wife, in view of the ban on polygamy.[38]

Another method of evading legal punishment, and which indeed involved a certain risk, was to divorce one's wife without her knowledge, amend the marital status entry in the Population Registry, take another wife, and continue living with the first wife as well without a formal marital bond. The author discovered only one case of this kind, but it sheds light on a mechanism for protection against the Knesset's innovations which was sometimes developed with the cooperation of the *ma'dhūn*. In this particular case, the wife (both she and the husband being of the Abū Ruqayyiq tribe) alleged that her husband had divorced her at a date unknown to her, concealed this from her and continued to have marital relations with her until she learnt of the divorce. The husband denied that he had divorced her, but admitted taking an additional wife. In fact, it transpired that the husband, who had wished to take an additional wife, had told the *ma'dhūn* that his wife agreed to his doing so. The *ma'dhūn* thereupon said to him: "When I ask you in the presence of people: 'Are you divorced'?; you must say: 'Yes, I am.' The certificate of divorce which I shall make out will be quite worthless; its only purpose will be to convince the Government." The *ma'dhūn* sent the certificate of divorce to the Population Registry, and the divorced man took another wife. The *qāḍī* found that the man had circumvented the law by concealing the divorce from the wife "in order that he might be able to live with her as well as take another wife."[39]

The Decline of Polygamy

From a variety of sources it may be inferred that polygamy is on the decline in Israel. About 70% of the cases discovered during the hearing of various actions in court involved marriages concluded before the establishment of the State.[40] The prohibition of polygamy by criminal legislation has undoubtedly made its mark on whatever inclination toward polygamy still exists. Witness the various means employed to circumvent the ban. But quantitatively the most significant manifestation of the deterrent effect, of the criminal sanction is that the traditional motives for polygamy, viz., barrenness of the wife, lack of male issue, advanced age of the wife or illness incapacitating her for sexual intercourse, the desire for a young wife as a symbol of status and social prestige, etc..,[41] had now become frequent causes of divorce.[42]

As will be seen below, the Knesset's ban on polygamy, well-intentioned though it certainly was, did women more harm than good because divorce was considered by most worse than polygamy. If there is no normative or economic bar to a polygamous marriage, there is no reason for a husband to divorce his first wife when wishing to take a second: on the contrary, he has good reason for not divorcing her: if he does, he will lose her working power and have to pay her the deferred dower in addition to maintenance for the waiting-period.[43] There is express evidence that men who desired another wife instead of one who was old, barren or away in some Arab country were reluctantly compelled to divorce the first wife for no reason but the ban on polygamy. This happened especially in the Little Triangle villages, where the inclination to marry young wives had increased because of economic prosperity. Since polygamy was prohibited, it became usual to divorce the ageing wife, pay her what was due to her under matrimonial law and even compensate her in various ways.[44]

But Israeli legislation was not the only, or even the principal, cause of the decline of the polygamy rate. In most of the cases in which a person was convicted of polygamy, the law was not applied with full rigour; small fines were imposed which could have no deterrent effect. A judge of the District Court of Beersheba, whose attitude toward polygamy in Beduin society was one of tolerance, remarked in one of his judgments: ". . . it may be said that there is actual disregard of the law here and perhaps that the risk is worthwhile and not deterrent. A man who pays several thousand pounds for a new wife will not mind paying several hundred or even more as a fine; the fine at most puts the price up a little."[45] The author found only one case of a man applying to the *sharī'a* court for permission to take a second wife on one of the grounds recognized by the Knesset. He contended that his wife was mentally ill and had been in hospital for a long time, and that there was no hope of recovery. In another case, a man applied to the court for registration of his second marriage on the ground that his first wife had borne him six daughters and no son and that he had been "compelled to take a second wife in order that Allāh might bless me with a son who would bear my name after my death"[46]; this was of course an application for confirmation of a polygamous marriage *ex post facto*. Muslims did not seem to be aware of the grounds recognized by the Knesset or at any rate did not use them. In some of the dozens of cases in which a man divorced a wife absent from the country a good defense could have been set up to a charge of polygamy.[47] Except for one case,[48] there is no evidence of a wife intending to bring a criminal action against her husband in the event of his taking an additional wife. Women seemed to be unaware of this right, or in so far as they were aware, not to have attained a degree of social freedom enabling them to take criminal proceedings. Divorce probably worried them more than polygamy.[49]

The decline of polygamy has become a general phenomenon in the Middle East, known also in countries where polygamy is not prohibited by law.[50] The causes of this decline should therefore be sought first and foremost, in economic, cultural and social factors: in the spread of education and in the resulting change in the normative values and in attitudes toward the institution of marriage; in the rise in the standard of living and in the economic expectations of both spouses, in the increase in the amounts of the dower: in the transformation of traditional society, and especially in the liberation of woman.[51]

Owing to these factors, polygamy would have receded even if it had not been prohibited. In sum, the decline of polygamy has not necessarily been a boon to women as far as the balance-sheet of marriages and divorces is concerned. Indeed, there was a correlation between the decline of polygamy and the rise of the divorce rate.[52] This was particularly noticeable in the Little Triangle villages, where according to Shaykh Ḥasan Amīn al-Ḥabash the rate of divorces exceeded that of marriages.[53]

In several cases, a woman had two husbands at one and the same time.[54] This does not indicate a material change in the position of women, but laxity in compliance with the law of marriage and divorce. This phenomenon was found especially among Beduin, but also in recently-settled rural society and even among the urban population.[55] The polyandrous marriage is irregular (*fāsid*) and liable to immediate termination under religious law[56]; it is criminal under general law, in one case, a woman was punished for polyandry.[57]

The *Qāḍīs* and Polygamy

The attitude of the *qāḍīs* to polygamy in the context of religious and secular law was perplexed and ambivalent. On the one hand, they welcomed the ban imposed by the Knesset; they even tried to find support for it in the Qur'ān and for this purpose adopted elements of modernistic interpretation in the spirit of Muḥammad 'Abduh (1849-1905), who led the movement to adapt Islam to modern Western civilization, and who with regard to polygamy attempted to interpret the Qur'ānic verses as a legally binding injunction in favour of monogamy. On the other hand, they were concerned for the substantive validity of religious law in this matter and at times even found some social justification for it. Shaykh Ṭāhir Ḥamād held that the treatment of polygamy in the Qur'ān expressed a subtle intent in favour of monogamy since it was usually impossible to maintain justice and equality between several wives in all circumstances in the *sharī'a* itself contends that if one cannot do so one should content oneself with one wife. Shaykh Tawfīq 'Asaliyya said that the Qur'ān ordered fair treatment of one's wives and that polygamy was conditional on one's ability to treat them justly.[58] Both referred to the well-known "polygamy verses" in the Qur'ān. They made their remarks in connection with the Knesset's ban on polygamy in order to show that secular legislation in this matter was consonant with the spirit of the *sharī'a*. But it seems that the *qāḍīs* did not, like the modernists, mean to go so far as to give binding legal validity to the Qur'ānic moral prohibition.[59] Shaykh Ṭāhir Ḥamād stressed that the Knesset's ban on polygamy sprang from the same religious-legal consideration as was expressed in the Qur'ān, but that the Knesset could not "attack the *sharī'a* or the heavenly laws," i.e., detract from the substantive validity of the Qur'ānic permission. The idea that the Knesset's legislation is intended to strengthen the validity of the Qur'ānic norm recurs in various formulations. Shaykh Ṭāhir Ḥamād considered that the ban on polygamy (like other prohibitions in criminal legislation) not only did not abrogate the religious law but strengthened it by means of the penal sanction, because the moral command, being without teeth, was ineffective. Shaykh Tawfīq 'Asaliyya was likewise careful to point out, praising the Knesset's criminal legislation in matters of marriage and divorce, that it was framed "whilst maintaining the validity of the religious law."[60]

In 1954, Advocate Muhammad Nimr al-Hawwārī applied to the Supreme Court sitting as the High Court of Justice for an order against the *qāḍī* of the *Sharī'a* Court of Acre to show cause why he should not agree to the bigamous marriage of a certain man. Shaykh Māsā al-Ṭabarī had refused to do so on the ground that although there was no bar to such a marriage under the *sharī'a* it was forbidden by secular law. Advocate al-Hawwārī contended in the High Court of Justice that the Knesset's ban on polygamy constituted an infringement of the freedom of religion of the Muslims and that it conflicted with section 5 of the Women's Equal Rights Law, which provides that "this Law shall not affect any religious-legal prohibition or permission relating to marriage or divorce." The court rejected these arguments, holding, *inter alia*, that freedom of religion (within the meaning of the general law) was the freedom to do what religion commands, and not what it permits, and that, since Islam did not command, but merely permitted polygamy, its prohibition did not infringe the freedom of religion. In this connection the Indian modernist Ameer Ali was mentioned, who tried (like 'Abduh) to prove by reference to Qur'ānic verses that Islam forbids polygamy.

Shaykh Ṭāhir Ḥamād was not satisfied with this judgment. In a letter to the President of the Supreme Court, he maintained that the orthodox interpretation of the "polygamy verses" should be adhered to and stressed that the main criterion of equality was economic; although it was not possible to adopt the same emotional attitude toward several wives, he said, the resulting restriction was merely moral, not legally binding—a matter of piety (*wara'*), left to the individual conscience. Shaykh Ṭāhir utterly rejected Ameer Ali's interpretation, since Allāh could not have permitted and forbidden polygamy at the same time. Lastly, Shaykh Ṭāhir held that freedom of religion was not only freedom to do what religion commanded, but also what it permitted; more exactly, the Muslim marriage should be considered in terms of the five religious qualifications under which any aspect of Muslim behaviour is categorized (*al-aḥkām al-khamsa*—obligatory, recommended, indifferent, reprehensible, and forbidden). In his opinion, the Knesset's ban on polygamy conflicted with all but the last (*ḥarām*) of these qualifications and therefore constituted an infringement of the freedom of religion promised in the Declaration of Independence.[61]

Shaykh Ḥusnī al-Zu'bī also welcomed the ban on polygamy, but considered that the range of "good defenses" should be widened. He suggested adding in the Penal Law Amendment (Bigamy) Law, 5719-1959, a provision to the effect that the wife's refusal to comply with a judgment for obedience, her chronic illness, barrenness "and the like" should entitle the husband to take an additional wife without this being considered a criminal offense. The ban on polygamy and on divorce against the wife's will had barred the two traditional remedies available to the husband against a disobedient wife, and the *qāḍī's* proposal was intended to restore the equilibrium upset by the secular law, which, in his opinion, was misused by the wife.[62] Shaykh Amīn Qāsim Mudlij shared the view that rebelliousness of the wife should be a justification for polygamy.[63] In effect, the *qāḍīs* asked for the legalization of what were the commonest reasons for polygamy in traditional society.

The Egyptian Personal Status Bill of 1966 would not have abolished polygamy (had it been approved), but entitled the first wife to demand dissolution of the marriage (*tafrīq*) on the ground of *ḍarar* (damage, legal cruelty), which was in itself a new ground for dissolution. The *qāḍīs* rejected the proposed reform most categorically because, in their opinion, it expressly contradicted the *sharī'a*. Shaykh Tawfīq 'Asaliyya thought it impossible to regard the taking of an additional wife, which is expressly permitted by the Qur'ān, as causing damage to the first wife; he suggested some orthodox remedies instead. Shaykh Amīn Qāsim Mudlij held that any allegation of damage was a matter of "discord" within the meaning of article 130 of the Ottoman Family Rights Law and should be dealt with by arbitration. Shaykh Ḥusnī al-Zu'bī added that the problem of the ban on polygamy had found its solution within the framework of the "existing law," in other words, by means of criminal legislation.[64]

Polygamy as a type of marriage, apart from the ciminal aspect, did not preoccupy the *qāḍīs* in their day-to-day practice. In their view, polygamy was a legitimate institution, anchored in the *sharī'a* and in social reality. Where between the spouses questions arose that were rooted in this type of marriage, such as allegations of deprivation or discriminatory treatment of one of the wives as to maintenance, housing or conjugal rights, the *qāḍīs* dealt with them in the context of the rights and duties of the spouses under the *sharī'a*.[65] They were well aware of the Knesset's ban on polygamy. Thus, in one case of a polygamous marriage in East Jerusalem, Shaykh Tawfīk 'Asaliyya was careful to indicate in the record that while the marriage was contrary to Israeli law, it had been concluded when the latter was not yet in force there, before the, Six-Day War.[66] Shaykh Amīn Qāsim Mudlij once noted, when about to confirm a marriage, that no other wife had remained in the husband's *'iṣma* since his first wife's death.[67] Moreover, when about to confirm the divorce of one of the wives in a polygamous marriage, he was accustomed to warn the husband not to take the divorced wife back so long as there was another wife in his *'iṣma*, "having regard to the Women's Equal Rights Law" or "in order that he might not incur the legal liability" attached to such a marriage.[68]

On application for confirmation of a marriage concluded without registration and in violation of the ban on polygamy, the *qāḍīs* would validate the marriage retroactively if it was valid under the religious law and confirm the *nasab* (blood-relationship) between the children and the parents. As stated, most of these offenses were committed by Nagev Beduin, in whose case some *qāḍīs* either ignored the offense completely or treated it with leniency. In one instance, Shaykh Amīn Qāsim Mudlij, on confirming the marriage of Beduin of the al-Huzayyil tribe remarked: "These two do not know the law that forbids polygamy because life in the desert makes it impossible to know the laws that are to be observed in this country, especially the recently enacted ones."[69] According to one source, Shaykh Ṭāhir Ḥamād used to advise men who wanted to take an additional wife to do so in a ceremony performed in accordance with the *sharī'a* but not before the *ma'dhūn*, and then to apply to the *sharī'a* court for a declaratory judgment. In one case, he advised man who had taken an additional wife to have her sue him for maintenance and then to agree to pay maintenance while admitting her to be his wife, whereupon the *qāḍī* would award maintenance while incidentally confirming the marriage on the basis of his admission. In this way, the question of the criminality of the polygamous marriage would not arise.[70]

On the other hand, there were *qāḍīs* who, with certain differences in style and wording, took care to note the fact of the offense in the record. Shaykh Tawfīq 'Asaliyya did so on several occasions. He would confirm the validity of the polygamous marriage, but add at once that it had been performed in contravention of Israeli legislation.[71] In one case, the man applied for confirmation of his marriage while his identity booklet already described him as married. He alleged that he had divorced his first wife but had not amended the entry of his marital status in the Population Register owing to ignorance of the law. The *qāḍī* confirmed the second marriage, adding that it had been performed in contravention of the law and that the man was obliged to prove that he had divorced his first wife or face the legal penalty.[72] In the case of the man who had divorced his wife without her knowledge so as to be able to take another wife and at the same time keep the first one, Shaykh Ṭāhir Ḥamād found that the use of this device involved two offenses: polygamy and divorce against the wife's will, and that the man was liable to the legal penalties.[73]

All these cases, in which the *qāḍīs* envinced sensitivity to the question of the criminality of polygamy, were actions for confirmation of a marriage (or divorce). The *qāḍīs* seemed to be less sensitive where the offense was disclosed incidentally to the hearing of some matrimonial claim, as for maintenance or obedience. The reason for this may be a purely formal one, viz., that in the latter kind of case the legality of the marriage was not at issue, so that the *qāḍīs* were not obliged to take a stand on it. But it is also possible that the *qāḍīs* were not anxious to upset the life of the family where it seemed to them that the first wife had accepted the situation. Thus, in one case, a woman claimed maintenance until such time as her husband would agree to provide a legal dwelling (*maskan shar'i*) for her. She contended that he had installed her rival in close proximity to her, remarking in this connection that he had married the other woman illegally. The husband maintained that he had married the second wife "in accordance with the *sharī'a* and the general law, under special circumstances," which he did not specify, and voluntarily agreed to pay maintenance to the first wife until he had provided her with suitable accommodation. The wife agreed to the amount of the maintenance, and the *qāḍī* Shaykh Ḥasan Amīn al-Ḥabash, confirmed it without in any way referring to the quesiton of the criminality of the second marriage.[74] In several actions for maintenance heard by Shaykh Tawfīq 'Asaliyya, the husband did not deny the offense at all, but this question was not dealt with by the court. Thus, in one case, a woman claimed maintenance on the ground that her husband had badly treated her, thus compelling her to return to her father's house. The husband replied that his wife had left him not because of any ill-treatment but because he had taken another wife (from Gaza). The *qāḍī* awarded maintenance.[75] In another maintenance claim, it appeared during the inspection (*kashf*) of the dwelling that the man's first wife and her grown-up children were living in one of the rooms, whereupon the *qāḍī* declared that the dwelling was not legal and ordered the man to pay maintenance. The couple later reached a compromise and the wife asked the *qāḍī* to quash the claim, which he did.[76]

Although the grounds recognized by the Knesset as justifying polygamy are technical and do not leave much scope for judicial discretion, the manner in which the *qāḍīs* relied on them is a significant criterion of their attitude toward polygamy; but they had little opportunity to invoke them for the simple reason that Muslims, as stated, did not usually ask permission for polygamy. In one case, Shaykh Ḥasan Amīn al-Ḥabash, in express reference to the law of 1959, permitted an additional marriage on the ground that the wife suffered from an incurable mental illness. In another case, a man's application to approve and register his polygamous marriage because his wife had borne him no son (though he had borne him daughters) was dismissed by Shaykh Ḥasan on the unprecedented grounds that polygamy was forbidden by law and that the registration of marriages was not his business but that of the *ma'dhūn,* who would register a marriage after it had been proved to his satisfaction that there was no bar to it under the *sharī'a* or secular law.[77] In other words, Shaykh Ḥasan refused relief in these circumstances because an offense had been committed and apparently also because the plea of lack of male issue did not satisfy him.[78]

Notes and References

1. See Paper on "Stipulations Inserted in Contracts of Marriage."
2. *FRL*, arts. 14, 74. See Qadrī, arts. 19, 30; *ENFRL*: 'Abduh and Ridā, pp. 348-9; Amīn, pp. 139-40; Linant de Bellefonds, pp. 134-6; Hinchcliffe, *Polygamy,* pp. 13-16; Anderson, *Contract of Marriage,* pp. 122-4; *idem, Islamic Law*, pp. 41-2, 46, 49; Coulson, *History,* pp. 18-19, 208; *idem, Conflicts*, pp. 30, 93; Meron, pp. 515-16, 519, 521; Goitein and Ben-Shemesh, pp. 132-3, 218-19; Levy, pp. 101-2.
3. Par. *(c)* of the proviso to sec. 181 of the Criminal Code Ordinance, 1936. See Meron, p. 516.

4. Women's Equal Rights Law, 5711-1951, sec. 8 (repeal of par.(c) of the proviso to sec. 181 of the Criminal Code Ordinance).
5. During the debate on the Bill in the Knesset, the Prime Minister said: "We regard polygamy as an insult to the human race, an insult to woman as a human being. If we permit polygamy among Muslims, it means that we abandon the Muslim woman and discriminate between women, and as we are pledged to grant equal rights to women, we must not retain discrimination against the Muslim woman." *KP,* vol. 9, p. 2191 col. 1; see also the remarks of the Minister of Justice in the Knesset, *ibid.*, p. 2006 col. 2; the Explanatory Note to the Women's Equal Rights Bill, 5711-1951, *Bills*, No. 75 of 1951 (5711), p. 192; Silberg, pp. 426-7; Meron, p. 530 *seq.*
6. Par. *(b)* of the proviso to sec. 181 of the Criminal Code Ordinance. This defense was reformulated in the Penal Law Amendment (Bigamy) Law, 5719-1959 (in connection with the repeal of the said sec. 181), as follows: "the spouse by the earlier marriage is missing under circumstances raising a reasonable presumption of his [or her] death, and all trace of him [or her] has been lost for at least seven years." (*Ibid.*, par.(2) of the proviso to sec. 6).
7. Penal Law Amendment (Bigamy) Law, 5719-1959, par.(1) of the proviso to sec. 6.
8. *Ibid.*, sec. 6.
9. Absence and mental illness of the spouse are grounds for dissolution of the marriage on the wife's initiative. See the chapter "Divorce," pp. 199 *seq.*
10. See Glasner, pp. 276, 279-80. The Minister of Justice told the Knesset that it appeared from an opinion submitted to the Ministry of Religious Affairs by a *qāḍī* that although there might seem to be no need to permit polygamy in the event of mental illness of the spouse because of the case with which divorce could be effected, it was repugnant to the humane outlook of the Muslims to divorce a wife who was mentally ill and that they therefore sought something like a *hetter de-me a rabbanim* (permit signed by a hundred rabbis). *KP,* vol. 23, pp. 263-6, 313.
11. This attitude is expressed in sec. 5 of the Women's Equal Rights Law, 5711-1951. See Silberg. p. 428; Zadok, pp. 74-6.
12. They are guided in their decisions by considerations such as the man's ability to support his wives and treat them impartially, and the benefit to be expected from the polygamous union. See Linant de Bellefonds, pp. 137-8; Hinchcliffe, *Polygamy,* p. 19 *seq.*; Coulson, *History,* pp. 208-13; *idem, Conflicts*, p. 93; Anderson, *Islamic Law,* pp. 48-50; *idem, Syria,* pp. 36-8; *idem, Tunis*, pp. 267-9; Meron, pp. 527-8; Fyzee, pp. 60, 93.

13. For polygamous marriages revealed on dealing with the confirmation of a marriage see, e.g., *JfQ3*, p. 156: no. 253-f.160/64 (the man contended that since the death of one of his wives he had only one wife), p. 297: no. 437-f.133/66 (the *qāḍī* noted that the marriage was contrary to the Women's Equal Rights Law); *NzI4*, p. 368:no.3/ 33-f.89/68 and p. 368: no. 4/34-f.68/90 (two women applied for confirmation of their marriages to the same deceased main); *AcQ5*, p. 84: f.230/63 (a man said that he had divorced one of his wives and had only one wife left in his *'iṣma*). For reference to *sijill* entries relating to polygamy disclosed in the course of actions for maintenance, obedience or divorce see the chapters "Maintenance and Obedience," pp. 98-9, and "Divorce," p. 129.
14. See Rosenfeld, *Peasants*, p. 126; Marx, *Bedouin*, p. 139.
15. *AcT4*, p. 79: f.17/67, p. 94: f.32/67, p. 139: f.28/68; *ṬbḤ1*, p. 182: no. 11 (four wives), Cf. Marx, *Bedouin*, p. 139; Muhsam, *Marriage Habits*, pp. 71-2.
16. Cf. Marx, *Bedouin*, p. 139; *idem, Marriage Patterns*, pp. 405-6; *idem, Social Structure*, p. 6; al-Ārif, p. 133; Baer, pp. 37-8.
17. See, e.g., *JfQ1*, p. 63: no.101-f.14/52 (the husband lived in a tented camp (*mukhayyam*) at Ramla): *JfQ4*, p. 113: no.126-f.82/ 68 (the wife, from Lod, the husband from Ramla, both of Negev Beduin origin).
18. *JfMC68*, nos.10313, 9515, and *AcMC68*, no. 3441, respectively. The author has not found such stipulations in other types of settlement. See also *JfQ3*, p. 145: no.230-f.108/64 the wife stipulated that if the husband preferred her rival to herself, she might divorce herself by delegation). See the chapter "Divorce." pp. 153 *seq.*
19. See, e.g., *JfQ3*, p. 155: no.251-f.150/64 (the second marriage was concluded in 1959), p. 374: no.515-f.95/7; *ṬbI1*, p. 188: no.9-f.15/61 (the wife revealed in an action of maintenance that her husband had "illegally" taken another wife). Cf. Anderson, *Islamic Law*, p. 88.
20. Unpublished data of the Central Bureau of Statistics. See also *Criminal Stats*. 1968, pp. 34-5. Cf. Meron, p. 524; *The Jerusalem Post* of June 15, 1971.
21. Rosenfeld, *Peasants*, pp. 39-40, 141.
22. The petition was of September, 1954. See the Archives of the Bureau of the Adviser on Arab Affairs, Prime Minister's Office. In the Little Triangle villages, there were those who interpreted the ban as a deliberate attempt to reduce the natural increase of the Israeli Arab population See Cohen, p. 135.
23. Cf. Marx, *Bedouin*, p. 139.
24. See, e.g., *JfQ3*, p. 297: no.437-f.133/66, p. 312: no.451-f.5/66.

See Layish, *Custom*, p. 382. To conceal polygamy offenses, it is usual in Turkey to register the children in the name of only one wife. See Dirks, p. 80.

25. *Ṭbl1*, p. 160: no.1-f.3/60.

26. They said so at a symposium at Beyt ha-Gefen in Haifa on May 26, 1971.

27. Interviewee District Judge Muhammad Nimr al-Hawwārī explained that the expression *barrānī* was borrowed from the terminology of the land registry: a *barrani* transfer of land is made outside the land registry by consent of the parties, while a transfer made at the registry is described as *jawwāni* (internal).

28. Through the head of the Demography Section, interviewee Zion Rabi.

29. *AcD8*, p. 97: no.14/70-f.125/69. See also *Ṭbl1*, p. 226: no.18-f.14/63; *JfQ4*, p. 94: no.97-f.38/68; *AcD8*, p. 76: f.97/69 (the wife alleged that her husband has deserted her and was living with a young woman on the West Bank).

30. Sec. 9 of the Penal Law Amendment (Bigamy) Law, 5719-1959, permits a wife to testify against her husband concerning an offense under this law, but does not require her to do so, and in the absence of such testimony it is difficult to prove the offense.

31. *Ṭbl1*, p. 278: no.26-f.33/64 (at the time of the hearing, the man had not yet taken a second wife).

32. See, e.g., *JfQ4*, p. 84: no.83-f.16/68, p. 185: no.239-f.57/69.

33. See the chapter "Dower," p. 60.

34. Penal Law Amendment (Bigamy) Law, 5719-1959, sec.4(3).

35. District Judge Muhammad Nimr al-Hawwārī refused to hear such a case on the plea of lack of jurisdiction because the offense had been committed outside Israel, but the Supreme Court directed him to hear it and the man was convicted. Particulars were given by interviewee Judge al-Hawwārī. See *AI*, vol. 12(1970), Nos.1-2, p. 119-26; Meron, p. 525. See also *ha-Aretz* of February 9, 1970, and *Ma'ariv* of February 3, 1970.

36. The author was told about this subterfuge by S. Nawi. The *sijills* contain evidence that a divorced wife sometimes remained at the house of the husband, who provided for all her needs. See the chapter "Divorce," pp. 147-8.

37. *JfQ5*, p. 124: no.210-f.2/70.

38. See, e.g., *AcṬ4*, p.38:f.3/66, p. 107: f.45/67.

39. *JfQ2*, p. 401: no.564-f.12/59.

40. Cf. Rosenfeld, *Peasants*, p. 126. See there for data on polygamy at Arṭās, studied by Granqvist, and in five Muslim villages in Palestine studied in the 1940s.

41. See Rosenfeld, *Peasants*, pp. 39-40, 64, 127-8, 136 150; Granqvist, vol. 2, pp. 174, 208-12; Marx, *Bedouin*, pp. 139-40; Muhsam, *Polygamy,* pp. 88-90; Baer, p. 37; *Ma'ariv* of February 3, 1970 (the man said the reason for his second marriage was that his first wife had borne him two daughters, while the second wife had borne her former husband four sons).
42. See the chapter "Divorce," pp. 125 *seq.* and *Ma'ariv* of February 3, 1970 (the man took a second wife only after the first wife had refused to agree to a divorce).
43. Cf. Rosenfeld, *Peasants*, p. 131.
44. See the chapter "Divorce," pp. 143 *seq.* Cf. Cohen, p. 72.
45. Quoted from Meron, pp. 524-5. See also *ibid.*, p. 539. The person guilty of bigamy is liable to five years' imprisonment and the person who solemnizes the marriage is liable to six months' imprisonment. Sec. 181 of the Criminal Code Ordinance and sec.8(a) of the Penal Law Amendment (Bigamy) Law, 5719-1959. District Judge Muhammad Nimr al-Hawwārī said that the court usually sentenced such offenders to small fines and up to three months' imprisonment. He personally imposed a fine of IL 2,000 on a man who had contracted a polygamous marriage on the West Bank. The District Court of Haifa sentenced a resident of Kafr Qar' to six months' imprisonment for polygamy. The prosecution maintained that polygamy was widespread in Israel and that a heavy penalty should therefore be imposed as a deterrent, but the court took into account the pregnancy of the second wife, who asked clemency for her husband. Judgment 13/59, *AI,* vol. 7(1959), no. 1, p. 28.
46. *ṬbḤ4*, p. 65: no.26; and *ṬbḤ2*, p. 90: no.1, respectively.
47. See the chapter "Divorce," p. 131.
48. *JfQ2*, p. 528: no. 510-f.93/61, Cf. Marx, *Bedouin,* p. 139 n.1.
49. In Iraq, too, women rarely invoke the penal sanction attached to polygamy. This is because disputes in matrimonial matters are frequently settled out of court—by arbitrators—and custom and conditions in traditional society assign a passive role to women, el-Naqeb, pp. 57-9.
50. See Baer, p. 38.
51. See Rosenfeld, *Peasants*, p. 126; Marx, *Social Structure*, p. 6; Baer, p. 37: Levy, p. 101; Anderson, *Patriarchal Family,* p. 231: Woodsmall, p. 117; Granqvist vol. 1. p. 138.
52. Cf. Baer, p. 38 and the sources indicated there; Woodsmall, pp. 125-6.
53. See the chapter "Divorce," pp. 180 *seq.*
54. See, e.g., *JfQ2*, p. 290: no.451-f.63/57: *AcD6*, p. 48: no.49-f.124/64; *NzI4*, p. 49: no.1/9-f.14/49; *NzḤ20*, p. 75: no.6/68 (the wife married another man while the husband was in prison).

55. See, e.g., *JfQ1*, p. 94: no.150-f.74/52 (a woman married a well-known public figure in Lod before her earlier marriage had been properly dissolved).
56. *FRL,* arts. 13, 54.
57. *Ha-Aretz* of June 7, 1966 (a Jewess converted to Islam and married a Muslim before her marriage to a Jew had been terminated).
58. *AI*, col. 9(1964), Nos.1-2, p. 9 and *AI*, vol. 11 (1968), Nos. 1-2, p. 11, respectively.
59. See ʻAbduh and Riḍā, pp. 350-1; Amīn pp. 139-40; Shafik, pp. 43-9; Goitein and Ben-Shemesh, pp. 133, 218-19.
60. *AI*, vol. 8(1963), Nos.1-2, pp. 1-2, and *AI*, vol. 11(1968), Nos.1-2, pp. 10-11. respectively.
61. Shaykh Ṭāhir Ḥamād remarked incidentally that keeping a common-law wife was a form of polygamy not subject to legal punishment. The correspondence between him and the President of the Supreme Court was published in *AI*, vol.7 (1959), No.4, pp. 1-9. The case in question was High Court of Justice 49/54, Mulḥim Na if Mulḥim vs. the Religions Judge in Acre, *PD,* vol. 8, pp. 910, 913-14. Parts of the judgment are quoted by Silberg, pp. 419-20, 427-8, and by Goitein and Ben-Shemesh, pp. 239-41. See also Arami, pp. 116-17. For Knesset member A. Jarjūra's objection to the withdrawal of permission for polygamy among Muslims see *KP,* vol. 9, p. 2189. See also Schacht, pp. 120 *seq.*; Meron, pp. 517 *seq.*, 526-7.
62. *AI*, vol. 8 (1963), Nos. 3-4, pp. 1-2; *AI*, vol. 9 (1964), Nos.1-2, p. 8; *AI*, vol. 11 (1968), Nos.1-2, p. 6. For a more extensive discussion see the chapter "Maintenance and Obedience," pp. 110-11.
63. So did Advocate Maḥmūd al-Mādī, a former director of *sharīʻa* courts. Shaykh Amīn Qāsim Mudlij suggested that disobedience of the wife should also be a "good defense" to the charge of divorcing her against her will. *AI*, vol. 9 (1964), Nos. 3-4, pp. 2-3, 8-9.
64. *AI*, vol. 10(1967), Nos. 3-4, pp. 7-8, 12-13, 18.
65. See the chapter "Maintenance and Obedience," pp. 98-9.
66. *JfQ4*, p. 137: no.164-f.148/68.
67. *JfQ3*, p. 156: no.253-f.160/64. See also *AcṬ4*, p. 57: f.27/66.
68. *AcṬ4*, p. 38: f.3/66, and p. 80: f.18/67, respectively. See also *AcṬ4*, p. 50: f.17/66 (the *qāḍī* confirmed the divorce, adding that the man might only marry his divorced wife again "after he had become single"), p. 88: f.26/67 (the reinstatement of the divorced wife was "prohibited by law"), p. 94: f.32/67 (the *qāḍī* wanted the man not to take his divorced wife back so long as he had two wives in his *ʻisma*), p. 98: f.36/67, p. 107: f.45/67 (the *qāḍī*

explained that although the main might take back divorced wife according to the *sharī'a*, he might not do so according to secular law so long as he had another wife).

69. *JfQ3*, p. 155: no. 251-f.150/64.
70. Based on information supplied by Advocate S. Darwish.
71. *JfQ3*, p. 297: no. 437-f.33/66, p. 312: no. 451-f.5/67.
72. *JfQ3*, p. 374: no. 515-f.95/67.
73. *JfQ3*, p. 401: no. 464-f.12/59.
74. *ṬbI1*, p. 188: no. 9-f.15/61.
75. *JfQ4*, p. 84: no. 83-f.16/68. See also *JfQ4*, p. 185: no. 239-f.57/69.
76. *JfQ4*, p. 92: no. 95-f.121/67 and p. 133: no. 158-f.130/68. See also *JfQ4*, p. 113: no. 126-f.82/68: *JfQ5*, p. 133: no. 218-f.317/69.
77. *ṬbḤ4*, p. 65: no.26; and *ṬbḤ2*, p. 90: no.1, respectively. Permission for polygamy sought from *qāḍīs* in Iraq on the plea of "legal benefit" is granted automatically and the law is thus made a mockery. Also, ignoring offenses subject to penal sanctions (imprisonment up to one year and a fine up to 100 dinars), the *qāḍīs* confirm polygamous marriages *ex post facto*, el-Naqeb, pp. 51-4, 58.
78. For his attempt to turn the mechanism of registration into an effective bar to divorce against the wife's will see the chapter "Divorce," pp. 191 *seq*.

4

"Bride Price": Customary Law and Dower

Law and Convention

According to the customary law prevailing before Islam, marriage was the sale of a woman, in return for whom her father or guardian received a dower. Muḥammad changed the wife from a mere object of sale into a party to the marriage contract, enabled her to own property and prescribed that the dower should be given to *her* in return for marital relations[1]; the husband has no status with regard to the dower. Islamic law knows no community of property between spouses. Property relations are based on the principle of separation of the property of husband and wife. Each remains the owner of the property he or she acquired before, in consequence of, or during the marriage and manages it independently.[2] The Ottoman Family Rights Law stresses that the dower belongs to the wife and that she cannot be forced to spend it on the acquisition of *jihāz* (equipment, clothing and household effects). Moreover, the parents and relatives of the bride are forbidden to accept money or any other consideration for giving her in marriage or handing her over to her husband. The wife may deal with the dower in the manner of an owner, transmit it by way of inheritance and perform any act of transfer in respect of it.[3]

According to the Ḥanafī school of law, the minimum dower payable to the wife is ten dirhams. In view of the small purchasing power of this sum, the Ottoman legislator, relying on the Ḥanbalī school of law, ignored this question completely.[4] The Family Rights Law distinguishes between a specified *(musammā)* dower, stipulated in the marriage contract, and a fair (*mithl*) dower, equal to that of another woman of her father's kin similar to the bride in social status and personal (physical and moral) qualities, or in the absence of such a woman, equal to the dower of residents of her locality. In accordance with the Hanafī school, the law provides that the specified dower may be wholly or partly paid as a prompt dower (*mahr mu'ajjal*), that is, dower payable immediately on marriage, or after a time. Where no date has been fixed for its payment, it is assumed to be payable on divorce or on the death of one of the parties as a deferred dower (*mahr mu'ajjal*). The amount of the dower due to the woman depends on the type of dower (specified or fair), the type of marriage (*ṣaḥīḥ,* valid, or *fāsid*, irregular), on whether the marriage has been consumated, and the like. Thus, for instance, if in the case of a valid marriage and amount has not been agreed on, and divorce takes place before valid privacy (*khalwa ṣaḥīḥa*), the woman is entitled to *mut'a*, an indemnity fixed in accordance with custom, consisting of a set of clothing, provided that its value does not exceed half the amount of the fair dower.[5] The marital bond requires the husband to pay his wife the dower, but the dower is not a condition of the validity of that bond. If the prompt dower has not been paid, the wife is not bound to share the husband's dwelling and may refrain from intercourse with him, provided the marriage has not been consummated.[6]

The Knesset has not intervened in the matter of the dower in any way. Section 2 of the Women's Equal Rights Law was implicitly intended to make Jewish women capable of owning and disposing of property and to introduce for them the system of separation of the property of the spouses.[7] These reforms brought nothing new to Muslim married women.[8] In 1966, the Knesset debated a private member's bill designed to prohibit the taking of a dower exceeding IL 50. The bill was rejected.[9]

Prompt Dower

The prompt dower has increased enormously since the establishment of the State of Israel in 1948, as the Tables 4.1 and 4.2 indicate. In the two decades from 1950 to 1969, the average prompt dower increased from IL 230 to IL 3,700, that

TABLE 4.1
Average Prompt Dower by Districts and Subdistricts Selected Years, 1950-61[a]

District and Subdistrict	*Average Amount of Dower in IL*			
	1950	*1955*	*1958*	*1961*
National Average	229	1,187	1,603	1,974
Northern District	237	1,160	1,486	2,666
Safad Subdistrict	—	—	1,762	2,064
Kinheret Subdistrict	222	1,362	1,486	1,847
Jezreel Subdistrict	218	1,199	1,552	2,068
Acre Subdistrict	250	1,088	1,427	2,066
Haifa District	257	1,400	1,792	1,923
Haifa Subdistrict	—	1,130	1,838	2,095
Hadera Subdistrict	257	1,500	1,785	2,451
Central District	200	1,315	1,880	2,405
Sharon Subdistrict	211	1,396	1,764	3,031
Petah Tikva Subdistrict	163	1,195	2,545	—
Ramla Subdistrict	170	980	1,346	1,870
Rehovot Subdistrict	—	—	1,000	—
Tel Aviv-Jaffa District	171	708	1,386	1,400
Jerusalem District	238	836	1,433	1,381
Southern District	—	—	—	—
Ashkelon Subdistrict	—	—	1,500	—
Beersheba Subdistrict	—	—	1,315	2,188

(a) Data of the Central Bureau of Statistics, as published (with slight variations in *AI*, vol. 5(1957), Nos.1-2, pp. 23-4: *AI*. vol. 7(1959), Nos. 2-3, p. 35; *AI*. vol. 8(1963), Nos. 3-4, p. 34: *Marriages*, 1957-1958, p. 54.

TABLE 4.2
Average Prompt Dower by Type of Bride's Settlement Selected Years, 1960-69[a]

Type of Bride's Settlement	*Average amount of Dower in IL*				
	1960	*1962*	*1965*[c]	*1967*	*1969*[d]
National Average	1,196	2,341	3,114	3,267	3,654
Urban National Average	1,088	2,079	2,596	2,411	2,469
Nazareth and Shafā Amr	—	2,338	2,537	2,080	2,558
Mixed Towns	845	1,796	2,687	2,671	2,273
Jewish Settlements	—	2,900	1,000	2,740	5,333[e]
Rural National Average	1,221	2,405	3,195	3,383	3,826
Northern District	1,088	2,344	3,191	3,329	3,860
Haifa District	1,426	2,466	3,236	3,738	3,737
Central District	1,526	2,642	3,702	3,509	4,239
Ṭayyiba and Umm al-Faḥm[b]	—	—	—	2,963	3,399
Jerusalem District	2,167	2,220	2,824	2,667	4,000[f]
Beduin National Average	—	—	—	—	4,436
Negev	1,756	2,344	3,110	4,416	4,632
Galilee	144	2,224	2,979	3,612	3,727

(*a*) Data of the Central Bureau of Statistics, as published (with slight variations) in *AI*, vol. 8(1962), Nos.1-2, p. 16; *AI*, vol. 9(1964), Nos. 1-2, p. 49, *AI*, Nos. 3-4, p. 24, *AI*, vol. 10 (1966), Nos. 1-2, p. 93; *AI*, vol. 12(1970), Nos. 1-2, p. 54 (variations in accordance with unpublished data of the Bureau).
(*b*) These two villages are treated as urban settlements under the new classification.
(*c*) See also *Vital Stats., 1965: 1966,* p. 62 where there are slight differences from the material published in *AI*, due to different definitions of the settlements.
(*d*) Based on unpublished data of the Central Bureau of Statistics. See also *AI*, vol. 12 (1971), Nos. 3-4, p. 67 (amounts rounded off; differences due to different definitions of the settlements).
(*e*) Based on the average of three cases.
(*f*) Based on one case.

is, about sixteenfold. Even allowing for the decline in the purchasing power of the Israel pound, it is no over-statement to say that the dower went up by leaps and bounds. Using the consumer price index as a measure of the real increase of the dower, it works out at 300%.[10] Rosenfeld found that the real value of the dower in the villages was two-and-a-half times as great in the early 1960s as compared with 30 to 40 years earlier. Y. Ben-Porath found that in the decade from 1950 to 1961 the dower increased faster than the gross national product per capita: its average annual increase was 8.8% as against 5.5% annual increase of the gross national product in the years 1950-1960.[11] This was due to the improvement of the economic situation in Israeli Muslim society. The phenomenon is especially striking in the villages of the Central District and in the Hadera Subdistrict of the Haifa District, i.e., in the villages of the Little Triangle.[12] Throughout the period the average amount of the dower was higher in the villages than in the towns, and highest in the villages of the Central District, where in 1969 it was IL 4,200 as against a national average of IL 2,500 in urban settlements and of IL 3,800 in rural settlements.[13] The differences in the amount of the dower in the Northern and Haifa Districts are without significance. The amount for Tayyiba and Umm al-Fahm, IL 3,400, was considerably smaller than that for the Central District.

The amounts of the prompt dower in the towns were the lowest in the whole country throughout the period under review; in the mixed towns, the amount was smaller than in Nazareth and Shafā 'Amr—IL 2,300 as against IL 2,600.[14] This seems to be mainly due to the deferred dower customary in the towns: its amounts were inversely proportional to those of the prompt dower.[15]

The most impressive discovery is that of the large amounts of prompt dower among the Beduin. In fact, in recent years, the amounts among the Negev Beduin have approximated and even exceeded those in the villages of the Central District; in 1969, the respective figures were IL 4,600 and IL 4,200. The average amounts among the Galilee Beduin exceeded those in the towns and in recent years have not been much smaller, and sometimes even larger, than the average for all types of rural settlements; the respective figures are IL 3,600 and IL 3,400 for 1967 and IL 3,700 and IL 3,800 for 1969.[16] It should, of course, be remembered that the registration of marriages among the Beduin was not complete, and it may be assumed that the amounts of dower were larger in the case of registered marriages than in the case of marriages performed in accordance with custom, without resort to the *ma'dhūn,* on the fringe of Beduin society. In 1969, 191 marriages were registered among Negev Beduin and 53 among Galilee Beduin. The average dower thus reflects the position as to a relatively small, unrepresentative sample of marriages and so quantitative conclusions should be guarded against.

Nevertheless, there can be no doubt that these data are significant and that there is one basic fact which accounts for them: the registered marriages were largely those of members of the ruling class in Beduin society: shaykhs, heads of clans and tribes. Marx, in his study on the Negev Beduin, notes that the shaykhs frequently contracted short-term marriages (in addition to polygamous unions) in order to have more children.[17] The economic position of the Beduin shaykhs in the Negev was among the best of any section of Israeli Muslim society. They had grown rich in various ways since the establishment of the State. Hundreds of thousands of dunams of land in the areas where the Negev Beduin were concentrated had been leased to the farmers among them through the intermediary of the tribal chiefs; large amounts of drought compensation were until recent years paid to the shaykhs; they enjoyed what amounts to a monopoly on agricultural machinery (tractors etc.)[18]; they maintained close relations with real estate dealers and various agricultural companies; moreover, there were certain highly lucrative pursuits traditionally engaged in this transit zone. Since the shaykhs, the tribal chiefs, served as *ma'dhūns* in their tribes, it may be assumed that they also registered their own frequent marriages, for which they paid large sums as prompt dower. Large sums are also not unexpected in view of the fact that the Negev Beduin quite often married town girls, for whom they paid handsomely. There is much evidence of this in the marriage contract registers and in the *sijills*.[19]

The dower was usually paid in money,[20] sometimes by instalments, and by means of promissory notes.[21] It might take the form of a plot of land, an olive grove, or a vegetable garden (*ḥakūra*), a house,[22] or livestock.[23] The wife frequently inserted in the marriage contract stipulations (*shurūṭ*) to the effect that the husband must give her various household articles (*athāth, 'afsh al-bayt)*, such as furniture and bedding, or jewellery and ornaments (*ḥaly, maṣāgh*), a room of a house, livestock and the like; the things themselves were likewise referred to as stipulations. Such stipulations were part of,[24] or additional to, the prompt dower.[25] The wife was sometimes careful to note that they were *her* property. The monetary value of the stipulations was occasionally indicated alongside the prompt and deferred dowers and included in the total amount of the dower.[26] The Central Bureau of Statistics estimates that the custom of indicating the monetary value was much more widespread than is reflected in the marriage contracts and that it mainly related to gold coins and gold jewellery.[27] The marriage contract registers of 1968 show more than 130 stipulations, which constitute about 70% of all stipulations inserted in marriage contracts in that year. Stipulations were especially customary in mixed towns and in the Little Triangle villages—more than in villages in other areas. The author did not come across a single instance of such stipulations among Negev or Galilee Beduin.

The Central Bureau of Statistics, which had examined this question both by interview and in the marriage contracts, found that it was usually the wife who had to bring the household effects and the bedding and that the stipulations in marriage contracts imposing this duty on the husband were contrary to accepted practice.[28] From research and various sources it is known that the practice with regard to the purchase of household effects, jewellery and clothing varied from place to place. According to one view, it was customary for a woman to leave her father's house and join her husband with the *jihāz*, which included bedding and various utensils.[29] Rosenfeld found that part of the prompt dower which did not remain with the bride's father was expended on the requirements of the young people.[30] A survey in Nazareth in 1965 revealed that prompt dower was not as common that town as in the villages but that, on the other hand, the economic demands made by the bride's family in return for its consent to the marriage were much weightier than the dower payments; an appartment and most modern conveniences had to be assured prior to the marriage.[31]

It was customary for the groom to pay the prompt dower at or before the drawing up of the marriage contract. There were differences in this respect between different types of settlement. In 1968, prompt dower was paid in full in four-fifths of the marriages contracted in the towns (including Ṭayyiba and Umm al-Faḥm) as against two-thirds in the villages (including Beduin settlements in the Negev and in Galilee). It was partly paid in 13% of the marriages in the towns as against 9% in the villages, and it was not paid at all in 8% of the marriages contracted in the towns as against one-quarter of the marriages in the villages.[32] It seems that in the towns the wife and her family were more insistent about receiving the whole or part of the prompt dower than in the villages or in Beduin society. At the same time, the mode of paying the prompt dower was essentially a custom varying from place to place.[33]

The *sijills* contain a fair amount of evidence of women not receiving the whole or part of the prompt dower. The fact emerges at the hearing of actions for maintenance, obedience, divorce and the like.[34] A woman might allege that she had not received the prompt dower although her husband would assert that he gave it to her.[35] There was sometimes a discrepancy between the amount indicated in the marriage contract and that claimed by the wife.[36] All the foregoing shows that although the wife was careful to stipulate her rights to prompt dower in the marriage contract and usually in fact obtained it, there were cases when it was not paid, and it might happen that the wife sought to realize her right years after the marriage, sometimes at the very moment of divorce. The parties might agree at the time of the marriage that the prompt dower should be paid a specified time after the signing of the marriage contract.[37] Sometimes a divorced woman was entitled to half the specified dower or waived this right; this refers to cases where a divorce was performed before consummation of the marriage or valid privacy. Hence it may be deduced that a woman was not always ready to move into her husband's house before the prompt dower had been paid to her.[38]

There is a definite connection between dower customs and the type of marriage, especially exchange marriage (*tabādul al-zawjāt, shighār*). The *raison d'etre* of this institution is the mutual waiver of the dower for the two exchanged women. According to customary law, each of the two women constitutes the substance (*'ayn*) of the dower of the other. This type of marriage creates a mutual dependence between the two women and is very injurious to family life. Islam sought to eradicate exchange marriage indirectly by laying down that the dower belonged to the wife; according to the Ḥanafi school, where no dower was agreed on at the time of the marriage, each of the two exchanged wives was entitled to a fair dower. In other words, the exchange marriage was incorporated into Islamic law and at the same time distorted and emptied of its main content.[39] But social custom is stronger than religious law. In many of the approximately 100 exchange marriages which the author came across in the *sijills*,[40] the two women received no dower. Thus, in one case, it was stated in court that a girl had been given to a man, in a gift (*'aṭā'*) marriage, by way of exchange for the man's sister, who was given to the girl's brother, without anything being paid to either bride. In another case, in which the husband demanded that his wife should obey him, the wife replied that she was prepared to do so if her exchange partner (*badīla*) did likewise or, alternatively, if she received her dower.[41] Of course, it was usual to indicate in the marriage contracts identical amounts of dower for the two brides, but it seems that this was a fiction and that in reality the two dowers cancelled each other out. Thus, in one case, the *ma'dhūn* testified that no dower had been paid in his presence although identical amounts of dower had been indicated in the marriage contracts.[42] In another case, a woman renounced the whole (including the deferred) dower on divorce, alleging that she had not received the prompt dower—"not one mil"—because it had been an exchange marriage.[43] The wife's renunciation of the dower on divorce by mutual consent was frequent in exchange marriages and may support the assumption that she did not really receive the prompt dower at the time the marriage was contracted.[44]

At the same time, there is evidence, though not much, of exchanged wives, receiving all or part of the dower. Thus, in one case, two such wives were divorced on the same day and it was decided that each should receive the balance of the prompt dower, since the total prompt dowers had not been received at the signing of the marriage contracts. In another case, it was noted in the marriage contract that the wife's father had received half the dower on contraction of the marriage and that it had been stipulated that the husband should pay a certain sum as deferred dower. In a further case of divorce by agreement between the parties to an exchange marriage, it was stated that the wife had received the whole dower at the time of contraction of the marriage and that the husband had waived its return.[45] In several cases, the marriages of the two couples were not consummated and the exchanged wives waived half the dower, from which it may perhaps be concluded that they had received one-half.[46] In one case, one of the wives was divorced, while her *badila* received the prompt dower and remained with her husband.[47] Payment of dower to one of the exchanged wives infringes the principle of equality of treatment for them; the dissolution of the marriage of one of the couples does not automatically entail the dissolution of the marriage of the other.[48] It might happen that instead of the dower the wife was given or promised its equivalent in clothing (*jihāz*), jewellery (*maṣāgh*), household effects and the like.[49]

Many researchers have found that in marriages of paternal cousins the dower was smaller than in exogamous marriages.[50] The author came across only one express testimony to a reduction of the dower under these circumstances. A witness testified in court that the girl's father had said: "I allow my brother's son a reduction of IL 200 [on a dower of IL 2,500]."[51] The author did indeed come across many cases of dissolution of cousin marriages by consent of the parties where the wife waived both the prompt the deferred dowers,[52] as well as cases where the dower was not mentioned at all in the terms of divorce,[53] but such phenomena were not peculiar to cousin marriages and do not permit the conclusion that this type of marriage had any effect on the amount or mode of payment of the dower.

According to religious law, as stated, the dower belongs to the wife. To what extent did she enjoy this property right in practice? An exhaustive reply to this question cannot be obtained from the sources because a woman was generally given in marriage by a marriage guardian, who might be her father or brother or another relative, and who received the dower on her behalf.[54] Hence, it cannot be ascertained whether the dower was given to the bride or what became of it. At the same time, scattered evidence permits one at least to say that the wife did not always enjoy this right. Sometimes a woman declared in court, during the hearing of some matrimonial matter, that the dower had been given to her father or brother.[55] In several cases, a woman alleged that she had not received the whole or part of the dower, and afterward it appeared that her father had received it without her knowledge.[56] In one case, a woman alleged that she had received the dower, and afterward it appeared that her father had received it.[57] In another case, the dower was given to the woman, who declared before the court that she was making it over to her father as a *shar'i* gift *(hiba)* and was not allowed to revoke this act.[58] There is also express evidence of husbands taking control of their wives' dower without their consent. In one case, the husband took back the whole dower and spent it on his farm and on medical treatment for himself. In other cases, he reassumed possession of a plot of land or of some goats or olive trees that had been given the wife as part of the dower.[59]

On the other hand, there is a great deal of evidence in marriage contracts of women receiving the dower either directly or through a marriage-guardian. When a woman married without a guardian, she took the dower herself. This was usually a widowed or divorced woman,[60] but sometimes even a spinster married without a guardian and the dower was given her without an intermediary.[61] There is evidence also in the *sijills* of women receiving the dower from their guardians after the marriage, or "through" their guardians, but it is not always certain that they actually got it.[62] In one case, a man alleged that his deceased wife's father had appropriated her estate (dower and gifts) and asked that it be distributed in accordance with *shari'* rules, whence it may be deduced that in the wife's lifetime the dower was in her possession.[63]

There is a great deal of evidence of women insisting on their rights to dower and the stipulations connected with it. In many cases, women left their husband's houses on the ground that they had not been paid the whole or part of the dower and that the *jihāz* and various stipulations connected with the dower, such as household effects and jewellery and other ornaments, had not been delivered to them; they refused to return until they had received these things and in the meantime they claimed maintenance from their husbands. In one case, a woman of Jaffa contended that the household effects "belonged to her personally and were bound up with the dower in accordance with accepted custom." She also alleged that the husband had given her two radio sets, a piano and other articles, but had not yet registered them in her name. She asked the court to decide that these articles were hers and that her husband be forbidden to use them without her consent.[64] As stated, the wife sometimes refused from the outset to move into the husband's house before she had received the dower, but it seems that as a rule she wished to realize her right to dower after the marriage had been consummated and offspring born. Non-payment of the whole or part of the dower was a frequent cause of divorce on the wife's initiative. Instances of the wife's struggle for realization of her property rights were common in urban and rural, but not in Beduin, society.[65]

Most of the women who married without a guardian and received dower directly came from urban types of settlement, especially from mixed towns,[66] and the same applies in cases where the dower was given through a guardian. There is less evidence of rural women receiving dower, and the author found only one instance of a woman being given dower in Beduin society (in Galilee).[67] These findings are confirmed by other sources. Rosenfeld found that among the Muslims of Tur'ān 40% of the dower was given to the wife for the purchase of clothing and gold and the remainder was left to her father. Cohen found that in 56% of the cases surveyed in a sampling carried out in the late 1950s in the village of Bint al-Ḥudūd, the dower was given to the wife's father or brother and that the wife was sometimes given monetary compensation by the person who had taken the dower.[68] Yūsuf Dasūqī, Secretary of the *Sharīʻa* Court of Ṭayyiba, reported in 1965 that the practice of the bride's father pocketing the dower was diminishing in the Little Triangle villages. Fathers, except the very poor, wished to help the young couple at its first steps and therefore generally returned the dowers to the daughters.[69] Marx notes that among the Negev Beduin the whole or the largest part of the dower was given to the bride's father or brother.[70] G. Kressel found that in the 'Arab Jawārīsh housing project in the Ramla municipal area many fathers returned the whole or part of the dower in the form of gold jewellery or furnishings for the daughter's home.[71] In a survey conducted in Nazareth in 1965, it appeared that in most cases the dower was given to the daughter for her personal requirements and for domestic arrangements and did not remain with her father.[72] Shaykh Muḥammad Ḥubayshī reported that in Acre it was usual for the daughter to receive the whole dower, while in rural areas the father took part of it and used the remainder to buy her jewellery and clothes.[73] There are also indications—though not in the *sijills*—that beside the dower, the institution of the dowry (the contribution of the bride's father to the marriage) was spreading. Rosenfeld found such indications in several places.[74]

What did the wife do with the dower she received? The author could discover information as to this in only one instance. A woman who had married at the beginning of the 20th century had received 5,000 Turkish Kurush as dower, partly in cash and partly in the shape of seven olive trees; with the cash she had bought gold coins, for which her husband had sold her six olive trees in the the village.[75]

Deferred Dower

Deferred dower *(mahr muʻajjal)* and its proportion to the whole dower are not matters of law but of custom recognized by the Hanafi school. If the deferred dower was of a considerable amount, it might deter the husband from hasty or arbitrary divorce and also give a certain measure of economic security to the wife after divorce,[76] for according to the *sharī'a* she is only entitled to maintenance during the *idda* (the waiting-period of a woman after termination of the marriage), which is normally three months.[77] According to the testimony of Shaykh Muḥammad Ḥubayshi, it was then usual to regard the deferred dower as the wife's insurance policy. In several, cases the wife, on contraction of the marriage or subsequently, demanded that the deferred dower should be increased.[78] In functional respect, there is thus a distinct material difference between prompt and deferred dowers.

Until recently, deferred dower was not an object of study[79]; this was chiefly on account of its rarity. It was not accounted in the sense that its realization was a matter for the future. Table 4.3 shows that deferred dower was not particularly frequent in Israeli Muslim society.

TABLE 4.3
Muslim Marriages Without Deferred Dower in 1969 by Type of Bride's Settlement[a]

Type of Bride's Settlement	*Total Number of Marriages*	*Mariages without Deferred Dower*	
		Number	*% (rounded off)*
National Total	1,910	1,117	58
Total Urban	355	83	23
Nazareth and Shafā 'Amr	212	65	31
Mixed Towns	143	18	13
Total Rural	1,295	981	76
Northern District	712	541	76
Haifa District	278	230	83
Central District[a]	304	210	69
Jerusalem District	1		
Total Beduin Tribes	244	53	23
Negev	191	3	2
Galilee	53	50	94

(*a*) Including Ṭayyiba and Umm al-Faḥm.

Nearly 60% of the national total of marriages were concluded without deferred dower. At the same time, there are noticeable differences in the frequency of this practice between and even within the various ecological groups. Deferred dower was particularly frequent in urban society: more than three-quarters of the total number of cases. It was more usual in mixed than in purely Arab towns: 87% as against 69%. In rural society it was comparatively rare: one-quarter of the total number of cases; there were no significant differences between villages in different areas. The frequency of the deferred dower in the large villages of Ṭayyiba and Umm al-Faḥm (12%) was below the national average. Surprisingly enough, it was widespread among, the Negev Beduin. Although caution is required in evaluating the phenomenon there on the basis of percentage figures,[80] there can be no doubt that its extent was significant: it occurred in almost all the marriages performed by the *ma'dhūn*. This seems mainly to be due to marriages between Beduin and women from mixed towns—as is also the case with large amounts of prompt dower.

Considerable differences between the various types of settlement (urban, rural, and Beduin), and within each type existed also with regard to the amounts of deferred dower, as is illustrated in Table 4.4. The amounts of the deferred dowers were larger in towns than in villages—IL 2,700 as against IL 950—and slightly larger in mixed towns than in Nazareth and Shafā 'Amr. The rural sector showed striking differences in different districts. The amounts of deferred dower were smallest in Ṭayyiba, Umm al-Faḥm and the villages of the Haifa District (about IL 400) and largest (IL 2,700) in the Central District of the Little Triangle, where they approximated to the average of the mixed towns. The deferred dower was smallest among the Beduin (IL 700), but three-and-a-half times as large among the Negev Beduin as among the Galilee Beduin (IL 820 as against IL 230, approximately equal to that customary in the villages of the Northern District), which was probably due to the sizeable representation of shaykhs in registered marriages.

TABLE 4.4
Average Amounts of Prompt Dower and Deferred Dower in 1969 by Type of Bride's Settlement[a]

Type of Bride's Settlement	*Average Amount of Dower in IL*		
	Prompt	*Deferred*	*Ratio of Prompt to Deferred Dower*
Overall National Average	3,654	1,247	2.9
National Average, Urban	2,469	2,694	0.8
Nazareth and Shafā Amr	2,558	2,660	0.9
Mixed Towns	2,273	2,767	0.8
Jewish Settlements	5,333[b]	1,667	
National Average, Rural	3,826	943	4.0
Northern District	3,860	855	4.5
Haifa District	3,737	439	8.2
Central District	4,239	2,727	1.5
Ṭayyiba and Umm al-Fahm	3,399	421	8.0
Jerusalem District	4,000	4,500	
Beduin National Average	4,436	694	6.2
Negev	4,632	822	5.6
Galilee	3,727	231	16.1

(a) Derived from unpublished data of the Central Bureau of Statistics.
(b) Based on three cases.
(c) Based on one case.

On the national average, the prompt dower was about three times as large as the deferred dower (IL 3,600 as against IL 1,200), but there were differences as to the ratio of the two kinds of dower between and within the various types of settlement. In the towns, the deferred dower slightly exceeded the prompt dower (IL 2,700 as against IL 2,500). On the other hand, in the villages and among the Beduin, the prompt dower was four and six times, respectively, as large as the deferred dower; the gap was particularly wide in the villages of the Haifa District and in Ṭayyiba and Umm al-Fahm (eight times) and among the Galilee Beduin (16 times).[81] In the Little Triangle villages, the prompt dower exceeded the deferred dower by only 50%; the ratio between the two kinds of dower was here nearest to that customary in the towns. The two kinds of dower were inversely proportional: the larger the deferred dower, the smaller the prompt dower, and vice versa. This is clearly apparent in all types of settlement. In the mixed towns were found the largest deferred dowers side by side with the smallest prompt dowers: IL 2,800 as against IL 2,300, and among the Beduin, the smallest deferred dowers alongside the largest prompt dowers: IL 700 as against IL 4,400. Exceptions to this rule were the Little Triangle villages (not including (Ṭayyiba and Umm al-Faḥm), where the amounts of deferred and prompt dower were the largest in the country: IL 2,700 as against IL 4,200.

The negative correlation between prompt and deferred dower arose from different conceptions of the function of dower. In the villages and in Beduin society, where the traditional conception was still very much alive, the amount of deferred dower was but a small fraction of that of prompt dower. In the towns, where women's freedom is greatest, the idea that the main object of the dower is economic security for divorced and widowed women was gaining ground, as a result, deferred dower was eclipsing prompt dower to the extent of reducing it to a mere token payment. In the Little Triangle villages, which had enjoyed increasing prosperity since the late 1950s, the two conceptions, the traditional and the modern, seemed to exist side by side, which probably accounts for the large amounts of both prompt and deferred dower. Rather surprisingly, in Ṭayyiba and Umm al-Faḥm, two of the most developed and progressive villages in Israel, a small deferred dower was found beside a large prompt dower (IL 400 as against IL 3,400).

The negative correlation between the two kinds of dower becomes clear if the dower is viewed in connection with women's education one of the accepted criteria of their social liberation.[82] Table 4.5 shows that where the wife was completely uneducated the prompt dower was .largest and the deferred dower smallest: IL 4,000 as against IL 600, whereas in the case of a woman with a secondary education the prompt dower was smallest and the deferred dower largest: IL 2,900 as against IL 3,100. The gap between the two kinds of dower narrowed the better the woman's education: where she had no schooling at all, the prompt dower was six times or more the amount of the deferred dower, and where she had nine to 12 years of schooling, the two dowers were almost equal.

TABLE 4.5
Averages of Prompt and Deferred Dowers in 1969 by Number of Years of Schooling of the Bride[a]

Number of Years of Schooling	*Average Amount of Dower in IL*		*Ratio of Prompt to Deferred Dower*
	Prompt	*Deferred*	
Overall Average	3,654	1,247	2.0
0	3,964	626	6.3
1-4	3,923	948	4.1
5-8	3,365	1,712	1.9
9-12	2,941	3,145	0.9
13+[b]	4,333	1,667	2.5

(a) Derived from unpublished data of the Central Bureau of Statistics.
(b) The averages in this group are based on six cases.

An anomaly exists with regard to the relation between dower and higher education of the wife: the prompt dower was largest (IL 4,300) and the deferred dower comparatively small (IL 1,700). Although caution is needed in drawing conclusions as to this group in view of the small number of cases, it may be significant that both the smallest[83] and the largest amounts of prompt dower were to be found here (the median prompt dower being IL 750 in 1966 and IL 4,500 in 1969). This phenomenon may be due to the bride's family background. A woman with a higher education is likely to be among the most liberated socially—to have adopted (and imparted to her family) the modern conception of the choice of the marriage partner and the function of the dower, but on the other hand, she may belong to a prominent, wealthy family which has preserved the traditional approach to marriage; such families tend to be punctilious about social origin and economic status, one of the symbols of which is the fair dower. Some researchers have already noticed that upper-class women tend to be less liberated than their middle-class sisters.[84]

The Problem of Excessive Dower

The problem of the soaring dower never ceased to exercise the Muslim public, and some considered it "the most serious problem facing a Muslim youth in Israel on reaching maturity."[85] The young men complained that they had to incur heavy debts, at usurious interest, or work for years to save up money for the dower, the gifts for the bride and her family, the wedding festivities and the dwelling with all the necessary equipment. Especial criticism was levelled at the increase of the dower in the Little Triangle villages: it was contended that fathers sold their daughters like cattle to the highest bidder, that young men had to forego their betrothed because the fathers had withdrawn their consent to the marriages and demanded exorbitant dowers.[86] As a result of all this, the young men were utterly bewildered. Some of them accused the Government of encouraging the prevailing practice in order to limit the Arab birth-rate. The marriage rate in Muslim society was generally on the decline: it had dropped from eight per mille in 1953 to six per mille in 1968, and in some years, there had even been an absolute decline in the number of marriages.[87] One of the causes of this phenomenon was the enormous increase in the prompt dower.[88]

The young men reacted to this irksome problem in different ways. According to one, there were three courses open to them: old bachelor-hood, theft (to finance the dower), or abduction of the girl of their choice. Some of them had threatened to declare a marriage strike "in order that the fathers might learn a lesson and let them marry their daughters free of charge."[89] There were several criminal cases and acts of despair in this connection.[90] Many had asked the Ministry of Religious Affairs to intervene, for example, by introducing criminal legislation to prohibit excessive dower.[91]

The first organized expression of the young men's point of view occurred early in 1960. Intellectuals from the Little Triangle villages held a meeting in Ṭayyiba to create an organizational framework for a movement to fight excessive dower. One of the leaders of this movement, Abd al-Salām Yūsuf Maṣārwa, opened the conference "in the name of Allāh and tortured humanity, which collapses under the yoke of reaction" and read out letters of encouragement from Shaykh Mūsā al-Ṭabarī and from Knesset Members and other public figures, Muslim and non-Muslim. The local *imām* quoted passages denouncing excessive dower from the Qur'ān and *ḥadīths* (formal traditions) attributed to the Prophet. The young men made it clear that they did not intend to abolish dower altogether, since it was ordained by religion, but to reduce it to token proportions. They demanded that it should be limited by legislation to a minimal amount. A young teacher asked excitedly. "How can such a disgraceful trade [in daughters] be carried on in the 20th century, the era of the conquest of space?" The meeting decided to convene a national Muslim conference to discuss measures for a reduction of the dower, and to conduct a large-scale propaganda campaign in the press and at local, regional and national meetings. A second rally of the movement took place soon afterward on a Friday at the mosque of Kafr Qāsim, when the villagers were urged to content themselves with a token dower after the manner of the Prophet and the Caliphs and to contribute to a fund to finance the activities of the movement. Following this rally, 'Abd al-Salām estimated that "our victory is near, for among the Muslim public, and especially the intelligentsia, support and solidarity are forthcoming which in part already found practical expression at Kafr Qāsim." About two months later, a national rally was held at the Israel Labour Federation's club in Jaffa, attended by youths from Galilee, the Little Triangle, Jaffa and Ramla. For the first time, girls had been invited to take part actively in discussing means to reduce the dower. The rally was under the patronage of Shaykh Ṭāhir Ḥamād.[92] The movement continued its activities for some time longer. Thus, for instance, the Minister of Religious Affairs was asked to ensure, by criminal legislation, full freedom for women in the choice of their spouses, to assist in a large-scale propaganda campaign among the general public, and to urge that the *qāḍīs* support the movement both materially and morally.[93]

However, the great enthusiasm that had seized the public subsided quickly. 'Abd al-Salām emigrated to the United States, and so ended the movement. From time to time, young people attempted to revive it, as in Majd al-Kurūm in 1965, but afterward feelings cooled again.[94] The expected response from wide sections of the public and assistance from the Government did not materialize.[95] The Minister of Religious Affairs did not bring in a bill to limit the amount of the dower. On the contrary, he strongly opposed the initiative of Knesset Member U. Avneri, whose private member's bill entitled the Prohibition of Dower Bill, 5726-1966, was designed to impose a penal sanction for taking dower of a value exceeding IL 50. Mr Avneri thought that the problem could not be solved by public action but only by legislation, as according to him had been done by the revolutionary regime in Egypt.[96] The Knesset rejected the bill. The Minister of Religious Affairs based its rejection on social, legal and practical considerations. In his opinion, limiting dower by legislation would not have stood the test of reality and the law would have been ridiculed; the problem could only be solved by a change in social habits. He added that Knesset intervention would produce angry reactions from the Arab states and Israel would be accused of attacking the *sharī'a*. Knesset Member 'Abd al-'Aziz al-Zu'bī denounced excessive dower, but expressed the view that it should not be combatted by legislation forbidding something permitted by the Qur'ān and warned that there might be those who would say that "the Jews want to change the Qur'ān."[97]

Though the movement for the fight against excessive dower did not succeed in getting the Knesset to introduce prohibitive or restrictive legislation, it probably contributed, by influencing public opinion, to the speeding-up of far-reaching changes in dower practices in Israeli Muslim society. There is evidence of a number of instances of token prompt dower, usually amounting to IL 10, alongside deferred dower running into thousands of pounds, sometimes IL 10,000 or more.[98] This arrangement placed no financial obstacle in the way of marriage, and on the other hand provided a deterrent to arbitrary divorce, and was a means to ensure the wife's subsistence in the event of divorce or the husband's death. Still, the token prompt dower might become meaningless, for the husband sometimes undertook in the marriage contract to give the wife, in addition to the prompt dower, various household effects, high-quality furniture for their dwelling, jewellery, and occasionally even an appartment or house, of an aggregate value exceeding the average amount of the prompt dower. Thus, in one case, the prompt dower was IL 5, but in addition, the wife received a fully appointed house worth IL 15,000 and was moreover, promised a deferred dower of IL 10,000.[99] From the point of view of the husband, this arrangement was thus not always advantageous. But neither was it from the point of view of the wife: instead of the prompt dower, which passed into her ownership for her own exclusive use, she received its equivalent in property used by the whole family. In places where custom required the husband to provide the household effects at his own expense, the wife was deprived in that they were bought with her money.

Though not particularly frequent, the token prompt dower seems to have become established in Israeli Muslim society. In 1968, it occurred in about 140 marriages, i.e., about 7% of the total number, in amounts up to IL 10, but there were remarkable differences in this respect between different types of settlement. About one-fifth of the marriages in towns involved token prompt dower, as against approximately 4% in villages.[100] Token dower was a recent phenomenon (since the mid-1950s), found especially in Acre, or where at least the bride was from that town, among intellectuals and members of relatively prestigious callings[101]; the author came across some instances also in exchange marriages.[102] In such cases, token prompt dower met the demands of both social custom and religious law.

Since the early 1960s, a new practice has emerged in Israeli Muslim society: marriage with no dower at all, prompt or deferred. The press gave great prominence to "the first case" of this kind in Mazra'a village near Acre. The bride's family agreed to take no dower from the groom, a member of the "Arab pioneer youth," and the *qāḍī* did not believe his ears. This was regarded as "an historic precedent in the fight against excessive dower."[103] Thirteen dowerless marriages took place in 1968, all in urban types of settlement.[104] Instead of paying dower, the groom probably bought household effects, clothes and the like for the bride with his own money, as he often did in cases of token prompt dower.

Militating against renunciation of the dower were not only consideration of finance, but also of status and prestige. A small dower, let alone the total lack of dower, was apt to impair a woman's standing,' which was identified with the family honor (*'ird*).[105] This notion underlay the fair dower, i.e., the dower to be given to a woman according to her value by criteria of a traditional society. There is evidence of dozens of girls imploring families to forego the dower and let them marry the penniless boys they loved and not some wealthy old man, and quite often the family would have been ready to comply but for the fear that this would mean a loss of face.[106] To overcome this obstacle, the bride and her family sometimes contributed to the dower or even paid the whole of it or secretly returned it to the groom after he had paid it in the presence of many people.[107] Methods of circumventing the dower with the consent of the girl but against the will of the family included the borrowing of equipment and jewellery, to be returned to the owners after the marriage,[108] and the abduction of the bride.[109] Informed persons pointed out a further way of circumventing the problem: marriage to Jewish and Christian girls. Such marriages had the added advantage of providing educated brides, who were in great demand in Muslim society.[110] Marriages between Muslim men and non-Muslim women (but not the other way round) were widespread in Israel, but the evidence of the *sijills* does not convey the impression that they were contracted without dower.[111] Relief to those wrestling with the problems of excessive dower came from an unexpected quarter. After the Six-Day War of 1967, many dozens of brides began to be imported from the West Bank, the Gaza Strip and East Jerusalem and its rural vicinity at comparatively low rates of dower.[112]

The *sijills* mention hundreds of cases in which women renounced their right to dower, viz., prompt dower (the whole or the outstanding part), deferred dower, or half the specified dower where the marriage had not been consummated; in almost all cases; the renunciation was made on divorce by mutual agreement of the parties.[113] In other words, the divorced woman did not in fact enjoy her right to deferred dower[114] or even, sometimes, to the whole or part of the prompt dower. In this context, it is significant that the *sijills* afford no evidence of widows realizing or demanding the realization of their right to dower out of the estates of their late husbands before distribution thereof among the heirs. Renunciation of the dower was frequent in all ecological groups and must be understood in the light of changes in the status of women, of which the extremely widespread dissolution of marriage on the wife's initiative was one of the most notable manifestations. The wife was ready to forego monetary and other rights in order to obtain her freedom.[115]

The *Qāḍīs* and Dower

As a rule, the *qāḍīs* sought to apply the religious-legal norm which made the dower the exclusive property of the wife and rejected social custom as far as it was inconsistent with this conception. This approach was of course in keeping with the wife's interest. In one case Shaykh Ṭāhir al-Tabarī rejected a husband's demand that his wife obey him when he became aware that theirs was an exchange marriage and the wife had not received her dower.[116] In another case, in which a man contended that the marriage had been contracted without dower with the wife's consent, Shaykh Ṭāhir Ḥamād decided that a *fair* dower was obligatory whether dower was agreed on or not. In yet another case, he decided that the dower belonged to the wife and that the husband should not use it without her permission. On the other hand, he once dismissed a wife's contention that a clause in the marriage contract concerning dower was fictitious and that neither of the two exchanged wives had received anything.[117] In similar circumstances, Shaykh Ḥusnī al-Zu'bī dismissed a woman's claim for dower on the ground that a wife's contention that she had not received the whole dower should not be heard after she had given herself to her husband.[118]

Shaykh Ḥasan Amīn al-Ḥabash once declared that he insisted on the dower being given to the wife and not to anyone else.[119] He ordered a woman to return to her deserted daughter-in-law a cupboard the latter had bought with her dower, and a husband to pay his wife the balance of the prompt dower.[120] In another case, he rejected a wife's demand that her husband pay her the balance of the dower and took no account of the fact that the dower had been handed to a proxy (*wakīl*), who had not transmitted it to the wife.[121] Shaykh Amīn Qāsim Mudlij considered that the dower belonged to the wife along and that neither her father nor her husband had any share in it. The dower, he believed, was in part designed to enable the wife to buy jewellery and clothes, and in part to be saved for emergencies, such as divorce or the husband's death. In his opinion, a wise father would give his daughter money to supplement her dower.[122] But these sentiments were not reflected in his judgments. Shaykh Mūsā al-Ṭabarī stated that according to custom prevailing in Muslim localities of Israel a woman moved from her father's house to that of her husband equipped with various household effects.[123] When a woman was divorced before consummation of the marriage, the *qāḍīs* took care to ensure that she was aware of her entitlement to one-half of the specified dower.[124] They did not intervene in any way when a woman renounced the dower—prompt or deferred—in the event of divorce.[125]

The problem of excessive dower frequently preoccupied the *qāḍīs* outside their judicial activity. They renounced excessive dower on religious and social grounds. Shaykh Ṭāhir Ḥamād thought that this problem did not exist at the inception of Islam or in the days of the *tabi'un,* the followers of the Prophet. At the same time, both he and Shaykh Ḥasan Amīn al-Ḥabash quoted *hadīths* attributed to the Prophet and the earliest Caliphs deprecating excessive dower. Shaykh Mūsā al-Ṭabarī revealed that he was "greatly perturbed by the position with regard to excessive dower and the heavy burden it imposed on the husband because of debts or the necessity to sell his property in order to finance the dower . . ." He also stressed that he wholeheartedly supported the movement for the fight against excessive dower.[126] Shaykh Amīn Qāsim Mudlij, in one of his Friday sermons, expressed the view that excessive dower was "contrary to honor (*sharaf*) and religion"; he attacked the fathers who "make their daughters objects of trade and treat them like cattle" for monetary gain, who exposed them to contempt and humiliation by their husbands, who later blamed them for their economic straits. In his opinion, excessive dower corrupted morals and encouraged prostitution and suicide among women, as well as marriages between Muslims and Jewish and Christian girls, which were foredoomed to failure. He, too, invoked *ḥadīths* in repudiating excessive dower.[127]

At the same time, all the *qāḍīs*, for religious and practical reasons, categorically rejected a solution of the problem by means of legislation forbidding or limiting dower. Shaykh Ḥasan Amīn al-Ḥabash thought that dower "was not set an upper or lower limit by the *sharīʻa*" and relied in this connection on interpretations of the term *qinṭār* (a measure mentioned in Qurʻān IV: 19 and in *ḥadiths* attributed to the Prophet). Shaykh Ṭāhir Ḥamād voiced the opinion that a law fixing grades for dower—high, medium and low—would be of no practical value.[128] At the first *qāḍīs* conference in 1950, proposals were made to limit dower and were all rejected.[129] The question was again discussed at a conference in 1966 following the tabling of Knesset Member U. Avneri's bill. The *qāḍīs* sharply objected to Knesset interference in Islamic custom and law.[130] The only means they thought they could adopt without fear of infringing religious law was to exhort fathers to agree of their own free will not to demand excessive dowers for their daughters. The 1950 conference resolved that *qāḍīs* and religious functionaries should advise *maʻdhūns* to persuade those concerned to exert moderation with regard to dower. Such activities were indeed conducted from time to time by mosque functionaries, *maʻdhūns*[131] and also *qāḍīs*. Shaykh Ṭāhir Ḥamād said, on the one hand, that "the best method is to point out to preachers (*waʻiẓs*) and instructors (*murshids*) that they should urge the people to follow the straight path." On the other hand, he doubted the effectiveness of such activities in view of the experience of the Supreme Muslim Council in Mandatory times. Shaykh Ḥasan Amīn al-Ḥabash called for the "launching of a campaign" *(shann ḥamla)* of enlightenment against excessive dower; he participated personally in such a campaign. In 1950, Shaykh Mūsā al-Ṭabarī called on *imāms* to urge people to reduce dower and fix limits for it: a lower limit of IL 500 and an upper limit of IL 1,000; he declared his willingness to conduct a campaign in the villages for this purpose.[132] In 1966, Shaykh Amīn Qāsim Mudlij undertook a campaign in Galilee villages to combat excessive dower. He reportedly intended to propose the introduction of fixed norms for dower on the basis of voluntary arrangements.[133]

The fact that the problem remained on the agenda of the *qāḍīs* for years suggests that propagandistic activities against execessive dower bore no real fruit. It is doubtful whether the *qāḍīs* were in fact capable of solving this problem. Their personal authority was not sufficient to uproot a social custom supported by religious law. Moreover, this was not a question of a legal norm, religious or secular (it is also doubtful whether intervention by the Knesset would be of use), but of a social norm, which by nature changes slowly, in the course of a long period. The *qāḍīs* were aware of this, and at their 1966 conference they expressed the view that the problem would find its solution with the passage of time.[134] They seemed to have had in mind the token prompt dower alongside a large deferred dower, an arrangement which, as noted, has begun to evolve in recent years. This was a practical solution which involved no violation of Islamic law. Such, at any rate, was the view of Shaykh Amīn Qāsim Mudlij.[135]

Shaykh Ḥasan Amīn al-Ḥabash advocated increasing the specified dower beyond the *qinṭār* mentioned in the Qur'ān as deferred dower, so as to discourage divorce.[136] At their 1966 conference, the *qāḍīs* recommended that the provision in the marriage contract providing for deferred dower by strictly adhered to in order that it might assure the wife's future in the event of divorce or the husband's death.[137] This recommendation sprang from a new social motive, not rooted in Islamic law. At the same time, it is very doubtful whether the *qāḍīs* had any influence on contemporary practices with regard to deferred or token dower. It seems more likely that they desired to give such practices *shar'i* sanction. Thus, for instance, Shaykh Ḥasan related how during a visit to a village the people who had gathered on that occasion told him that the Ministry of Religious Affairs ought to limit prompt dower; they stressed that there was nothing to prevent deferred dower being three or four times as large as prompt dower. The *qāḍī* transmitted their wish to the Ministry of Religious Affairs with the remark that it seemed reasonable to him.[138]

Notes and References

1. The origin of dower has been variously explained by reference to marital, kinship or property relations, matters of manpower, etc.

See Robertson Smith, pp. 93-6; Gibb, p. 237; Anderson, *Islamic Law,* pp. 40-1; Coulson, *History,* p. 14; Schacht, p. 161; Abu Zahra, p. 144; Levy, pp. 95, 115; Baer, p. 41: Granqvist, vol. 1, pp. 132-4, 139, 145-7; Rosenfeld, *Peasants,* pp. 117, 136, 166, 187.

2. Schacht, p. 167; Qadrī, art. 206; Goitein and Ben-Shemesh, p. 223.
3. *FRL,* arts. 89-90; Qadrī, arts, 97, 99; Fyzee, pp. 134-6, 374-5.
4. The Qur'ān, IV: 20, mentions the *qinṭār.* The Ḥanbalī and Shāfi'ī schools do not recognize a lower limit for dower. No school recognizes an upper limit. Qadrī, art. 70; *ENFRL*; Linant de Bellefonds, pp. 207-8; Coulson, *History,* p. 40; Abu Zahra, pp. 141-2.
5. *FRL*, arts. 80-8; Qadrī, arts. 70-111; Linant de Bellefonds, pp. 213 *seq.*; Schacht, pp. 167, 191-2; Fyzee, pp. 131-2; Goitein and Ben-Shemesh, pp. 130-1. The matter of the *mut'a* is based on Qur'ān, II:236, and other verses.
6. *FRL*, arts. 69, 71; Qadrī, art. 104; Linant de Bellenfonds, pp. 201-2; Abu Zahra, pp. 141-2; Fyzee, p. 135; Levy, p. 114; Schacht, p. 197.
7. Silberg, p. 400; Zadok, pp. 67, 69; Women's Equal Rights Bill, 5711-1951, *Bills,* No. 75 of 1951 (5711), p. 191; remarks of the Minister of Justice in the Knesset, *KP,* vol. 9, p. 2005 col. 1, p. 2171 col. 2; remarks of Knesset Member Jarjūra, *ibid.*, p. 2089 col. 1.
8. The position is not clear with regard to unmarried women. See Gibb, p. 240.
9. See Prohibition of Dower Bill, 5726-1966, *Private Member's Bill,* No. 26; *ha-Aretz* of June 23, 1966. See above, pp. 57-8.
10. The calculation is based on Table IX/I, *SAI*, 1970, No. 21, p. 241.
11. Rosenfeld, *Peasants,* pp. 66-7, 117, 138; Ben-Porath, pp. 78-9. Cf. Marx, *Bedouin,* p. 159.
12. See Ben-Porath, pp. 72, 78. See also *AI*, vol. 5 (1959), Nos. 1-2, p. 25. Shaykh Amīn Qāsim Mudlij explained the increase of dower as a consequence of competition, especially in recent years, for educated brides, who are few, and in great demand. *Ma'ariv* of July 3, 1966.
13. Cf. Chatila, pp. 184, 192, 195; Granqvist, vol. 1, pp. 122, 124, 132.
14. See *AI*, vol. 9 (1964), Nos. 1-2, English Summary.
15. For deferred dower see above, p. 51.
16. Cf. Marx, *Bedouin*, p. 159; Granqvist, vol. 1, p. 124.

17. Shaykh Salmān al-Ḥuzayyil, e.g., was married 39 times, and shaykhs had an average of eight living children as against three to four for Beduin generally. Marx, *Bedouin*, pp. 139-40.
18. Marx, *Bedouin*, pp. 42-5. See also the appendix relating to leased lands. *Ibid.*, p. 244.
19. See, e.g., *JfMC68* no. 10132 (husband for the al-Huzayyil tribe, wife of Jaffa; total dower IL 10,000, prompt IL 5,000, deferred IL 1,000, value of household effects forming part of the dower IL 4,000), no. 10032 (husband of the Abū Ruqayyiq tribe, wife of Jaffa; total dower IL 7,500, prompt IL 7,000). For references to *sijill* entries concerning marriages between Beduin and town women see the chapter "Maintenance and Obedience.' pp. 96 *Seq.*
20. It may be paid in foreign currency. See, e.g., *JfQ1*, p. 131: f.112/52 (Egyptian pounds) *JfQ5*, p. 86: no. 146-f.219/69 (300 Jordanian dinars).
21. See, e.g., *JfQ2*, p. 567: no. 578-f.88/62; *NzḤ24*, p. 216: no. 1/28-f.64/69.
22. See, e.g., *NzḤ15*, p. 46: no. 20/73; *AcṬ2*, p. 120; *AcṬ1*, p. 10. Cf. Granqvist, vol. 1, p. 119; Chatilla, p. 193.
23. *NzḤ19*, p. 160: f.5/52. Cf. Granqvist, vol. 1, p. 120; al-'Ārif, pp. 130-1; Chatila, pp. 193, 195.
24. See, e.g., *JfMC68*, nos. 10033, 10147, 10149: *ṬbMC68*, nos. 8027, 8028, 8037; *AcMC68*, nos. 2636, 2848.
25. See, e.g., *JfMC68*, nos.10163, 10027; *ṬbMC68*, nos. 8030, 8040; *AcMC68*, no. 3022.
26. See, e.g., *JfMC68*, nos. 9520, 10132, 10315.
27. See Palmon.
28. *Ibid.*
29. *AcI2*, p. 21: no. 18-f.1/51.
30. Rosenfeld, *Recent Changes*, p. 23. Cf. al-'Ārif, pp. 130-1; *Ma'ariv* of July 3, 1966.
31. *NzDS*, p. 39. Cf. Granqvist, vol. 1, p. 126; Chatila, pp. 185-6, 194; Baer, p. 41.
32. Derived from unpublished data of the Central Bureau of Statistics.
33. See Rosenfeld, *Peasants*, pp. 121-2. Among Negev Beduin it is usual to pay the whole dower before consummation (not on contraction) of the marriage, and the father does not agree to hand over his daughter before receiving the dower. Marx, *Bedouin*, pp. 104, 159. Cf. Granqvist, vol. 1, p. 111; Chatila, pp. 192-3.
34. Scc, e.g., *JfQ1*, p. 116: no. 198-f.62/53; *JfQ4*, p. 102: no. 114-f.70/68; *NzḤ20*, p. 128: no. 2/56 (the wife alleged at the time of the divorce that she had received nothing of the prompt dower); *NzḤ22*, p. 133: no.3/28-f.52/64; *NzḤ24*, p. 93: no.10/64-f.136/67; *NzI4*,

p. 108: no.2/20-f.76/51; *AcI2*, p. 26: f.32/51; *AcṬ3*, p. 12: f.7/51; *ṬbI1*, p. 15: no.1-f.1/51, p. 175: no. 16-f.38/60.

35. See, e.g., *JfQ1*, p. 101: no. 163-fs.63/52, 12/53; *JfQ3*, p. 359: no. 501-f.31/67.

36. See, e.g., *AcD6*, p. 15: f.29/65.

37. See, e.g., *JfQ4*, p. 88: no. 87-f.3/68.

38. *FRL.* art. 83, See, e.g., *ṬBI1*, p. 5: no.713-f.17/50, p. 266: no. 17-f.22/64 and p. 280: no. 1-f.51/64; *JfQ4*, p. 126: no. 146-f.119/68 and p. 138: no. 165-f.126/68. In one case, the husband was given time to prove his virility, and he agreed that if he did not succeed in doing so within a month the wife should be regarded as divorced and be entitled to receive back one-third of the prompt dower. See *AcI1*, p. 85: f.59/50.

39. See Qadrī, arts. 15, 76; Ibn 'Ābidīn, p. 361; Linant de Bellefonds, pp. 209 *seq.* See also Levy, p. 105; Robertson Smith, p. 112; Granqvist vol. 1, pp. 111-17, 136, 140; *ibid.*, vol. 2, p. 13; Rosenfeld, *Peasants,* pp. 117, 122-5, 136; Marx, *Bedouin*, p. 121; al-'Ārif, pp. 131-2; Shaykh Hasan Amīn al-Ḥabash, *AI,* vol. 11 (1968), Nos. 1-2, p. 3. See also *AD*, vol. 3 (1966), Nos.1-2, p. 14.

40. See the chapters "Divorce," pp. 129-30, and "Maintenance and Obedience," pp. 100-1.

41. *AcD6,* p. 19: no.58/65; and *NzI4*, p. 87: no. 4/45-f.114/50, respectively.

42. *ṬbMC68*, nos. 8045, 8046. See also *JfQ5,* p. 102: no. 171-f.258/69.

43. *AcṬ3,* p. 172: f.15/60.

44. See, e.g., *NzḤ18*, p. 212: no.9/34 and p. 212: no. 10/34; *JfQ5*, p. 26: no. 46-f.144/69 and p. 27: no. 47-f.145/69.

45. *ṬbḤ1*, p. 103: no. 2/70 and p. 103: no. 3/71; *AcMC68,* nos. 2694, 2695; and *ṬbḤ1,* p. 108: no. 1/78 and p. 109: no. 2/79, respectively.

46. But this is not certain; it is perfectly possible that the waiver of half the dower is purely formal, devoid of practical significance. See, e.g., *AcṬ4*, p. 4: fs.7/64, 8/64, p. 6: f.12/64, p. 8: f.15/64, p. 10: f.20/64, p. 11: f.22/64 and p.12: f.23/64.

47. *AcṬ3*, p. 172: f.15/60.

48. For instances of equal treatment in various spheres, of the wives in exchange marriages, see the chapters "Maintenance and Obedience," pp. 100-1, and "Divorce," pp. 100-1.

49. *JfQ3*, p. 97: no.154-f.21/64; *NzI4*, p. 284: no.1/6-f.165/65.

50. Granqvist, vol. 1, pp. 70, 122-3; Rosenfeld, *Peasants,* p. 117; Chatila, pp. 184, 192: Kressel, p. 25; Baer, p. 66 and the sources indicated there.

51. *AcD6,* p. 71: f.177/64.
52. See, e.g., *NzḤ23*, p. 16: no. 6/92-f.157/64.
53. See, e.g., *ṬbH2*, p. 53: no. 19; *NzḤ18*, p. 160: no. 6/262; *JfQ4*, p. 65: no. 61-f.12/68.
54. Cf. Chatila, p. 185.
55. See, e.g., *NzḤ23*, p. 163: no. 2/22-f.32/66; *ṬbI1*, p. 10: no. 1/11-f.25/50; *JfQ1*, p. 8: no. 15-f.13/51, p. 94: no. 150-f.74/52.
56. See, e.g., *JfQ2*, p. 520: no. 495-f.6/61; *NzI4*, p. 59: no.2/26-f.43/49, p. 126: no. 24/4-f.102/52 (the groom had paid the dower to the bride's father in two instalments, and the bride did not know of the second instalment). See the remarks of the Minister of Justice in the Knesset in the debate on U. Avneri's private member's bill for the limitation of dower; *KP,* 74th meeting of June 22, 1966.
57. *NzḤ22*, p. 82: no. 2/75-f.127/63.
58. *NzḤ17*, p. 133: no. 34/285 the girl, of the Arab al-Subayh tribe, was not yet 17 years of age, and it had been agreed to marry her to her fiance, who had paid the dower, after her age had been corrected to 17 years; in the meantime, the dower was to remain "until called for" with two persons with whom the father had deposited it.
59. See, e.g., *ṬbI1*, p. 25: no. 9-f.24/51; *NzḤ15*, p. 46: no. 20/73; *NzḤ19*, p. 160: no.5/52; and *Nz14,* p. 61: no. 5/59-f.?/49, respectively.
60. See, e.g., *JfMC68*, nos. 10094, 10148, 10149, 10291; *AcMC68*, nos. 2834, 3445.
61. See, e.g., *JfMC68*, nos. 9520, 10080, 10081, 10097, 10098, 10150, 10166, 10279, 10299, 12561, 12601, 12606, 12610, 12615, 12617, 12621, 12623, 12624; *ṬbMC68,* no. 9399 (the dower was handed to the wife and the proxy (*wakil*); *AcMC68*, nos. 2828, 2831, 2835, 3022.
62. See, e.g., *ṬbI1*, p. 249: no. 50-f.8/64 (the wife received the dower through her father and was only then asked to let herself be conducted to the husband's home); *JfQ2*, p. 323: no. 505-f.53/58 (received the dower "by the hand of" her father); *NzḤ23*, p. 43: no. 4/24-f.48/65; *NzḤ24*, p. 35: no. 4/84-f.147/66, p. 95: no. 11/65-f.137/67, p. 114: no. 4/4-f.5/68.
63. *ṬbI1*, p. 5: no. 3/7-f.17/50.
64. *JfQ2*, p. 403: no. 565-f.55/59. Cf. Granqvist, vol. I, p. 145.
65. For more details, and source references, see the chapters "Maintenance and Obedience," pp. 92-3, and "Divorce," p. 131.
66. This statement is based on marriage contracts in which the wife made some stipulation.

67. *Nz14*, p. 44: no. 4/4-f.147/67 (the wife, of the Arab al-Subayh tribe, affixed her signature to the judgment for divorce).
68. Rosenfeld, *Peasants,* pp. 117, 166, 187; *idem, Recent Changes,* p. 23; *idem, Change and Conservation,* p. 211: Cohen, pp. 87-8.
69. D. Goldstein, *Ma'ariv* of June 25, 1965. See also interview with Shaykh Hasan Amīn al-Ḥabash, Z. Lavi', *Ma'ariv* of June 12, 1970. Cf. Granqvist, vol. 1, pp. 128, 132, 139-40; Chatila, p. 194.
70. Marx, *Bedouin,* pp. 159, 199; *idem, Social Structure,* p. 3. Cf. Canaan, p. 194; Chatila, p. 196; Baer, p. 40.
71. Kressel, p. 25.
72. *NzDS,* p. 39. Cf. Chatila, p. 185.
73. Interview with Shaykh Muḥammad Ḥubayshī.
74. Rosenfeld, *Peasants,* p. 166. This was confirmed by the *Mukhtār* of Bayt Safāfā, Musṭafā 'Alayān. See also *Ma'ariv* of June 25, 1965. Cf. Chatila, pp. 185-94; Abu Zahra, p. 144.
75. *Nz14,* p. 61: no. 5/59-f.?/49. Cf. Granqvist, vol. 1, p. 146. For the use of the dower by the bride's father see Rosenfeld, *Peasants*, pp. 23-4, 117-9; Granqvist, vol. 1, pp. 135, 137; Baer, p. 41, and the sources indicated there.
76. *FRL.* art. 71, See Coulson, *History,* pp. 207-8; Schacht, p. 167; Abu Zahra, p. 142; Fyzee, pp. 134-6, 140, 374-5; Chatila, pp. 184, 191, 199; E. Hare'uveni, *Ma'ariv* of July 3, 1966 (quotes persons who held that a connection exists between the amount of dower and the rate of divorces).
77. See the Chapter "Divorce," p. 177.
78. See, e.g., *AcI3,* p. 43: no. 4-f.9/57; *AcQ5*, p. 31: f.63/63.
79. See Chatila, p. 190. The author is indebted to Messrs. Ziyon Rabi and Refa el Palmon, of the Demographic Section of the Central Bureau of Statistics, for allowing him to use their statistical analysis, the first of its kind, on deferred dower in marriage contracts in Israel, prepared on the basis of unpublished data of the Bureau for the year 1968.
80. The performance of marriages without registration and without observing the niceties of the *sharī'a* is particularly widespread among the Negev Beduin. See Layish, *Custom,* pp. 381-3.
81. Cf. Chatila, pp. 185, 191-3, 195.
82. Dower is fixed according to the status and personal qualities of the bride and not according to the financial ability of the groom.
83. In 1966, the average prompt dower was smallest in the highest educational group—smaller by IL 100 than in the group with nine to 12 years of schooling. See *AI,* vol. 11 (1968), Nos. 1-2, p. 94.
84. Cf. Berger, p. 128: Baer, p. 52 n. 1.

85. *ha-Aretz* of May 7, 1956.
86. See, e.g., *AI*, vol. 3 (1955), No. 4, p. 13: *AI*, vol. 5 (1957), Nos. 1-2, p. 26; *AI*, vol. 7 (1959), No. 4, pp. 4-8; *ha-Aretz* of May 7, 1956; Su'ād Qaramān and Ahmad Safadī, Beyt ha-Gefen of May 16, 1968. Cf. Rosenfeld, *Peasants*, p. 187; Chatila, pp. 188-9.
87. See *Marriages*, 1957-1958, p. 46; *Vital Stats*. 1967; 1968, p. 6.
88. See *AI*, vol. 5 (1957), Nos. 1-2, *Hebrew Summary*, p. 3.
89. Y. Hame iri, *Yedi'ot Aḥaronoth* of August 17, 1956. Cf. Chatila, p. 197.
90. See, e.g., *ha-Aretz* of May 7, 1956; *ha-Tzofeh* of December 12, 1960.
91. See, e.g., an appeal by the Imām Ghālib Aḥmad Shibi, *AI*, vol. 1 (1950), No. 6, pp. 8-9; a letter from a young man to the Minister of Religious Affairs, *AI*, vol. 5 (1957), Nos. 1-2, p. 27; *Lamerḥav* and *Al ha-Mishmar* of October 10, 1955, *Davar, Lamerḥav, ha-Boqer* and *Ḥerut* of March 17, 1956.
92. *Al ha-Mishmar* of February 1, 1960; *Davar*, *'Al ha-Mishmar* and *ha-Boqer* of January 6, 1960; *Herut* of February 24, 1960; *Yedi'ot Aḥaronoth* of March 16, 1960.
93. *Davar* and *ha-Boqer* of March 24, 1960. Cf. Chatila, pp. 187-91, 197.
94. D. Goldstein, *Ma'ariv* of June 25, 1965 ('Abd al-Salām's sister was married off with a large dower).
95. See Rāshid Ḥusayn, *al-Mirṣād* of January 11, 1960, and January 21, 1960.
96. Prohibition of Dower Bill, 5726-1966 (Private Member's Bill No. 26), secs. 1, 3-6, 10; *KP*, 74th meeting of June 22, 1966. Neither Egypt nor any other Arab state has prohibited or limited dower. On the contrary, the relevant legislation was designed to increase the rates of dower by bypassing the minimal amounts, devoid of real value, prescribed by the Ḥanafī and Mālikī schools. See Linant de Bellefonds, pp. 251-2.
97. *KP*, 74th meeting of June 22, 1966. Knesset Member E. Ḥabībī, a Christian and a Communist, likewise said that the Knesset was not the appropriate place for solving the problem of excessive dower, for which he held the Government responsible *(loc. cit.)*. Interviewee Judge Eliyās Kteylī thought that the problem would not be solved, as demanded by the young, by legislation, but by change from below, and especially by education.
98. See, e.g., *AcMC68*, no. 3441 (IL 5 prompt, IL 10,000 deferred), no. 2644 IL 10, IL 5,000), no. 2426 (IL 10, IL 12,000), no. 2848 (IL 10, IL 15,000), no. 2946 (IL 1.60, IL 3,000), no. 2432 (10 agorot, IL 5,000); *ṬbMC68*, no. 18304 (IL 5, IL 10,000);

NzḤ23, p. 131: no. 7/111-f.173/65 (IL 10, IL 10,000); *JfMC68,* no. 10083 (IL 50, IL 2,000).

99. *ṬbMC62,* no. 18304. See also *AcMC68,* nos. 2644, 2826, 2841, 2848 (IL 10 and IL 15,000; the wife stipulated that the house with all its contents should be registered in her name as part of the prompt dower), no. 2432 Cf. E. Hare uveni, *Ma'ariv* of July 3, 1966.

100. According to unpublished data of the Central Bureau of Statistics. The category "villages" includes over 200 Beduin marriages, a few of them with token dower. See Palmon.

101. See, e.g., *AcMC68,* no. 2426 (the spouses had a secondary education and were employed as teachers), no. 3441 (the husband had a secondary education and was employed as a clerk; the wife had an elementary education), no. 2848 (the husband had a university education and the wife a secondary education: the husband was a teacher and the wife a clerk); *ṬbMC62,* no. 18304 (the husband was a school principal and the wife a teacher). See 'Abd al-Azīz al-Zu'bī in *Al ha-Mishmar* of July 17, 1966: E. Hare uveni, *Ma'ariv* of July 3, 1966 (interview with Shaykh Amīn Qāsim Mudlij). See also the remarks of the Minister of Religious Affairs in the debate on U. Avneri's private member's bill; *KP,* 74th meeting of June 22, 1966. In Iraq, too, token dower (commonly of one dīnār) is a new phenomenon, having developed in recent years in the educated strata; on the other hand, the groom is expected to prepare the dwelling at his expense, while the bride shares in the cost only if she is a woman of means; see el-Naqeb, p. 62. Cf., on the other hand, Chatila, p. 191).

102. See, e.g., *NzḤ23*, p. 131: no. 7/111-f.173/65, p. 158: no. 11/15-f.20/66 and p. 159: no. 12/16-f.21/66; *NzḤ24*, p. 106: no. 2/79-f.169/67 and p. 107: no. 3/80-f.170/67.

103. *Davar* and *Lamerḥav* of June 30, 1960. For further instances, see *Davar* of November 7, 1960, and *al-Yawn* of January 28, 1963 (both quoted from *AI*, vol. 8 (1963), Nos. 3-4, p. 48). See also Baer, p. 62 and the sources indicated there.

104. According to unpublished data of the Central Bureau of Statistics.

105. Cf. Berger, p. 108.

106. Knesset Member U. Avneri, *KP,* 74th meeting of June 22, 1966. Cf. Granqvist, vol. 1, pp. 120-2.

107. See E. Hare'uveni, *Ma'ariv* of June 3, 1966. Yusuf Dasūqī reported that youths in Little Triangle villages tended to marry girls with occupational skills "in order to recoup themselves for the dower they pay to them." See *AI*, vol. 8 (1962), Nos. 1-2, pp. 4-5. Cf. Chatila, pp. 191, 195.

108. In one case, the deception came to light when the bride's mother visited the young couple a week after the wedding "and saw that her daughter's hands were bare." The bride's family was convinced that the young man had duped them, relations between the two families became strained, and the bride was regarded as a traitress by her family. The younger generation, at any rate, admired the couple's pluck. *ha-Aretz* of August 31, 1960.

109. Interviewee Judge Eliyās Kteylī knew of many abductions in which the woman consented and waived the dower. Cf. Granqvist, vol. 1, pp. 153-4.

110. See, e.g., *Ma'ariv* of June 3, 1966, and 'Aṭāllāh Manṣūr, *ha-Aretz* of January 19, 1968. In one case, a well-known Muslim public figure converted to Judaism in order to marry a Jewess and afterward returned to Islam. See *al-Ittiḥād* of March 18, 1960.

111. The dower question is referred to in many cases. See, e.g., *JfQ1*, p. 106: no. 169-f.47/53; *NzḤ22*, p. 150: no. 13/46-f.78/64.

112. See, e.g., 'Aṭāllāh Manṣūr, *ha-Aretz* of January 19, 1968, February 5, 1969, and March 13, 1970; Z. Lavi, *Ma'ariv* of June 12, 1970, *al-Anbā* of November 4, 1970. Jalāl Abū Ṭu'ma, former Chairman of the Council of Bāqa al-Ghrabiyya, reported that dozens of young men of his village had since the Six-Day War brought brides from the West Bank for the low rate of dower of IL 2,000. See also *JfQ4*, p. 175: no. 220-f.73/69; *JfQ5*, p. 53: no. 89-f.194/69; and the chapter "Polygamy," p. 76.

113. See, e.g., *JfQ1*, p. 76: no. 118-f.88/52, p. 196: no. 318-f.60/55; *JfQ5*, p. 138: no. 229-f.6/70; *AcṬ2*, p. 7; *AcṬ3*, p. 32: f.23/57, p. 162: f.5/60, p. 173: f.16/60; *AcṬ4*, p. 16: f.31/64; *AcI3*, p. 71: f.7/58.

114. There is only sporadic evidence of divorced women insisting on realizing their right to deferred dower. See e.g., *JfQ2*, p. 498: no. 458-f.75/61 (a divorced woman sued her ex-husband for deferred dower after a lapse of years, when he had remarried and had children by his new wife); *JfQ4*, p. 162: no. 199-f.25/69; *ṬbI1*, p. 8: no. 1/9-f.22/50.

115. See the chapter "Divorce," p. 159.

116. *NzI4*, p. 87: no. 4/45-f.114/50.

117. *JfQ1*, p. 6: no. 12-f.10/51; *JfQ2*, p. 403: no. 565-f.55/59; and *JfQ3*, p. 97: no. 154-f.21/64, respectively.

118. In reliance on art. 104 of Qadrī's collection. *NzI4*, p. 284: no. 1/6-f.165/65.

119. Interview with Shaykh Ḥasan Amīn al-Ḥabash. See also Z. Lavi', *Ma'ariv* of June 12, 1970.

120. *NzI4*, p. 54: no. 2/17-f.28/49; and *ṬbI1*, p. 175, respectively.

121. *NzI4*, p. 59: no. 2/62-f.43/49.
122. *AI*, vol. 1(1950), No. 8, p. 9.
123. *AcI2*, p. 21: no. 18-f.1/51.
124. See, e.g., the decisions of Shaykh Tawfīq Maḥmūd 'Asaliyya. *JfQ4*, p. 126: no. 146-f.119/68, p. 138: no. 165-f.126/68.
125. See the chapter "Divorce," p. 198.
126. *AI*, vol. 3 (1955), No. 4, pp. 13-14; *Davar*, *'Al ha-Mishmar* and *ha-Boqer* of January 8, 1960.
127. *AI*, vol. 1 (1950), no. 8, pp. 9-11; *Ma'ariv* of July 3, 1966.
128. *AI*, vol. 3 (1955), No. 4, pp. 13-14. Shaykh Ḥasan Amīn al-Ḥabash's opinion as to minimum dower was inconsistent with the view of the Ḥanafī school (but conformed with those of the Shāfi'ī and Ḥanbalī schools. See Linant de Bellefonds, pp. 207-8). On the other hand, he declared during an interview that the *qāḍīs* had opposed the limitation of dower by legislation on the ground that the *qinṭār* mentioned in the Qur'ān constituted a minimum quota.
129. *AI*, vol. 1 (1950), No. 7, p. 4.
130. *AI*, vol. 10 (1966), Nos. 1-2, English Summary, p. 6. *KP*, 74th meeting of June 22, 1966. In a letter to the Minister of Justice of March 13, 1966, the Minister of Religious Affairs said that the *qāḍīs* regarded the bill as contrary to Islamic law because dower is mentioned many times in the Qur'ān and therefore cannot be banned or limited in any religious-legal way and that any interference by the Knesset in the matter of dower would be considered by them interference in religious affairs. See also Z. Lavi', *Ma'ariv* of June 12, 1970.
131. *AI*, vol. 1 (1950), No. 7, p. 4; *AI*, vol. 6 (1958), No. 4, pp. 8-9.
132. *AI*, vol. 1 (1950), No. 5, p. 5; *AI*, vol. 3 (1955), No. 4, pp. 13-14; *AI*, vol. 11 (1968), Nos. 1-2, p. 5; *'Al ha-Mishmar* and *Lamerḥav* of October 10, 1955.
133. See E. Hare'uveni, *Ma'ariv* of May 31, 1966, and July 3, 1966.
134. *AI*, vol. 10 (1966), Nos. 1-2, English Summary, p. 6.
135. See E. Hare'uveni, *Ma'ariv* of July 3, 1966.
136. *AI*, vol. 9 (1964), Nos. 1-2, p. 11.
137. And also act as a bar to rash *ṭalāq* divorces. *AI*, vol. 10 (1966), Nos. 1-2, p. 83. See *ha-Tzofeh* and *ha-Yom* of July 19, 1966; *ha-Aretz* of July 22, 1966.
138. *AI*, vol. 1 (1950), No. 5, pp. 14-15.

5

Women's Rights: Succession in Islamic Law and Practice

Historical Background

The Islamic system of succession is based on the customary law of pre-Islamic Arab tribal society, a law adapted to the structure of the patrilineal, patriarchal family. In that family, only male agnates (*'asabāt*) inherited; women and cognates were excluded from the succession. Muhammad did not abrogate the customary law, but sought to naturalize it in Islam by superimposing religious norms on it. He did so by placing the "Qur'ānic heirs" (*dhawū al-farā'iḍ*) first in line. In other words, he wished to stress the importance of the heirs who belonged to the inner family and to improve the status of woman in this connection. Eight of the 12 members of that group are women of different degrees of kinship to the deceased, both agnates and cognates. Nevertheless, the male agnatic heirs have remained the most important element in the Islamic system of succession. The Qur'ānic female heir usually takes half the share of the male of the same class, degree and strength of the blood to the deceased. Placing the *dhawū al-farā'iḍ* first in line is designed to assure them of a fixed portion of the estate without affecting the senior status of the male agnatic heirs, who take the lion's share. From the point of view of the status of woman, this system, in spite of the important Islamic amendments, involves discrimination against her in favour of man and against her family in favour of that of her husband.[1]

The Islamic law of wills affords protection, though not complete, to female heirs against deprivation of their shares in the estate at the whim of the deceased. The Sunnite Islamic system is one of the legal systems that do not give the testator absolute freedom to determine the devolution of his property after his death to the exclusion of the legal heirs. Wills are subject to two restrictions: they may not be made in respect of more than one-third of the estate and not in favour of a legal heir. A will disregarding these restrictions is valid only with the consent of the legal heirs (which is only taken into account after the testator's death).[2]

The Ottoman legislator introduced a revolutionary change in the status of women, to the extent of complete equally with men, as regards the transmission by inheritance of *mīrī* property (lands owned by the State, right of possession of which is granted to the individual). The Ottoman Law of Succession of 1913 is a replica of a German law with certain modifications.[3] It does not distinguish between males and females or between agnates and cognates. It only relates to *mīrī* property and certain kinds of *waqf ghayr ṣaḥīḥ* (endowed *mīrī*). It is thus not possible, circumventing its provisions, to deprive women of their rights in the inheritance by creating *waqf ṣaḥīḥ* (an endowment of property in which the individual has full ownership) or by means of a will.[4] The Mandatory legislator went even further in that he wished to enact a general law of succession. For this purpose, he adopted the Ottoman Law of Succession of 1913, appending it to the Succession Ordinance, 1923, at the Second Schedule. All judicial authorities, including the *shari'ā* courts, were ordered to have *mīrī* property inherited in accordance with the provisions of the Ottoman law, and their circumvention by will or otherwise was forbidden (section 21). *Mulk* property (in which the individual has full ownership and possession) and movables were indeed distributed, as in the past, in accordance with the provisions of religious law (section 8(1)), but on intestacy the religious court had to distribute them in accordance with the provisions of the Ottoman law if one of the parties so requested (section 8(2)).[5]

The Knesset closed the circle: the Women's Equal Rights Law, 5711-1951, extended the Ottoman Law of Succession to *mulk* property and movables (section 4*(a)*). This turned that secular law into a general law of succession applicable to all categories of property and all inhabitants of the State—nationals and foreigners, members of recognized religious communities and persons not belonging to any such community. This reform was, however, subject to two reservations: the Ottoman law was not to apply to *mulk* property and movables in the case of testacy (section 4*(c)*) or where all the parties were over 18 and had, of their own free will, consented before the religious court to litigate in accordance with the law of their religious community (section 7). Barring these reservations, it may be said that a fundamental reform had been achieved: the Islamic law of succession, one of the most characteristic branches of Islamic law, had been superseded by a complete secular law.[6]

The Succession Law, 5725-1965, was a step backward from the point of view of the status of Muslim women in the *shari'ā* courts, although in substantive respect it maintains the principle of complete equality of men and women and of agnates and cognates of all classes and degrees of relationship to the deceased (sections 12 and 13). The principal innovation is the primacy of the spouse in succession (sections 10-11 *(a)*).[7] This is a deviation from the orthodox concept of inheritance, according to which the latter's main purpose is the linking of the generations.[8] Islamic law and the Ottoman Law of Succession accord decisive precedence to heirs by virtue of blood-relationship. The Israeli Succession Law reaffirms the principle embodied in the Mandatory Succession Ordinance of absolute freedom of testation in quantitative and personal respect (including legal heirs) (sections 40 and 46-7) and, moreover, abrogates in matters of succession the special provisions relating to immovables of the *mīrī* category (section 149), that is to say, lifts the restriction placed on disposal of *mīrī* by wil'[9] This removes the protection given legal heirs, including the women, against dis-inheritance. Along with absolute freedom of testation, the Knesset introduced maintenance out of the estate, intended to serve as a remedy against a will depriving an heir and to give expression to the principle that the needs of the relatives who had been dependent on the deceased must be satisfied first and that only the residue of the estate should be distributed among the heirs. *Inter alia,* there is a tendency to turn the widow's right to maintenance into a permanent and independent right (sections 56-9).[10] Maintenance out of the estate is unknown in Islam law.[11] To facilitate the concentration of the estate in the hands of the nuclear family after the death of the deceased, the Israeli Succession Law, so long as the estate has not been distributed does not permit an heir to renounce his share in favour of anyone but the deceased's spouse or children. This provision (section 6), as well as a similar provision relating to beneficiaries under a will (section 50), are mainly designed to benefit the widow, since the family property usually belongs to the husband.[12]

At the same time, the law downgrades the jurisdiction of the *shari'ā* courts in matters of succession, and wills from exclusive to concurrent, *i.e.,* jurisdiction in these matters is transferred to the district court unless all the parties concerned in the matter under the law have consented in writing to the jurisdiction of the religious court (section 151*(a)* and 155*(a)*).[13] The provisions of the law apply only if the matter is heard before the district court, while the religious court, after the parties have consented to its jurisdiction, may "follow its religious law" (section 155*(b)*); consent to the jurisdiction of the religious court is thus sufficient also to allow for the application of religious law not only to *mulk* and movables but also to *mīrī*. In other words, the religious law of succession and wills applies in the religious courts provided that if the parties include a minor (under 18) or a person declared legally incompetent, his rights of succession, either on intestacy or under will, and his rights to maintenance out of the estate are not to be less than they would have been under the Succession Law (section 155). The law has an adverse effect on the status of Muslim women both because their succession rights are generally less under *shari'ā* than under Ottoman law and because—with the well-known limitations—they may be deprived of their rights in *mīrī* by means of a religious will.

Succession Order on a Woman's Initiative

From the establishment of the State to the end of the 1960s, the *shari'ā* courts in Israel granted approximately 2,500 succession orders. Some 30% were issued on the initiative of women,[14] and over 50% of the latter on the initiative of the deceaseds' widows. Rosenfeld found that even in recent times the wife did not succeed the husband and that the property of the family head passed to the sons.[15] However, findings in the *sijills* reveal that except for some 20 cases where the widow inherited alone or along with other women, she inherited along with the children of the deceased and their descendants, who are first in the line of heirs, as well as with agnates of other classes. The interval between the death of the deceased and the issue of the order was usually short,[16] which strengthens the assumption that the widow was interested in the distribution of the estate and the determination of the rights of succession. Moreover, the widow was in many cases appointed guardian of her minor children at an early date, sometimes on the same day as she initiated the succession order, which indicates that she intended to actually hold their share until they came of age.[17] Occasionally the widow was appointed guardian of her husband's children by another woman and thereupon hastened to initiate a succession order.[18] The aforesaid assumption is confirmed by Rosenfeld's researches in Ṭur'ān village. He found there a number of families consisting of unmarried children and their mother as head of the household after the death of the father.[19]

In 30% of the cases, the woman initiating the order was a daughter of the deceased. In only one-quarter of these cases did the daughter inherit alone or along with women of different degrees of relationship to the deceased; in the latter case, she took the major part of the estate as a Qur'ānic heir. In three-quarters of the cases, the daughter inherited along with a son or several sons, which made her an agnatic heir taking half the share of a brother of hers of the same strength of the blood-tie, and along with other agnates.[20] Rosenfeld and Cohen found that a daughter, like the widow, did not inherit in the presence of a son or sons. They explain this in terms of property and kinship relations.[21]

It may be inferred that a daughter who initiated a succession order was grown up and married. The interval between the death of the deceased and the issue of a succession order on the initiative of the daughter was usually great (sometimes 20 years or more).[22] An unmarried daughter at her father's house, even if she has reached the qualifying age for owning property, does not in fact enjoy this qualification either during her father's lifetime or after his death. At any rate, her dependence on her brothers and her family is greater before her marriage than afterward.[23] A woman is more likely to succeed her husband than her father or brother.[24] Rosenfeld and Cohen, in their researches on Galilean and Little Triangle villages, found that a woman sometimes claimed her share in her father's estate under pressure from her husband.[25] There is no evidence of this in the *sijills,* except perhaps for a few hints.[26] On the other hand, in some cases, a man initiated a succession order with a view to realizing a woman's right in the estate of her father, husband or other relative; in all these cases, the order was only issued after the woman had died.[27]

In 5% of cases, the woman initiating the order was the deceased's mother. Except for some isolated instances, the order was issued in respect of the estate of a son, and in most cases, the mother inherited along with the children and other relatives of the deceased. In some cases, the mother was appointed guardian of the property of her grandchildren on the day when she initiated the succession order.[28] Only rarely did the mother inherit during the lifetime of the father, *i.e.*, her husband.[29] In 4% of cases, the woman initiating the order was a sister of the deceased.[30] In 2% of cases, she was his granddaughter.[31] In the rest of the cases, she was a cousin, niece, daughter-in-law[32] or other relative.[33]

It may be surmised that the principal motive inducing women to initiate succession orders was their wish to realize their right in the estate. There is no reason to doubt this where the woman was the sole heir or inherited along with women only. In 13% of the orders issued on the initiative of women, there were no agnatic or other relatives. More than half of these orders were issued on the initiative of a daughter of the deceased,[34] one-fifth on that of the widow[35] and the remainder on that of a germane sister (*shaqīqa*),[36] the mother,[37] a granddaughter[38] or some other relative.[39] The absence of a son removes the main obstacle to a woman's realizing her rights in an estate. Even Rosenfeld and Cohen confirm that the daughter inherits in the absence of a son.[40] In many cases, the woman did not initiate the succession order until all the agnatic relatives had died. Sometimes several years elapsed between the death of the deceased and the death of the agnatic relative, while on the other hand, a short time passed between the death of the latter and the issue of the succession order on the woman's initiative.[41] In many other cases, a woman initiated the succession order while there were agnatic relatives who in the circumstances did not inherit under religious law or the Ottoman Law of Succession owing to the order of priority of heirs or the rules of exclusion[42]; this situation, too, may have been conducive to the woman's initiative.

There may have been a causal connection between the issue of the succession order on a woman's initiative and the fact of the deceased having been a woman. One-tenth of the orders on a woman's initiative were issued for the estates of women of different classes and degrees of relationship: mother,[43] daughter[44] grandmother,[45] and others.[46] It seems that in families in which a woman, and particularly a divorce[47] or widow, had property of her own the position of a daughter or other female relative was more favourable than it usually was in families in which the property was in male hands.

Again, one can easily imagine disputes between a woman and other members of the deceased's family arising from structural antagonisms and making her wish to take her share of the estate. Thus, by the side of the widow initiating the order, there often were, at the time of its issue, one or several rival wives,[48] children by another wife,[49] the deceased's parents (*i.e.*, her parents-in-law), his uncles and other agnatic relatives.[50] Similarly, beside the daughter, there were consanguine brothers and sisters (in the case of polygamy or death of the first wife) or uterine brothers and sisters (in the case of the mother's divorce and remarriage). A woman's initiative is particularly understandable in those cases in which she was the daughter of a divorced or deceased wife and the widow and children of the deceased inherited along with her.[51]

The rapid disintegration of the extended family and transition to the nuclear family in Israeli Muslim society encourage women to take their share of the estate. In the nuclear family, the integrity of immovable property and personal security based on kinship protection are, by the nature of things, less important. The issue of a succession order on the initiative of a widow is certainly a manifestation of her aspiration to economic independence and to the termination of her structural dependence on her husband's family with all the tensions it involves (domination by the mother-in-law and the husband's brothers etc.).[52] The issue of a succession order on the initiative of a granddaughter is likewise particularly understandable in the light of changes in the family structure, since the customary law underlying the Islamic system of inheritance is adapted to the structure of the extended family, in which the children of the deceased take precedence over his grandchildren,[53] whereas the principle of representation can be applied in the nuclear family, in which grandchildren take precedence over their uncles.

The proportion of Muslim urban women initiating succession orders was higher than the proportion of city dwellers in the total Muslim population about a quarter as against one-sixth. This is because urban women enjoyed a greater measure of social freedom and economic independence than women in other types of settlement. The proportion of Beduin women initiating succession orders was considerably lower than the proportion of Beduin in the total Muslim population—6% as against one-sixth. But the very fact that several dozen Beduin women initiated succession orders seems to be a significant indication of changes taking place in Beduin society, especially in Galilee.[54] About 70% of the orders were issued in rural types of settlement, a considerable proportion thereof in large, developed villages in the Little Triangle and near towns (such as Yafi'a and Furaydīs). These and other villages were undergoing an intensive, all-round process of modernization: in fact, from a social cultural point of view, the usual ecological division between urban and rural types of settlement was in many respects blurred in Israeli Muslim society. The effects of this modernization are particularly obvious with regard to the change in the structure of the family, *i.e.*, the rapid transition from the extended to the nuclear family, which is extremely significant in the context of inheritance customs.

More than half of the orders issued on the initiative of widows in respect of the estates of their late husbands relate to cases in which no blood-relationship existed between the spouses. Forty-four per cent relate to cases in which the spouses belonged to the same clan (*ḥamūla*), and in 20 cases the spouses were first cousins.[55] In cases in which the deceased left two widows, one a blood-relation and the other a stranger, the initiative for the issue of the succession order came sometimes from the blood-relation[56] and sometimes from the stranger.[57] Such a high percentage of endogamous marriages indicates that blood-relationship between the spouses was at any rate no serious obstacle to the wife's wish to realize her right to her husband's estate, although it may be assumed that in this type of marriage she was exposed to pressures from her relatives to avoid fragmenting the family property[58]; in exogamous marriages no such interference could occur, and the wife may even have been encouraged to take her share.

Education does not seem to have been a determining factor in the issue of succession orders on the initiative of women. The *Shari'ā* Courts of Ṭayyiba and Nazareth (but not those of Jaffa and Acre) had the initiator of the order sign it.[59] Only about 2% of the orders issued on the initiative of women were signed by them: the others were thumbmarked. Most of the signatures were made in very recent years,[60] which may herald a new stage in the development of women's status with regard to inheritance, when the education provided to girls in the State of Israel will find its expression besides other changes in women's economic and social status.

Women and the Law Applicable to Inheritance

The question of the law applicable to matters of inheritance is of great significance with regard to the position of women. As stated, the secular law leaves the heirs wide discretion to determine under which law, the religious or the secular, the estate is to be distributed. Consent under the Succession Law, 5725-1965, to the jurisdiction of the *shari'ā* court determines also the substantive law which is to apply to the succession. Until the coming into force of the Israeli Succession Law, the prevailing practice was for the initiator of the succession order to ask that the estate be distributed in accordance with the *shari'ā* and the Ottoman law.[61] This meant that *mulk* property and movables were to be distributed under religious law and immovables of the *mīrī* category under the Ottoman Law of Succession.

After the adoption of the Women's Equal Rights Law, there were several cases of women asking the *shari'ā* court to distribute the estate in accordance with Ottoman law only, which the court was then bound to do in any case. The reason for this request is generally clear and understandable. The widow's share in the estate in greater under Ottoman law than under the *shari'ā*[62] and, moreover, the widow (like the widower) does not enjoy the *radd, i.e.,* the residue of the estate when the Qur'ānic heirs have taken their shares and there are no other heirs. In other words, the maximum the widow can get is one-quarter, and in the absence of heirs in the inner family (all male agnates and Qur'ānic heirs) and outer family (all other heirs), the residue, in accordance with the doctrine of the Ḥanafī school, passes to the *bayt al-māl* (treasury).[63] In fact, there were two cases in which the widow of a deceased who had left no other heirs asked for the estate to be divided solely according to Ottoman law, under which she took everything.[64] Under Ottoman law, a daughter takes a share equal to that of a son and may, in certain circumstances, inherit a much larger share than under the *shari'ā*[65]; a granddaughter, under Ottoman law, takes the share of the parent through whom she inherits, while the principle of representation is unknown in Sunnīte law. Under Qur'ānic law, an agnatic granddaughter, in the absence of sons, takes one-sixth where there is one daughter and is *de facto* excluded from the succession where there are two daughters.[66] In sum, the motive of the women seeking the succession orders seems in those cases to have been the wish to increase their shares.

The most significant test in this context is the extent to which the woman took advantage of the Women's Equal Rights

Law, which permanently extends the Ottoman Law of Succession to *mulk* property and movables, save, as stated, where the heirs agree otherwise—in other words, all the woman had to do to increase her share was to avoid giving her consent to the application of religious law. It seems that women, and the public in general, were not alive it all to this reform. When seeking a succession order, the woman would, as in the past, ask for the estate to be distributed according to both the *shari'ā* and the Ottoman law. The author did not come across a single case in which a woman, either as the initiator of a succession order or as an heir, insisted that the application of religious law required her consent. The question of the consent of all the heirs (and not only of the women among them), their ages, etc., did not arise in at all until the adoption of the Israeli Succession Law.

The question of the consent of the parties, under the Women's Equal Rights Law, to the application of the *shari'ā* to *mulk* and movables arose only in 1969. In 1965, the *Shari'ā* Court of Acre issued a succession order distributing the estate, as usual, according to both laws. The widow of the deceased, an Acre woman, requested the Land Registry official, through an advocate, to refrain from registering the rights of the heirs according to the *shari'ā* distribution, as set out in the succession order, on the ground that she had not agreed to litigate in a religious court in accordance with religious law. She also asked that her share in the estate be determined according to the Ottoman Law of Succession alone. She contended that, owing to ignorance of the law, she had not discovered the flaw in the distribution of the estate at the time the order was issued and that only at the land registration stage had she realized that the succession order was contrary to law and therefore void *ab initio*.[67] There was not a single case of recourse to the High Court of Justice regarding excess of authority by the *shari'ā* court as to consent of the parties to litigate before it in a succession case, although there were such recourses in other matters of personal status.

Why did women not take advantage of the freedom of choice given them by the Women's Equal Rights Law as to the law applicable to succession? The principal reason seems to have been that they did not know of the existence of this right. Land Registry officials would honor succession orders of *shari'ā* courts without going into the question of the parties' consent to litigate in accordance with religious law,[68] and this practice, too, seems to have contributed to women's inaction. Some people, such as the *mukhtār* of Bayt Ṣāfāfā, said that women did not insist on the estate being distributed in accordance with Ottoman law for the simple reason that such a demand would generally have been without practical significance since most village lands were of the *mīrī* category and officials would in any case register the rights of heirs in such property in accordance with Ottoman law; but as will be seen below, succession orders were seldom registered in the Land Registry. Others, such as Advocate Darwish, said that women dared not oppose the *qāḍīs* practice of distributing *mulk* and movables according to religious law out of regard for religion and tradition (the borderline between these two was blurred) or for fear of sanctions by their families and social environment.

In some cases, a woman asked for an estate to be distributed in accordance with the *shari'ā* only although this was not to her advantage.[69] In these cases, and also in cases where the order was sought by a man, the property in question was usually money and movables,[70] and the applicants probably assumed in their ignorance that such property could only be dealt with in accordance with the *shari'ā*, as before the adoption of the Women's Equal Rights Law. The author found some such cases in records prior to the adoption of that law, and even in the *sijills* of the late Ottoman and Mandate periods.[71]

To be sure, the question of the consent of women, and of heirs in general, did not arise on a significant scale until after the adoption of the Israeli Succession Law. This law, as stated, provides that the written consent of all the heirs is a condition for the jurisdiction of the religious court, but not for the application of religious law. The relevant provisions were properly applied in only a limited number of cases, in which all the heirs, including the women, in the presence of the *qāḍī*, gave their written consent to the jurisdiction of the religious court, and the estate was distributed in accordance with the *shari'ā*. This proper application is only reflected in the *sijills* of Nazareth (for the last few years) and Acre,[72] so that it must probably be attributed to the *qāḍīs* of these courts. Usually the law was given a distorted interpretation: the party interested in the issue of the succession order asked for the estate to be distributed in accordance with the *shari'ā* and sometimes added a written declaration signed by all the heirs in which they consented to such a distribution. The *sijills* record dozens of cases in which the law was interpreted in this way, sometimes on the initiative of a woman.[73] In one case a widow asked for the estate of her husband to be distributed in accordance with the *shari'ā* on the ground that the ought to have the largest share in the estate.[74]

In many cases, a woman asked for or consented to the distribution of the estate in accordance with the *shari'ā*, or the jurisdiction of the *shari'ā* court, on behalf also of her minor children by virtue of her being their natural guardian or after being appointed guardian by the *shari'ā* court.[75] It is doubtful whether in consenting to the distribution in accordance with the *shari'ā* the woman was guided by considerations of her interest in the inheritance; on the contrary, distribution according to the *shari'ā* is to the detriment of the widow and tantamount to her renunciation of succession rights.[76] It therefore seems reasonable to assume that the woman's request or consent related to the vesting of jurisdiction in the *shari'ā* court, which, in turn, distributed the estate in accordance with religious law.

The Muslim public had over the years become used to the idea of the *shari'ā* court distributing the estate or certain kinds of estate property in accordance with secular law, but it did not seem to be used to the reduction of the jurisdiction of the *shari'ā* court in matters of succession from exclusive to concurrent. It was mostly not aware of this reform at all, and even those who realized its significance preferred the religious to the civil judicial authority. At any rate, expert testimony indicates that Muslims, and especially Muslim women, did not in matters of succession resort to any significant extent to the district court and thus did not take advantage of the mechanism placed at their disposal by the Knesset for the application of the Israeli Succession Law to all categories of estate property, without distinction between *mulk* and *mīrī*.[77] There is no trace of any such tendency in the *sijills*, except, perhaps, for one isolated case.[78]

Disinheritance of Women

Studies on inheritance customs in Middle Eastern society describe various means of disinheriting women or curtailing their succession rights.[79] In the following, the author will try to evaluate, from *sijill* material, to what extent these and other means were applied to Muslim women in Israel.

(i) Renunciation of Succession Rights

Renunciation (*tanāzul*) of rights in the estate was the simplest way of circumventing the succession laws. It was made before the *shari'ā* court at the time of the issue of the succession order or at a later stage, by amending the order before the estate had been distributed. Of course, it was stressed from time to time that the renunciation was made "voluntarily," "without coercion or force," or the like,[80] but when a woman renounced in favour of her father or brother, it may be assumed that she did so under pressure and not of her own free will.[81] Although in the *sijills* the author found only two dozen or so cases of legal heirs renouncing all or part of their rights in favour of other heirs, in reality this phenomenon was undoubtedly much more frequent, despite the lack of formal expression. One of the reasons for formalization, especially after the issue of a succession order, was the wish to carry out transfer operations involving registration in the land register and the provision of other legal safeguards.

In most of the cases, it was a woman who renounced her right in favour of agnatic relatives: the daughter or daughters renounced her or their share in the father's estate in favour of a germane brother (*shaqīq*)[82] or consanguine brother[83]; the daughters renounced their share in the mother's estate in favour of the father[84]; a widow of the deceased renounced in favour of her sons[85] or of another widow and her children[86]; the deceased's mother renounced in favour of his sons (*i.e.*, her grandsons)[87]· or of his father (*i.e.*, her husband)[88]; and other combinations.[89] In two-thirds of the cases, the renouncing woman came from a rural, and in one-third of the cases, from an urban type of settlement. The author did not come across a single instance of renunciation among Beduin, but this of course does not warrant the conclusion that the Beduin woman took her share of the inheritance. On the contrary, according to tribal custom she does not inherit at all,[90] but not formal steps are resorted to deprive her of this right. The possibility that some compensation was received for the renunciation cannot be ruled out.[91]

On the other hand, in some cases, the order states expressly that the woman did not renounce any rights in the estate or that she confined her renunciation to a particular item of property. In two cases, it was indicated that all the daughters except one renounced their shares in favour of the son or sons (their brother(s)), and the one who did not renounce had her right in the estate reaffirmed by an amended succession order. In another case, the daughters renounced in favour of the son—but not the mother, who realized her right.[92] In a case of a different kind, the daughters, who had renounced their right in favour of their brother, asked for the succession order to be amended to the effect that the renunciation was confined to their shares in a certain *hākūra* as to the other estate property, each of them reserved her rights, under-religious and secular law, in her father's estate, which right she declared to be "mine and not my brother's."[93] Lastly, in two cases, agnatic relatives renounced their shares in the estate in favour of a woman. In one of these cases, the deceased's brothers and sisters renounced under both laws in favour of their mother on the day when the succession order was issued. In the other, the eldest son renounced his share in his father's estate under the *shari'ā* and asked for it "to be added" to that of his mother.[94] Both cases occurred in an urban type of settlement. These isolated cases may denote a new development in the status of Muslim women in Israel with regard to succession.

(ii) Wills

Wills were not widely resorted to in Israeli Muslim society. There is evidence of about 40 wills made since the establishment of the State—nearly all of it in the *sijill* of Jaffa. Isolated instances were found recorded in Acre and Nazareth, but not a single one in the *sijill* of Ṭayyiba. All but four wills were made in towns.[95] It might seem that one of the causes of the rarity of wills was the dearth of lands of the *mulk* category (especially in non-urban areas), since, as stated, it was not possible to will *mīrī* legally before the adoption of the Israeli Succession Law. But in the towns, too, where a considerable proportion of the property was *mulk,* the absolute number of wills was small, and anyway, there was no legal bar to making a will in respect of movables, money and the like (with the known limitations imposed by the *shari'ā*). It may indeed be assumed that the number of wills was greater than would appear from the *sijills*, for according to the Ḥanafī school of law a will need not be made before a *qāḍī* or even in writing. An oral will is valid so long as its contents can be verified by means of ear witnesses who were present at the time of the declaration.[96] There were in fact many instances of wills being made out of court, orally or in writing, and registered in the *sijill* in the testator's lifetime or after his death.[97] But this does not alter the basic finding that wills were not particularly frequent.

An analysis of the wills confirmed by the *shari'ā* courts does not disclose a distinct and unambiguous tendency to disinherit women *qua* women, although many wills were made in respect of more than one-third of the estate and in favour of a legal heir. There seem to have been only a few cases of women being disinherited or in any way having their rights of succession curtailed—sometimes with their own express consent. In one case, a woman willed all her property to her grandson while her daughter, the grandson's mother, was alive; the daughter, who was the only legal heir, attested in court that she consented to the will. In another case, a man alleged that a relative of his, a member of the al-Huzayyil tribe in the Negev, had willed all his property and rights to him and that the legal heirs had consented to the will; these heirs were the claimant's paternal aunt, his male cousin on the father's side and his uterine sister. All these, except the uterine sister (who was not present in court), attested before the *qāḍī* that they consented to the will.[98] As is known, the consent of all the legal heirs is required to give effect to a will relating to more than one-third of the estate and in favour of a legal heir. The effectiveness of this requirement as a means to prevent circumvention of the law of succession and the exclusion of women from the inheritance depends on the extent of their ability to withstand pressures arising out of a complex of kinship and property relations, and this seems to be the principal weakness of the Islamic system of wills from the point of view of the status of women. In the first-mentioned case, it was probably not difficult to obtain the woman's consent to renounce the whole of the estate in favour of her son, let alone in the other case, where a half-sedentary tribal society was involved and with women of a comparatively distant degree of relationship to the testator. The curtailment of a woman's right of succession, though not her complete disinheritance, occurred in a further case, where a man willed his property to his daughter and her husband in equal shares.[99] But for the will, the daughter would have taken the whole of the estate since there were no other heirs. Other wills disclose no intention of dispossessing a woman *qua* woman.

Moreover, wills were occasionally made for the benefit of women. In some cases, the purpose was probably to prevent rights vested by the *shari'ā* in women of various degrees of kinship to the deceased from being frustrated in some way or other.[100] In one case, a man willed his property to his as yet unborn descendants on a basis of equality between males and females, in express deviation from the distribution of the estate under the *shari'ā*, which discriminates against females.[101] In two cases, a man willed his property to his wife, who was apparently the only legal heir[102]; as according to the Ḥanafī school spouses do not enjoy the *radd*, he probably wanted to ensure that his wife inherited the whole of the estate. In one of these cases, there was probably still another motive. On the day following the confirmation of the will, the man applied for a certificate that his marriage was valid (*ithbāt zawjiyya*),[103] whence it may perhaps be inferred that at the time of making the will a doubt had arisen as to whether the spouses were legally married. According to the *shari'ā*, if there is any flaw in the legality of the marital union, the spouses do not inherit one from the other,[104] and this is probably what the man wished to prevent by making the will.[105] In another case, a man willed all his property to a strange woman in recognition of services rendered to him and his blind wife.[106]

About one-half of the wills were made by women. Women enjoyed great freedom of testation: they willed their property to relatives of different degrees and to strangers. True, where the will was in favour of a son, brother or other agnatic relative, doubts might arise as to the measure of the woman's freedom of action. Thus, in one case, two sisters gave their brother a general power of attorney to protect and dispose at will of their property and rights, and a year later they willed that property to him.[107] In another case, a widow made a will in favour of a relative, who subsequently alleged that she had willed to him all her property, including her share in her husband's estate, in return for his having provided for her upkeep.[108] The orders contain nothing to explain the motives of the wills or whether they involved the exclusion of legal heirs, but the beneficiary in each case is known to have been a wealthy Jaffa resident, a shrewd and adroit person, who may have pressured the woman into making the will so as to avoid the family's considerable fortune being fragmented by intestate succession. In yet another case, a woman willed all her property to her son in return for a sum of money she had borrowed from him and been unable to repay; she directed that all the heirs should consent to the will after her death (failing which it would be invalid) and that he who refused to do so should pay her debt [out of his share in the estate] to the beneficiary.[109]

On the other hand, there can be no doubt that the woman's will was freely made in cases where the beneficiaries were her daughters or her son and daughter in equal shares. In one case, the woman did not will her property to her daughters in equal shares within each category of property (lands and houses), as usual on intestacy, but the distribution was by categories, with a view to preserving as complete and economically sound units as possible. In another case, it was provided that the children (of both sexes) entitled under the will might rejected or accept the inheritance after the death of the testatrix but must accept it in her lifetime.[110] In some cases, a woman willed her property to the children, of both sexes, of a son or daughter who had predeceased her; in one case, she left it to the children of a daughter still alive at the time and who was thus disinherited.[111] That the will was freely made is certain beyond a doubt in cases where a woman left her property to a stranger. In the absence of legal heirs, the motive was gratitude for services received from the beneficiary.[112] Sometimes a woman willed her property to a stranger with a definite intent to disinherit an agnatic relative. In one case, it was the testatrix's brother[113] and in another a relative of an unspecified degree.[114] The decision to exclude a legal heir, and especially a brother, betokens a great measure of self-confidence and the woman's complete control over her property.

In sum, the abovementioned orders do not leave the impression that wills were used to curtail or nullify womens' rights of succession, though they seem to have been sometimes used to restore a woman's share in her father's property to the family estate, *viz.*, in cases where the will was in favour of near agnatic relatives, and especially of the testatrix's son or brother.[115] Moreover, in many cases, the will indicates that a woman effectively enjoyed the right to own property and was able, with the well-known *shar'i* limitations, to determine the devolution of her property after her death to the exclusion of legal heirs. The foregoing applies mainly to urban environments. As far as can be judged from the *sijills,* wills were not frequent in rural society.[116] The author did not come across a single instance of a will disposing of *mīrī* property under the provisions of the Israeli Succession Law.[117] From interviews with experts,[118] the author gained the impression that Muslims did not make use of the complete freedom of testation obtaining in the civil courts.

(iii) Gifts

A gift (*hiba*) makes it possible to circumvent the Islamic law of succession without any quantitative or personal limitations. Not being a matter of personal status, within the meaning of article 51 of the Palestine Order in Council, it does not come within the jurisdiction of the *shari'ā* courts. Nevertheless, some documents are found relating to gifts in the Jaffa *sijill*. The gift might be made in favour of sons only, sometimes with a definite intent to curtail or completely nullify a woman's right of succession. In one case, a man bestowed his property on his wife's son (by another man) as a gift after his death in return for services rendered to him when lying ill and also that he might bury him next to his son and pay all the burial expenses. The gift was revoked a few months later, but for our purposes it is important to note that it was to have deprived the wife and daughter of the donator (*wāhib*) of their shares in the estate. This may be inferred from other transfer operations in respect of the property in question. The man had earlier given it to his wife, but after a time she had given it back to him, and in addition had given him her own property.[119]

In another case, the gift was clearly a means to disinherit women, but also other heirs. A wealthy man gave all his property to his minor sons and none of it to his daughter[120] or to his wife, whom he had appointed guardian on his behalf for his children.[121] He also had sons and daughters by a divorced wife, who were likewise disinherited by the gift. After his death, a grown-up son by the divorced wife contested the gift on the ground that it had been made while his father was mortally ill, and the *qāḍī* indeed invalidated the gift. The *wāhib's* wife thereupon appealed to the *Shari'ā* Court of Appeal and the district court.[122] The limited number of the orders does not permit general conclusions to be drawn as to the use of the gifts as means for the disinheritance of women, but a tendency to such use is apparent from the orders reviewed above.[123]

(iv) Waqf

The *waqf* (endowment) is one of the principal means of circumventing the Islamic law of succession. Unlike the will, a person may dedicate the whole of his estate, or more exactly, the enjoyment of its proceeds, without any restriction, denying the rights of legal heirs. This denial may take two principal forms: exclusion from the right of enjoyment of the *waqf* and from its administration. The second element is of great importance because the *mutawallī (waqf* administrator) is vested with considerable authority, which, in the absence of appropriate supervision, he may exercise to his personal advantage.[124]

It is doubtful, however, whether the *waqf* was used in Israel as a means to disinherit women. For one thing, the inclination of Muslims to dedicate property, considerable in the past, had virtually ceased. There are indeed dozens of judgments and orders relating to endowments—the great majority of them in the *sijills* of Jaffa and Acre—but they deal mainly with the appointment or dismissal of *mutawallis* of existing (mostly family) endowments, permits to sell *waqf (istibdāl)*, and other similar matters. The author met with only three new endowments, founded after the establishment of the State. Their number may of course be really greater,[125] but this does not basically alter the assumption of a small number of endowments founded in Israel. Some of the main causes—social, religious, economic and cultural[126]—of the strengthening of the *waqf* in the course of centuries seem to have lost their significance and validity in Israeli Muslim society. In addition, the radical reforms introduced by the Knesset probably made a considerable contribution to its decline.[127]

Moreover, the endowments founded in Israel point to no unambiguous tendency to deprive women of rights they would have had in property had it been transmitted by inheritance in the ordinary way. In one case, the man dedicating his property directed in the *waqfiyya* (deed of endowment) that its income should after his death be evenly divided between his daughter on the one hand and charitable, welfare and educational purposes of the Muslims of Jaffa, Ramla and Lod on the other. The daughter's beneficial interest was after her death to pass to her children and be divided "between males and females in equal shares" and thereafter to their descendants until the end of all generations in accordance with the same principle of equal division between the sexes. As his partner in the administration of the endowment (*tawliya*), the dedicator appointed his wife's son by another man, who was not his legal heir. The *waqfiyya* also indicated that the dedicated property had partly been the dedicator's and partly been inherited by him from his son or given him by his wife.[128] The dedication was chiefly injurious to the man's wife (if she was alive at the time of the dedication). The daughter's rights were only partly prejudiced because her Qur'ānic share in the estate (one-half) was assured to her.[129] In the presence of a widow, who would have taken one-eighth, the daughter would have taken seven-eighths, and as sole heir she would have taken everything. The appointment of the stepson as co-administrator also prejudiced the daughter's rights. If she had inherited the property in the ordinary way, she would, at least in theory, have been able to administer it herself.

Another case involved flagrant, unambiguous discrimination in favour of daughters. The dedicator directed that the enjoyment of the proceeds should after his death pass to his daughters and from them to his granddaughters and so on until the end of all generations, and when there were not more daughters, to the holy cities, Mecca and Medina. On the other hand, it is true, the dedicator directed that his (apparently only) son should be the *mutawalli* of the endowment, but he was to be succeeded by female beneficiaries who would be in Jaffa, and only in the absence of such was the *tawliya* to pass to other descendants of the dedicator who would be found worthy, while in the absence of such others the court was to appoint a stranger as *mutawallī*.[130] In a third case, a woman of the Old City of Acre dedicated her property to the Shādhilī Dervish center of worship (*zāwiya*) in Acre and to the local poor.[131]

In two cases, a woman was the administrator of a family *waqf*. One of them concerned the well-known 'Alī and 'Abdallāh Pasha *waqf* which had property in Haifa, Acre and Mazzra'a. The woman, probably of the family of the dedicators, acting at her place of residence, Istanbul, empowered her representative in Israel to carry out various transfer operations in respect of the property.[132] In the other case, the *Shari'ā* Court of Jaffa appointed an East Jerusalem woman as administrator of the *waqf*—established by her father—after the previous incumbent had left the country during the Six-Day War. She was instructed, *inter alia*, to see that the income was distributed among the beneficiaries in strict adherence to the terms of the endowment.[133] But these cases were exceptional. The persons appointed to be *mutawallis* were usually men, either of the dedicator's family or strangers.[134]

In sum, the *waqf,* as far as it existed in Israel Muslim society, was not used as a means to deprive women of the family property or to curtail their rights.

(v) Appointment of Estate Administrator

Another way of circumventing the laws of succession, even after the issue of the succession order and the determination of the shares of the legal heirs, was the appointment of an estate administrator at the stage preceding the registration of the rights in the land register. It was not a widespread phenomenon, and it does not appear to have been specifically used to disinherit women. Its main purpose (apart from the formal purpose of paying the debts of the deceased) was to prevent the fragmentation of the family property. It usually concerned large estates of well-known Jaffa families, the division of which among the heirs was likely to diminish their value. In most cases, the deceased's son was appointed to this office, and he was thus in actual possession of the shares of the women and other heirs. This appointment was frequently made on the initiative of the other heirs, including the women.[135] It cannot, of course, be certain that the women's initiative in these matters was voluntary. The author come across only one case in which the appointment of the son was definitely intended to debar a woman from the actual enjoyment of her inheritance.[136] At the same time, in two cases, women—the deceased's widow and daughter, respectively—were appointed administrators. In the first of these cases, the deceased's children were minors.[137]

(vi) Omission from the List of Successors

Another mode of disinheritance was probably the omission of an heir from the list of successors. In several dozen cases, persons applied for a correction of the succession order on the ground that their names or those of other heirs had been omitted from it. The application was mostly made after the issue of the order and not at the stage of publication of the *maḍbaṭa* in the press, the main reason being that the applicant, especially if a woman, could not read and was not able to look out for newspaper advertisements.[138] It may therefore be assumed that the number of cases of omission of the names of heirs from the list of successors was greater than is reflected in the *sijills*, and it is not impossible that when an omission was detected after a time,[139] the heirs came to some arrangement without going to court.

The omission of the widow was rare; in fact, the author met with only two instances, in which the omission seems to have been due to the fact that a doubt had arisen as to whether the woman had been married to the deceased at the time of his death.[140] In other cases it appeared that the woman had been divorced from the deceased and had cohabited with him without a religious-legal marital bond and was therefore not entitled to succeed him.[141] It has happened that an heir applied for an amendment of the succession order so as to exclude the wife from the list of successors on the ground that she and the deceased had been divorced.[142] The comparatively great frequency of the omission of grand-daughters from the list of successors[143] may be due to the fact that only an agnatic granddaughter inherits according to the *shari'ā*, either as the taker of a Qur'ānic share or as an *'aṣaba*.[144] In fact, in one case an heir contended that the omission of the children of his sister, who had predeceased their father, had been in good faith because a daughter's children did not inherit under the *shari'ā*.[145] In other cases, the initiator of the original order contended that he "had not remembered" that there were any heirs but those indicated in the *maḍbaṭa* or that he had not known that women were entitled to a share in the estate. Such a contention cannot be taken seriously when the omission concerned the deceased's daughter.[146] In several cases it was the woman who disputed the contents of the *maḍbaṭa* or applied for an amendment of the succession order denying her rights.[147]

There is no doubt that the omission was sometimes made in good faith or intended for a purpose other than disinheritance of a woman. Finally, this mode of excluding heirs did not, as far as applied consciously, affect only women. In some cases, men appealed against their non-inclusion among the heirs and asked for the succession order to be amended accordingly, and it has happened that a woman initiating a succession order wronged other heirs by such non-inclusion.

(vii) Appointment of a Guardian Over the Property of a Minor

Another method of frustrating a woman's right of succession was via guardianship over the property of a minor. The guardian enjoys great freedom of action in managing the property, being allowed to perform various acts in respect thereof, such as a sale, an exchange or consolidation,[148] and it does not seem to have been very difficult to convince the court, on applying for permission to do the act, that it was in the interest of the minor. It is doubtful, moreover, whether the guardian always troubled to apply for permission. The deceased's brother, *i.e.,* the uncle of the minor, was generally more anxious than any other relative to preserve the family property, which accounts for the frequency of his appointment as guardian.[149] Since the children, according to the *shari'ā* and the Ottoman Law of Succession, take the lion's share of the inheritance, he in fact hold the greater part of the estate. Elsewhere instances have been noted of an uncle's attempts to prevent the partition of the estate between the daughters by marrying them to his sons or by gaining control of their property.[150] In the *sijills*, there is evidence of daughters considering themselves aggrieved by the way the guardian managed the property. Thus, for instance, a daughter complained that on the uncle's application the estate had been distributed in accordance with the *shari'ā*; having reached puberty and become free of his tutelage, she asked that the succession order be amended and she be given a share equal to that of her brother, *i.e.,* that the estate be distributed in accordance with the Ottoman Law of Succession.[151]

The Extent to which Women Inherit in Practice

The issue of the succession order, even on her initiative, is not proof that a woman actually inherits. The court's function ends with the definition of the rights in the estate under the relevant laws. It has no authority to implement the order. In the areas in which land settlement has been completed, the land registers under the new system of registration are supposed to reflect the position, and any change, with regard to ownership.[152] A right registered in the land registers to a share in an estate (ownership in the case of *mulk*, possession rights (*taṣarruf*) in the case of *mīrī*) is *prima facie* evidence that the heir has realized his right and become the owner in all respects. Inquiries at the land registries in Jerusalem, Netanya and Nazareth[153] showed that only a small proportion of succession orders were registered, and this none too soon after the issue of the order. The *sijills* and the land registers contain a great deal of evidence that heirs did not hasten to register the succession order in the latter and distribute the estate,[154] which of course might have facilitated and exclusion of heirs.

Moreover, even where the succession order had been registered in the land register, there were still ways of disinheriting a woman. The most notable of them was the transfer defined in the land registers as "sale without consideration." This transfer made it possible to avoid various taxes, such as land appreciation tax and estate duty, and, which is more relevant to our subject, to circumvent the laws of succession. A well-informed source[155] estimated that in the Little Triangle region about 90% of "sales without consideration" registered in the Netanya land register were made within the family. The suspicion of disinheritance of a woman arises in cases where a man transferred property in this way to his son or where women transferred their shares in an estate to their brother.[156] In many other cases, women transferred their proerty or shares in an estate by "sale without consideration" to men who were apparently their sons.[157] Transfers in these circumstances were generally made under pressure from family members interested in preventing fragmentation of the property. The author was told of several cases where married women who had taken their shares in an estate and registered their rights formally in the land registers transferred those shares years later to their brothers by "sale without consideration" since they were no longer able to withstand family sanctions. Women sometimes received monetary compensation or part of the land in return for renunciation of their shares in the inheritance. The volume of transfers of this kind was greater than in reflected in the land registers because the sale was usually not to be effected until after the seller's death, on the basis of an irrevocable power of attorney. In hundreds of cases, persons renounced their shares in an estate in favour of other heirs in the course of land settlement proceedings (at the stage preceding the publication of the schedule of rights); a strikingly large proportion of these persons were women. It also frequently transpired in settlement proceedings that heirs had sold their shares to relatives, and here, too, there were many "sales without consideration," *i.e.,* renunciations by women in favour of agnatic relatives. Renunciation was usually made by means of an irrevocable power of attorney and sometimes in the presence of the settlement officer.[158]

There can be no doubt that many matters of succession were settled out of court and not in accordance with any law of succession, either secular or religious—in other words, without women inheriting at all. Indirect evidence of this can be found in the *sijills*. Sometimes many years elapsed between the death of the deceased and the issue of the succession order, and in the meantime the property was held and administered in accordance with the local custom of a patriarchal society, a custom usually discriminating against women. A whole generation of heirs might be skipped before the issue of the order.[159] Rosenfeld, Cohen and Marx, who carried out research on Galilean and Little Triangle villages and Negev Beduin, declared that Muslim women did not as a rule inherit; this was said to be due to a desire to prevent the removal of property from the control of the family and clan (*ḥamūla*) and to the system of kinship relations in traditional society, which is so vital to the protection and security of women that they are willing to renounce property rights for its sake. These findings would seem to be confirmed by other research conducted in Palestine and elsewhere in the Middle East.[160]

It nevertheless seems possible to state as a basic fact that Muslim women in Israel did inherit. As mentioned, some 30% of succession orders were issued on the initiative of women, the smaller part in the absence, the greater in the presence of agnatic relatives. Women appealed against their omission from the list of successors or their deprivation at the distribution of the estate and claimed their share according to a system of succession that would assure them of a larger portion. Men appealed against a woman's right to inherit or asked her to pay debts of the deceased out of the estate.[161] Some 400 succession orders for the estates of women, being about one-sixth of the total number were issued by the *shari'ā* courts during the period under review. Nearly 60% of them were in favour of the children—sons and daughters[162]—and the remainder in favour of the husband,[163] agnatic brothers and sisters,[164] a brother's children,[165] parents,[166] grandchildren,[167] cousins[168] and other relatives (son-in-law, daughter-in-law, father-in-law).[169]

Moreover, the *sijills* record many dozens of cases in which a woman left property she was to have inherited from the deceased but had not yet received by the time of her death, *i.e.,* she died after the deceased but before the issue of the succession order for his estate, so that she left the share she had taken of his estate to her own heirs.[170] Women willed their property to legal heirs and to strangers, dedicated it as an endowment and bestowed it as a gift. The land registers contain evidence of women leaving their share in an inheritance to their heirs (see below), some wills state expressly that the testatrix had carried out an act of transfer in respect of "what came to her by way of inheritance" (*mā āl ilayhā biṭarīq al-'irth*).[171] But the willed property may have come from other sources (dower, purchase and personal efforts). All this evidence in its cumulative effect, supports the assumption that women realized their right of succession and enjoyed freedom to own and dispose of property.

This conclusion is confirmed by proceedings in other matters dealt with by the *shari'ā* courts. Women were very active as guardians over the property of minors who had inherited from relatives[172]: in many dozens of cases, a woman asked the *qāḍī's* permission to carry our a transfer in respect of property administered by her: a sale, or exchange, consolidation or the like. She might, *inter alia*, ask permission to transfer property registered in the land registers in the name of daughters of the deceased or to register rights in the land registers in their names.[173] From maintenance claims by women against their sons there is evidence that every now and then a woman inherited from her husband or received from him in his lifetime a house, or other property, which was thereupon registered in the land registers in her name.[174] Judgments for divorce and other judgments sometimes show that a woman compensated her husband for her divorce by ceding to him her rights in the estate of her father or agnatic relatives[175] or that a house or dwelling belonged to a woman,[176] and a wife might stipulate in the marriage contract that the house or dwelling should be wholly or partly hers.

The means used for the disinheritance of women, as far as reflected in the *sijills,* do not always point to a definite tendency to discriminate against women *qua* women. On the contrary, they were sometimes used for women's benefit. The enjoyment of the proceeds of endowments was assigned to them and rights in estates were renounced in their favour. Women occasionally used those means in order to supplant legal heirs, male and female alike. But anyhow, the very resort to means of disinheriting women, and especially to "sales without consideration" or paternal-cousin marriages as far as intended to maintain the integrity of the family property, strengthens the assumption that were it not for them women would have taken their shares of the inheritance.[177]

The fact that only a small proportion of succession order were registered in the land registers does not prove that women did not realize their rights of succession, at least in cases in which the orders were issued on their initiative. Inquiries the author made revealed that the Land Registry was hardly ever resorted to, except where one of the heirs wished to sell his share and on the occasion of the transfer his rights and those of the other heirs were registered. In all these cases the two acts—the registration of the rights of succession and the transfer on sale—were carried out one immediately after the other on the same day.[178] In other words, the transaction was registered only where the buyer wanted complete legal security; there seem to have been no other incentives. On the contrary, several factors militated against resort to the Land Registry: the wish to avoid expenses involved in carrying out transfers (including the registration of rights of succession) in the land registers; the widespread tendency in the Arab sector to reduce contacts with the various government departments to a minimum for fear of exposing oneself to the grip of taxation authorities and for other reasons; fear of the intervention of the Custodian of Absentees' Property where the deceased or one of the heirs was an absentee. Many thought that actual possession of the property was sufficient guarantee against challenges from whatever quarter and relieved them of the need to establish their rights formally in the land registers. A succession order issued by the *shari'ā* court affords the members of the family certainty and security as regards the distribution of the estate, and every heir can transfer his share to another person by means of a sale agreement[179] or an irrevocable power of attorney.[180] In fact, most land transactions were effected outside the Land Registry.[181] In this sense, the Land Transfer Ordinance, 1920, did not achieve its objective.[182] Lastly, in many rural and some urban areas, land settlement was not complete and there was no orderly land registration.

On the other hand, land registers faithfully reflect the position as to ownership on the date of completion of land settlement under the Mandatory Ordinance. Here registration was carried out on the initiative of the land settlement officer after the rights in the land had been proven to his satisfaction by means of succession orders and other documents. The particulars of registration permit the certain conclusion that the rights of women in an estate were in many cases registered in accordance with the original distribution indicated in the succession order. In cases in which a plot was registered wholly in a woman's name, it is impossible to tell whether the property came to her by way of inheritance (in the absence of other heirs) or purchase, but in many cases the property was registered in the names of several members of the inner family in accordance with their proportionate shares in the deceased's estate, and since the property was usually *mīrī*, a woman's share was equal to that of a man of the same degree of relationship to the deceased.[183] In most of these cases, the succession order was probably issued on the initiative of the man who maintained contact with the settlement officer. In dozens of cases, a woman carried out an act of transfer—a sale, a purchase or the like—within the family or, which is more important, outside it, an act which from the time land settlement was completed was duly registered in the land registers.[184]

Further confirmation of the assumption that Muslim women inherited may be obtained from the files relating to claims for compensation for land vested in the Development Authority under various laws. The Development Authority does not compensate persons claiming shares in estates acquired by it until the claimants have produced succession orders from the *sharīʻā* court; and compensation is paid on a personal basis, to each claimant according to his share in the estate. Among the recipients of compensation were women of different degrees of relationship to the deceased. And again, these files clearly reflect women's wide freedom of action in the field of ownership relations: they bought, sold, transmitted and inherited property.[185]

Lastly, on submitting the question under discussion to experts, the author received contradictory answers. Some insisted that women did not inherit to all. Advocate Darwish thought that it was not difficult, in case of need, to persuade a woman to renounce her right in an estate in favour of her agnatic relatives. Shaykh Ḥusnī al-Zuʻbī believed that women did not take their shares in an inheritance and that the issue of a succession order on a woman's initiative was not proof that she intended to realize her right. At the same time, cases of women inheriting were in his opinion more frequent than they had been in the past.[186] Others declared that women did as a rule inherit. Advocate Fārūq al-Zuʻbī thought that a woman initiating the issue of a succession order intended to realize her right to the inheritance and regarded the order as a full legal guarantee of the preservation of this right.[187] A person well-versed in land matters in the Jerusalem area believed that the daughters of the deceased actually inherited along with the sons. He knew of cases in which daughters had applied to the civil court in order to realize their right in the estate after an attempt had been made to deny them this right. At any rate, according to him, a daughter seldom renounced her share in the inheritance in favour of her brother; this occurred mainly where she was unmarried, lived at the brother's house and was supported by him. Sometimes she was compensated for the renunciation by a monetary payment or a plot of land. On the other hand, a woman sometimes claimed her share of her father's estate in order to transmit it to her son or her children. It happened that fathers sold land to their sons while representing the sale as a gift so as to secure exemption from land registration fees. They did so when they wished to exclude one of the heirs.[188] The *mukhtār* of Bayt Ṣāfāfā. Muṣṭafā 'Alayān, likewise confirmed that women actually inherited on frequent occasions. He assumed that women initiated the issue of a succession order in two cases: where the deceased had left no sons and where the sons withheld her share of the estate. Mrs. Su'ād Qaramān said that women received more than was allotted to them by the *shari'ā* and less than was allotted to them by secular law, but that a brother sometimes bought his sister's share, which practically meant that he excluded her from the succession against payment of compensation.

The diversity of opinion on this subject is probably due to the fact that inheritance customs differed from region to region and were constantly changing. One thing seems to be beyond doubt; the phenomenon of Muslim women inheriting was neither marginal nor new, and although no quantitative estimate can be given, the degree of frequency is significant. Of course, this was a transition period, and beside women inheriting (and enjoying considerable freedom in regard to property relations) women were sometimes excluded from the succession (and debarred from owning and disposing of property). A. Granott noted women inheriting during the Mandate. In his opinion, it was one cause of the formation of what he calls the "detached areas of a village," *i.e.,* areas of land belonging to owners in others villages. Nor, as far as can be judged from Mandatory and Ottoman *sijills,* was the issue of succession orders on the initiative of women an innovation. But it was greatly encouraged in Israel by social, legal and administrative fators, such as the rapid disintegration of the extended family and transition to the nuclear family and, in close connection therewith, manifestations of women's social liberation and economic independence, the speeding-up of land settlement proceedings and the registration of ownership rights in the land registers;

changes in the system of land tenure and, especially, the transition from *mushā'* (joint ownership) to individual ownership; a change in the economic role of land and its inclusion in the cycle of economic transactions; and large-scale nationalization of lands along with personal compensation to the owners. All these led to intensified activity in the field of property relations, one of the forms of which is inheritance, and created conditions which enabled the changes in the structure of the family and the status of women to find expression; the weight of these factors was of course different according to region, type of settlement and social stratum. Although some of them already existed in the past, they were never so important, both qualitatively and quantitatively, as in Israel during the period under review.

The *Qāḍīs* and Succession

The Women's Equal Rights Law made almost no impression on the *shari'ā* courts. The *qāḍīs* went on issuing succession orders under *shar'i* and Ottoman law as if nothing had happened. The distribution of the estate under both systems of succession, the religious and the secular, was appropriate before the enactment of the Women's Equal Rights Law. For the court then had to "transfer" *mīrī* property under the provisions of Ottoman law and to apportion the inheritance of *mulk* property and movables under *shar'i* law unless one of the heirs asked that they, too, be distributed under Ottoman law. The *shari'ā* court was not competent to determine the category of the estate property (*mulk* or *mīrī*), and by determining the rights of the heirs under the two systems of law the *qāḍī* implied that the Land Registry official was to register the rights of the heirs in accordance with the classification of the property in the land register. In other words: the distribution of rights took place under the Ottoman Law of Succession in respect of *mīrī* property and under the Islamic law of succession in respect of *mulk* and movables.

There is no basis for distributing *mulk* and movables under the *shari'ā* after the enactment of the Women's Equal Rights Law unless all the parties are 18 years of age or over and have voluntarily agreed before the *shari'ā* court to litigate under the law of their community. Yet, the author came across only a few cases in which the *qāḍīs* did so with express or implied reference to the Women's Equal Rights Law, and in all cases they deviated from its provisions in one way or another. Thus, in one case, Shaykh Mūsā al-Ṭabarī dismissed the application of the deceased's daughter for an amendment of the succession order and distribution of the estate under the Ottoman Law of Succession, holding that the application was contrary to the *shari'ā* and to section 7 of the Women's Equal Rights law because all the adult heirs and the guardians of the minor heirs had agreed in writing before the court that the estate should be distributed under the *shari'ā* and the Ottoman Law of Succession; it is doubtful whether this is a correct interpretation of the Women's Equal Rights Law, for where the heirs include minors it is from the outset impossible to distribute the estate under the *shari'ā*. As the procedure of making a succession order does not involve the presence of all the heirs, the *qāḍī* was unable to ascertain their wishes as to the law to the applied to the estate. He distributed the estate under both systems of law, apparently in reliance on the request of the initiator of the order and the signatories to the *maḍbaṭa*, at any rate not on the basis of the agreement of all the heirs, as required by the Israeli law.

The *qāḍīs* deviation in this matter seems in part to be a *bona fide* practice carried over without a break from the Mandate period. At the same time, it is difficult to assume that they should so long have been unaware (until the enactment of the Succession Law in 1965) that the agreement of the parties was required for the application of religious law to *mulk* and movables. It seems that they felt strongly impelled to oppose the Knesset's intervention because of the substantive character of the legislation concerned.

On the other hand, the impact of the Israeli Succession Law on the *shari'ā* courts is clearly discernible although their interpretation of it was not always in accord with the Knesset's intention. Only Shaykh Amīn Qāsim Mudlij and, in recent years, Shaykh Ḥusnī al-Zu'bī were careful to obtain the agreement of the heirs to the *shari'ā* court's *jurisdiction,* as required by law. Most of the *qāḍīs*, in so far as they attended to the matter of the agreement of the heirs, did so with reference to the applicability of religious law (instead of to the competence of the religious court). They seem to have been unaware that their jurisdiction had been reduced from exclusive to concurrent. Some were careful to obtain the agreement of the heirs in writing, as required by law, but others contented themselves with the initiator of the succession order or with only those of the heirs who requested that the estate be distributed under the *shari'ā*. The author was informed by the Ministry of Religious Affairs that the *qāḍīs* had been requested to obtain the written agreement of *all* the heirs to the *jurisdiction* of the *shari'ā* court (and not to the application of religious law).

The *qāḍīs* usually applied *shar'i* law to *mulk* and movables, as they had done before approval of the Israeli Succession Law. Surprisingly enough, in one case, Shaykh Ḥusnī al-Zu'bī distributed the whole estate under the Israeli Succession Law, although the legislator had meant that law to apply in civil courts only. The *qāḍīs* were divided as to the law applicable to *mīrī*. As already stated, the Knesset empowered the religious court "to follow its religious law" after the parties had agreed to its jurisdiction, *i.e.,* the religious court is authorized to distribute also *mīrī* property under religious law. Indeed, the *qāḍīs* are expected to do so, since the agreement of the parties to the jurisdiction of the religious court apparently implies the application of the religious law, although it is not obligatory. But only Shaykh Ḥasan Amīn al-Ḥabash. Shaykh Tawfīq 'Asaliyya and Shaykh Amīn Qāsim Mudlij applied religious law to all categories of property, without distinguishing between *mulk* and *mīrī,* and the two latter did not do so regularly. Shaykh Amīn Qāsim Mudlij noted in many cases that as far as the estate consisted of *mulk* and movables he distributed it under the *shari'ā*; he passed over in silence the mode of distribution of *mīrī*. Shaykh Ḥusnī al-Zu'bī in many cases distributed the estate under *shar'i* law and the Ottoman Law of Succession, as in the past, after obtaining the agreement of the parties under the new law. In other cases, he and Shaykh Amīn Qāsim Mudlij and Shaykh Tawfīq 'Asaliyya distributed the estate under *shar'i* law and the Israeli Succession Law, that is to say, they applied the new law to *mīrī* property. In fact, Shaykh Ḥusnī usually did so, and he explained to the author that in his opinion this was the meaning of Section 155*(b)* of the Succession Law.

As stated, the Knesset imposed a restriction on the application of religious law to the whole estate, *viz.*, that where the parties included a minor his succession rights should not be less than they were according to the Israeli Succession Law. Shaykh Amīn Qāsim Mudlij and Shaykh Tawfīq 'Asaliyya were alive to this point, and in several cases in which they distributed the estate under *shar'i* law they stressed that this mode of distribution was of advantage and benefit (*al-ḥazz wa'l-maṣlaḥa*) to the minors among the heirs. The impression is sometimes gained that where there were minors among the heirs, the *qāḍīs* meant to satisfy the requirements of the law by obtaining the agreement of the heirs including the guardians of the minors, to the application of religious law, as required by section 7 of the Women's Equal Rights Law, or to the jurisdiction of the religious court, instead of by being alive to the succession rights of the minors. In one case, Shaykh Tawfīq 'Asaliyya combined the agreement aspect with the succession rights aspect. The order stated that all the heirs except an absent daughter (*viz.*, sons and another daughter) had asked for the estate to be distributed under *shar'i* law, and in reliance on section 155 of the Israeli Succession Law he granted their request but awarded to the absent daughter a share equal to that of the sons, *i.e.*, double that of her sister who had agreed to the *shar'i* distribution. In no case did the *qāḍīs* refer to the matter of maintenance out of the estate, which was introduced by the Israeli Succession Law.

The original Succession Bill of 1952 was more radical: exclusive jurisdiction in matters of succession was to be transferred to the district court, and religious law was to be superseded entirely by the provisions of the new law. The publication of the bill led to vehement opposition from the *qāḍīs* and the Muslim public in general. Protest meetings were held in mosques, telegrams and delegations were sent to State leaders with a view to preventing the enactment of the law or to toning down its provisions. Under pressure from the Jewish religious parties, the sting was largely taken out of the bill:

the religious courts were to retain concurrent jurisdiction, and within these limits the application of religious law was to be extended to all categories of property. This may account for the careful—if sometimes incorrect—implementation of this law by the *qāḍīs* as against their disregard of the Women's Equal Rights Law in matters of succession.

Shaykh Ḥasan Amīn al-Ḥabash and Shaykh Tawfīq Mahmūd 'Asaliyya took care that a woman's renunciation of succession rights was "without compulsion or constraint" and that a person renouncing declared before the court that he or she did so voluntarily, but it is difficult to assess whether such declarations were meaningful or merely routine. Shaykh Ḥusnī al-Zu'bī insisted that the renunciation be in writing and Shaykh Ṭāhir Ḥamād that it be under both *shar'i* and Ottoman law. Shaykh Muḥammad Hubayshī, who for many years served as secretary of the *Shari'ā* Court of Acre, told the author that Shaykh Mūsā al-Ṭabarī would refuse to accept a woman's renunciation of succession rights, and if she insisted, would, after issuing the succession order, refer her to the Land Registry or the Land Settlement Officer;´the author found no instances of renunciation of succession rights in the Acre *sijills* of Shaykh Mūsā's period of tenure. In one case, in which the daughters renounced their share in the succession in favour of the son and subsequently restricted their renunciation to some particular property of the estate, Shaykh Tawfīq 'Asaliyya allowed the retraction, declaring that the renunciation was in the nature of a gift and might be withdrawn so long as the property existed unchanged.

As stated, the deceased's wife is not, according to the Ḥanafī school, entitled to enjoy the *radd,* the residue which remains of the estate when the Qur'ānic heirs have taken their shares and there are no other heirs. In the absence of heirs in the inner family, the residue passes to members of the outer family or, if there are none, to the *bayt al-māl* (public treasury). The *qāḍīs* adopted different modes of action, in this matter. Shaykh Ṭāhir Ḥamād and Shaykh Amīn Qāsim Mudlij awarded to the widow that was her maximum Qur'ānic share in the absence of children (one-quarter) and assigned the remainder to the public treasury for distribution to the Muslim poor. One the other hand, in some cases, Shaykh Ṭāhir al-Ṭabarī and Shaykh Mūsā al-Ṭabarī decided, contrary to the Ḥanafī school, that the widow should take the whole estate.

It seems that the *qāḍīs* were generally alive to the question of the agreement of the legal heirs to the contents of the will where the latter related to more than one-third of the estate or was in favour of a legal heir. Shaykh Ṭāhir Ḥamād and Shaykh Amīn Qāsim Mudlij were careful to obtain the agreement of the heirs before confirming the will. Shaykh Tawfīq 'Asaliyya took evidence when it was alleged that there were no legal heirs. The *qāḍīs* acted in accordance with the *shar'i* norm and there is no indication that they specifically were guided by the wish to prevent the disinheritance of women.

Notes and References

1. Coulson, *Succession,* pp. 3, 22, 29, 33. For a systematic discussion of the order of priority and shares of the heirs see *ibid.*, chs. 2-7; Qadrī, arts. 582 *seq.*; Fyzee. ch. 13; Goitein and Ben-Shemesh, pp. 142, *seq.*
2. See Coulson, *Succession,* pp. 1-2, chs. 13-14; Qadrī, arts. 530 *seq.*; Anderson, *Islamic Law,* pp. 72-3.
3. Silberg, pp. 178-88, 207-10; *SB52*, Explanatory Note, p. 52.
4. Ottoman Law of Succession, arts. 1, 7; see Ben-Shemesh, pp. 115-16, 166, 198-9; Goadby, p. 121.
5. See Silberg, p. 182; Goadby, p. 122; Vitta. p. 206. The Ordinance also permits the making of a will in civil form for *mulk* property and movables (but not for *mīrī* property). This innovation, however, does not affect Muslims (sec. 20).
6. See Silberg, pp. 417-19, 425-6; Zadok, pp. 71-2; Weines, p. 319; Goitein and Ben-Shemesh, p. 246.
7. See Yadin, *Reflections*, pp. 134-6; Succession Bill, 5718-1958, Explanatory Note, pp. 59-61.
8. See the remarks of the Chairman of the Constitution, Legislation and Juridical Committee of the Knesset, *KP,* vol. 42, p. 964, col. 2-p. 965 col. 1.
9. See Succession Bill, 5718-1958, Explanatory Note, p. 234; Yadin, *Reflections*, p. 137; Remarks of Minister of Justice in the Knesset, *KP*, vol. 24, p. 2106; *KP,* vol. 32, p. 195.
10. See remarks of the Chairman of the Constitution, Legislation and Judicial Committee of the Knesset, *KP,* vol. 42, p. 955 col. 1.
11. *FRL*,. art. 152.
12. See Yadin, *Reflections*, p. 136.

13. *Ibid.*, p. 133.
14. Over 70% of the orders were issued on the initiative of men of different degrees of relationship to the deceased, but may indirectly serve the interests of women as well since the *qāḍī* in the order—either under religious or secular law—determines the rights of the heirs, including female heirs. Anyhow, only orders issued on the initiative of women were analysed.
15. Rosenfeld, *Peasants*, p. 120.
16. See, e.g., *JfQ1*, p. 68: no. 109-f.68/52 (inheriting along with sons and daughters; order issued three months after husband's death), p. 239: no. 369-f.13/56 (along with husband's brother; a few months after husband's death); *ṬbḤ2*, p. 207: no. 103 (along with sons and daughters, father and brothers; after a year).
17. See, e.g., *ṬbḤ1*, p. 124: no. 9/13 and p. 125: no. 10/14; *NzḤ19*, p. 89: no. 10/90 and p. 142: no. 5/35; *AcIr2*, p. 76: no. 19/51 and p. 77: no. 20/52. For a more extensive discussion see the chapter on "Guardianship," pp. 265-6. Cf. Marx, *Bedouin*, p. 185 (Marx found that Beduin women did not inherit but watched over the rights of their sons until they reached adulthood).
18. See, e.g., *JfQ1*, p. 90: no. 144-f.3/53 and p. 93: no. 148-f.15/53.
19. Ṛosenfeld, *Recent Changes*, p. 29.
20. These may include her father. See, e.g., *NzḤ18*, p. 94: no. 29/188, p. 102: no. 41/194; *ṬbḤ4*, p. 270: no. 1-f.89/66.
21. See Rosenfeld, *Peasants*, pp. 80, 144-9; cf. Cohen, p. 124.
22. See, e.g., *ṬbḤ2*, p. 24: no. 46; p. 79: no. 46; *ṬbḤ3*, p. 84: no. 55 in all these cases, the orders were issued 50-60 years after the death of the deceased.
23. Through marriage, a woman reaches the status of a legal personality, while Islamic law is not clear on this point as regards an unmarried woman. See Gibb, p. 240; Coulson, *Succession*, p. 247.
24. This was confirmed to the author by the *mukhtār* of Bayt Ṣāfāfā, interviewee Muṣṭafā 'Alayān.
25. Rosenfeld, *Peasants*, p. 29; Cohen, pp. 77, 122. This was confirmed to the author by interviewee S. Amir, an expert on land affairs in the Jerusalem region.
26. Thus it was said in one case in the order that the daughter who initiated it "refers (*muntasiba*) to her husband's family." See *AcIr2*, p. 98: f.40/51. In the Jaffa *sijill* of the Mandate period the author came across a case in which a woman initiating a succession order for her mother's estate was represented by her husband as a proxy (*wakīl*) for this purpose. See *JfḤ19*, p. 82: no. 376.

27. See, e.g., *ṬbḤ1*, p. 163: no. 4; *ṬbḤ2*, p. 12: no. 31; *NzḤ21*, p. 74: no. 1/62-f.91/60; *NzḤ22*, p. 59: no. 2/50-f.78/63; *ṬbḤ4*, p. 140: no. 3; *JfQ1*, p. 172: no. 283-f.15/55; *ṬbḤ4*, pp. 152, 156: no. 19; *AcIr2*, p. 168: no. 62-f.139/52; *AcIr6*, p. 43: f.87/61; *AcIr7*, p. 15: f.74/65.
28. See, e.g., *ṬbḤ2*, p. 133: no. 8 and p. 134: no. 9; *AcIr2*, p. 146: no. 41-f.105/52 and p. 147: no. 42-f.106/52.
29. See, e.g., *ṬbḤ1*, p. 4: no. 7/8.
30. See, e.g., *JfQ2*, p. 509: no. 470-f.58/61; *NzḤ14*, p. 137: no. 4/4.
31. See, e.g., *JfQ1*, p. 129: no. 218-f.50/53; *NzḤ20*, p. 6: no. 9/100.
32. See, e.g., *AcIr3*, p. 25: no. 23/55-f.89/55; *AcIr7*, p. 34: f.141/64; *JfQ3*, p. 164: no. 265-f.11/65; *ṬbḤ2*, p. 34: no. 59.
33. See, e.g., *AcIr6*, p. 26: no. 33/62, p. 57: f.135/63.
34. See, e.g., *JfQ2*, p. 557: no. 561-f.55/62; *NzḤ17*, p. 49: no. 54/178.
35. *AcIr4*, p. 81: no. 55-f.100/59; *NzḤ19*, p. 103: no. 6/106.
36. See, e.g., *NzḤ20*, p. 114: no. 1/37; *NzḤ21*, p. 42: no. 6/6-f.5/60.
37. See, e.g., *JfQ2*, p. 457: no. 469-f.18/61; *ṬbḤ4*, p. 206: no. 35.
38. See, e.g., *JfQ2*, p. 512: no. 477-f.106/61; *AcIr3*, p. 114: no. 34/57-f.64/57.
39. See, e.g., *JfQ2*, p. 317: no. 495-f.32/58.
40. Rosenfeld, *Peasants*, p. 145; Cohen, p. 122. Cf. Granqvist, vol. 1, p. 128.
41. See, e.g., *NzḤ19*, p. 220: no. 7/30 (the woman who left the estate died in 1950; her husband died in 1956, and the daughter initiated the issue of the order three months later); *AcIr2*, p. 55: no. 52/56-f.17/56; *ṬbḤ1*, p. 148: no. 5/25; *ṬbḤ4*, p. 84: no. 51 (in both cases, 14 years elapsed until the issue of the order on the daughter's initiative; meanwhile, several of the legal heirs died; shortly before the issue of the order, the initiating daughter's only brother died).
42. See, e.g., *JfQ4*, p. 132: no. 156-f.97/48 (under the Ottoman Law of Succession, the daughter took everything (*mīrī*); under *shar'i* law, the daughter took one-half (*mulk* and movables), and the deceased's germane brothers took the residue); *NzḤ20*, p. 86: no. 8/82 (a widow inherited along with two daughters, the mother, and germane brothers and sisters who did not inherit under Ottoman law); *AcIr6*, p. 2: no. 2/62-f.31/61 (three germane sisters and two consanguine sisters; the latter inherited only under the Ottoman Law of Succession).
43. See, e.g., *JfQ2*, p. 305: no. 472-f.13/58; *ṬbḤ1*, p. 17: no. 7/33; *NzḤ17*, p. 49: no. 54/178; *AcIr3*, p. 221: no. 55-f.66/59.
44. See, e.g., *JfQ3*, p. 221: no. 360-f.31/66; *ṬbḤ1*, p. 35: no. 17/63; *NzḤ21*, p. 86: no. 1/75-f.114/60. Cf. al-'Ārif, p. 126.

45. See, e.g., *ṬbḤ3,* p. 109: no. 18.
46. See, e.g., *ṬbḤ1*, p. 56: no. 2/95 (aunt); *ṬbḤ2*, p. 34: no. 59 (mother-in-law); *NzḤ20*, p. 114: no. 1/37 (sister).
47. See, e.g., *ṬbḤ2,* p. 222: no. 129.
48. See, e.g., *ṬbḤ1*, p. 59: no. 6/99; *NzḤ21*, p. 122: no. 7/43-f.71/61 (along with two wives and mother-in-law); *AcIr2*, p. 14: no. 11/50 (along with second wife and her children and a daughter by a divorced wife).
49. See, e.g., *ṬbḤ2,* p. 45: no. 8, p. 125: no. 50 (in both cases, the initiating wife had only daughters, while the rival wife had a son or sons); *NzḤ21*, p. 96: no. 5/5-f.4/61 (along with sons and daughters by a deceased wife and with the deceased's mother); *AcIr1*, p. 12: no. 10 (along with a son by another wife).
50. See, e.g., *NzḤ17*, p. 238: no. 4/9; *NzḤ22*, p. 27: no. 1/11-f.23/63; *AcIr5*, p. 133: f.189/58; *NzḤ24,* p. 76: no. 44/2-f.67/98; *NzḤ18,* p. 38: no. 22/107; *ṬbḤ2*, p. 181: no. 66.
51. See, e.g., *ṬbḤ1*, p. 46: no. 6/80; *NzḤ18,* p. 19: no. 25/178; *AcIr3*, p. 175: f.182/57. For the problem of the distribution of the inheritance among consanguine brothers by polygamous marriages see Cohen, p. 77.
52. See Rosenfeld, *Peasants*, pp. 32 *seq.*
53. The son excludes not only the descendants who inherit through him, but also who inherit through other sons who predeceased the deceased.
54. See, e.g., *AcIr2,* p. 12: f.9/50 ('Arab al-Sa'diyya); *AcIr3*, p. 117: no. 37/57-f.104/57 ('Arab al-Sawā'id); *AcIr7,* p. 12: f.41/66 ('Arab al-Maksūr, Hajīrāt), p. 14: no. 14/67-f.175/66 ('Arab al-Ka'biyya); *NzḤ17,* p. 278: no. 25/55 ('Arab al-Hayb, Ṭūbā); *NzḤ19,* p. 65: no. 8/67 ('Arab al-Shiblī), p. 198: no. 6/6 ('Arab al-Ṣubayh); *JfQ4*, p. 90: no. 90-f.32/68 ('Ashīrat Abū Ruqayyiq).
55. See, e.g., *JfQ3*, p. 189: no. 309-f.63/65; *ṬbḤ4*, p. 302: no. 7-f.79/67; *NzḤ19,* p. 165: no. 1/56.
56. See, e.g., *ṬbḤ2*, p. 45: no. 8; *NzḤ21*, p. 122: no. 7/43-f.71/61; *AcIr7*, p. 2: no. 2/66-f.109/65 (in all these cases, the exogamous wife was alive at the time the order was issued).
57. See, e.g., *ṬbḤ3,* p. 7: no. 8; *NzḤ16*, p. 66: no. 12/12; *AcIr3,* p. 184: no. 21-f.4/58 (in all these cases, the endogamous wife was alive at the time the order was issued).
58. Cf. Cohen, pp. 77, 122, 124; Rosenfeld, *Peasants*, pp. 29, 102, 145. In cousin marriages, the husband succeeds the wife in two capacities; *qua* husband who takes the Qur'ānic share and *qua* agnatic heir (*aṣaba*).
59. This practice was not regular. It was abandoned in the Little Triangle in late 1966.

60. See, e.g., *NzḤ24*, p. 99: no. 4/70-f.149/67, p. 130: no. 3/23-f.42/68, p. 151: no. 2/49-f.88/68; *ṬbḤ4*, p. 176: no. 3.
61. See, e.g., *JfQ1*, p. 248: no. 385-f.39/56 (the heirs applied for the issue of a succession order "that would clarify the portion of each of them according to the *shar'ī* distribution and according to the (secular) legal distribution" *(fī al-mas alaṭayn al-shar'iyya wal-qānūniyya)*.
62. See, e.g., *NzḤ18*, p. 16: no. 15/78; *NzḤ19*, p. 103: no. 6/106 (the widow inherited along with another widow and a daughter by a deceased wife; according to Ottoman law, each of the two widows received one-eighth of the estate, while according to the *shari'ā*, they would have received one-eighth together).
63. See Qadrī, art. 638; Coulson, *Succession*, pp. 31, 49-50.
64. *NzḤ18*, p. 1: no. 26/56, p. 17: no. 16/79.
65. See, e.g., *NzḤ19*, p. 98: no. 1/101 (the deceased left a daughter, a son and several sisters; the sisters inherited under *shar'ī* law, while under Ottoman law they took nothing and the estate was evenly divided between the son and the daughter).
66. See Coulson, *Succession*, pp. 54-7. See, e.g., *NzḤ19*, p. 35: no. 2/32; *NzḤ20*, p. 6: no. 9/100.
67. Sources for this case: Advocate J. Mehrez, who represented the woman in her application to the Land Registry; Advocate S. Darwish, who represented her in the *shari'ā* court (his office file: P/24-3-appeal to *Shari'ā* Court of Appeal against refusal of *Shari'ā* Court of Acre to amend and/or revoke Succession Order No. 68 of 1965); Dr. A. Link and D. Etun of the Ministry of Justice, Jerusalem.
68. Only after the enactment of the Israeli Succession Law were they directed to insist on consent to jurisdiction in the case of *shari'ā* court orders, as they had even previously done in the case of orders of Rabbinical and Christian courts, which throughout the whole period had only had concurrent jurisdiction. In the absence of consent, they returned the orders to the court *(ibid.)*.
69. See, e.g., *NzḤ18*, p. 117: no. 13/211 (the mother, under the *shari'ā*, took one-third of the estate along with a germane sister and paternal uncle of the deceased, while under Ottoman law the estate would have been evenly divided between her and the germane sister).
70. *NzḤ18*, p. 117: no. 13/211 (estate being compensation for the death of the deceased in a work accident), p. 146: no. 8/246 (salaries and compensation in consequence of death of the deceased in a road accident).
71. See, e.g., *NzḤ14*, p. 68: no. 1/10; *NzS26*, p. 238: no. 18; *JfḤ19*, p. 89: no. 390.

72. *NzḤ24,* p. 163: no. 4/62-f.123/68, p. 18, no. 24/93-f.165/68, p. 210: no. 4/21-f.153/69, p. 241: no. 6/61-f.122/69, p. 250: no. 7/73-f.141/69, p. 263: no. 33-f.7/70; *AcIr7*, p. 14: no. 14/67-f.175/66 (the widow and all the heirs filed "an affidavit vesting power in the court to ascertain the share of each of them in the estate according to the *shar'ī* method"; all the heirs signed the declaration vesting this power), p. 31: f.128/66; *AcIr8*, p. 18: f.63/68.
73. See, e.g., *JfQ3,* p. 346: no. 488-f.142/66; *JfQ4*, p. 70: no. 66-f.4/68, *ṬbḤ4*, p. 302: no. 8-f.17/68.
74. *JfQ3,* p. 344: no. 486-f.18/67.
75. See, e.g., *JfQ4*, p. 59: no. 55-f.139/67: *JfQ5,* p. 109: no. 183-f.291/69; *ṬbḤ4,* p. 302: no. 7-f.79/67, p. 309: no. 17-f.37/68; *AcIr7,* p. 1: no. 1/67-f.146/66: *AcIr8,* p. 17: f.144/68.
76. In one case, grand-daughters (and grandsons) were deprived of rights in the estate of their grandfather, a wealthy Jaffaite, because their guardian (an agnatic relative) had asked that the estate, which had previously been distributed according to both laws, be distributed according to *shar'ī* law only. As a result, the deceased's son, the granddaughters uncle took the whole estate. The granddaughters indeed certified in writing, on reaching puberty, that they agreed to distribution according to the *shari'ā*, but it is doubtful that they did so of their own free will. See *JfQ2*, p. 302: no. 467-f.64/57 and p. 573: no. 590-f.99/62.
77. This was attested by Muḥammad Nimr al-Hawwārī, Judge of the District Court of Nazareth, A. Shrem. Registrar of Lands, Nazareth District, B.Z. Cohen, Assistant Registrar of Lands, Netanya Region (who recalled no instance of a Muslim of the Little Triangle taking out a succession order in a district court). Shaykh Ḥusnī al-Zu'bī (who knew of several women applying to the district court in matters of succession) and S. Nawi.
78. *JfQ4,* p. 188: no. 244-f.66/69 (the file was transferred from the district court to the *shari'ā* court on the ground that until November 26, 1965, the power to issue succession orders was vested in the latter: this shows at least that application was made to the district court).
79. See, Baer, p. 39, and the sources mentioned there.
80. See, e.g., *JfQ3*, p. 293: no. 433-f.109/66, p. 302: no. 442-f.118/66.
81. This is what Shaykh Muḥammad Ḥubayshi maintained during an interview.
82. See, e.g., *JfQ3,* p. 293: no. 433-f.109/66; *NzḤ24*, p. 71.
83. *JfQ4*, p. 95: no. 100-f.90/62, p. 187: no. 243-f.42/69.

84. *JfQ4*, p. 4: no. 4-f.87/67.
85. See, e.g., *JfQ2*, p. 574: no. 591-f.112/62; *JfQ3*, p. 45:no. 456-f.9/67; *NzḤ24*, p. 199: no. 1:7-f.69/18.
86. *NzḤ24*, p. 270: no. 3/13-f.24/70 (renouncing widow was childless).
87. *ṬbḤ2*, p. 168: no. 51: *NzḤ14*, p. 68: no. 1/10; *NzI4*, p. 84: no. 2/41-f.106/50.
88. *JfQ4*, p. 144: no. 173-f.11/69.
89. *NzḤ24*, p. 197: no. 5/5-f.12/69.
90. See Marx, *Bedouin*, p. 185.
91. The author found evidence of monetary compensation in Jaffa of the Mandate period. Renunciation of a right in an estate in favour of a relative in return for economic assistance from him is practically maintenance out of the estate, such as is found in systems of succession—e.g., the Jewish—under which a woman does not inherit along with certain relatives.
92. *JfQ3*, p. 292: no. 432-f.114/66; *JfQ4*, p. 95: no. 100-f.90/62; and *NzḤ24*, p. 71: no. 4/39-f.76/67, respectively.
93. *JfQ4*, p. 101: no. 111-f.90/62 (the order was amended in accordance with their request).
94. *JfQ2*, p. 443: no. 436-f.30/60 and p. 443: no. 437-f.33/60; and *JfQ4*, p. 70: no. 66-f.4/68, respectively.
95. Two wills were made in villages, one among Negev Beduin (al-Huzayyil) and one among Galilee Beduin ('Arab al-Shiblī). See *JfQ2*, p. 558: no. 564-f.106/62 ('Abū Ghūsh); *AcD6*, p. 1: f.1/64 (Tarshīhā); *JfQ2*, p. 521: no. 497-f.21/62; and *NzḤ24*, p. 110: no. 5/82-f.174/67, respectively.
96. Coulson, *Succession*, pp. 215-16.
97. See, e.g., *JfQ2*, p. 76: no. 116-f.1/64, p. 140: no. 219-f.110/64, p. 142: no. 224-f.119/64.
98. *JfQ2*, p. 601: no. 646, and p. 521: no. 497-f.21/62, respectively (in the latter case, it is not indicated how, if at all, the uterine sister's consent to the will was obtained). In a further case, a man of the 'Arab al-Shiblī tribe in Galilee willed his property to his wife and four sons, directing that they (also the wife?) should take equal shares. One of the sons was appointed executor. The man revoked all the wills that preceded this one. See *NzḤ24*, p. 110: no. 5/82-f.174/67.
99. *JfQ3*, p. 8: no. 14-f.97/63 (no indication of the testator's motives). See also *JfQ3*, p. 16: no. 24-f.55/63.
100. *JfQ2*, p. 475: no. 498-f.34/61 (the man willed all his property to his two sons and his daughter; his daughter was to have "her right *(istiḥqāquhā)* in the estate under the *sharī'ā*, as if he had died intestate"); *JfQ3*, p. 111: no. 174-f.58/64 (the head of the

family made a will assuring the rights of all the legal heirs, *viz.*, the widow, the daughters and the sons, under the *sharī'ā;* at the end of the will, it is expressly stated that it was made "for fear of denial and abandonment [of the rights of the heirs]"; he probably meant to protect the rights of the wife and daughters rather than of the sons).

101. *AcQ5*, p. 44: f.80/63 (and in the event that he should have no offspring, he willed his property for the renovation of the mosques in Acre; this is structurally very similar to prescribing the order of beneficiaries of an endowment).
102. *JfQ2*, p. 311: no. 481-f.29/58, p. 385: no. 539-f.23/59.
103. *JfQ2*, p. 312: no. 483-f.28/58.
104. See Coulson, *Succession*, p. 16.
105. In the *sijills* of the courts of Jaffa and Nazareth of the Ottoman period, the author also found a will in favour of the widow and other female relatives; see *JfS43*, p. 85; no. 89 (will in favour of the widow despite the existence of legal heirs, viz., sons and daughters); *JfS88*, p. 83: no. 316; *NzS26*, p. 166: no. 56, p. 205: no. 49 (will in favour of testator's sister-in-law and her children).
106. *AcQ5*, p. 45: 4.82/63 (the order does not indicate if the blind woman was alive at the time the will was made).
107. *JfQ1*, p. 252: no. 392-f.47/56. For a further will by one of the sisters in favour of the same brother see *JfQ2*, p. 474: no. 497-f.49/61.
108. *JfQ2*, p. 392: no. 550-f.20/59.
109. *NzH15*, p. 34: no. 5/58. For further wills in favour of the son see *JfQ2*, p. 506: no. 566-f.101/61; *JfQ3*, p. 59: no. 48-f.42/63 and p. 124: no. 197-f.89/64 (in the latter case, the son applied for a decision that his mother's property was his by virtue of the will and of his being the sole heir).
110. *JfQ3*, p. 62: no. 96-f.202/63; and *JfQ2*, p. 540: no. 532-f.69/62, respectively.
111. *JfQ2*, p. 601: no. 646; *JfQ3*, p. 19: no. 29-f.29/63, p. 20: no. 31-f.109/63.
112. *JfQ2*, p. 329: no. 516-f.60/58, p. 570: no. 584-f.130/62, p. 571, no. 589-f.4/63 and p. 591: no. 627-f.49/63; *JfQ3*, p. 194: no. 321-f.99/65.
113. *JfQ2*, p. 524: no. 53-f.34/62.
114. *JfQ3*, p. 76: no. 116-f.1/64, p. 90: no. 139-f.5/65. See also *JfQ3*, p. 96: no. 151-f.38/64.
115. There is a resemblance here to a family endowment which entitles the daughter to enjoy the income of the *waqf* and to use the

dedicated property so long as she is single, while her right terminates on her marriage. The resemblance lies in the principle that the woman may not transfer the family property to her husband, but that she has rights in it in her lifetime or until her marriage.

116. A noteworthy phenomenon is the occurrence of two wills made among Beduin in Galilee and the Negev in accordance with the *sharī'ā*. This is a clear sign of the Islamization that tribal society is undergoing. This process was at the time confined to tribes in an advanced stage of sedenterization (al-Huzayyil in the Negev and al-Shiblī in Galilee).

117. The author indeed came across a will made in relation to *mīrī* in 1964, but such a will was contrary to the law then in force. See, *JfQ3,* p. 124: no. 197-f.64/89. In another case the court, relying on the Israeli Succession Law, confirmed a will leaving the entire property—movables and immovables—to a stranger, but there is no certainty that it was made under the new law (it states that there were no legal heirs) and that the property (situated in Jaffa) included also *mīrī*. See *JfQ5,* p. 96: no. 162-f.279/69.

118. Nazareth District Judge Muḥammad Nimr al-Hawwārī and the Directors of the Land Registries at Nazareth and Netanya.

119. Which she had obtained "by civil purchase." See *JfQ1*, p. 34: no. 59-f.13/52.

120. According to another version, the gift comprised only part of the property and was made also in favour of the daughter. See *JfQ1*, p. 200: no. 324-f.20/55.

121. *JfQ1,* p. 168: no. 277-f.14/55 and p. 169: no. 279-f.20/55.

122. *JfQ1*, p. 197: no. 319-f.23/55, p. 200: no. 324-f.20/55 and p. 205: no. 328-f.20/55.

123. Since gifts are not within the jurisdiction of the *sharī'ā* courts, no clarification of the position can be expected from the *sijills*.

124. Cf. Baer, pp. 39-40.

125. Registration of a *waqf* with the court is not a condition of its validity. See Qadrī, *Waqf,* art. 2.

126. See Baer, pp. 142-3; Goitein and Ben-Shemesh, pp. 154-7.

127. See Layish, *Waqf,* pp. 41-72.

128. *JfQ1*, p. 38: no. 68-f.29/52. The son afterward resigned his position as *mutawallī* and claimed an appropriate remuneration for his services, *JfQ1,* p. 69: no. 110-f.51/52.

129. This may be the reason for the proportion fixed between the daughter's share in the proceeds and the share assigned for public purposes.

130. *JfQ1,* p. 235: no. 363-f.16/56.

131. *AcD6*, p. 21: no. 45/64. For other endowments established by women during the Mandate and perhaps even earlier see *JfQ3*, p. 193: no. 311-f.102/65; *AcQ4*, p. 87: f.82/60.
132. *AcD7*, p. 18: no. 80/66; *AcD8*, p. 23: no. 23/68.
133. *JfQ5*, p. 66: no. 113-f.223/69.
134. See, e.g., *NzḤ24*, p. 228: no. 6/42-f.94/69; *AcI3*, p. 7: no. 9/55-f.26/55.
135. See, e.g., *JfQ1*, p. 22: no. 37-f.52/51; *JfQ2*, p. 440: no. 431-f.4/60; p. 441: no. 432-f.19/60, p. 565: no. 577-f.123/62; *JfQ3*, p. 236: no. 375-f.64/66.
136. The reference is to the succession of a wealthy real estate dealer of Jaffa. In a dispute between his two wives, with their respective sons, one of the sons was appointed administrator. See *JfQ3*, p. 236: no. 375-f.64/66. On a subsequent occasion, a stranger was appointed administrator of the same estate for fear that the son might nullify or curtail the rights of the other heirs. See *JfQ3*, p. 185: no. 304-58/65 and p. 224: no. 364-f.58/65.
137. *NzḤ14*, p. 100: no. 1/53 (widow): *JfQ5*, order of October 16, 1969 (unmarried daughter).
138. See, e.g., *JfQ2*, p. 576: no. 599-f.24/63.
139. See, e.g., *JfQ3*, p. 31: no. 52-f.148/63.
140. *JfQ2*, p. 576: no. 595-f.24/63; *JfQ3*, p. 31: no. 52-f.148/63.
141. *ṬbḤ*, p. 21: no. 7-f.12/51 (the woman, who had been irrevocably divorced, contended that her husband had taken her back after three or four days and that she had even borne him a child, but she was not able to prove that he had legally remarried her); *AcD6*, p. 37: f.32/64 (the legal wife opposed the confirmation of the marriage of the divorced wife); *Ap1*, p. 14: no. 14 (a woman's claim to a share in the inheritance was dismissed because she had been divorced in the deceased's lifetime and it had not been proven that he had remarried her).
142. *NzḤ17*, p. 78: no. 32/212; *NzḤ24*, p. 12: no. 8/58-f.93/66.
143. See, e.g., *JfQ2*, p. 492: no. 444-f.32/57; *ṬbḤ3*, p. 34: no. 46; *NzḤ17*, p. 59: no. 10/190; *AcIr2*, p. 45: no. 38.
144. Coulson, *Succession*, pp. 54-7.
145. *NzḤ17*, p. 128: no. 28/278. He was correct, but their omission prejudiced rights they had under the Ottoman Law of Succession.
146. See, e.g., *NzḤ19*, p. 163: no. 2/54; *JfQ4*, p. 167: no. 207-f.8/69.
147. See, e.g., *ṬbḤ3*, p. 34: no. 46; *NzḤ17*, p. 204: no. 32/382.
148. See Coulson, *Succession*, p. 245.
149. See, e.g., *JfQ2*, p. 563: no. 569-f.110/62 (the *maḍbaṭa* notes that the uncle was "the worhtiest of persons" to act as guardian in the absence of the father).

150. See the chapter "Guardianship," pp. 269-70.
151. *AcQ4,* p. 82: f.60 (her application was dismissed). See also *NzḤ15,* p. 38: no. 10/63.
152. See Weines, pp. 274-5; Ben-Shemesh, p. 274.
153. In the *JrLR,* the transactions in blocks 29520-29525 in Abū Ghūsh village were examined; in Netanya, some of the transactions in block 7824 and in Ṭayyiba village; and in Nazareth, at random, transactions in recent years.
154. See, e.g., *JfQ1*, p. 22: no. 37-f.52/51; *ṬbḤ3*, p. 118: no. 31 (one year after the issue of the succession order, the widow of the deceased notified that the heirs had agreed to distribute the estate between them in accordance with the succession order); *NzḤ19,* p. 163: no. 2/54 (five years after the issue of the succession order one of the heirs applied for its amendment remarking on this occasion that "the order has not yet been made use of). p. 259: no. 6/77. See also *JrLR*, f. 2570/65 (registration 13 years after issue of the order). f.2161/64 (ten years), f.2109/64 (nine years).
155. What follows was recorded at an interview with P. Kvitt.
156. See, e.g., *JrLR*, deed of sale no. 1730/66.
157. This cannot be proved from the land registers because a woman bears her father's name even after her marriage while her son is named after her husband (his father). See, e.g., *JrLR,* deed of sale no. 3049-3050/61.
158. This was communicated to the author by Dr. J. Tartakover, formerly Director of the Department of Land Registration and Land Settlement at the Ministry of Justice.
159. See, e.g., *JfQ2*, p. 291: no. 452-f.53/57 (the deceased had died 35 years before the succession order was issued on the initiative of a son: in the meantime, the widow, the two daughters, and one of the two sons had also died); *JfQ3*, p. 356: no. 498-f.36/67 (the deceased died in the early days of the Mandate, and the succession order was issued in 1967 on the initiative of a grandson; in the meantime, the widow and most of the children had died); *ṬbḤ4*, p. 135: no. 115 (the deceased died 50 years before the succession order was issued on the initiative of a son); *NzḤ19,* p. 212: no. 14/23 (the deceased died 70 years before the order was issued on the initiative of a grandson after the children and many of the grandchildren had died); *NzḤ23,* p. 103: no. 7/27-f.51/65 (the deceased died 46 years before the issue of the succession order; the number of shares according to *shar'ī* law was over 400 million, and according to Ottoman Law six million); *AcIr7,* p. 26: f.57/67 (the deceased died 50 years before the order was issued on the initiative of his son-in-law; the widow and the daughter had died by then).

160. Rosenfeld, *Peasants*, pp. 29-30, 96, 102, 120, 144-5, 148-9; Cohen, pp. 77, 122, 124; Marx, *Bedouin*, p. 185. Cf. Groadby, p. 122; al-'Ārif, p. 125; Baer, pp. 35, 38-40.
161. See, e.g., *JfQ1*, p. 27: no. 45; *JfQ3*, p. 35: no. 57-f.107/63, p. 35: no. 60-f.15/52.
162. See, e.g., *JfQ2*, p. 305: no. 472-f.13/58; *NzḤ18*, p. 55: no. 17/129; *AcIr3*, p. 81: no. 2/57-f.27/56. Cf. al-'Ārif, p. 126.
163. See, e.g., *JfQ1*, p. 135: no. 228-f.30/54; *NzI4*, p. 74: no. 5/24-f.63/50.
164. See, e.g., *NzḤ19*, p. 266: no. 7/85; *NzḤ17*, p. 144: no. 3/298; *AcIr5*, p. 112: f.114/60; *AcIr3*, p. 204: no. 39/58-f.179/57.
165. See, e.g., *JfQ3*, p. 3: no. 5-f.64/63; *NzḤ19*, p. 90: no. 11/91.
166. See, e.g., *ṬbH1*, p. 35: no. 17/63: *ṬbH3*, p. 43: no. 1; *NzḤ18*, p. 95: no. 31/184; *NzḤ20*, p. 162: no. 105.
167. See, e.g., *JfQ2*, p. 459: no. 474-f.68/60, *ṬbH2*, p. 47: no. 11, *NzḤ20*, p. 112: no. 9/35; *AcIr3*, p. 69: no. 67/56-f.82/56.
168. See, e.g., *NzḤ17*, p. 91: no. 11/226; *AcIr4*, p. 15: no. 90-f.179/58.
169. See *AcIr4*, p. 8: no. 83-f.164/58; *AcIr7*, p. 3: no. 3/66-f.40/65: *ṬbH2*, p. 34: no. 59; *NzḤ19*, p. 112: no. 4/4.
170. See, e.g., *JfQ2*, p. 578: no. 599-f.114/62.
171. See, e.g., *JfQ2*, p. 392: no. 550-f.20/59, p. 506: no. 566-f.101/66, p. 601: no. 646: *NzḤ15*, p. 25: no. 32/47, p. 26: no. 33/48.
172. See the chapter "Guardianship," pp. 265-6.
173. See, e.g., *NzḤ14*, p. 116: no. 9/77; *NzḤ17*, p. 85: no. 5/220; *NzḤ23*, p. 173: no. 5/32-f.44/66. See also *NzḤ19*, p. 151: no. 2/45.
174. See, e.g., *AcI2*, p. 64: f.26/54: *TbI1*, p. 49: no. 10-f.24/53, p. 194: no. 15-f.25/61 and p. 196: no. 18-f.25/61; *JfQ3*, p. 199: no. 327-f.84/65.
175. See, e.g., *JfQ1*, p. 275: no. 424-f.29/57; *JfQ4*, p. 102: no. 114-f.70/68; *NzḤ14*, p. 85: no. 14/30; *NzḤ24*, p. 29: no. 7/77-f.134/66; *AcṬ3*, p. 28: f.19/57.
176. See, e.g., *JfQ2*, p. 426: no. 413-f.59/79, p. 434: no. 421-f.27/59; *JfQ3*, p. 163: no. 264-f.13/65; *NzI4*, p. 182: no. 1/12-f.43/57.
177. See, e.g., *Nz14*, p. 71: no. 1/20-f.51/50; *NzḤ18*, p. 29: no. 11/96. Cf. Baer, pp. 39-40, 64-6.
178. See, e.g., *JrLR*, fs. 2161/64, 2153/66, 2819/67. This was also confirmed to the author by S. 'Amir.
179. For specimens to such agreements see *JfILA*, f.821/79.
180. For specimens of such powers of attorney see *JrLR*, fs. 2109.64, 2153/66.
181. Such a transaction is popularly called *bay 'barrānī* (external sale). Interviewee Shrem estimated that tens of thousands of

transactions were effected in the Northern District in this way, and Advocate Fārūq al-Zu'bī, of Nazareth, estimated that 90% of all transactions in immovable property in the Nazareth area were effected outside the Land Registry.

182. See the remarks of the Minister of Justice in the Knesset, *KP*, Fifth Knesset, third session, no. 32, p. 2128 col. 2, p. 2129 col. 1. Cf. Weines, p. 274; Ben-Shemesh, p. 189.

183. There are many dozens of cases in the blocks examined by the author in 'Abū Ghūsh (land settlement completed in 1942) and Ṭayyiba (1937). See, e.g., *JrLR*, f.2161/64 (the widow owned one quarter of the property and all the children, sons and daughters alike, owned equal shares, in accordance with the Ottoman Law of Succession), f.2987/65 (as above), f.2153/66 (property registered in the name of two sisters in equal shares), f.1699/64 (property registered wholly in the name of a woman). For instances in the Little Triangle see *NtLR*, block 7824.

184. See, e.g., *JrLR*, f. 2153/66 (when the sons wished to register their mother's estate in their name, it appeared that she had sold the property to several persons by means of an irrevocable power of attorney), f.1588/64 (a woman bought some tens of dunams of *mīrī* land from her husband), f.394/58 (a woman sold some property wholly owned by her to two persons), *NtLR*, block 7824.

185. See, e.g., *JrILA*, f.79/821, f.119/821 (a woman sold a parcel of land registered wholly in her name to a resident of the village; after his death, his daughter initiated a succession order and applied to the Israel Lands Administrative for compensation for property which had been vested in the Development Authority), f.137/821 (three brothers and a sister of the deceased received equal shares of the estate in accordance with the Ottoman Law of Succession and divided the land among them; an affidavit states expressly that the sister also received a parcel of land).

186. Recorded at an interview with Shaykh Ḥusnī al-Zu'bī.

187. Recorded at an interview with Advocate Fārūq al-Zu'bī, a son of the *qāḍī* of the *Shari'ā* Court of Nazareth and frequently present in that court.

188. Recorded at an interview with S. Amir. Cf. al-'Ārif, p. 125. The author indeed found instances in the *sijills* of aged fathers dividing their property among their sons and even registering it in their names in the Land Registry and then claiming maintenance from them.

6

Divorce in Islam: Women in Cross-Cultural Perspective

Divorce: A Sociological Profile

The causes of divorce on the husband's initiative, some traditional and some modern, are rooted in socio-economic, legal and political circumstances. The main purpose of marriage, according to a conception deeply rooted in traditional society, is the production of offspring, especially sons. Where this purpose is not achieved, the marriage has no *raison d'être*.[1] Thus, in one case, a man asked permission to divorce his wife because she was barren and "the legal object of marriage is the bringing forth and raising of children," and in another case, a husband told the court that since his wife had borne him no children he was "compelled, in order to ensure progeny, to dissolve the marriage. . . ." In some further cases, the husband wished to divorce the wife either because she had borne him no children at all or because "she had borne him no male children."[2] The *sijills* contain many instances of barrenness, childlessness[3] or of the birth solely of daughters being the reason for divorce.[4] In several cases, the marriage was dissolved after the couple had half a dozen or more daughters.[5] It might happen that a mother of girls was divorced during pregnancy.[6] The wife often admitted that failure to bear children or sons was a ground for dissolution of the marriage,[7] which might account for the high proportion (90%) of divorces by mutual agreement under these circumstances.[8]

In the traditional view, barrenness or the absence of male issue is not necessarily a ground for divorce since the position may be remedied by taking a second wife without divorcing the first,[9] unless the husband is unable to support two wives or is unwilling to do so for other reasons. One such reason was provided by the Knesset, which prohibited polygamy. If the husband did not wish to run foul of the law, the only way for him to have children was by his divorcing his wife and taking another wife. There are clear cases of the Knesset's ban being the direct cause of the divorce of a barren woman. Most of them occurred in the Little Triangle villages. Thus, one man sought to divorce his barren wife in order to take another wife because "her [the first wife's] remaining within my *'iṣma* prevents me from doing so."[10]

In many cases, the wife on divorce was of advanced age or had been married a long time (20 years or more). As a rule, no definite reason for the divorce was given but vague formulas were used, such as "incompatibility" or "lack of normal matrimonial relations."[11] But from various indications it appears that one of the main reasons for divorce under such circumstances was the husband's wish to take a young wife to replace his aging one.[12] This was indeed a common motive for polygamy, but since the latter had been forbidden by the Knesset (and for other reasons), the husband was now compelled to divorce his first wife in order to take a second. He sometimes explained that the wife had "aged and [was] unable to fulfil her marital duties," or that she was "unable to serve him,"[13] but he might say quite openly that the purpose of the divorce was to enable him to take another wife.[14]

Divorce of an elderly wife in order to take a young one was particularly widespread in the Little Triangle villages, probably owing to the economic prosperity of the region. Men suddenly grown rich wished to marry young women of a social status appropriate to their new economic position. Shaykh Ḥasan Amīn al-Ḥabash dwelt disapprovingly on this phenomenon. Frequently, he said, the cause of divorce was "the lightheadedness that seizes him who has become rich after having known poverty; he has a sudden feeling of ease; it spreads and pulsates powerfully in his veins, and this is the source of the evil. Instead of being thankful for the ease and wealth that has been vouchsafed him he becomes ungrateful. Heaven forfend, and chooses to divorce the wife who has been his partner in times of trial and borne him children; after becoming rich, he repays her by divorcing her for a strange, astonishing reason: love for another woman. This phenomenon is unfortunately a frequent subject of court cases." In this connection, Shaykh Ḥasan quoted a *ḥadith* with the moral that there were people whom wealth corrupted and for whom it would have been better to be poor.[15] The phenomenon in question was also clearly reflected in the testimony of some women.. In one case, a woman said that her husband was trying to get rid of her by various devices "because he has become wealthy after knowing dire poverty, which I shared with him during the best years of my youth. . . After he had become one of the well-known, rich people in the village, he cut himself off from me, who had borne him seven children, because I had in his eyes become unworthy of one like him, one of the rich people in the village. . . ." In another case, a woman asserted that "people talked him [her husband] into taking another wife because I am old."[16]

But for the Knesset's ban on polygamy, sudden wealth would probably have caused an increase in the polygamy rate. Paradoxically, this ban, prompted by good intentions, led to an increase in the divorce rate[17] and thus harmed more than helped women. As regard the legal and financial consequences, divorce was apt to be much worse for them than polygamy.[18]

The husband might be dozens of years—sometimes half a century[19]—older than the wife, and there were cases when the wife was considerably older than the husband.[20] Great age differences tend to disrupt married life; in some cases, the marriage was probably never consummated owing to the husband's advanced age.[21] Other instances of incompatibility involved differences as to type of settlement, education or religion. A townswoman might be loath to move to her husbands village, tribe or even town for reasons of status and prestige.[22] Sometimes the wife was better educated than the husband, which might become apparent in cases in which the divorce judgment bore the wife's signature beside the husband's fingermark (*baṣma*).[23] In marriages of a Muslim man and a Jewish or Christian woman, the difference in religion usually involved also social, economic and cultural differences, and although the wife sometimes adopted Islam to facilitate integration within her husband's environment, this formal act could not obliterate or blur those differences. Many dozens of marriages failed for this reason.[24]

In many cases, divorce took place after the wife had claimed maintenance or been awarded maintenance for non-payment of dower, non-provision of a legal dwelling or the like.[25] In one case in which a wife was divorced in the course of the hearing of her maintenance claim the *qāḍī* remarked that "it seems the husband meant to get rid of her in the hope that he would not have to pay maintenance to her and her daughters."[26] The very fact of litigation over maintenance might lead to divorce. Sometimes feelings ran so high in the course of the hearing that the husband divorced the wife spontaneously[27] or the spouses reached the conclusion that it was impossible or pointless to continue their marriage and decided on divorce by mutual agreement.[28] The wife might be alive to this possibility and therefore delay the filing of the maintenance claim, sometimes for years, "in order to preserve our marriage."[29]

More frequent causes of divorce were the wife's disobedience and rebelliousness: her leaving the husband's house without his permission and without a legal reason, for instance, in order to visit her relatives at other than the permitted and agreed times[30]; her going out to work against the husband's will[31]; the dismissal of the husband's claim for obedience[32]; the wife's refusal to comply with a judgment for obedience[33]; her rebelliousness or her having been declared rebellious (*nāshiza*).[34] Under such circumstances the husband divorced the wife because he did not agree to her deviating from the norm accepted in traditional society as regards freedom of movement, economic activity, and so on. Divorce is the husband's last resort when the economic sanction against a rebellious wife (denial of the right to maintenance) does not achieve its purpose, because a judgment for obedience is not enforceable.[35]

Rebelliousness was a particularly frequent ground in cases of suspended repudiation, which was intended to deter the wife from doing something (such as going out) or to get her to do something (such as to return home).

Another, less frequent motive for divorce was behaviour on the part of the wife which, according to the traditional scale of values, was disgraceful. The reference was mainly to deviation from the accepted norm in relations with the husband or to matters of chastity and female honour (*'ird*). A man might divorce his wife with the contention that she had caused him humiliation or brought him into contempt, for example, that her behaviour toward him was "intolerably" bad; "that she [was] depraved"[36]; that at the time of the consummation of the marrigae she had not been a virgin[37]; that she refused to have sexual intercourse with him[38]; that she did not live in his house, loitered, crossed the frontier from time to time or sullied her womanly honour; that she fled from his village home to the city[39]; that she was not faithful to him, that she went with another man for a long trip on the West Bank without his knowledge and consent and thus "impairs my good name and stains my honor"[40]; that she fled with a strange man or a relative to a distant place and he did not even know where she was.[41] The fact that these matters were solved by divorce and not by the traditional methods of dealing with a wayward wife is one of the manifestations of the process of modernization Israeli Muslim society has been undergoing.

Another cause of divorce was polygamy. A man might simply wish to divorce one of his wives "in order that only one wife may remain in his *'iṣma*"[42] or he might explain that "he cannot support both wives"[43] or there might be "constant quarrels between the two rivals."[44] The divorced in these cases were oldish women who had 20 to 30 years of marriage, which suggests that the man wished to keep the younger woman. At any rate, the divorce of a polygamous wife did not appear to have anything to do with the Knesset's ban on polygamy.

Exchange marriages were a fairly frequent cause of divorce. It has already been noted that this type of marriage creates a mutual dependence between the two wives.[45] The tendency to give them equal treatment found its expression also in the matter of divorce. The divorce of one of them, whatever its cause—barrenness, lack of male offspring or anything else—was in itself an incentive for divorcing the other even if no such disability attached to her.[46] In one instance, a man divorced his wife conditionally on another man's divorcing her *badīla,* who was the first man's sister, that is to say, the divorce was to become effective automatically on the *badīla's* divorce.[47] There were indeed cases where the very same cause, *viz.,* the wife's having left the husband's house, was invoked in the divorces of both *badīlas,* or where actions for obedience or maintenance ended with the simultaneous divorce of both couples,[48] but it seems that even in these cases only one of the women had a concrete reason for acting the way she did, while the other merely reacted to the behaviour of the first. Only in one case did the dispute not end with the dissolution of both marriages. One woman was divorced and waived both dowers, while her *badīla,* who insisted on staying with her husband, received the prompt dower.[49]

Characteristic features of exchange marriages were a relatively high proportion (25%) of cases in which the union was never consummated and the short duration of such marriages (usually between one and four years). In other words, exchange marriages appear in many instances to have been doomed in advance to failure. This has also been noted by Shaykh Ḥasan Amīn al-Ḥabash,[50] and there is also evidence from some of the parties concerned which confirms that a form of marriage that links the fates of the two couples or the two wives leads to quarrels and conflicts and makes divorce almost inevitable.[51] Another characteristic of exchange marriages was that the divorces all involved mutual renunciation of matrimonial rights—dower and maintenance during the *'idda*[52]—and, ostensibly, mutual agreement of the parties. The dissolution of exchange marriages, similarly to their contraction required the prior definition of the rights of the two women on a basis of equality. Almost two-thirds of the divorces of exchange marriages occurred in rural settlements, one-half in the Little Triangle villages. Particularly striking is the comparatively large share (more than one-quarter) of the Negev and Galilee Beduin.[53] About one-tenth of the cases occurred among the urban population.

Another type of marriage particularly likely to end in divorce was the cousin marriage. Dissolutions of marriages of this kind, though not very frequent, are significant in the context of the modernization of Israeli Muslim society, a principal manifestation of which has been the disintegration of the extended family. Cousin marriages have many advantages in terms of kinship and property relations,[54] but these advantages accrue to the two families concerned and not to the spouses themselves. In fact, since the individual has a natural tendency to seek his mate outside his near kin, marriage within the extended family, the basic unit of traditional society, is likely to be less than successful. The following case is symptomatic: after a marriage had not been consummated for five years, the husband wished to dissolve it with the wife's consent, *inter alia,* on the ground that "we, I and my wife, have lived together all our lives within the same family."[55] The *sijills* record further cases of cousin marriages that were never consummated.[56]

A dispute between the spouses into which the two families were drawn or a "family rift" (*khilāf 'ā'ili*)[57] with which the spouses had in fact nothing to do might also be a cause of divorce. Sometimes there was serious inter-family fighting, involving bloodshed, which left no alternative to the dissolution of the marriage.[58]

A physical defect, chronic or mental illness of the wife or her invalidity as the result of an accident, preventing normal marital relations, were further causes of divorce. The husband might contend that the wife was unable to fulfil her marital duties, serve him, raise the children; that relations between them had deteriorated owing to her defect or illness and that he wished to take another wife in her place.[59] A defect preventing marital relations, or mental illness, as grounds for judicial dissolution of marriage, were reserved to the wife[60]; moreover, they were not good defenses to a charge of divorce against the wife's will. In 1959, the law was amended to the effect that the wife's mental illness should be a good defense to a charge of polygamy, but the *sijills* reflect a tendency of men in such circumstances to resort to divorce rather than take an additional wife.[61] In a case of a different kind, a man wished to dissolve his marriage on the ground that he had fraudulently been married to a wife with an eye defect, having been promised that the eye could be cured, while afterward it transpired that it could not.[62]

In numerous cases, the ground for divorce was the wife's being in a neighbouring Arab country. This situation was basically a consequence of the 1948 War: either the family had been separated by the new border or the husband had married his wife in an Arab country and then somehow entered Israel, while the wife had remained in her country of origin. The problem was largely solved by the family reunion scheme, but in several dozen cases the wife refused to rejoin the husband although he had obtained permission for her to come to Israel. The main reason for her refusal was unwillingness to leave her family (her father's house) and especially her grown-up children, who were not included in the reunion scheme.[63] Other cases concerned women who fled from their husbands to an Arab country after the 1948 War and there joined their relatives, and especially their children; sometimes all trace of them was lost.[64]

The husband usually stated as the reason for the divorce that he could not live alone, that he needed a wife to serve him, to run the household, to raise his children, and the like[65]; that his marriage to the absent woman had never been consummated[66]; that the divorce was necessary in order for him to take another wife because of the Knesset's ban on polygamy.[67] Here, too, the tendency was to divorce one's wife rather than take an additional one, even in those cases where it would have been possible to invoke the Knesset's good defense that the wife had been absent for a consecutive period of seven years and that her whereabouts were unknown.[68] It sometimes happened that a man divorced his wife when she insisted on leaving Israel for an Arab country to join her kinsfolk and children there.[69]

The causes of dissolution on the wife's initiative were, briefly, as follows[70]: non-payment of the whole or part of the prompt dower, appropriation of household articles (*'afsh al-bayt*), clothing and jewellery bought by the wife with her dower[71]; location of the wife's dwelling in the house of the husband's family[72]; non-provision of maintenance to the wife and children[73];

non-provision of maintenance to a deserted wife and fear for her good name and chastity owing to the husband's absence; the husband's being outside Israel[74] or in prison[75]; cruelty and injury (*ḍarar*) to the wife, such as beating, assault and locking her up in the house[76]; charges of immoral conduct, such as infidelity and adultery, against the wife and disownment of the children[77]; the wife's being forced to work away from home[78]; social, cultural or religious incompatibility of the spouses[79]; inability of the wife to fulfil her marital duties owing to advanced age, illness infirmity and the like[80]; impotence, various defects and diseases preventing marital relations or endangering the wife[81]; reprehensible conduct of the husband, such as depraved habits or transgression of Qur'ānic and other prohibitions[82]; religious-legal defects in the marriage, such as incest, and difference of religion (*ikhtilāf al-din*).

Divorce on the Husband's Initiative

1. Legal Background

Islamic law recognizes dissolution of a marriage without legal proceedings. The right to this mode of divorce (*ṭalāq*) is reserved to the husband. The wife is a passive party to such a divorce; her consent is irrelevant. The husband may divorce her in her presence or in her absence; the *shari'ā* court has no standing in a *ṭalāq* divorce. The wife is thus under a permanent threat of divorce, whereas the husband is liable to no legal sanction, although arbitrary divorce is disapproved by the *shari'ā*.[83] True, Muḥammad introduced several important reforms in this institution, such as the *'idda* (waiting-period), which enables the husband in the case of a revocable divorce (*ṭalāq raf'i*), to take the divorced wife back without the need for the conclusion of a new marriage, and the *taḥlil*, designed to discourage hasty divorces by requiring a thrice-repudiated wife to undergo an intermediate marriage before being again permitted to her original husband. But these reforms not only did not affect the husband's unilateral right to divorce the wife, but sometimes aggravated the wife's position, as will be seen below.

Nor did the Ottoman Family Rights Law, which introduced important changes in the law of divorce with a view to improving the status of the wife, abrogate the husband's unilateral right of repudiation. It is true that divorces pronounced in a state of intoxication or under compulsion were declared invalid and that the validity of divorces pronounced in metaphorical expressions was made dependent on proof of intent (*niyya*), but the law reaffirmed the principle that *ṭalāq* divorces do not require legal proceedings and that "explicit utterances or metaphorical expressions the meaning of which is customarily known and clear" are sufficient to make them valid. Suspended repudiation (*ta'liq al-ṭalāq*) and divorce made effective from a specified future date (*ṭalāq muḍāf ilā al-mustaqbal*) also remained unchallenged by the Ottoman legislator.[84] The Family Rights Law indeed laid down the new provision that the husband must notify the divorce to the *shari'ā* court, but this is not a substantive but a procedural provision: the husband does not need the *qāḍī's* consent and the divorce is valid even without notification to the court.[85]

On the other hand, the Muslim woman has no unilateral freedom of divorce in any form. She may indeed obtain her release by mutual agreement with her spouse or by judicial proceedings, but this does not counterbalance the husband's freedom of *ṭalāq*. The seriousness of divorce from the point of view of the wife lies not only in the ease with which the husband can effect it but also in its legal and financial consequences. According to Islamic law, the father alone is the natural guardian of the children, and on the expiration of the period of custody (*ḥaḍāna*) the children pass from the control of the mother to that of the father. Divorce thus means severance of the wife from her children, and this is probably the most serious sanction threatening her. A divorced woman also loses her rights in the family property, although she sometimes had a fair share in its acquisition. She does not succeed her ex-husband. She is entitled to maintenance during the waiting-period (*'idda*), which usually lasts three months (*qurū*) or, if she is pregnant, until the birth of the child, to deferred dower and to other connected stipulations if provided for in the marriage contract. Divorce is thus worse from the point of view of the wife than polygamy.[86] The husband's almost unlimited freedom of *ṭalāq* and the adverse consequences of divorce for the wife faithfully reflect the structure of the patriarchal family.

The Women's Equal Rights Law provides that divorce against the wife's will, in the absence of a court judgment imposing divorce on the wife, is a criminal offense carrying a sentence of five years' imprisonment.[87] In other words, the criminality of this kind of divorce does not affect its legal validity insofar as it is valid according to the *shar'i* personal law applicable to the Muslim parties, but it entails a penal sanction.[88] Although couched in general terms, the provision is intended especially for Muslims.[89] In 1959, section 181A of the Criminal Code Ordinance was replaced by the provision that "where the husband dissolves the marriage against the will of the wife, and there is not, *at the time of the dissolution,* a final judgment of the (civil) court or the competent religious court imposing divorce on the wife, the husband shall be liable to imprisonment for a term of five years" (the italicized words were added to the original section).[90] In this way the Israeli legislator meant to bar the husband from divorcing his wife against her will and afterward obtaining the formal approval of the religious court.[91]

In sum, the Knesset did not intend to negate the validity of the Islamic law which recognizes the dissolution of a marriage by unilateral action of the husband. This finds its explicit expression in section 5 of the Women's Equal Rights Law, which provides that this law is not to affect any legal prohibition or permission relating to marriage or divorce. The intention was to preclude the husband's exercise of the right of *ṭalāq* if the wife did not agree to the divorce, compelling his resort to the court by means of a penal sanction. The question of the wife's consent to divorce by the husband and the dependence of divorce on a judgment making it binding on the wife are elements alien to the spirit of Islamic law.[92] The court's permission provides the husband with a good defense to the charge of divorce against the wife's will, but the divorce is performed by him. If he divorces her without such permission, the divorce is valid, but he is guilty of a criminal offense.

Thus, by means of a procedural provision supported by a penal sanction, the Knesset created a mechanism affording the religious court an opportunity to consider each case, in the light of its particular circumstances, whether there was justification for approving the divorce (on other than religious-legal grounds).[93] If the wife agrees to the divorce, there is no room for intervention by the court and so, *ipso facto,* no question of a criminal offense. Knesset Member Uri Avneri proposed by way of a private member's bill that a divorce against the wife's will should be invalid, but his proposal was not adopted.[94]

2. Divorce Against the Wife's Will

More than 1,800 *ṭalāq* divorces have been confirmed and registered since the establishment of the State. Striking among them is the high proportion of the various forms of "renunciation and compensation" divorces (around 1,300) as against other *ṭalāq* divorces (see Table 6.1 below); and adding divorces conditional on the wife's renunciation of rights and compensation to the husband, it may be said that about three-quarters (around 1,350) of all *ṭalāq* divorces were by agreement between the parties, whereas unilateral *ṭalāq* divorces made up only about

TABLE 6.1
***Ṭalāq* Divorces by Main Categories and by Courts, During the Period Studied in the *Sijills*[a]**

Court	*Total*	*Ṭalāq*	*Tawfīḍ al-Ṭalāq*	*Ordinary*	*Ṭa'liq al-Ṭalāq Conditional on wife's Renunciation of Rights*	*Total*	*Renunciation and Compensation Divorces*
Jaffa	369	116	7	10	34	44	202
Ṭayyiba	236	65	—	20	—	20	151
Nazareth	488	67	1	17	5	22	398
Acre	714	135	3	7	4	11	565
Total	1,807	383	11	54	43	97	1,316

(*a*) Divorces confirmed by *qāḍīs*, including divorces revealed during the hearing of various matrimonial claims; not including judicial dissolutions and annulments of irregular (*fāsid*) or void (*bāṭil*) marriages (total 80).

one-quarter (approximately 450; see Table 6.2 below). The data on divorces by agreement reflect the position relatively faithfully because the parties were interested in registration.[95] On the other hand, the estimate of *ṭalāq* divorces not by agreement is probably too low for a number of reasons.

Awareness of the duty of registering divorces has not yet taken root in all strata of society. This duty is an innovation introduced in 1919,[96] and has no substantive significance from the *shar'i* point of view. In the transitional period from the Mandate to the State of Israel, the work of the *shari'ā* court, including the whole registration machinery, was disrupted and the proper confirmation and registration of divorces was impossible.[97] Since the Six-Day War of June 1967, the Muslims of East Jerusalem have also been in a state of transition; they brought their matrimonial matters before two *shari'ā* courts, in which differing systems of material law applied.[98]

TABLE 6.2
***Ṭalāq* Divorces by Agreement Between the Parties and Otherwise, by Courts**

Court	*Total*	*Ṭalāq Divorces by Agreement*	*Ṭalāq Divorces Otherwise than by Agreement*
Jaffa	369	236	133
Ṭayyiba	236	151	85
Nazareth	488	403	85
Acre	714	569	145
Total	1,807	1,359	448

A divorce was usually registered for a specific purpose, such as realization by the wife of the rights accruing to her in consequence of the divorce; remarriage of one or both of the parties[99]; or an increased old-age pension from the National Insurance Institute for the wife as a lone woman.[100] The motive might arise long after the divorce, and sometimes one or even several decades passed between the divorce and its confirmation.[101] The divorce might not be registered in time because the spouses honestly believed that it was not valid, or were interested in concealing it, and continued to cohabit without a *shar'ī* bond; the divorce might then come to light at a later stage, sometimes during the hearing of another matter, such as a claim for maintenance or obedience.[102] Lastly, the ban on divorce against the wife's will also contributed to the non-registration of divorces (especially since the amendment enacted in 1959), because the husband was not anxious to expose himself to the penal sanction.

Ṭalāq divorces otherwise than by agreement were still, at any rate, a significantly frequent phenomenon. Their rates were lower in the areas of jurisdiction of the *Shari'ā* Courts of Nazareth (17% of all *ṭalāq* divorces) and Acre (20%) than in those of the *Shari'ā* Courts of Jaffa and Ṭayyiba (36%). These differences were probably due to the high concentration of an urban population (mixed towns) in the area of jurisdiction of the *Shari'ā* Court of Jaffa and to the economic prosperity of the Little Triangle villages. Hardly any divorce not by agreement had in recent years been registered at the *Shari'ā* Courts of Nazareth[103] and Ṭayyiba.

Divorce against the wife's will took various forms: usually she was divorced out of court, sometimes even in her absence, and she might learn of it accidentally or from someone other than her husband[104]; occasionally a husband divorced his wife in court in the presence of the *qāḍī,* but in her absence.[105] It could happen that a wife was divorced in court in her presence without being asked to agree to the divorce and even against her express opposition and without the husband having asked or received permission for the divorce.[106] The husband frequently did not even take the trouble to assign reasons.

One of the most striking manifestations of the husband's freedom of divorce is suspended repudiation (*ta'liq al-ṭalāq*). The Ottoman legislator did not restrict the husband's right in this matter.[107] Resort to this mechanism has two traditional purposes: the threat of divorce is to get the wife to do or refrain from doing a certain act; the husband may wish to reinforce by an oath a pronouncement he has made in a matter not connected with the wife—that is to say, the element of intent (*niyya*) to divorce is absent here (see below).[108]

Suspended repudiation, usually of the first-mentioned kind, was resorted to in about a hundred cases, that is, about one-quarter of all *ṭalāq* divorces without the wife's consent. It arose out of problems connected with obedience, the dwelling, duties toward the family and the household, property relations between the spouses, family rifts, the type of marriage, etc. Thus, for instance, the husband said ". . . if the wife does not come at once, or at least within the hour, to my house which has been prepared for her, she shall be deemed repudiated by triple repudiation" or "if you do not return to our house by seven o'clock tomorrow morning. . . ." or "if you do not return to my house with the bearer of this letter . . . ."[109] The wife's leaving the house without the husband's permission, especially her going to the house of her father, brother or mother or some other relative, was a very frequent ground for suspended repudiation: "if you go to the house of your relatives or your relative comes to you. . . ," "if you leave the house after sunset without my written permission . . . ," "if you leave your home and go outside the village . . . ," "if you go to see the doctor . . . ."[110] Sometimes the husband threatened to divorce the wife if she remained at his house for another night or returned to his house.[111]

Suspended repudiation might be prompted by the wife's refusal to move with the husband to a dwelling in another locality. In some cases, the wife was asked to do so to prevent the splitting up of the family as a result of the 1948 War.[112] Other grounds were the wife's working away from home, for example, as a teacher or labourer[113]; her negligence in the performance of household duties[114]; disputes over financial matters: "if you do not return the money you have taken. . . ," "if you touch it [the money] of use it as you please. . ."[115]; quarrels between the wife and her mother-in-law: "if you cross the threshold of my mother's room. . ."[116]; quarrels between the husband and wife concerning her loyalty to her family: one husband divorced his wife by suspended repudiation, effective if within a stated period she did not give him the power of attorney she had given her brother and undertake in writing never to give a power of attorney in matrimonial matters to a member of her family so long as they were married[117]; in another case, the husbnad swore an oath [to divorce her] as a chastisement (*yamīn al-ta'dib*)—"*'alayya al-ḥarām*, may she not return to my house until she becomes a human being"[118]; suspended repudiation also occurred in exchange marriage: "if [X] divorces his wife, my sister, then my wife [Y, X's sister] shall be divorced."[119]

Sometimes the fulfilment of the condition of the divorce did not depend on the wife but on the husband; for instance, one stated: "if I beat or humiliate her or ask her a favour, she shall be considered divorced"[120]; another swore not to eat anything his wife had prepared as long as he lived[121] and another not to receive her into his house or take her to the town in which he resided.[122] In one case, the husband did not succeed in consummating the marriage for two years and the wife returned to her father's house; then it was agreed between them that she should return to his house for 30 days and that if he was still unsuccessful at the end of that period she should be considered divorced.[123]

Suspended repudiation as a means to reinforce a pronouncement by the husband unconnected with the wife's behaviour was less frequent: a man who had quarreled with his brother swore to leave the house, failing which his wife would be considered divorced (he subsequently returned to the house and the divorce became effective); a man having a fight with another swore to rip his opponent's belly open with a knife (the contestants were separated, but the wife was divorced): a man swore to leave Israel for an Arab country (he gave up the idea when his application for permission to emigrate was rejected, and again the wife was divorced); a man caught a thief in his encampment and when he got away swore that he was a certain person; he was unable to prove the charge because his wife denied having seen the thief, and the divorce became effective.[124]

In dozens of cases the husband declared, sometimes before the court: "If she [the wife] releases me (*idhā abra'atni*) [from certain matrimonial obligations, such as deferred dower and maintenance during the waiting-period], I shall be prepared to divorce her."[125] In all these cases, the wife renounced her rights and was divorced. Such a renunciation may play the part of a condition of suspended repudiation, the husband saying:

"You shall be divorced . . . if you release me from . . ." and the divorce becoming effective when the wife fulfils the condition.[126] Sometimes suspended repudiation preceded agreement between the parties as to the conditions of divorce and renunciation and might be regarded as an invitation (or pressure[127]) to agree to a divorce on the husband's terms. The process was thus as follows: the husband at first repudiated the wife on certain conditions, and then the wife appeared in court announcing that she agreed to the conditions, whereupon the divorce was complete and effective.[128] Where dissolution involved not only renunciation of rights by the wife but also monetary compensation, the husband expressly stipulated that the divorce should only become effective when the money had been deposited with him.[129] Sometimes several months elapsed before the wife succeeded in raising the money, which she then deposited with the court, whereupon the husband collected it, thus completing the divorce.[130]

In one case, the mechanism of suspended repudiation was applied by arbitrators within the meaning of article 130 of the Family Rights Law. When their efforts to restore domestic peace failed, they decided that the wife should be divorced if the spouses did not become reconciled within six days; they did not, and so the court decided that the wife was divorced.[131] The author did not come across a single case of a wife's being divorced with effect from a specific future date (*ṭalāq muḍāf ilā al-mustaqbal*). Suspended repudiation was particularly frequent in mixed towns and in Nazareth; it was more widespread in the Little Triangle villages of Ṭayyiba, Umm al-Faḥm and Ṭira than in the villages of Galilee.[132] It was rare in Beduin society.[133] Suspended repudiation, in its various forms, was common also in the Ottoman period, especially in urban society,[134] but, as will be seen below, it received considerable impetus in Israel as a result of the ban on divorce against the wife's will.

There are clear cases of husbands being undeterred by the penal sanction from divorcing their wives against their wills. Sometimes the husband declared in court, before or after the divorce, that he knew that the wife was opposed to it, that he did not care whether or not she agreed, that the divorce was performed before he had received permission for it from a *shari'ā* court, that he was well aware that it was contrary to secular law and subject to a penal sanction, and that he was "prepared to bear legal responsibility" or "criminal responsibility." The husband might go through with the divorce even after the *qāḍī* had warned him not to divorce the wife against her will.[135] The husband's readiness to bear criminal responsibility is rooted in the belief that the right of *ṭalāq* must not be curtailed in any way because it is given him by the *shari'ā* or by God. Thus, in one case, the husband declared that he had divorced his wife because "Islamic law has placed the marital bond in the man's charge . . . and in reliance on this legal right granted me by God . . . ." In another case, the husband said he wanted to follow "the path of the *shar'i* law only."[136] This attitude toward the institution of *ṭalāq* is part of the Muslim's religious belief, which is reinforced by his social outlook. In fact, the borderline between the social and religious was blurred in his consciousness, and he often sought support in the *shari'ā* for his traditional attitude in social matters.

The restriction of the right of *ṭalāq* by the Knesset is a measure which not all Muslims were able to live with, and under such circumstances social custom reinforced by the *shari'ā* proved stronger than secular law backed by a penal sanction. There were various ways of circumventing the ban on divorce against the wife's will: until the enactment of the Penal Law Amendment (Bigamy), Law, 5719-1959, it was possible to divorce one's wife and afterward seek permission for the divorce from the court. This was the most usual way of achieving a divorce without becoming guilty of a criminal offense. It is doubtful whether this device was used consciously. It seems rather that application to the court *ex post facto* was not intended to obtain permission but confirmation and registration. In any case, circumvention of the ban diminished greatly after the 1959 amendment, which, as stated, provides that the court's permission must be obtained beforehand.

The simplest way to evade the penal sanction was to divorce one's wife without registering the divorce[137] or to register it after a long time, when the question of the form of the divorce had ceased to be of actual concern. This way was of course effective where the wife was not alert to her rights. Bullying the wife into consenting to the divorce, false pretences, and false and falsified documents as to her consent were also resorted to.[138] Yet another circumvention of the ban on divorce against the wife's will was to drag the wife to court by a ruse, such as by filing an action which required her presence, and in the course of the hearing of that action divorcing her in the presence of the *qāḍī* and ostensibly with his knowledge and permission. It is doubtful whether by such a stratagem the husband really met the requirement of asking the court's permission for the divorce. Thus, in one case, the husband had the wife come to court in connection with a maintenance claim, and then, in the presence of the *qāḍī*, divorced her without having first asked permission. The *qāḍī* entered the divorce in the record and asked the wife to confirm it by her signature. The wife refused to sign and brought a criminal action against the husband for infringing the ban on divorce against the wife's will.[139]

Divorce also sometimes took place before the court in the wife's absence, after she had failed to appear in time for the hearing. Some *qāḍīs* regarded dissolution under these circumstances as lawful.[140] In one case a husband used the mechanism of *tafwiā al-ṭalāq* (delegated repudiation) to make sure that he could divorce his wife against her will without becoming guilty of a criminal offense. He had her sign an agreement to the effect that "he had the right to divorce her . . . with her consent . . . whenever he liked, in her presence or absence."[141]

The most sophisticated, though not widely used, device for circumventing the ban on divorce against the wife's will was suspended repudiation. In many cases, the husband contended that he had not been the active party in giving effect to the divorce, so that there was no basis for charging him with a criminal offense. The choice between continuation and dissolution of the marriage had rested with the wife, he claimed, and if she had opted for the latter alternative she had done so of her own free will. The husband's allegation that the wife had "opted for divorce of her own free will" (*ikhtārat linafsihā hādhā al-ṭalāq wabimaḥḍ irādatihā*) occurred very frequently in different formulations.[142] These formulations were undoubtedly intended to suggest that the situation was one of *tafwīḍ al-ṭalāq*, that is, delegation to the wife of power to divorce herself, and they should be regarded as equivalent to the expressions *takhyir* and *ikhtāri nafsaki* within the meaning of articles 260 and 261 of Qadrī's collection. This was explicitly confirmed by Shaykh Ṭāhir Ḥamād, who on one occasion used an expression typical of the context of delegated repudiation: *ja'ala al-amr biyadihā*.[143] In one case, the husband asserted that suspended repudiation was "*shar'i'*" and "*qānūnī*,"[144] by which he apparently meant that it was valid under the *shari'ā* and not contrary to secular law. Some husbands carried out suspended repudiation by means of a letter to the wife with a copy to the court, apparently in order to create a kind of alibi in support of the plea that the wife had known of the divorce "and opted for it."[145] In one case, the wife said that she had asked and received the husband's advance permission for a visit to the pediatrician and that on her return he had told her that she had left the house without his permission and that he had made the divorce contingent on her going out. She said that this had been a "manoeuvre" in order to divorce her so as to be able to marry another woman[146]; she apparently did not think that such a divorce involved a criminal offense since a husband was always able to divorce his wife. The use of suspended repudiation as a means to circumvent the ban on unilateral divorce was particularly widespread in mixed towns within the jurisdiction of the *Shari'ā* Court of Jaffa and in the Little Triangle villages.[147]

Those who infringed or circumvented that ban were undoubtedly encouraged by the policy of the competent authorities, who were not unduly anxious to prosecute offenders. Infringements of the ban could without difficulty be traced in the *sijills*, at any rate, in those cases in which the judge noted expressly in the judgment that the wife had been divorced illegally and the husband admitted this and even declared that he was prepared to bear the criminal responsibility involved. The first trial of a Muslim for divorcing his wife against her will took place as late as 1959,[148] and the number of offenders punished thereafter was very small.

3. *The Deterrent Effect of the Penal Sanction*

On the other hand, there are indications that the penal sanction attached to the ban on divorce against the wife's will had made an impact as will be shown in the following:

(a) *The Wife's Consent to the Divorce*

Divorces with the wife's consent occurred, of course, even before the passage of the Women's Equal Rights Law in 1951, but it seems that her consent related to the mode of settlement of matrimonial rights rather than to the divorce itself.[149] At any rate, up to the prohibition of divorce against the wife's will, obtaining the wife's consent was voluntary, whereas afterward it became a statutory duty. One of the most impressive indications of the deterrent effect of the penal sanction is the husband's tireless effort to obtain the wife's consent in various ways. In hundreds of cases, he renounced his matrimonial rights and paid what was due to the wife; his renunciation related especially to dower. These cases mainly concerned marriages that had not been consummated.[150] Usually it was noted that "each of them [the spouses] renounces matrimonial rights"[151]; occasionally the expression "general renunciation"[152] was used, without any rights or conditions being specified. Sometimes it was noted that the spouses had agreed on the divorce "unconditionally and without qualification."[153] There were cases in which renunciation or other conditions were not referred to even vaguely. This was especially frequent where the marriage had not been consummated and in the case of exchange marriages.[154] These cases may be equated with others in which mutual renunciation of rights had taken place.[155]

The wife's matrimonial rights implemented on divorce by agreement included deferred dower and sometimes also prompt dower or the outstanding balance of it, maintenance for the waiting-period, stipulations connected with the dower, viz., household effects (*'afsh al-bayt*), jewellery, clothing etc.,[156] accumulated maintenance and maintenance for the children left in the custody of the wife[157]; the husband might also renounce *shar'i* and civil claims pending in *shari'ā* courts and civil courts,[158] promise to relinquish property of the wife and acknowledge the child she was expecting as his.[159] The husband's readiness to discharge all his obligations to the wife at the time of the divorce is extremely significant, even though he would seem bound to do so under religious law; in ordinary *ṭalāq* divorces, the realization of those rights involve legal proceedings.

Another, even more impressive, indication of the deterrent effect of the penal sanction is the compensation paid to the wife for her consent to the divorce. It was usually paid in cash in amounts ranging from several hundred to several thousand Israeli pounds.[160] Shaykh Ḥasan Amīn al-Ḥabash noted that in some cases it reached 15,000 pounds.[161] Occasionally compensation was paid in hard currency, such as pounds sterling, English sovereigns and even Ottoman gold liras, or in jewellery.[162] It was usually paid at the time of the divorce, but sometimes in monthly instalments or in promissory notes payable after several months (or a year) or the wife was left to demand the money "whenever she likes."[163] Frequently the compensation was paid in kind, mostly in immovables: a parcel of land, an olive grove or some fruit trees, a plot in a built-up area, a house or room with a yard, a well, etc. The property was usually transferred to her full ownership, sometimes with an undertaking to register it in her name in the Land Registry.[164] The husband might sell to his divorced wife a parcel of land or a building as a part of the compensation arrangement.[165] The compensation might take the form of livestock: goats, sheep, horned cattle, and so forth.[166]

Other arrangements related to the wife's dwelling. The couple might reach an agreement that the house or apartment in which they lived until their divorce should, with all its furniture and appurtenances, serve as dwelling of the woman until her death and that the man might not oust her from it as long as she lived. The man might undertake to leave the house and to pay her a fine *(gharāma)* of several thousand pound if he failed to do so; if he forced her out or if, for any reason, she moved out of her own accord, he was to pay her monetary compensation.[167] The man might undertake to provide a furnished apartment to the woman and to pay the rent for an agreed period.[168] Such arrangements were especially frequent in the towns of Acre and Haifa.

Another way of compensating the woman was by assuring her of an extension beyond the waiting-period of the maintenance which was prescribed by the *shari'ā* for that period: the husband might undertake to support the woman for life or until she remarried,[169] left the country and rejoined her family,[170] or became entitled to a National Insurance or welfare pension.[171] The principle was that the husband would provide for her upkeep until some other agency assumed that responsibility. Maintenance was often combined with compensation in the form of property or with the provision of living accommodation in the ex-husband's house.[172] Compensation in kind was intended to ensure the ex-wife's subsistence and economic independence.[173]

The chief reason for the payment of compensation to the divorced woman was undoubtedly the Knesset's ban on divorce against the wife's will, which is coupled with a penal sanction. The compensation was intended to secure the wife's consent to the divorce. Evidence of this is to be found in direct references by several *qāḍīs* and in their decisions. Shaykh Ḥasan Amīn al-Ḥabash stated that: ". . . what is called compensation is a quid pro quo given for the wife's consent to her husband's divorcing her, in circumvention of the criminal responsibility incurred in the event of his divorcing her without her consent and without obtaining a judgment of the competent court permitting him to perform the divorce . . . The phenomenon of compensation is clearly a consequence of the law forbidding divorce against the wife's will. . . ."[174] Shaykh Tawfīq Maḥmūd 'Asaliyya remarked: "The husband was the right of *ṭalāq* and is therefore not bound to pay compensation to the wife except in the event that the wife does not wish to be divorced and the husband wants to bring her round with money in order to avoid punishment. . . ."[175] Further confirmation that compensation was a consideration for the wife's consent to the divorce was given to the author by Shaykh Muḥammad Ḥubayshī.

In fact, almost all the divorce judgments mentioning compensation state that the wife consented to the divorce. Often they even state expressly that the compensation was a "consideration for her consent"[176] or that the wife made her consent conditional on compensation.[177] Significant in this context is the fact that all the cases in which compensation was paid were divorces by mutual agreement and performed in court. In one case, a man first divorced his wife out of court, but at the time of registration offered to pay compensation as he had done on the divorce of a previous wife.[178] The author did not come across a single instance of payment of compensation to a divorced wife prior to the enactment of the Women's Equal Rights Law on July 17, 1951.[179] Nor did he find any instances in the Ottoman or Mandatory *sijills* (of several years selected at random).

Some researchers note that the custom of compensating the divorced wife already existed before the establishment of the State, though not on a large scale. The compensation sometimes consisted in a part, usually one-third, of the dower which had been set aside for the eventuality of divorce or the husband's death.[180] Israeli *sijills* usually indicate that the compensation was paid in lieu of maintenance for the waiting-period, the dower being rarely referred to[181]; in these few cases, the compensation might have been identical with the dower. In other cases, a clear distinction was made between compensation and dower.[182] The compensation was often said to be for injury *(ḍarar)* caused to the wife by the divorce.[183] Shaykh Ḥusnī al-Zuʿbī, asked about the origin of the custom of compensation, said that compensation was stipulated in advance in the marriage contract.[184] In fact, at a *qāḍīs*' conference in 1963, it was recommended that *ma'dhūns* should safeguard the wife's rights in the marriage contract by providing for divorce compensation of an amount to be fixed according to the circumstances or by the court.[185]

But Shaykh Ḥasan Amīn al-Ḥabash, in whose area of jurisdiction compensation was particularly widespread, strongly emphasized that it had nothing to do with dower and that "not a mil" was paid to the divorced wife as compensation before the establishment of the State.[186] Nor is there any evidence in judgments of compensation being stipulated in the marriage contract and its realization sought on divorce; neither did the author find an instance of such a stipulation in the marriage registers of 1962 and 1968. It thus seems that although the practice of paying divorce compensation may not be new, its spread to its present dimensions is at any rate connected with conditions and circumstances which developed in Israel. The stipulation of compensation in the marriage contract must be regarded as still in the recommendation stage, the reference to the injury caused to the divorced woman being, as will be shown below, an attempt to give *shar'i* legitimation to a custom which has no basis in Islamic law.

The Knesset's ban on polygamy may also have contributed to the spread of the practice of compensation. As stated, the primary intent of the husband who divorced his wife in many cases had been polygamy. But for the ban on the latter, he would not have divorced her; on the contrary, the divorce caused him to lose her working capacity and experience, required him to pay her the deferred dower and maintenance for the waiting-period and might spoil his relations with her family; above all, he might not want to be separated from a wife whom he honoured and valued as the mother of his children and to whom he was still emotionally attached.[187] The ban on polygamy thus suddenly placed the husband in a situation where he was reluctantly compelled to divorce his ageing wife in order to be able to marry another younger one, and the compensation under these circumstances may have to be explained not only as the price of her consent to the divorce but also as an expression of his wish to repair the damage he had unwillingly inflicted on her and to provide for her future upkeep. Rosenfeld regards compensation as a structural solution for the elderly divorced woman, who does not return to her father's house.[188]

Support for the view expressed in the foregoing may be found in cases where the husband was willing to enable the divorced wife to reside "temporarily" or to the end of her days near or even in his house. He would build a room for her above his own dwelling, install her in part of his dwelling divided off by a partition "so that they may not see each other" or even allot a room to her within his dwelling without any partition.[189] In rare cases, it was agreed between the parties that the divorced woman should live in her former husband's dwelling and be "under his control." She was to be allowed to use all the household utensils; the ex-husband was to support her and her children; to supply them with food and clothing, provide for their medical needs, and so on. He also undertook "to behave well and properly, displaying all male virtues, be patient and courteous and protect her whenever necessary"; and if they moved elsewhere, it was to be to a dwelling of higher standard than that they had left. On the other hand, the divorced wife was forbidden to be absent from the dwelling without his consent, and if she left the dwelling with her children she was to lose all her rights except the right to maintenance at a specified rate until death or re-marriage.[190] It might be agreed that if he ousted her from the dwelling or if for any reason she left of her own accord she should be entitled to monetary compensation.[191]

The divorced wife's living in or near her former husband's house was of no significance where she was elderly, ailing or disabled, and this seemed to be so in most of the cases in question. At the same time, the possibility cannot be ruled out that the divorce was sometimes fictitious in the sense that the couple continued to live maritally together (or that the ex-husband took back or remarried his former wife, which was apt to be in contravention of the ban on polygamy).[192] The author came across a not inconsiderable number of cases in which the divorced wife lived at the former husband's house and maintained marital relations with him without the couple troubling to notify the court of the divorce or to register it until several years later.[193] The facts might come out in court incidentally to the hearing of a claim by the woman for maintenance or by the man for obedience.[194] The divorced wife's living at her former husband's house was more natural and understandable where the parties were cousins who lived in one dwelling-unit within the framework of the extended family. Thus, in one case, a man said that he had divorced his wife by triple repudiation and pointed out to her that her living at his house was prohibited: "I considered her to be living near me [in the dwelling] as my cousin, not as my lawful wife." Four years had passed since the divorce before he decided to apply to the court to make clear to her that she was divorced, so that she might leave his house.[195]

About three-quarters of the cases in which the divorced wife was compensated concerned intra-*ḥamūla* or cousin marriages. Blood-relationship is likely to strengthen a man's inclination to compensate his former spouse owing to family pressures. At the same time it should be noted that the rate of endogamous marriages was high in rural society and had been so even in the past, before the custom of compensating the divorced wife became established. Shyakh Ḥasan Amīn al-Ḥabash remarked that a smaller compensation was paid to a blood-relation than to a stranger and that the rate of compensation was lower in the case of exchange marriages "lest there be a bad influence on the other *badīla*."[196]

About three-quarters of the 120 cases in which compensation was paid were in the Little Triangle villages.[197] Shyakh Tawfīq Maḥmūd 'Asaliyya confirmed that compensation was not customary in localities in the area of jurisdiction of the *Shari'ā* Court of Jaffa[198] (in which all types of settlement were represented). The cases with compensation in the Little Triangle constituted almost 60% of divorces by agreement in that region, as against up to 3% in the areas of jurisdiction of the *Shari'ā* Courts of Jaffa. Nazareth and Acre. The frequency of the practice in the Little Triangle was probably due to the economic prosperity of that region, which fostered the inclination in married men to seek younger wives: polygamy being forbidden, the older woman was divorced with compensation.

The institutionalization of the wife's consent to the divorce found various kinds of formal and structural expression: in most cases of divorce by agreement, it was declared that the parties wished to dissolve their marriage "by voluntary, mutual agreement" (*biriḍāhimā wa'khtiyārihimā*), and in addition, the *qāḍī* often recorded a statement by the wife, in the first person: "I agree (*rāḍiya*) to this divorce."[199] Occasionally the mechanism of suspended repudiation was used, the wife's consent being one of the conditions, or the only condition, of the validity of the divorce. The husband might say, for instance: "My wife . . . shall be considered divorced . . . if she consents to the divorce and grants me remission of . . ." and the divorce then took effect as soon as the wife consented to it and renounced various matrimonial rights in accordance with the husband's demand. Divorce conditional on the wife's consent was chiefly practiced in the towns of Jaffa, Lod and Ramla.[200] It was not uncommon to designate the wife's consent as one of the conditions of a comprehensive divorce agreement drawn up in writing with the signatures of the parties.[201] Sometimes it was expressly noted that compensation was paid to the wife "in return for her consent" (*liqā' muwāfaqatihā*) or the wife made her consent conditional on receipt of compensation.[202]

The wife's consent to the divorce was undoubtedly meaningful in those cases in which she initiated or demanded the divorce and probably in most of the cases in which she renounced matrimonial rights or even paid compensation to the husband in order to obtain her freedom and in the cases in which divorce was conditional on her consent and the fulfilment of this condition was left to her. But in many other cases in which the wife consented to the divorce, including cases in which she obtained her matrimonial rights and even compensation for her consent, a suspicion arises that she did not always do so of her own free will and in awareness of her status and legal rights. It is often quite clear, especially when the divorce took place out of court, that her consent was given in the innocent belief that the *ṭalāq* was the husband's indisputable *shar'ī* right, given him by Allāh; in other words, she resigned herself to her fate for religious reasons.[203] The wife's submission had also social, traditional causes. In many cases, she gave her consent when she was elderly, disabled or ill, unable to fulfil her marital duties, attend to the household, etc., or when she was barren or had only borne daughters.[204] Shyakh Ḥusnī al-Zu'bī confirmed that the wife's barrenness or inability to fulfil her duties toward the husband and the family were frequent causes of divorce by agreement. The wife consented to the divorce in order to enable the husband to marry another woman "for a family purpose," *i.e.*, the production of offspring.[205]

Other causes of divorce that the wife regarded as legitimate in view of the norm accepted in traditional society were disputes between rival wives in polygamous marriages,[206] and especially, the divorce of one of the *badīlas* in exchange marriages.[207] Needless to say, the wife's consent to the divorce in cases of exchange marriages was not meaningful in the sense intended by the Knesset. The wife in such a marriage rarely opposed the divorce. The only institutionalized way to preserve the surviving marriage in such cases was by paying dower to the wife who did not wish to leave her husband.[208] Family pressures were also the probable cause of the wife's consent in cases where the spouses were blood-relations, especially where they were cousins,[209] and where there were disputes between the two families.

One may also be sceptical of the wife's consent in cases where she was represented by a proxy (*wakīl*). This proxy, who was usually her father or brother, not only formulated the conditions for her divorce (renunciation, compensation, and so forth) in her name, but also consented in her name to the divorce.[210] She was often not in court on those occasions, and thus her view of the divorce was not heard. The possibility cannot be ruled out that she was forced to appoint the proxy precisely because she was herself opposed to the divorce. The same measure of scepticism should apply in cases where the wife was absent from the session of the court and the husband presented her consent in writing or had people testify to it or alleged that she had consented. It sometimes transpired that she was divorced against her will although the husband alleged that she had consented.[211] In one case, it was ascertained that the wife's signature on the document purporting to attest her consent had been forged and the matter went as far as the Supreme Court sitting as a High Court of Justice.[212] Many cases are on record where the husband put various kinds of pressure on the wife—harassment, humiliating treatment, beating, non-payment of maintenance and ejection from the house—so as to force her to consent to the divorce.[213] In numerous instances, the divorce preceded the wife's consent, which was given only at the registration stage. In other words, she was faced with an accomplished fact and her consent did not relate to the divorce itself but to her matrimonial rights.[214]

Thus, the wife's consent to the divorce should not be taken at face value; the particular conditions under which it was given should be examined in each case. It is much more meaningful in this connection to examine to what extent the wife opposed the divorce in reliance on the secular law. In fact, the author observed the following phenomenon: a wife vehemently opposed the husband's intention to divorce her and when he nevertheless did so "placed on record" that the divorce was against her will[215]; she declared that Israeli law was on her side and that she reserved the right to take legal steps in the competent courts[216]; and in one case the wife threatened to have jailed both her husband who had divorced her, and the *qāḍī* if he confirmed the divorce[217]; she misinterpreted the law to the effect that the divorce was not valid so long as she did not consent to it[218]; in another case, the wife declared that she would only consent to the divorce after she had "scratched his [the husband's] eyes out" and that "Israeli law is on the side of the wife," and in another she opposed the divorce although the husband put pressure on her in various ways and offered her whatever she might ask in return for her consent.[219]

These phenomena are unmistakable signs of a revolutionary change in the traditional mechanism of unilateral divorce by the husband. The requirement of the wife's consent to the dissolution of the marriage has turned her from a passive into an active factor[220]; she has been given a new weapon—the power to threaten the invocation of a penal sanction against the husband. There are clear indications of the wife's growing self-confidence and awareness of her legal rights. The fact that the husband resorted to various devices to obtain her consent is in itself significant. The wife is essentially in a position to refuse her consent, to withhold it as long as she wishes, to attach to it conditions satisfactory to herself and even to retract it.[221] At the same time, the process of change is still in its beginnings. It is particularly widespread in mixed towns, and more so in the villages of the Little Triangle than in those of Galilee. As yet, it is not noticeable at all in Beduin society.

(b) Permission for Divorce Granted by the Court

The most significant criterion for the effect of Israeli legislation in the sphere of divorce was the husband's resort to the *shari'ā* court in order to obtain permission for the divorce where the wife did not consent to it. As stated, what is involved here is a procedural mechanism designed to provide something like a good defense for the husband to the charge of divorce against the wife's will. Requiring the husband to apply to the court in matters of *ṭalāq* was in itself a revolutionary innovation. Only in a few dozen cases did the husband ask the court's permission, and it is not even certain that this was always the real purpose of his application. In some cases, he probably intended to divorce the wife with the knowledge or in the presence of the court, as had already been customary before the enactment of the Women's Equal Rights Law,[222] or to have the divorce registered.[223] Moreover, in a few instances, the wife had consented to the divorce and the court's permission was thus not really needed.[224] There is sometimes the impression that recourse to the court in cases where the wife opposed the divorce was rather in the nature of a request for a religious-legal opinion (*fatwā*); at any rate, the religious and the secular elements were closely linked.[225]

At the same time, there are clear instances of the husband's application in one case, he made the application "in order to escape legal punishment," and in another case he admitted that he did not wish to divorce his wife out of court, against her will and without a court judgment "for fear of doing something contrary to the law."[226] In a further case, when the court refused permission for the divorce, the husband appealed to the *Shari'ā* Court of Appleal.[227] Moreover, significant in this context were cases where the husband at first tried to get permission and only when he encountered difficulties contended that he had divorced his wife already, before applying to the court.[228] The chief grounds of applications for permission to divorce a wife were her being an absentee or staying in an Arab country, her barrenness, illness or misconduct, and conflicts arising out of polygamous marriages. The cases of application for permission encountered by the author mark the beginning of a revolutionary change in the sphere of divorce.

(c) *Reliance on Grounds Provided for Judicial Dissolution*

A further indication of the deterrent effect of the penal sanction is the husband's endeavour to dissolve the marriage on one of the grounds provided by the Ottoman Family Rights Law, although they were mainly intended to offset the wife's lack of freedom of *ṭalāq*. The number of cases of this kind is indeed not great but they are symptomatic of the disturbance of the traditional system of balances in the sphere of divorce. Thus, in one case, the husband asked the court to dissolve his marriage on the ground that his wife was mentally ill (article 123 of the Family Rights Law).[229] According to the *sharī'ā,* the husband needs no protection by the court in the event of the wife's disability or illness since he can divorce her by *ṭalāq* or take an additional wife. Mental illness, as stated, is a good defense to the charge of polygamy, but not to the charge of divorce against the wife's will.

Dissolution of the marriage by arbitration (article 130) may release the husband from the obligations to the divorced wife to which he would be subject had he divorced her by ordinary *ṭalāq*, provided that the arbitrators decide that she is responsible for the dissolution.[230] But there were cases in which this mechanism was apparently used in order to obtain dissolution without becoming guilty of a criminal offense through the wife's opposition to the divorce. Thus, in one case, a husband resorted to article 130 after all his efforts to get rid of his wife by "legitimate" methods, such as various harassments and suspended repudiation, had proved unsuccessful. The wife said that the purpose of his application was "obvious," viz., to attempt to rid himself of her "by every possible means."[231]

Dissolution on the Wife's Initiative

The wife's position is reflected not only in her reaction to unilateral divorce; she also plays an active part in dissolving the marriage, trying to obtain her freedom in various ways: by *ṭalāq* and by legal proceedings.

1. Talāq Divorces

(a) Delegated Repudiation

The most effective means at the wife's disposal to secure a dissolution without recourse to legal proceedings is delegated repudiation (*tafwīḍ al-ṭalāq*).[232] By this mechanism the husband confers on the wife power—a kind of irrevocable power of attorney—to divorce herself in his name and thus to become the active party to the divorce.[233] Of course, the decision as to the delegation itself rests with the husband, who may, in principle, grant it to someone other than the wife,[234] and only the timing of the divorce is left to her or depends on cetain pre-agreed conditions. Although according to orthodox doctrine *ṭalāq* is the unilateral privilege of the husband, in actual fact, delegated repudiation is undoubtedly a clear manifestation of the wife's freedom of divorce, albeit limited and structurally controlled.

As far as can be ascertained from the *sijills* this type of divorce was not frequent in Israeli, Muslim society. The author encountered only 11 cases, although, of course, there might be more.[235] The most usual formula for empowering the wife to divorce herself was *takūn 'iṣmatuhā biyadihā* ("her 'protection' will be in her hands"), whereas the formula customary in *shar'i* literature, *yakūn amruhā biyadihā* ("she will be responsible for herself"), which is the most serious one as regards the legal effect, since it entails irrevocable or triple repudiation, was rarely employed. The author encountered no other formulas.[236] In most cases, *tafwīḍ al-ṭalāq* in the marriage contract, in others it was granted in the course of the marriage, following a dispute or crisis between the spouses.

The delegation may be absolute or conditional.[237] An absolute delegation is formulated in a general, indefinite way, and sometimes it is said expressly that the wife may divorce herself whenever she wishes.[238] A conditional delegation becomes operative, for instance if the husband leaves the country without the wife's consent, as during the 1948 War, deserts her, makes her live in another locality than the one chosen by her or takes an additional wife.[239] Other conditions, arising out of the experience of married life, relate to the way the wife is installed in the house of the husband's family, his treatment of the wife, maintenance, equality and justice between rival wives, etc. In all the cases in question, the delegation was the consequence of a dispute between the spouses, the nature of which may be inferred from the conditions. The dispute ended in a compromise, with a saving formula that included empowerment of the wife to divorce herself. Thus, in one case, the wife fled to her father's house and refused to return to the husband's house unless he set up a partition between her dwelling and that of his family, built her a separate kitchen and separate sanitary facilities and paid her a sum of money in cash; if he failed to fulfil these conditions within a week, she was to have the right to divorce herself. The husband accepted the conditions "of his own volition and by free choice" and signed an agreement in court.[240]

In another case, a dispute arose between the spouses and the wife filed a claim for maintenance in the *shari'ā* court. The *qāḍī* succeeded in restoring domestic peace on the basis of the wife being empowered to divorce herself if the husband did not treat her well, if he beat her, cursed her, did not supply her needs as to clothing and footwear, or gave her rival preference over her in any way. The parties agreed on these conditions thanks to the intervention of Shaykh Salāma al-Huzayyil and also agreed that he should act as arbitrator (*ḥakam*) between them, deciding whether one of the said contingencies had arisen. In yet another case, where after falling out with her husband the wife sued for divorce, the *qāḍī* proposed a reconciliation on the basis of the husband undertaking to pay maintenance to his wife and children. The husband agreed and declared on this occasion: "If I beat or humiliate my wife without there being a good reason for a beating or a humiliation . . . her *'iṣma* shall be in her hands," but added that a divorce resulting from this should require the consent of the court.[241]

The wife exercised her right to divorce herself on the ground that the husband did not treat her well, that there was no harmony or compatibility between them, or that she was dissatisfied with him.[242] In one case, she did not even trouble to give a particular reason but simply said that according to the marriage contract she was entitled to divorce herself "as she wished."[243] In other cases, the wife exercised her right when the contingency in which she was authorized to divorce herself had in her opinion arisen. Thus, one wife divorced herself as soon as her husband had left the country, and married another man even before the *shari'ā* court had confirmed the divorce and before the expiry of the waiting-period.[244] In another case, the wife divorced herself although the husband made desperate efforts to prove that he had fulfilled all the conditions agreed between them and that she, therefore, had no grounds for exercising her right of divorce: the wife emphatically insisted on the divorce and applied to the court to register it.[245] In all these and other cases, the wife effected an irrevocable divorce, i.e., one which did not enable the husband to bring her back to him except by a new marriage contract and a new dower. In one case, she divorced herself by triple repudiation.[246]

In the cases described above, the wife was the active party to the divorce and the husband the passive party, opposing it. This clearly conflicts with the structure of the patriarchal family underlying the *shar'i* law. There may be a certain symbolism in the fact that in one case the husband wished to avail himself of the device of *tafwīḍ* intended for the protection of the wife, to empower *himself* to dissolve the marriage: a year after the wife had been divorced for the first time, the husband wanted to marry her again, but stipulated "that the *ṭalāq* should be in his hands at his will and choice, whether she consents or not." He was probably prompted to do so by the ban on divorce against the wife's will.[247] This is a vivid illustration of the disturbance of the balance of the Israeli Muslim family by the intervention of secular legislation. An anomaly has been created in that, on the one hand, the wife may divorce the husband against his will (in those cases where she has been empowered to do so), and on the other, the husband may not divorce the wife against her will, although this is his elementary right according to the *shari'ā*, but needs permission from the *shari'ā* court or her authorization.

As stated, dissolution by way of delegation to the wife was not common in Israeli Muslim society.[248] In most of the cases referred to, the spouses, or at least the wife, originated from urban settlements. One case occurred in the Circassian village of Kafr Kamā[249] and another in the al-Huzayyil tribe in the Negev. No conclusions should be drawn from the latter isolated case as to the status of women in Beduin society; for this was a case not of a stipulation in the marriage contract but of an agreement suggested by the court and a shaykh of the tribe as a solution to a crisis between the spouses[250]; in other words, this was yet another instance of the encounter between *shari'ā* and custom: a successful linking of a legal device with the institution of arbitration.

(b) Suspended Repudiation

Suspended repudiation is indeed one of the most striking manifestations of the husband's freedom of *ṭalāq*. However, this sharp weapon, mainly intended to ensure the wife's obedience and submission, sometimes became a double-edged sword, used by her to obtain her freedom. In many cases, the wife hastened to bring about the fulfilment of the condition and then proceeded forthwith to the *shari'ā* court to have the divorce confirmed and registered. Thus, in one case, the husband swore that the wife would be considered divorced if she left the house. A quarter of an hour later, she left the house and applied to the court to confirm the divorce.[251] In another case, the husband stipulated that the wife should be considered divorced if she did not return to his house within ten days. Even before the time was up, she informed the court that she refused to return and wanted a divorce.[252]

Occasionally the husband regretted a hasty divorce but could not forestall the wife's prompt action. He would then try to empty the suspended repudiation of its contents by qualifying the condition. Thus, in one case, the husband at first denied having divorced the wife at all, but when she brought witnesses to prove her allegation, he claimed to have stipulated that she should be considered divorced if she spent the night at her mother's house; he added, however, that the condition referred only to the night on which the divorce had been pronounced and that, since she had spent that night at his house, the divorce was ineffective.[253] In another case, the wife alleged that the husband had sworn she would be considered divorced if he ate any food prepared by her and that he had subsequently done so; she accordingly asked that the divorce be declared effective. The husband admitted eating half of some meat she had served him after he took the said oath, but added that he had made the effectiveness of the divorce contingent on "the absence of sincere feelings for him on her part"; he swore that she had again shown tenderness to him but could produce no witnesses to prove it, and she denied it emphatically.[254]

In another case, the wife refused to move into the husband's house after the marriage because she had not received the whole of the prompt dower. The husband stipulated that if she did not move into his house within five days she would be considered divorced. The wife did not move in within the time allowed. In court, the husband contended that the divorce was not effective because, according to him, he had reached an agreement with the wife as to the payment of the balance of the dower. The wife denied the existence of such an agreement and asked the court for "a judgment in accordance with the Muslim *shari'ā*"; her request was granted. In yet another case, the wife maintained that she should be considered divorced because she had left the house, but her husband contended that he had meant to make the divorce contingent on her re-entering the house, and since she had not yet done so she was still his lawful wife.[255]

The wife sometimes took advantage of a vow of divorce by the husband intended to reinforce a statement in a matter that had nothing to do with her. Thus, a man who had quarreled with his brother swore that if he did not leave the house his wife would be considered divorced; he in fact left the house, but the wife alleged in court that he had returned the same morning, whereby the divorce had become effective.[256] In several cases, the wife alleged that there had been a suspended repudiation, but was unable to prove it.[257] Sometimes there is a distinct impression that the wife resorted to making up a story in order to obtain the dissolution of her marriage.[258]

The stipulation of suspended repudiation in the marriage contract on the wife's initiative was not customary in Israeli Muslim society. The marriage registers of 1968 record only one case of this kind. The wife compelled the husband to stipulate that if he married an additional wife the latter should be considered divorce.[259]

(c) Rebelliousness

It sometimes appears that the wife strove to attain the status of *nāshiza* (rebellious wife) in order to wrest a divorce from the husband when she had no legal ground for dissolution or the husband did not agree to divorce her.[260] This impression is particularly strong in those cases in which she initiated the declaration of rebelliousness; she might even openly admit that she did not wish the marriage to continue.[261] In fact, in several instances, the stage of the wife's rebelliousness was followed by divorce.[262] Nor can the possibility be ruled out that a wife might use a maintenance claim as a device to obtain dissolution of the marriage.

(d) Divorce Pronounced in a State of Intoxication

The Ottoman legislator, in contrast to the Ḥanafī school, laid down that a divorce pronounced in a state of intoxication was not valid.[263] The plea of the husband's intoxication was provided for the protection of the wife. This plea was in fact made in a few isolated cases (all in urban settlements), but here it was not the wife but the husband who used it to avoid divorce; in some instances, he contended that the wife had extorted the divorce from him by provocation while he was drunk. Thus, in one case, some persons testified that the husband had been sitting in a cafe, drinking "large quantities of wine until he became besotted," when suddenly the wife appeared, hurled abuse at him and demanded that he divorce her in court. Other people present also urged him to divorce her and be rid of her. Giving in to all this pressure, he had divorced his wife in court. The *qāḍī* accepted the testimony of the witnesses and decided that the divorce was not valid.[264]

In dozens of cases in which the wife sought a judgment confirming her divorce, she did not succeed in proving that a divorce had really taken place.[265] A suspicion sometimes arises that the wife tried to take advantage of the husband's freedom of *ṭalāq* and the lack of formality attending divorce in order to obtain her freedom by falsely claiming that she had been divorced and, by conspiring with false witnesses, getting the court to confirm the alleged divorce.[266] In some cases, in court the wife retracted the allegation that she had been divorced.[267] Occasionally she achieved her purpose during the hearing of her suit by getting the husband to divorce her before the *qāḍī*.[268]

(e) "Renunciation Divorces" and "Compensation Divorces"

The means most frequently used by the wife to obtain her freedom was divorce by agreement between the parties. According to traditional classification, this kind of divorce comprises two main varieties: mutual renunciation by the spouses of their matrimonial rights and payment of compensation (*'iwaḍ*) to the husband in return for the divorce. Without the husband's consent to the divorce, renunciation and compensation are meaningless. The court cannot compel the husband to divorce the wife or itself dissolve the marriage by *ṭalāq* divorce.[269] It is the husband who performs the divorce, and he does so of his own free will; resort to the court is merely for confirmation of the terms of the divorce with all the attendant effects on legal and property relations.

In "renunciation divorces," the most usual arrangement was for the wife to renounce what would have been due to her by virtue of her matrimonial rights if she had been divorced by ordinary *ṭalāq*. This included maintenance during the waiting-period (*'idda*) and —if stipulated in advance in the marriage contract—deferred dower. The wife might also renounce the whole of the prompt dower (if she had not received it) or the balance of it (if she had received part of it on contraction of the marriage).[270] She might renounce half the dower (or half of both dowers); this was mostly in cases where the marriage had not been consummated.[271] She might renounce "the stipulations connected with the dower" enumerated in the marriage contract, such as household effects, *jihāz,* jewellery and clothing.[272] She sometimes forewent the implementation of other provisions of the marriage contract, such as that if the husband divorced her against her will he was to pay her an agreed sum of money "for the education of her children" or a fine (*gharāma*), or her entitlement to a sum of money from him "whenever she demands it."[273]

The wife occasionally renounced maintenance awarded her by the court and accumulated with the husband. She might renounce various claims pending in court and agree to discontinue the proceedings.[274] She often renounced her *shar'i* right of custody (*ḥaḍāna*), and the children were handed over to their father or some other person. Sometimes the spouses agreed on a division (*taqsīm, tawzī'*) of the children between them. The wife might retain *ḥaḍāna* but undertake to support the children throughout the legal period and not to claim maintenance for them (suckling and *ḥaḍāna* money) from their father. It might be agreed that the children should remain with the wife until she remarried, or that she should bring up her husband's children by another woman.[275]

The wife's renunciation might relate to rights and claims un-connected with matrimonial matters, such as monetary debts of the husband to her or her family, deposits, promissory notes, and so forth.[276] Often it was stated vaguely that the wife renounced civil (*niẓāmiyya*) claims or claims pending in a civil court. Sometimes reference was made to criminal charges connected with the ban on divorce against the wife's will.[277]

In "compensation divorces" the wife paid compensation to the husband in return for her freedom.[278] It might be in money, in kind or both.[279] It ranged from a few Israeli pounds to several thousand, sometimes 10,000 pounds.[280] Occasionally, it was paid in gold coins, such as Ottoman gold liras.[281] The wife might return the dower, especially in cases where the marriage had not been consummated,[282] the expenses of performing the betrothal and the marriage, or other sums of money received from the husband.[283]

Monetary compensation was normally paid at or about the time of the divorce. In a few exceptional cases, the wife undertook to compensate the husband when she remarried: in one instance, it was expressly stipulated that she was not permitted to remarry before she had paid compensation to her former husband. In most of these cases, security for the payment of compensation was given in the form of an undertaking by the wife's family or of a promissory note signed by the wife's father payable on her remarriage. In one case, the wife undertook to pay an amount equal to half the prompt dower "in order to safeguard her children," who were to be handed over to their father.[284] In two cases, arrangements for deferred compensation were prescribed by arbitrators.[285] It seems that this was because the wife had no money at the time of the divorce and that the intention was that she should compensate the husband out of the dower she would receive on remarriage. This assumption is confirmed by a case in which arbitrators decided on dissolution of a marriage while requiring the wife to pay a certain sum to the husband, and her father promised that on her remarriage he would take some of the prompt dower "and satisfy the [former] husband."[286] Shaykh Muḥammad Ḥubayshī explained that an undertaking to compensate the husband at the time of the wife's remarriage must be honoured like a promissory note.[287] What is involved here is a social custom for which there is no support in the *shari'ā*, but Shaykh Tawfīq 'Asaliyya attested that the *shari'ā* court did not interfere in voluntary arrangements of this kind and respected the wishes of the parties.[288]

Compensation was sometimes paid in the form of immovable property: a parcel of land, an olive grove, a house, or a right of the wife in the estate of her father or of members of her original family; the wife undertook to transfer the asset registered in her name in the Land Register to the husband.[289] The asset given as compensation might be the dower she received from him.[290]

In dozens of cases, the parties came to court with the texts of detailed agreements, which they asked to have confirmed as part of the legal effects of the divorce and which thereupon were sometimes attached to the judgment.[291] But it seems that usually the parties formulated the terms of the agreement in court and that immediately afterward the husband divorced the wife and the wife renounced her rights or compensated the husband, or he first divorced her and then she renounced her rights.[292]

Another frequent form of divorce by agreement was, as stated, a combination of renunciation or compensation and suspended repudiation. In this context, the main purpose of suspended repudiation was to ensure in advance that the wife renounced certain rights or compensated the husband before the divorce became effective. Sometimes the wife made her renunciation conditional on the husband's divorcing her. The customary formula was: "I renounce . . . . on condition that you divorce me" or ". . . and this renunciation is conditional on divorce. . . ."[293] The act of renunciation or compensation and the divorce might take place on separate occasions. When the wife renounced her rights or deposited a sum of money intended for the payment of compensation, she usually did so at her residence in the presence of the secretary of the *shari'ā* court, and the husband subsequently divorced her before the court in her absence. The spouses did not meet during these proceedings.[294]

Occasionally the wife was represented by a proxy (*wakīl*) or an advocate authorized to negotiate the terms of the divorce (renunciation, compensation etc.) with the husband and to agree to the divorce in her name.[295] The *wakīl* was usually the father or a brother of the wife, but sometimes her son or even another woman.[296] The husband might also be represented by a *wakīl*,[297] and sometimes all the proceedings involved in divorce by agreement (renunciation, compensation and even divorce itself) were conducted by proxies of the parties without the latter meeting at all.[298] The spouses might agree on a "renunciation divorce" or "compensation divorce" in the course of a proceeding before a civil court and afterward resort to the *shari'ā* court for implementation of the agreement.[299] It would seem that the timing of the divorce was of secondary importance compared with the terms of the agreement. Yet, under certain circumstances, the time factor was so material as to become part of the terms. Thus, in one case, it was agreed between the parties that if the husband divorced the wife within 40 days the matrimonial maintenance should be regarded as including maintenance for the waiting-period, but if he divorced her later, he should have to pay maintenance for the waiting-period in addition to the matrimonial maintenance.[300]

In many dozens of instances, there is express evidence that the initiative for dissolution by agreement came from the wife.[301] More than two-thirds of all divorces by agreement involved renunciation by the wife of certain rights, or compensation to the husband. In most of these cases, especially where compensation was paid to the husband, the initiative probably came from the wife.[302] But it is not impossible that even under such circumstances it came from the husband.[303] Moreover, initiative by the wife may be doubted in dozens of cases of exchange marriage.[304]

Dissolution along with the wife's renunciation of rights or the payment of compensation to the husband was practised mainly in towns, and in mixed towns—where women's social liberation had made most progress—more than in Arab towns. The rate of such divorces in mixed towns was three times as high as in villages and Arab towns: 0.9-1.0 per mille as against 0.3 per mille (in 1967).[305] Such divorces also occurred among the Beduin, especially those Galilee, who were at an advanced stage of sedentarization. They were more frequent in exogamous than in endogamous marriages: in exogamous marriages, the wife who wanted a divorce was free from pressures arising out of blood-relationship. It seems, however, that the type of settlement was more important in this connection than the type of marriage. The wife's education had not yet had significant bearing on the measure of her initiative in bringing about a divorce. Only in a few cases did the wife sign her name to the divorce agreement or divorce judgment.[306] As a rule, her fingermark (*başma*) appeared on these documents.

2. *Judicial Dissolution*

In theory, the most important mode of effecting a divorce on the wife's initiative is by judicial proceedings on grounds recognized by law, without need of the husband's consent. Dissolution by the court is alien to the Ḥanafī school, which is stricter in this respect than the three other Sunnī schools.[307] The two Sultanic decrees of 1915 provided to the wife a limited number of grounds for judicial dissolution. These grounds were considerably widened by the Ottoman Family Rights Law of 1917. Most of the Ottoman amendments were based on orthodox schools of law other than the Ḥanafī.

As appears from Table 6.3 below, judicial dissolution was not very common.

TABLE 6.3
Judicial Dissolution and Annulment According to Grounds and Courts[a]

Court	*Total*	*Defect or Illness of Husband*	*Non-Payment of Maintenance by Absent Husband*	*Discord and Incompatibility*	*Irregular and Void Marriages*
Jaffa	43	—	26	14	3
Ṭayyiba	1	—	—	1	—
Nazareth	21	2	7	11	1
Acre	15	1	9	2	3
Total	80	3	42	28	7

(*a*) The data relate only to actions which ended a dissolution.

(a) Option of Puberty

According to the prevailing view in the Ḥanafī school, the option of puberty (*khiyār al-bulūgh*), *i.e.*, the right of a minor girl to terminate her marriage on reaching sexual maturity, exists only where the guardian is not the father or paternal grandfather.[308] The author came across only one case where a wife asked to terminate her marriage in reliance on this option. Her husband having crossed to the West Bank before the 1948 War without the marriage having been consummated, she declared: "I have opted for myself" as soon as she had her first menstruation.[309] The infrequency of this plea had several causes: the great majority of marriages were arranged by the father or grandfather; the wife was not aware of her right, which lapsed on consummation of the marriage[310]; and the age of marriage of Muslim women in Israel had risen.[311]

(b) Dissolution by Mutual Imprecation

An unproved charge of adultery (*zinā*) against the wife is liable to be a ground for judicial dissolution on her initiative. This is an archaic type of dissolution, which belongs to the domain of criminal law; it is connected with the mechanism of denial of paternity,[312] and involves mutual curses (*li'ān*). *Li'ān* dissolutions were not customary in Israeli Muslim society. There was not a single dissolution of this kind, although several cases involving *li'ān* were dealt with by the courts, a few of them on the wife's initiative.[313] The wife was not inclined to use this mechanism to obtain her freedom, probably out of concern for her good name, and sought other ways to effect dissolution.[314] Nor did the husband readily resort to this device when he denied paternity; he preferred more scientific methods, such as examination of the child's blood-type.[315]

(c) Defects and Diseases of the Husband

A defect (*'ayb*) of the husband preventing intercourse is a ground for judicial dissolution on the wife's initiative under the Ottoman Family Rights Law (articles 119-121). If the defect is incurable, the court dissolves the marriage there and then; if it is transitory, the husband is given one year's respite, and if it persists, the marriage is dissolved. The acceptability of this ground is subject to several conditions: that the wife has not herself a defect preventing intercourse; that the application is not made after intercourse has taken place; that the wife did not know of the defect before the marriage (unless it be impotence, in which case she may demand dissolution even if she did); and that she did not accept the defect after the marriage. The scope of this ground is much wider under the Family Rights Law than it was prior to the latter's enactment.[316] A new more radical ground under that law (article 122) is an infectious disease of the husband not permitting continuation of the marriage without injury (*ḍarar*) to the wife. In this case, too, the husband is given a year's respite if there is hope that the disease will pass; if there is no hope, the marriage is dissolved there and then. If the wife knew of the husband's ailment at the time of the marriage or agreed to continue the marriage after she became aware of his condition, her right lapses. A further ground for dissolution (article 123) is mental illness of the husband discovered after the marriage. Here also, the husband is given a year's respite, and if he is not cured in the meantime, the court dissolves the marriage at the wife's request.

These grounds were not often invoked. The judgments indicate that the defects and diseases caused agony, humiliation and injury to the wife and might even lead to her being beaten by the husband.[317] She usually waited several years before applying to the court for dissolution.[318] In fact, marriages were dissolved on one of the said grounds in only three cases.[319] In some of the cases in which the application was dismissed, the suspicion arises that the wife had invented the ground in order to obtain her freedom. Thus, in one instance, she alleged that the husband was impotent and mentally defective and that she was still a virgin, but afterward she admitted that she had received medical treatment to enable her to become pregnant and that she was no longer a virgin: she added that she did not love her husband and would not have him "even if he were 'Antar ibn Shaddād or were capable of taking four virgins in one night"—all she wanted was an irrevocable divorce.[320] The rarity of reliance on these grounds for dissolution may be due to several causes: the infrequency of the defects and diseases in question; the fact that the disclosure of unpleasant intimate matters is involved; and the wife's ignorance of the new grounds made available to her by the Ottoman legislator. Moreover, the proof of contentions as to a defect or disease of the husband involves wearying errands and various proceedings, such as medical examinations, with which the wife finds it difficult to cope.

(d) Dissolution of Marriage to an Absent Husband

The Ottoman legislator provided two grounds for dissolution of the marriage to an absent husband: his absence and the impossibility of collecting maintenance from him; the marriage is dissolved after the necessary inquiries as to the husband's whereabouts have been made (article 126); and, if the husband has left property from which maintenance can be collected (*māl min jins al-nafaqa*), the marriage is dissolved four years after hope is given up of finding ouit his whereabouts or whether he is alive or dead; if he disappeared in an enemy country as a result of war, the marriage is dissolved one year after the fighting forces and prisoners have returned home (article 127). These two new grounds are based on elements from different schools, the teachings of which are more liberal from the point of view of the status of women. By contrast, according to the Ḥanafī school, a marriage to an absent husband cannot be dissolved.[321]

Many dozens of cases of wives of absent husbands have been dealt with by the courts. In most of them, the husbands had gone to Arab countries under circumstances connected with the 1948 War. The gravity of the probelm was greatly relieved by the family reunion scheme proclaimed by the Government of Israel after the armistice agreements with the Arab countries, by frontier rectifications in the Little Triangle area, and especially by the legitimation of infiltrators who had returned to Israel after the war. Still, the problem had not yet found its complete solution. Moreover, the political tension between Israel and the Arab countries, even without actual war, encouraged men who, for various reasons, wished to leave their wives and families.[322] In most cases, the wife knew nothing of the husband's whereabouts except that he had gone to an Arab country, nor whether he was alive or dead; she sometimes waited for him for years before she gave up and sought relief in court.[323] There were cases in which the wife was deserted before the marriage had been consummated.[324] In some instances, it is evident that the husband meant to harm the wife: he stole her jewels or his departure was prompted by a desire for revenge.[325]

The most frequent ground for dissolution under these circumstances was non-provision of maintenance to the wife. One stereotyped formula was that the husband "left her without maintenance and did not instruct anyone to support he and has no money deposited with anyone and no debt due to him from anyone and no house and no land and no-one from whom she might borrow and who might collect the debt from him [the husband]."[326] The wife might ask assistance from her family (her father's house), but it was not always possible to obtain it; here relatives might be old, poor or ailing. One wife started to work away from home, but could not continue because she had no-one to look after her young children. The wife might find herself in "a desperate plight" or her position could become "grievous owing to lack of food and clothing."[327] In many cases, the wife had definite knowledge of the husband's whereabouts, and sometimes she even succeeded in contacting him. Thus, in one instance, she claimed maintenance from him and when he refused she applied to the court to dissolve her marriage. The wife might face the husband with the alternative of returning to Israel and supporting her or dissolving the marriage.[328]

Another ground for the application of the wife of an absent husband for dissolution is connected with the protection of the reputation and chastity of women in traditional society.[329] Remarriage is a structural solution to this problem, especially in the case of a young woman. In several instances, the wife stated that she wished to dissolve her marriage so that she might carry someone who would protect her reputation and chastity and at the same time support her.[330] A further ground was the injury (*ḍarar*) caused to the wife by the husband's absence and failure to provide maintenance.[331] In one instance, the plea of injury arose out of the husband's imprisonment.

The wife insisted that her marriage to a prisoner was causing her injury and that this alone was a sufficient ground for dissolution even if he had left property from which maintenance might be obtained.[332] Injury and the husband's imprisonment are not grounds for dissolution under the Ottoman Family Rights Law, but they are recognized by modern legislation in Arab countries.[333]

The wife might be ready to join the husband at his place of residence outside Israel if only he would ask her to do so.[334] On the other hand, there are cases where the impression is received that the wife invoked non-provision of maintenance as a ground for dissolution although she had an opportunity to be reunited with the husband. In several instances, she learnt of his whereabouts but when contact had been established between them and she could have joined him abroad, she hastened to reject this chance on the formal ground that she was not bound to follow him because the distance between them exceeded the specified maximum (*masāfat al-qaṣr*).[335] In these cases, the husbands had migrated from Jaffa no further than the Gaza Strip or Khān Yūnis in the south or Sidon in the north.[336]

The author came across no case in which the wife asked for dissolution merely by reason of the husband's being absent, under article 127 (opening passage), *i.e.*, because, although he had left maintenance, she despaired of ever hearing of him again, having waited four years in vain for his return. On the other hand, the author did encounter one case in which the wife asked for the application of the closing passage of article 127. She pleaded, in addition to non-provision of maintenance, that more than a year had elapsed since the signing of the armistice agreement, *i.e.*, more than the period within which, in her case, the fighting forces and prisoners could have been expected to return home.[337]

In some cases, the wife of an absent husband did not ask at all for her marriage to be dissolved. Instead, she asked to be awarded maintenance and to be certified as a *mahjūra* (a woman whose husband has deserted her and disappeared). There may have been several motives behind this course of action: the wife might not yet have despaired of the husband's return to Israel; she might have considered the provision of maintenance more essential in her circumstance than divorce; thus, in several cases, wives asked that their husband's pay maintenance and that only if they failed to do so should they divorce them or the court dissolve the marriages. The question of marital status is immaterial to an elderly wife who does not expect to remarry or to a wife who for some reason does not wish to remarry. Moreover, in this situation, the wife has several advantages: she continues to live in the husband's house; she receives maintenance from him or collects it from his property; she is independent, not taking orders from anyone; she has a share in the family property; and as a married woman, she is largely immune to family pressures and social sanctions to make her remarry. These advantages are particularly apparent in the nuclear family, in which the wife becomes the family head. In other words, being tied to an absent husband may sometimes be a structural solution convenient to the wife. It does not prevent her from drawing a pension from the National Insurance Institute like a widowed or divorced woman. Shaykh Amīn Qāsim Mudlij and Shaykh Muḥammad Ḥubayshī said that women applied to the court for confirmation as *mahjūras* in order to obtain such pensions.

(e) Discord and Incompatibility

Another ground for dissolution of the marriage on the initiative of both spouses is "discord and incompatibility" (*nizā washiqāq*) between them (article 130 of the Family Rights Law). According to the relevant provision, the *qāḍī* is to appoint two arbitrators (*ḥakam*), if possible from the families of the spouses, and they, also referred to as "the family council" (*al-majlis al-'a'ilī*), are to try to the best of their ability to bring about a reconciliation. If they fail through the husband's fault, they are to decide on dissolution of the marriage; if through the wife's fault, she is to be divorced by *khul'* (a form of repudiation by which the wife releases herself from the marriage for a consideration) while losing the right to the whole or part of the dower. If the arbitrators fail to reach agreement between themselves, the *qāḍī* is to appoint other arbitrators from the families of the spouses or a third arbitrator from neither family. The arbitrators' award is final and non-appealable. Dissolution by arbitrators on this pattern, which is based on the teachings of the Mālikī school, constitutes a far-reaching reform in the status of women. According to the Ḥanafī school, arbitrators are not competent to dissolve a marriage unless the spouses have authorized them in advance to do so; if they have not, the arbitrator's task is confined to reconciliation.

Arbitration was indeed the most effective means available to the wife to obtain her freedom in legal proceedings when the husband ill-treated her and yet was unwilling to divorce her. A study of the circumstances in which the wife sought to apply article 130 reveals a tendency to widen the meaning of the term "discord and incompatibility" as much as possible, far beyond the sphere of matrimonial rights.

The most frequent ground adduced was cruelty and the infliction of injury. The husband's cruelty consisted in acts causing physical or mental harm: severe beatings and aggravated assault, to the extent of endangering the wife's life; locking up the wife in the house, forcing her to work away from home and hand her earnings over to him; accusing the wife of adultery (*zinā*) and disclaiming paternity of her child.

In cases of non-provision of maintenance, a court judgment requiring the husband to pay was not always an effective remedy although it was theoretically enforceable by execution. According to the testimony of Shaykh Amīn Qāsim Mudlij, there were husbands who preferred prison to paying maintenance, and the wife could not always obtain a loan for her upkeep. Under these circumstances, there were wives who sought dissolution by arbitrators. Cruelty, injury and non-provision of maintenance are recognized by modern legislation in several Arab countries as grounds for judicial dissolution.

It sometimes appears that the wife used the mechanism of arbitration as an expedient or device to obtain her freedom where she had no *shar'i* ground for dissolution. This was particularly so in cases where she was prepared in advance to be found guilty by the arbitrators, to bear responsibility for the dissolution and to renounce various rights, such as dower, maintenance during the waiting-period and custody of the children. In fact, in most of the cases in which the marriage was dissolved under article 130, the arbitrators found that the wife was to blame for the dissolution and was obliged to renounce various matrimonial rights. They might require the wife to pay the husband compensation "for her deliverance" (*badal mukhāla'atihā*) or "for her divorce" (*muqābil taṭliqihā*). This compensation was sometimes the equivalent of the whole or part of the dower, the amount of the expenses incurred by the husband on contraction of the marriage and consideration for the right to stay and live in his house and to use his household equipment. In addition, the wife might be required to return to the husband jewellery, gifts, clothes, a bedroom suite, and so forth, which she had received from him. She might also pay compensation for not having let the husband exercise his conjugal rights.

Sometimes the arbitrators found both parties guilty and determined the legal effects accordingly, having regard to the circumstances of the case. Thus, in one instance, the husband was ordered to pay the wife a part only of the deferred dower, and in another, mutual renunciation of rights was enjoined. On one occasion, the arbitrators reached the conclusion that both parties wanted the divorce but that neither wanted to disclose his or her position "so as not to incur the consequences this would entail."

Arbitration was not often resorted to. It was mainly practised in the towns. It seems that townswomen know their legal rights, including the possibilities of dissolving their marriages, better than countrywomen. Some actions for dissolution by arbitrators were brought by Beduin. The custom of arbitration, established in Beduin society, has received *shar'i* legitimation and become institutionalized in family law. The arbitrators are shaykhs and heads of subtribes of Beduin in the Negev and *mukhtārs* of Beduin in advanced stages of sedentarization in Galilee and are therefore experienced in the settling of disputes by traditional methods, which they apply also to matrimonial matters. Arbitration was thus practised especially in the most Westernized and the most traditional society, which accounts for its rarity.

In dozens of cases, the wife demanded in court that the husband divorce her or that the court direct or compel him to do so although this type of dissolution is not recognized in Islamic law. These cases did not involve *shar'i* grounds for judicial dissolution but circumstances connected with the husband's behaviour, for instance, his ill-treatment of the wife, or expulsion of her from the house, or simply her desire to live away from him, and detestation of him, etc. In some of these cases, the husband refused the wife's demand for a divorce, but, significantly enough, found it necessary to justify his refusal, declaring that he loved her, wanted her and was utterly unwilling to part from her. In other cases, he agreed to divorce her, but only because she had taken the initiative and the terms of the divorce that had thereby been formulated were favourable to him.

(f) Dissolution of the Marriage of a Girl Under 17

The Knesset not content itself with imposing a sanction on a person found guilty of marrying, performing the marriage of, or giving in marriage, a girl under 17, but wished to remedy the position also with regard to such a girl already married, and therefore created an additional, secular ground for judicial dissolution: the Age of Marriage Law provides that the fact of the wife having been married under the age of 17 is a ground for an action for dissolution by the religious court. An action for dissolution on this ground may be brought by the wife (before she attains the age of 19) or by either of her parents or her guardian or a welfare officer (before she attains the age of 18). The said law also provides that if the husband dissolves the marriage at the wife's request or complies with a judgment requiring him to dissolve it, the court shall take this into account as a mitigating factor. However, the Knesset added the proviso that the dissolution shall be carried out "in accordance with the provisions of the law applicable to matters of personal status of the parties." This addition blurs the distinction between the substantive and the technical-procedural character of the new ground. Despite its similarity to *khiyār al-bulūgh* in several respects, the new ground has no basis in the Islamic legal heritage. It is the legislative act of a secular, non-Muslim parliament guided by norms totally different from those of the *shari'ā*. Islamic law does not recognize the wife's having been under 17 at the time of the marriage as a ground for dissolution and this ground is not valid in a *shari'ā* court.

Ths *sijills* do not record a single instance of the wife, her parents or guardian or a welfare officer seeking to avail themselves of the new ground created by the Knesset in order to dissolve the marriage of a girl under 17. It seems that it is not to be expected that the girl, who does not know her legal rights, should take the initiative for dissolution, let alone her parents or guardian, who are responsible for her early marriage. The main reason for this situation is a basically social one, deriving legitimation from the *shari'ā*.

(g) Termination of an Irregular or Void Marriage

Another method of having her marriage terminated is open to the wife where there is a defect or flaw in it which makes it irregular (*fāsid*) or void (*bāṭil*). Such a marriage is illicit, and if the spouses do not themselves effect a separation, the court will do so. There are material differences between an irregular and a void marriage as regards the legal status of the children and the rights of the partners. The Ottoman legislator, guided by a liberal outlook, and especially by the interest of the children, confined voidness to marriages between a Muslim woman and a non-Muslim man. Other marriages defective from a *shar'i* point of view were classified as irregular.

Only in isolated cases were marriages terminated on such grounds. Thus, a wife contended that her husband maintained sexual relations with her germane sister and had a child by her and that this created a prohibited situation necessitating termination of their marriage; the court accepted her contention: although it had not been contended that the husband was married to both sisters, it treated his sexual relations with the plaintiff's sister as a marriage. In some cases, the court ordered termination of the "marriage" of an already married woman to a man other than her husband, or of the remarriage of a divorced woman before the expiration of the waiting-period.

Marriages between a Muslim woman and a non-Muslim man are considered void, also according to the Family Rights Law. In one case, a marriage was annulled on this ground: a Jewess married to a Jew had adopted Islam and immediately afterward applied to the *shari'ā* court for annulment of her marriage on the ground of difference of religion (*ikhtilāf al-*

dīn); the *qāḍī* allowed her suit and directed her to apply to the appropriate authorities for an annulment judgment in accordance with the *sharī'ā*.

Notes and References

1. See Rosenfeld, *Peasants,* pp. 39-40, 64, 127, 129-31, 136, 150; Baer, pp. 34, 37; Marx, *Social Structure,* p. 6; Granqvist, vol. 2, p. 283 n. 2.
2. *JfQ2,* p. 330: no. 518-f.72/58; *AcṬ3,* p. 10: f.5/57; *ṬbḤ2,* p. 238: no. 15, and p. 231: no. 5, respectively. Cases of this kind were numerous. See, e.g., *JfQ2*, p. 579: no. 600-f.16/63; *JfQ3,* p. 103: no. 159-f.49/64; *ṬbI1*, p. 112: no. 1-f.42/57, p. 139: no. 1-f.58/59; *NzḤ21*, p. 139: no. 2/69-f.110/61; *AcṬ2*, p. 94; *AcṬ3*, p. 137: f.33/59.
3. References to childlessness do not necessarily indicate barrenness of the wife. Thus, in one case, the ground for divorce is said to be that the couple "now has no living child," *JfQ4,* p. 53: no. 49-f.153/67.
4. Cf. Woodsmall, p. 124.
5. *AcṬ2*, p. 106; *AcṬ3,* p. 104: f.3/59, p. 236: f.13/62; *ṬbḤ2*, p. 157: no. 38 (nine daughters).
6. *AcṬ3*, p. 58: f.46/57; *AcṬ4*, p. 33: f.23/65.
7. See e.g., *JfQ3*, p. 170: no. 278-f.40/65, p. 205: no. 338-f.25/66 (after 23 years of a childless marriage, they decided to separate in the hope "that God will cause something to happen afterward," i.e., that the husband would have children by another wife); *ṬbḤ2*, p. 63: no. 29 (the wife consented to the divorce "because she has borne no children and so sons"); *ṬbḤ3*, p. 22: no. 28 (the wife consented to the divorce "in order that he may be able to take another wife: perhaps He will bless him with children").
8. Shaykh Ḥusnī al-Zu'bī confirmed that barrenness of the wife was a frequent cause of divorce by mutual agreement; the wife consented to the divorce in order that the husband might marry another woman and produce offspring (the *qāḍī's* letter to the author of January 2, 1971).
9. See Rosenfeld, *Peasants*, p. 127; Baer, p. 37. For a more extensive discussion see the chapter "Polygamy," p. 78.
10. *ṬbI1*, p. 86: no. 5-f.8/56. See also *ṬbI1,* p. 185: no. 6-f.9/61; *ṬbḤ4*, p. 177: no. 44.
11. See, e.g., *ṬbI1*, p. 100: no. 8-f.28/57 (after 50 years of marriage); *NzḤ16,* p. 26: no. 44/245.

12. Another possible reason for divorce was referred to by Shaykh Ḥusnī al-Zu'bī. He said that divorce "was in many cases aimed at obtaining a pension from [National] Insurance" (*AI,* vol. 11 (1968), Nos. 1-2, p. 7; see also English Summary, *ibid.*, p. 1). In other words, this kind of divorce is intended solely to entitled the wife to an increased old-age pension of several tens of pounds a month (a married woman was entitled to about half the amount due to a single woman). There was no confirmation of this point in the *sijills*.
13. See, e.g., *JfQ1*, p. 180: no. 296-f.38/55 (the wife "has reached the age of despair *(sinn al-ya's)*"); *JfQ4*, p. 142: no. 169-f.2/69; *AcṬ3,* p. 197: f.1/61, p. 224: f.2/62; *ṬbI1*, p. 147: no. 10-f.17/59.
14. See, e.g., *JfQ1*, p. 97: no. 156-f.30/53; *JfQ3,* p. 313: no. 452-f.4/67.
15. *AI,* vol. 9 (1964), Nos. 1-2, p. 5.
16. *ṬbI1,* p. 242: no. 30-f.34/63, and p. 116: no. 5-f.2/58, respectively. Cf. Cohen, p. 76; Anderson, *Islamic Law,* pp. 52-3. Professor Z. Falk told the author that divorce upon sudden enrichment for the purpose of marrying a young woman appropriate to the changed circumstances had been observed by him among Jews who had received compensation from Germany.
17. To such an extent that Shaykh Ḥasan Amīn al-Ḥabash believed the divorce rate in his area of jurisdiction to be several times higher than the marriage rate. *AI,* vol. 8 (1962), Nos. 1-2, p. 37. Cf. Baer, p. 38. See above, sec. V. "The Decline of the Divorce Rate," pp. 178 *seq.*
18. Cf. Anderson, *Patriarchal Family,* p. 231. The problem in his opinion was no longer polygamy but divorce for the purpose of another marriage or, as he called it, successive polygamy. See also Meron, p. 530.
19. *NzḤ24*, p. 29: no. 7/77-f.134/66; *AcṬ2*, p. 151; *AcṬ3*, p. 199: f.3/61.
20. See, e.g., *JfQ3,* p. 341: no. 481-f.50/67 (22 years); *AcṬ3*, p. 106: f.5/59 (16 years); *NzḤ22,* p. 1: no. 8/50-f.73/62 (ten years).
21. See, e.g., *NzḤ24*, p. 29: no. 7/77-f.134/63 (husband aged 77: were married for a week).
22. See, e.g., *JfQ1,* p. 37: no. 65-f.71/52 (the wife was unwilling to move into the husband's house in Jaffa because "it was unbefitting her status and such a one as she was"), p. 275: no. 423-f.31/57; *JfQ2,* p. 465: no. 482-fs.69/60. 75/60, 22/61. See also the chapter "Maintenance and Obedience," pp. 95 *seq.*
23. See, e.g., *NzḤ24,* p. 225: no. 3/39-f.91/69. Cf. Baer, p. 37.

24. See, e.g., *JfQ3*, p. 285: no. 425-f.116/66.
25. See, e.g., *JfQ1*, p. 79: no. 123-f.98/52; *JfQ3*, p. 29: no. 49-f.115/63; *NzI4*, p. 46: no. 1/1-f.1/49 and p. 49: no. 6/8-f.13/49; *AcI1*, p. 4: f.4/98, p. 56: f.3/50.
26. *JfQ4*, p. 57: no. 53-f.150/67. See also *AcI3*, p. 14: no. 17/55-f.55/55; *NzI4*, p. 235: no. 2/34-f.42/63, p. 237: no. 4-f.4/64, p. 239: no. 2/5-f.21/64, p. 247: no. 2/20-f.83/64, p. 256: no. 8/37-f.151/64. Cf. Coulson, *History*, p. 173.
27. See, e.g., *JfQ1*, p. 97: no. 1/55-f.28/53; *AcI1*, p. 72: f.41/50, p. 74: f.42/50, *AcI2*, p. 11: no. 9-f.14/51.
28. See, e.g., *JfQ2*, p. 235: no. 508-f.56/58, p. 542: no. 536-f.33/62.
29. *JfQ4*, p. 85: no. 84-f.22/68; see also *Ṭb I1*, p. 157: no. 21-f.23/59 (the wife delayed the filing of the claim for 11 years).
30. See, e.g., *JfQ1*, p. 144: no. 243-f.50/54; *JfQ2*, p. 317: no. 496-f.39/58; *JfQ3*, p. 294: no. 434-f.131/66; *ṬbI1*, p. 78: no. 18-f.30/55; *AcṬ2*, p. 11. Cf. Granqvist, vol. 2, p. 260.
31. See, e.g., *ṬbI1*, p. 220: no. 15-f.13/63 (schoolteacher); *NzI4*, p. 227: no. 1: 19-f.60/63 (labourer).
32. See, e.g., *JfQ1*, p. 55: no. 85-f.58/52 (claim for obedience dismissed) and p. 55: no. 86-f.21/52 (divorce); *JfQ4*, p. 88: no. 87-f.3/68 and p. 102: no. 114-f.70/68; *ṬbI1*, p. 129: no. 17-f.9/58 and p. 131: no. 20-f.26/58.
33. See, e.g., *JfQ4*, p. 183: no. 235-f.70/69 and p. 184: no. 237-f.87/69 (judgment for obedience and divorce); *ṬbI1*, p. 179: no. 19-f.37/60, p. 183: no. 4-f.11/61 and p. 184: no. 5-f.12/61, *NzI4*, p. 345: no. 1/1-f.177/67 and p. 369: no. 6/36-f.72/68; *AcI2*, p. 54: f.119/53 and p. 56: f.127/53.
34. See, e.g., *JfQ1*, p. 162: no. 268-f.3/55.
35. Cf. Faris Fallāh, *AD*, vol. 3 (1966) Nos. 1-2, p. 10.
36. *JfQ1*, p. 26: no. 43, p. 133: no. 224-f.33/54; *JfQ2*, p. 380: no. 533-f.18/59; *ṬbI1*, p. 60: no. 13-f.25/54, p. 61: no. 51-f.27/54, p. 116: no. 5-f.2/58.
37. *ṬbI1*, p. 119: no. 8-f.10/58 and p. 124: no. 12-f.18/58 (rumors had reached the husband that the wife's way of life prior to the marriage had been free and easy; he divorced her and left the village). Cf. Rosenfeld, *Peasants*, p. 130; E. Hare'uveni, *Ma'ariv*, July 3, 1966.
38. *ṬbI1*, p. 53: no. 2-f.3/54, p. 149: no. 11-f.22/59 (the marriage had not been consummated during the three years of its exitsence).
39. *ṬbI1*, p. 120: no. 9-f.13/58; *JfQ3*, p. 329: no. 470-f.30/67.
40. *ṬbI1*, p. 44: no. 4-f.11/53 (the wife, who was pregnant, had told the husband that she wished to marry another man); *NzḤ19*, p. 17:

no. 4/12; *NzḤ24*, p. 166: no. 9/67-f.133/68. Cf. Granqvist, vol. 2, p. 260; Rosenfeld, *Peasants,* pp. 120, 130.

41. *NzḤ20*, p. 72: no. 1/63 ("she abducted my brother" and they went to live in another village); *JfQ5*, p. 98: no. 84-f.191/69; *AcṬ2,* p. 95. Cf. Granqvist, vol. 2, p. 267.
42. See, e.g., *AcṬ4,* p. 80: f.18/67, p. 142: f.32/68; *ṬbḤ1*, p. 108: no. 1/78.
43. *AcṬ4,* p. 117: f.5/68. Cf. Granqvist, vol. 2, pp. 259-60.
44. *ṬbI2*, p. 82: no. 50/55, p. 83: no. 51; *JfQ4*, p. 153: no. 185-f.18/69. Cf. Granqvist, vol. 2, pp. 191, 263-5; Rosenfeld, *Peasants*, p. 129.
45. See the chapter "Maintenance and Obedience," p. 100-1.
46. See, e.g., *JfQ4,* p. 165: no. 203-f.49/69 (no children) and p. 166: no. 204-f.50/69 (two children); *NzḤ24*, p. 148: no. 6/46-f.83/68 (no children) and p. 149: no. 7/47-f.84/68 (two children *AcṬ4*, p. 53: f.21/66 (a son) and p. 54: f.22/66 (a daughter). Cf. Granqvist, vol. 2, p. 258; Rosenfeld, *Peasants,* p. 129.
47. *AcṬ4*, p. 7: f.13/64.
48. See, e.g., *JfQ3,* p. 294: no. 434-f.131/66 and p. 295: no. 435/f-132/66; *JfQ4,* p. 183: no. 235-f.70/69 and p. 183: no. 236-f.71/69.
49. *AcṬ3*, p. 172: f.15/60.
50. *AI*, vol. 11 (1968), Nos. 1-2, p. 4.
51. See e.g., *JfQ3,* p. 294: no. 434-f.131/66 and p. 295: no. 435-f.132/66; *ṬbḤ4*, p. 286: no. 19-f.34/67 and p. 287: no. 20-f.35/67; *NzḤ23,* p. 158: no. 11/15-f.20/66 and p. 159: no. 12/16-f.21/66.
52. See, e.g., *NzḤ15*, p. 15: no. 19/34 and p. 16: no. 20/35; *NzḤ18,* p. 212: no. 9/34 and p. 212: no. 10/35; *NzḤ22*, p. 109: no. 5/5-f.8/64 and p. 110: no. 6/6-f.9/64.
53. Cf. Marx, *Bedouin*, pp. 121, 160.
54. See Baer, p. 66.
55. *ṬbḤ3,* p. 104: no. 12.
56. See, e.g., *ṬbḤ1*, p. 114: no. 87; *NzḤ19*, p. 42: no. 5/40; *AcṬ3,* p. 159: f.3/60 p. 180: f.22/60, p. 190: f.33/60; *AcṬ4,* p. 19: f.1/65, p. 21: f.5/65.
57. See, e.g., *AcṬ2,* p. 112; *ṬbḤ2*, p. 166: no. 49.
58. See, e.g., *JfQ1*, p. 247: no. 384-f.17/56; *JfQ4*, p. 12: no. 12-f.108/67, p. 17: no. 17-f.67/67; *ṬbḤ4*, p. 259: no. 30-f.53/66; *ṬbI1*, p. 108: no. 15-f.31/57, p. 131: no. 20-f.26/58. Cf. Granqvist, vol. 2, p. 258.
59. See, e.g., *ṬbḤ2*, p. 227: no. 136; *NzḤ18,* p. 232: no. 8/60; *JfQ5,* p. 67: f.227/69; *AcṬ2,* p. 86.

60. See above, in sec. III, 2. "Judicial Dissolution," pp. 164-5.
61. *NzH20,* p. 124: no. 3/50; *NzH22,* p. 129: no. 5/24; *AcT4*, p. 41: f.6/66.
62. *NzI4*, p. 301: no. 2/28-f.188/65.
63. See, e.g., *JfQ1,* p. 157: no. 261-f.63/54, p. 167: no. 276-f.13/55, p. 199: no. 321-f.67/55, p. 237: no. 366-f.21/56, p. 252: no. 391-f.45/56; *JfQ2,* p. 333: no. 521-f.74/58, p. 544: no. 541-f.81/62; *JfQ3*, p. 182: no. 299-f.85/65; *AcT2*, pp. 32, 82, 87, 132, 136; *NzH18*, p. 257: no. 5/91.
64. See, e.g., *JfQ1*, p. 167: no. 275-f.10/55; *JfQ2,* p. 237: no. 512-f.65/58, p. 399: no. 559-f.47/59, p. 544: no. 544-f.81/62; *JfQ5*, p. 69: no. 118-f.230/69; *TbH1,* p. 139: no. 37; *TbH2,* p. 129: no. 1, p. 272: no. 63; *TbI1,* p. 53: no. 1-f.28/53, p. 54: no. 4-f.5/54; *AcT1*, p. 24. Cf. Cohen, p. 77; Rosenfeld, *Peasants*, p. 130.
65. See, e.g., *JfQ1*, p. 167: no. 276-f.13/55; *TbI1,* p. 51: no. 12-f.25/53; *AcT2*, pp. 32, 66, 132.
66. *NzH18*, p. 257: no. 6/92; *AcT4*, p. 77: f.15/67; *TbH1*, p. 157: no. 4/4.
67. *JfQ2*, p. 308: no. 476-f.20/58, p. 327: no. 2/5-f.65/58, p. 537: no. 526-f.65/62; *TbH2*, p. 60: no. 25; *TbH3*, p. 28: no. 37. Cf. Cohen, p. 72.
68. See, e.g., *TbI1*, p. 51: no. 12-f.25/53; *AcT4*, p. 2: f.3/64, p. 2: f.4/64; *NzH22,* p. 47: no. 11/36-f.55/63.
69. *NzH18*, p. 176: no. 3/286; *AcT3*, p. 19: f.12/57; *TbH1*, p. 182: no. 11.
70. For more detail, and source references, see above, in the discussion of the various forms of divorce, pp. 163 *seq.*
71. See, e.g., *JfQ1*, p. 37: no. 65-f.71/52; *JfQ2,* p. 430: no. 415-f.58/59; *NzH20,* p. 128: no. 2/56; *AcT3*, p. 83: f.17/58.
72. See, e.g., *TbI1* p. 249: no. 5-f.8/64; *AcI1*, p. 76: f.47/50. Cf. Granqvist, vol. 2, p. 286.
73. See, e.g., *NzH20*, p. 98: no. 13/13; *AcT3,* p. 57: f.45/57; *TbI1,* p. 238: no. 26-f.28/63 (the wife wished to stipulate that if the husband did not pay her the monthly maintenance or fell one week behind with the payments he should have to divorce her).
74. See, e.g., *AcT2*, pp. 152-4. Cf. Rosenfeld, *Peasants,* p. 130.
75. *JfQ1*, p. 56: no. 87-f.71/52; *NzH20*, p. 5: no. 8/99; *AcT4*, p. 136: f.25/68.
76. See, e.g., *JfQ2*, p. 296: no. 460-f.70/57; *JfQ3*, p. 46: no. 76-f.122/63; *JfQ4,* p. 146: no. 175-f.111/68; *JfQ5*, p. 105: no. 176-f.296/69; *TbI1,* p. 198: no. 20-f.24/62.
77. Cf. Granqvist, vol. 2, p. 260.

78. See, e.g., *JfQ2*, p. 300: no. 464-f.5/58.
79. See, e.g., *JfQ3*, p. 47: no. 77-f.152/63, p. 359: no. 501-f.31/67. Cf. Baer, p. 37.
80. See, e.g., *JfQ5*, p. 105: no. 176-f.296/69.
81. See, e.g., *TbḤ2*, p. 14: no. 33, p. 226: no. 135; *AcṬ3*, p. 235: f.12/62; *AcI1*, p. 85: f.59/50; *JfQ5*, p. 117: no. 198-f.322/69; *NzḤ23*, p. 143: no. 2/2-f.3/66. Cf. Granqvist, vol. 2, pp. 259, 266-7, 286; Rosenfeld, *Peasants*, p. 129.
82. See, e.g., *AcI1*, p. 83: f.56/50 (the husband "drinks wine, smokes hashish and has no occupation but stealing").
83. See Qadrī, art. 217. Cf. Baer, pp. 35-7; Anderson, *Islamic Law*, pp. 51-2; Hinchcliffe, *Divorce*, p. 14.
84. *FRL*, arts. 104-7, 109. See *ENFRL*; Qadrī, art. 218; Anderson, *Dissolution*, pp. 273-6; Goitein and Ben-Shemesh, pp. 225-6; Fyzee, pp. 149-49.
85. *FRL* art. 110. See Goitein and Ben-Shemesh, p. 138.
86. Cf. Anderson, *Islamic Law*, pp. 51-2; el-Naqeb, p. 165.
87. Women's Equal Rights Law, sec. 8(b) (addition of sec. 181A to Criminal Code Ordinance). See Explanatory Note to Women's Equal Rights Bill, p. 192.
88. Cf. Silberg, pp. 428-9; Zadok, pp. 76-7; Goitein and Ben-Shemesh, pp. 241-2.
89. See Silberg, pp. 429 *seq.*; Zadok, p. 77.
90. Penal Law Amendment (Bigamy) Law, sec. 7.
91. See Explanatory Note to Penal Law Amendment (Bigamy) Bill, 5717-1957; Glasner, p. 276; remarks by the Minister of Justice in the Knesset on the first reading of the bill, *KP*, vol. 23, p. 266, col. 2.
92. The ban on divorce against the wife's will is patterned on the Jewish norm of divorce. See Eisenman, p. 375; Schereschewsky, pp. 298-300; Silberg, pp. 429 sec.
93. This form of restriction of the freedom of divorce has no parallel in Islamic legal reformism in the Arab Middle East.
94. Dower (Prohibition) Bill, 5726-1966 (Private Member's Bill No. 26), sec. 8. See *KP*, 74th meeting of June 22, 1966.
95. Rosenfeld, too, on the basis of his research, reached the conclusion that 70-80 per cent of divorces were by mutual agreement of the spouses (interview with him).
96. Marriages and Divorces (Registration) Ordinance, 1919.
97. See, e.g., *JfQ1*, p. 67: no. 106-f.3/52.
98. See, e.g., *JfQ4*, p. 157: no. 191-f.33/69 (the couple was at first divorced in the *Shari'ā* Court of East Jerusalem and the divorce was then confirmed by the *Shari'ā* Court of Jaffa to give it effect *vis-a-vis* the civil authorities); *JfQ5*, p. 138: no. 229-f.6/70.

99. *AcṬ2*, pp. 82, 97.
100. See, e.g., *NzI4*, p. 215: no. 1/3-f.56/62; *ṬbḤ3*, p. 33: no. 45; *AcI3*, p. 95: no. 125-f.113/58.
101. See, e.g., *JfQ4*, p. 142: no. 169-f.2/69; *NzI4*, p. 215: no. 1/3-f.56/62; *AcṬ4*, p. 1: f.1/64; *ṬbḤ4*, p. 33: no. 45.
102. See, e.g., *NzḤ14*, p. 18: no. 71; *NzḤ18*, p. 176: no. 3/286; *JfQ1*, p. 101: no. 163-f.63/52, p. 193: no. 4/3-f.55/55; *JfQ3*, p. 218: no. 357-f.14/66, p. 273: no. 413-f.97/66; *JfQ4*, p. 149: no. 178-f.19/69, p. 162: no. 198-f.41/69, p. 153: no. 185-f.18/69.
103. Cf. Shaykh Ḥusnī al-Zu'bī, *AI*, vol. 11 (1968), Nos. 1-2, p. 7.
104. See, e.g., *JfQ3*, p. 230: no. 369-f.50/66.
105. See, e.g., *JfQ1*, p. 85: no. 133-f.114/52, p. 114: no. 193-f.63/53; *ṬbI1*, p. 33: no. 1-f.10/52, p. 36: no. 5-f.15/52; *NzI4*, p. 159: no. 1/6-f.13/54.
106. For more detail see above, in sec. II,3,a "The Wife's Consent to the Divorce," pp. 143 *seq*. See Ghālib Shiblī, *AI*, vol. 1 (1950), No. 8, p. 7.
107. *FRL*, art. 105; for a more extensive discussion see Qadri, arts. 251-9.
108. See Schacht, pp. 117, 119.
109. *ṬbI1*, p. 136: no. 24-f.21/58, p. 138: no. 26-f.32/58; and *NzḤ20*, p. 115: no. 3/39, respectively. See also *NzI4*, p. 12: no. 29-f.56/46 ("during the day"), p. 83: no. 1/39-f.93/50 ("tonight"), p. 147: no. 2/13-f.39/53 ("tonight"); *JfQ3*, p. 149: no. 240-f.180-63 ("within ten days"); *JfQ4*, p. 147: no. 176-f.118/68 ("now").
110. *ṬbI1*, p. 14: no. 1/16-f.34/50, p. 94: no. 2-f.43/56, p. 111: no. 17-f.40/57, p. 146: no. 9-f.16/59, p. 218: no. 13-f.10/62, p. 242: no. 29-f.28/62, p. 242: no. 30-f.34/63, p. 275: no. 23-f.36/64; *NzḤ18*, p. 182: no. 11/294; *NzḤ19*, p. 1: no. 5/115; *NzḤ4*, p. 125: no. 2/22-f.95/52, p. 237: no. 1/4-f.4/64; *JfQ1*, p. 30: no. 50-f.8/52; *JfQ2*, p. 486: no. 522-f.71/61.
111. *JfQ3*, p. 273: no. 412-f.94/66; *NzI4*, p. 31: no. 45-f.87/47, p. 58: no. 3/24-f-40/49.
112. *NzḤ14*, p. 18: no. 17; *NzḤ18*, p. 180: no. 8/8; *NzḤ19*, p. 2: no. 7/117.
113. *ṬbI1*, p. 220: no. 15-f.13/63 (her teaching job entailed absence from home for five days a week; on these days, she stayed at her mother's house); *NzI4*, p. 227: no. 1/19-f.60/63.
114. *ṬbI1*, p. 87: no. 6-f.15/56.
115. *ṬbI1*, p. 130: no. 18-f.14/58, p. 177: no. 18-f.32/60; *NzḤ20*, p. 7: no. 10/101.
116. *NzI5*, p. 114: no. 11/116.
117. *JfQ2*, p. 426: no. 413-f.79/59.

118. *AcI1*, p. 1: no. 1 (the husband contended in court that the wife had become a human being and that the divorce thus had not become effective).
119. *AcṬ4*, p. 7: f.13/64. See also p. 6: f.5/63; *AcṬ4*, p. 34: f.25/65.
120. *JfQ1*, p. 2: no. 4-fs.3/51, 4/51.
121. *JfQ1*, p. 112: no. 190-f.52/53.
122. *NzI4*, p. 31: no. 45-f.87/47; *JfQ1*, p. 53: no. 82-f.54/52.
123. *AcI1*, p. 85: f.59/50.
124. *NzḤ16*, p. 23: no. 41/242; *ṬbḤ2*, p. 101: no. 11; *ṬbḤ1*, p. 184: no. 15; and *NzI4*, p. 23: no. 37-f.44/47, respectively. Cf. Granqvist, vol. 2, pp. 273-4.
125. See, e.g., *AcṬ3*, p. 58: f.19/57, p. 261: f.22/63; *AcṬ4*, p. 14: f.27/64.
126. See, e.g., *JfQ3*, p. 306: no. 446-f.44/66, p. 309: no. 470-f.30/67, p. 350, no. 492-f.59/67.
127. Cf. Anderson, *Islamic Law*, pp. 52-3; *idem, Africa,* pp. 54, 209.
128. See, e.g., *JfQ3,* p. 285: no. 425-f.116/66; *JfQ5*, p. 60: no. 102-f.211/69.
129. *NzḤ17,* p. 139: no. 293, p. 146: no. 7/245; *NzI4*, p. 179: no. 1/7-f.5/57.
130. *NzḤ20*, p. 70: no. 72/61.
131. *JfQ3,* p. 122: no. 192-f.61/64.
132. Cf. Granqvist, vol. 2, p. 272.
133. See, e.g., *JfQ3*, p. 294: no. 434-f.131/66 and p. 295: no. 435-f.132/66.
134. See, e.g., *JfS6a*, no. 323; *JfS7*, p. 3: no. 20, p. 33a: no. 258, p. 56: no. 460; *JfS88*, p. 9: no. 180. Cf. Granqvist, vol. 2, pp. 272-4; Fyzee, p. 152 and the sources indicated there.
135. *ṬbI1,* p. 116: no. 5-f.2/58, p. 120: no. 9-f.13/58, p. 131: no. 20-f.26/58, p. 146: no. 9-f.16/59, p. 218: no. 13-f.10/62; *NzḤ18*, p. 253: no. 6/18, p. 257: no. 5/91, p. 257: no. 6/92; *NzḤ19,* p. 6: no. 4/121, p. 171: no. 7/62; *NzḤ20*, p. 72: no. 1/63; *NzI4*, p. 156: no. 1/3-f.8/54, p. 115: no. 3/39; *JfQ3,* p. 313: no. 452-f.4/67; *JfQ4*, p. 126: no. 146-f.119/68.
136. *ṬbI1,* p. 63: no. 17-f.35/54, and p. 116: no. 5-f.2/85, respectively.
137. See *ha-Aretz*, November 14, 1968.
138. For more detail see above, sec. II,3,a "The Wife's Consent to the Divorce," pp. 143 *seq.*
139. *JfQ1*, p. 436: no. 421-f.18/60. See Criminal File 340/60—Attorney-General *vs.* Shaykh Ṭāhir Ḥamād. The author was told of this device by S. Nawi.
140. For more detail see above, sec. VI "The *Qāḍīs* and Divorce," pp. 180 *seq.*

141. *AcṬ3*, p. 2.
142. *JfQ2*, p. 426: no. 413-f.79/59 ("of her own choice" (*bi'khtiyariha*)); *JfQ4*, p. 147: no. 176-f.118/68 (since the wife had refused to return to her husband, it was she who "had effected the divorce (*awqa 'at al-talūq*) . . . and she consents to the *ṭalāq* . . ."); *ṬbI1*, p. 136: no. 24-f.21/58, p. 220: no. 15-f.13/63, p. 242: no. 29-f.28/62, p. 242: no. 30-f.34/63; *NzḤ20*, p. 7: no. 70/101; *NzI4*, p. 227: no. 1/19-f.60/63, p. 237: no. 1/4-f.4/64.
143. *JfQ2*, p. 426: no. 413-f.79/59. See above, sec III,1,a "Delegated Repudiation," pp. 153 *seq.*
144. *ṬbI1*, p. 220: no. 15-f.13/63 (in his opinion, suspended repudiation did not require permission by the court).
145. *ṬbI1*, p. 218: no. 13-f.10/62, p. 266: no. 17-f.22/64; *NzḤ19*, p. 1: no. 5/115; *NzḤ20*, p. 115: no. 3/39; *JfQ3*, p. 149: no. 240-f.180/63.
146. *ṬbI1*, p. 242: no. 30-f.34/63.
147. Cf. Schacht, pp. 59, 164.
148. *Yedi'oth Aḥaronoth*, December 29, 1959.
149. See, e.g., *JfQ1*, p. 6: no. 11; *NzḤ14*, p. 45: no. 1, p. 85: no. 14/30; *AcṬ1*, p. 3: no. 4, pp. 18, 23-4, 48, 54.
150. In 170 cases, i.e., about 10 per cent of *ṭalāq* divorces, the marriage had not been consummated. See e.g., *NzḤ18*, p. 155: no. 18/256.
151. See, e.g., *NzḤ16*, p. 53: no. 5/283; *NzḤ22*, p. 36: no. 13/23-f.38/63; *JfQ4*, p. 65: no. 61-f.12/68; *JfQ5*, p. 78: no. 132-f.245/69; *AcṬ3*, p. 8: f.3/57.
152. See, e.g., *JfQ3*, p. 174: no. 285-f.48/65; *NzḤ22*, p. 18: no. 1/1-f.6/63; *AcṬ4*, p. 23: f.9/65.
153. See, e.g., *AcṬ3*, p. 164: f.7/60.
154. See, e.g., *ṬbḤ1*, p. 114: no. 87; *ṬbḤ2*, p. 114: no. 32 and p. 114: no. 33; *JfQ1*, p. 80: no. 126-f.104/52.
155. Qadrī, art. 281.
156. See, e.g., *JfQ1*, p. 196: no. 318-f.60/55; *JfQ2*, p. 591: no. 626-f.46/63; *NzḤ17*, p. 116: no. 9/260; *NzḤ19*, p. 63: no. 6/65; *AcṬ3*, p. 130: f.27/59, p. 191: f.34/60.
157. See, e.g., *JfQ1*, p. 96: no. 152-f.26/53; *JfQ2*, p. 415: no. 583-f.80/59; *NzḤ19*, p. 160: no. 5/52; *NzḤ20*, p. 79: no. 4/73; *AcṬ3*, p. 202: f.6/61.
158. See, e.g., *JfQ3*, p. 351: no. 493-f.15/67 (the husband will withdraw an application to the district court to restrain the wife from leaving the country).
159. *AcṬ3*, p. 99: f.30/58, p. 267: f.36/63.
160. In many cases, compensation in the Little Triangle reached IL 5,000, in some cases IL 6,000 or more. See, e.g., *ṬbḤ3*, p. 103; no. 11,

p. 131: no. 47; *ṬbḤ4*, p. 12: no. 45, p. 116: no. 92, p. 138: no. 1; *ṬbI1*, p. 192: no. 12-f.20/61.

161. Interview with Shaykh Ḥasan Amīn al-Ḥabash. No confirmation in the *sijills*.

162. See, e.g., *ṬbḤ1*, p. 115: no. 1/1; *ṬbḤ2*, p. 255: no. 37; *ṬbḤ4*, p. 198: no. 26, p. 306: no. 14.

163. See, e.g., *ṬbḤ4*, p. 58: no. 19, p. 115: no. 91, p. 116: no. 92, p. 127: no. 103; *ṬbI1*, p. 73: no. 13-f.19/55, p. 140: no. 3-f.3/59.

164. See, e.g., *ṬbḤ1*, p. 119: no. 1/5; *ṬbḤ2*, p. 59: no. 24, p. 142: no. 20, p. 166: no. 49, p. 237: no. 14; *ṬbḤ4*, p. 127: no. 103; *ṬbI1*, p. 100: no. 8-f.28/57, p. 112: no. 1-f.42/57, p. 113: no. 2-f.37/57, p. 140: no. 3-f.3/59, p. 161: no. 2-f.6/60; *NzḤ20*, p. 119: no. 2/43; *NzḤ22*, p. 13: no. 2/66-f.93/62; *NzḤ23*, p. 9: no. 9/86-f.145/64; *NzḤ24*, p. 183: no. 25/94-f.169/68, p. 265: no. 3/6-f.13/70; *AcṬ4*, p. 52: f.20/66; *JfQ3*, p. 159: no. 256-f.5/65, p. 246: no. 385-f.73/66; *JfQ4*, p. 101: no. 112-f.66/68, p. 103: no. 116-f.69/68, p. 170: no. 212-f.61/69.

165. See, e.g., *ṬbḤ2*, p. 57: no. 22 (a sale agreement was attached to the judgment); *AcṬ3*, p. 120: f.18/59. Shaykh Ḥusnī al-Zu'bī notes that compensation in land was usual in villages; his letter to the author dated November 22, 1970.

166. See, e.g., *ṬbḤ2*, p. 3: no. 20, p. 63: no. 28; *ṬbḤ4*, p. 56: no. 15, p. 191: no. 19; *JfQ4*, p. 101: no. 112-f.66/68 (a house and a cow were to be the property of the wife).

167. See, e.g., *AcI3*, p. 133: f.30/59, p. 177: f.20/60; *AcṬ2*, pp. 31, 46, 126-7; *AcṬ3*, p. 56: f.44/57 (a fine of IL 2,000), p. 132; f.29/59, p. 171: f.14/60; *AcṬ4*, p. 112: f.50/67.

168. *AcṬ3*, p. 142: f.38/59.

169. *JfQ1*, p. 219: no. 343-f.2/56; *JfQ3*, p. 97: no. 153: f.32/64; *JfQ4*, p. 130: no. 153-f.132/68; *ṬbḤ2*, p. 157: no. 38 (annual amounts of maintenance were fixed); *ṬbḤ4*, p. 218: no. 50; *ṬbI1*, p. 100: no. 8-f.28/57; *AcṬ2*, p. 86, 126-7; *AcṬ4*, p. 59: f.29/66.

170. *JfQ2*, p. 590: no. 624-f.45/63; *NzḤ23*, p. 10: no. 1/87-f.148/64.

171. *AcṬ3*, p. 206: f.10/61; *AcṬ4*, p. 133: f.22/68.

172. See, e.g., *JfQ1*, p. 219: no. 343-f.2/56; *ṬbḤ4*, p. 218: no. 50; *AcṬ2*, pp. 126-7.

173. See, e.g., *ṬbI1*, p. 100: no. 8-f.28/58.

174. Shaykh Ḥasan Amīn al-Ḥabash's letter to the author, No. 2/2 244 of November 19, 1970.

175. Shaykh Tawfīq 'Asaliyya's letter to the author dated December 13, 1970. See also *JfQ1*, p. 219: no. 343-f.2/56 (the husband "tried to induce the wife to consent [to a divorce]" by showing readiness to support her for life).

176. See, e.g., *JfQ3*, p. 246: no. 385-f.73/66; *NzḤ23*, p. 10: no. 1/87-f.148/64; *Ṭbl1*, p. 100: f.28/57.
177. Use is made of conditional particles and the words *muqābil, liqā'* and *badal* which have the connotation of "in return for." See, e.g., *ṬbḤ2*, p. 82: no. 50/55; *ṬbḤ3*, p. 38: no. 50, p. 41: no. 55, p. 64: no. 26; *Ṭbl1*, p. 100: no. 8-f.28/57, p. 112: no. 1-f.42/57; *NzḤ18*, p. 232: no. 8/60; *NzḤ22*, p. 17: no. 101/62, p. 123: no. 4/19-f.36/64; *NzḤ23*, p. 43: no. 4/24-f.48/65; *NzḤ24*, p. 265: no. 3/6-f.13/70; *JfQ3*, p. 246: no. 385-f.73/66; *JfQ5*, p. 8: no. 14-f.103/69.
178. *Ṭbl1*, p. 73: no. 13-f.19/55.
179. The earliest cases of payment of compensation to divorced women were in the Little Triangle at the end of 1951 and the beginning of 1952. See *ṬbḤ1*, p. 116: no. 90, p. 119: no. 1/5.
180. See Granqvist, vol. 2, p. 283 no. 2 and the sources indicated there. Cf. Anderson, *Africa*, p. 268.
181. See, e.g., *Ṭbl1*, p. 192: no. 12-f.20/61; *ṬbḤ3*, p. 51: no. 12, p. 73: no. 39: p. 91, no. 65; *ṬbḤ4*, p. 53: no. 12.
182. See, e.g., *Ṭbl1*, p. 82: no. 1-f.34/55; *ṬbḤ2*, p. 237: no. 14.
183. See, e.g., *Ṭbl1*, p. 73: no. 13-f.9/55, p. 161: no. 2-f.6/60, p. 165: no. 6-f.14/60.
184. Shaykh Ḥusnī al-Zu'bī's letter to the author dated November 22, 1970.
185. *AI*, vol. 9 (1964), Nos. 1-2, p. 11. For a more extensive discussion see above, pp. 212 *seq*.
186. Interview with Shaykh Ḥasan Amīn al-Ḥabash.
187. Cf. Granqvist, vol. 2, pp. 282-5; Rosenfeld, *Peasants*, pp. 127, 131, 150. See the chapter "Polygamy," p. 78.
188. Interview with Rosenfeld.
189. *ṬbḤ2*, p. 157: no. 38; *ṬbḤ3*, p. 165: no. 12; *NzḤ22*, p. 13: no. 2/66-f.93/62; *AcṬ4*, p. 26: f.13/65 p. 110: f.48/67. See *ha-Aretz* of November 14, 1968.
190. *JfQ1*, p. 96: no. 152-f.26/53; *AcṬ2*, pp. 126-7. Cf. Granqvist, vol. 2, pp. 265-6, 268; Anderson, *Africa*, p. 260.
191. See, e.g., *ṬbḤ3*, p. 218: no. 50.
192. See the chapter "Polygamy," pp. 76-7.
193. See, e.g., *JfQ2*, p. 511: no. 476-f.4/62.
194. See, e.g., *JfQ3*, p. 215: no. 352-f.21/66; *AcṬ3*, p. 97: f.28/58.
195. *Ṭbl1*, p. 116: no. 5-f.2/58.
196. Shaykh Ḥasan Amīn al-Ḥabash's letter to the author, No. 2/2 244/ of November 9, 1970.
197. There were women in the Little Triangle who regarded compensation as "a *shar'i* right." See, e.g., *Ṭbl1*, p. 82: no. 1-f.34/55.

198. Shaykh Tawfīq 'Asaliyya's letter to the author dated December 13, 1970.
199. See, e.g., *JfQ2,* p. 292: no. 457-f.3/58; *JfQ3,* p. 201: no. 331-f.11/66.
200. See, e.g., *JfQ2,* p. 496: no. 453-f.94/61; *JfQ3,* p. 285: no. 425-f.116/66: *JfQ4,* p. 95: no. 99-f.85/68; *AcṬ4,* p. 8: f.16/64.
201. See, e.g., *AcṬ3,* p. 56: f.44/57, p. 120: f.18/59; *ṬbḤ4,* p. 229: no. 60.
202. See, e.g., *ṬbḤ1,* p. 116: no. 90; *ṬbI1,* p. 100: no. 8-f.28/57; *AcṬ2,* p. 163.
203. See, e.g., *ṬbḤ1,* p. 159: no. 3/7, p. 166: no. 18; *ṬbḤ2,* p. 61: no. 26, p. 63: no. 29, p. 83: no. 51; *ṬbI1,* p. 47: no. 7-f.18/53, p. 52: no. 13-f.29/53, p. 73: no. 13-f.19/55.
204. See, e.g., *ṬbḤ2,* p. 59: no. 24, p. 63: no. 28, p. 63: no. 29, p. 227: no. 136, p. 231: no. 5; *NzḤ19,* p. 127: no. 7/19; *NzḤ20,* p. 2: no. 4/95; *NzḤ23,* p. 10: no. 1/87-f.148/64; *JfQ3,* p. 205: no. 338-f.25/66, p. 217: no. 355-f.40/66; *JfQ4,* p. 163: no. 200-f.44/69; *JfQ5,* p. 3: no. 5-f.95/69, p. 8: no. 14-f.103/69; *AcṬ2,* pp. 94, 106, 124 (the wife: "There are no children and I have therefore agreed with him on *ṭalāq*"), p. 86; *AcṬ3,* p. 22: f.15/57, p. 224: f.2/62.
205. Shaykh Ḥusnī al-Zu'bī's letter to the author dated January 2, 1971.
206. See, e.g., *ṬbḤ2,* p. 82: no. 50/55, p. 83: no. 51.
207. See, e.g., *ṬbḤ2,* p. 134: no. 10 and p. 135: no. 11, p. 141: no. 18 and p. 141: no. 19; *NzḤ19,* p. 227: no. 2/38 and p. 228: no. 3/39; *NzḤ21,* p. 23: no. 3/46 and p. 24: no. 4/47; *AcṬ2,* pp. 84-5, 166-7; *AcṬ3,* p. 50: f.38/57 and p. 51: f.39/57; *JfQ5,* p. 26: no. 46-f.144/69 and p. 27: no. 47-f.145/69.
208. See, e.g., *JfQ4,* p. 174: no. 219-f.90/68.
209. See, e.g., *JfQ3,* p. 64: no. 98-f.206/63; *ṬbḤ2,* p. 53: no. 19; *ṬbḤ3,* p. 21: no. 26; *NzḤ19,* p. 143: no. 6/36; *NzḤ24,* p. 108: no. 21/90-f.161/68; *AcṬ2,* p. 66.
210. See, e.g., *NzḤ16*, p. 82: no. 34/16; *AcṬ3*, p. 35: no. 25, p. 129: f.26/59, p. 265: f.31/63; *AcṬ4,* p. 15: f.29/64, p. 109: f.47/67, p. 134: f.23/68.
211. *JfQ2*, p. 523: no. 500-f.37/62; *JfQ3*, p. 338: no. 478-f.44/67; *JfQ4,* p. 138: no. 165-f.126/68; *JfQ5*, p. 55: no. 92-f.150/69, p. 102: no. 171-f.258/69.
212. *JfQ2,* p. 583: no. 608-f.35/63 (a document was submitted indicating that the wife had been divorced with her consent; the *qāḍī* noted that the wife had confirmed her consent in court), p. 591: no. 626-f.46/63 (the wife maintained that her signature had been

forged and that she had not consented to the divorce); *JfQ4,* p. 48: no. 48-f.89/66 (the wife's attorney maintained that it had been proven in the District Court of Tel Aviv (Criminal File 822/64) and the High Court of Justice (26/66) that the wife's signature had been forged in the presence of the *qāḍī* and asked that the judgment for divorce be set aside).

213. See, e.g., *JfQ5,* p. 93: no. 156-f.248/69, p. 106: no. 178-f.259/69; *NzI4,* p. 189: no. 1/9-f.30/58.
214. See, e.g., *JfQ1,* p. 123: no. 208-f.15/54; *JfQ3,* p. 230: no. 369-f.50/66 (the wife had heard from someone that she had been divorced "and I consented to what I had heard"); *AcQ6,* p. 1: no. 1/63-f.111/62.
215. See, e.g., *JfQ3,* p. 11: no. 19-f.77/63; *JfQ4,* p. 58: no. 54-f.155/67, p. 172: no. 215-f.63/69; *ṬbḤ2,* p. 53: no. 19; *NzḤ18,* p. 20: no. 21/84; *NzḤ19,* p. 179: no. 4/71; *NzI4,* p. 156: no. 1/3-f.8/54; *AcI3,* p. 85: no. 18-f.?/58.
216. *ṬbI1,* p. 108: no. 15-f.31/57, p. 124: f.18/58, p. 131: no. 9-f.13/58.
217. *JfQ3, p.* 5: no. 9-f.88/63.
218. *JfQ5,* p. 49: no. 85-f.89/69; *ṬbI1,* p. 131: no. 9-f.13/58.
219. *JfQ5,* p. 35: no. 58-f.30/69 and p. 93: no. 156-f.248/69, respectively.
220. In one case, the husband contended that the divorce was not valid because the wife had not consented to it. See *JfQ3,* p. 13: no. 22-f.81/63.
221. See, e.g., *NzḤ19,* p. 179: no. 4/71.
222. See, e.g., *AcI1,* p. 48: no. 41-f.30/49, p. 52: no. 45-f.40/49, p. 57: f.4/50; *AcI2,* p. 17: no. 14, p. 19: no. 16; *AcṬ1,* pp. 18, 23; *AcṬ2,* pp. 30, 32, 64-6, 79, 81; *AcQ5,* p. 35: no. 35-f.125/61 (the husband asked the court to "hear" the divorce); *JfQ1,* p. 148: no. 249-f.60/54, p. 158: no. 263-f.63/54.
223. See, e.g., *JfQ2,* p. 308: no. 476-f.20/58; *AcṬ2,* p. 136; *ṬbI1,* hearing of May 26, 1971.
224. See, e.g., *AcṬ2* pp. 2, 4; *AcṬ4,* p. 117: f.5/68.
225. See, *JfQ1,* p. 74: no. 117-f.74/52 (it was contended that the husband had divorced the wife after receiving a legal opinion (*fatwa shari'yya*) from the court for the divorce).
226. *JfQ2,* p. 330: no. 518-f.72/58, and p. 380: no. 533-f.18/59, respectively.
227. *ṬbI1,* p. 185: no. 6-9/61 and *Ap1,* p. 198: no. 19-f.21/62.
228. See, e.g., *ṬbI1,* p. 108: no. 15-f.31/57.
229. *AcD8,* p. 99: no. 16/70-f.139/68.
230. See, e.g., *JfQ5,* p. 35: no. 58-f.30/69 (the arbitrators decided that the husband had wished the marriage to continue and had

therefore applied for the establishment of a family council; but they were unable to mediate between the parties and dissolved the marriage, fixing responsibility on the wife for refusing to obey the husband); *NzI4,* p. 369: no. 9/36-f.72/68; *AcD8,* p. 107: no. 24/70-f.9/70; *NzI4,* p. 301: no. 2/28-f.188/65.

231. *NzI4*, p. 237: no. 1/4-f.4/64, p. 256: no. 8/37-f.151/64. See also *NzI4*, p. 264: no. 4/12-f.7/65; *JfQ4*, p. 172: no. 215/f-.63/69.
232. See Fyzee, p. 151.
233. See Qadrī, art. 260.
234. See *ibid.*, art. 222. This was so in many cases. In one instance, a man from Sidon empowered his father to divorce his wife in Israel in his name. See *NzH17*, p. 80: no. 35/215.
235. The registers of marriage contracts from 1968 onwards record but one such case. *JfMC68*, no. 9515.
236. Qadrī, arts. 261 *seq.*
237. See Coulson, *History,* p. 207.
238. See, *JfQ1,* p. 105: no. 167-f.43/53, p. 166: no. 273-f.5/55; *JfQ2,* p. 394: no. 552-f.42/59; *NzḤ20*, p. 121: no. 6/47, *AcI2,* p. 36: f.91/51. Cf. Schacht, p. 164.
239. *JfQ1,* p. 11: no. 20: *JfMC68*, no. 9515; *AcQ5,* p. 31: f.63/63.
240. *JfQ1*, p. 266: no. 415-f.13/57.
241. *JfQ3,* p. 145: no. 230-f.108/64, and p. 209: no. 344-f.10/66, respectively.
242. *JfQ1,* p. 166: no. 273-f.5/55, *JfQ2,* p. 394: no. 552-f.42/59; and *AcI2*, p. 36: f.91/51, respectively.
243. *NzḤ20*, p. 121: no. 6/47.
244. *JfQ1*, p. 11: no. 21.
245. *JfQ1*, p. 266: no. 415-f.13/57. See also *JfQ1*, p. 105: no. 127-f.43/53.
246. *JfQ1*, p. 11: no. 21.
247. *AcI3*, p. 43: no. 4-f.9/57.
248. This form of divorce is rare also in Egypt and Iraq. See el-Hamamsy, p. 593; el-Naqeb pp. 121-3. Cf., on the other hand, Fyzee, pp. 151-2, 466-8.
249. *NzḤ20,* p. 121: no. 6/47.
250. *JfQ3,* p. 145: no. 230-f.108/64.
251. *Ṭbl1,* p. 111: no. 17-f.40/57. See also *NzI4,* p. 97: no. 2/7-f.14/51.
252. *JfQ3,* p. 149: no. 240-f.180/63.
253. *JfQ1,* p. 74: no. 117-f.74/52.
254. *JfQ1*, p. 112: no. 190-f.52/53. Advocate S. Darwish told the author of this case, as reported to him by Shaykh Ṭāhir Ḥamād.

The husband contended that the food he had eaten had not been cooked by the wife but was tinned meat which the wife had merely heated. The *Shari'ā* Court of Appeal accepted this contention and set aside the judgment for dissolution. *Apl,* p. 8: no. 7.

255. *Ṭbl1,* p. 226: no. 17-f.22/64; and *Nzl4*, p. 58: no. 3/24-f.40/49, respectively.

256. *NzḤ16*, p. 23: no. 41/242.

257. See, e.g., *AcI2,* p. 39: f.132/51; *AcQ5*, p. 7: no. 7/63-f.153/62; *JfQ1*, p. 2: no. 4-fs.3/51, 4/51.

258. *Nzl4*, p. 12: no. 29-f.56/46 (their testimony was disqualified on the ground that they were "sinners"), p. 83: no. 1/39-f.93/50 (the witnesses were found incompetent and their testimony was contradictory), p. 215: no. 2/22-f.95/52.

259. *AcMC68*, no. 3441. Cf. Woodsmall, p. 127; Granqvist, vol. 2, p. 274 no. 1. On the other hand, this device was fairly common in various places in Africa. See Anderson, *Africa,* pp. 25-6, 29, 72.

260. See, e.g., *Nzl4*, p. 292: no. 2/19-f.30/66.

261. *AcQ4*, p. 46-f.105/95; *Nzl4*, p. 156: no. 2/2-f.4/54, p. 186: no. 2/4-f.16/58.

262. *Nzl4,* p. 207: no. 4/7, p. 369: no. 6/36-f.72/68.

263. Qadrī, art. 218; *FRL*, art. 104; *ENFRL*; see Eisenman, p. 124.

264. *JfQ2,* p. 539: no. 529-f.64/62. See also *JfQ1*, p. 66: no. 105-f.4/52, p. 112: no. 190-f.52/53; *AcI2*, p. 30 [40]-f.134/51. Cf. Fyzee, pp. 148-9.

265. See, e.g., *JfQ2*, p. 312: no. 484-f.24/58, p. 460: no. 475-f.35/61; *Nzl4*, p. 54: no. 3/18-f.29/49 (the wife: "There was no one present at the divorce but I, he, God and his second wife . . ."), p. 206: no. 1/3-f.9/61: *AcI2,* p. 41: f.189/52 (she has no witnesses and she does not wish to put her husband on his oath because he "does not fear God and does not heed the oath and does not know to what punishment he who perjures himself is liable"), p. 42: f.192/52.

266. See, e.g., *JfQ1*, p. 133: no. 224-f.33/54, p. 247: no. 384-f.17/56.

267. See, e.g., *Nzl4*, p. 52: no. 2/14-f.23/49, p. 285: no. 1/8-f.8/66; *Ṭbl1*, p. 271: no. 20-f.5/64.

268. See, e.g., *JfQ1,* p. 181: no. 299-f.39/55.

269. The former kind of divorce is called *ibrā* and *mubāra'a*, the latter *khul'*, in legal literature. See Schacht, p. 164; Coulson, *Conflicts,* pp. 53-4; *idem, Succession,* p. 19; Fyzee, pp. 155-8; Hinchcliffe, *Divorce*, pp. 15-16; Goitein and Ben-Shemesh, pp. 126, 138-9, 227-8. Qadrī's collection of personal status laws

blurs the distinction between these two concepts (see Qadrī, arts. 273-97). For simplicity's sake, these two kinds of divorce are hereinafter referred to as renunciation divorce and compensation divorce.

270. See, e.g., *AcṬ3,* p. 89: f.21/58; *JfQ1*, p. 77: no. 120-f.90/52, p. 265: no. 4/4-f.22/57; *ṬbḤ1,* p. 64; no. 60/108, p. 174: no. 31; *NzḤ23,* p. 25: no. 2/7-f.18/65.
271. See, e.g., *JfQ5,* p. 9: no. 16-f.105/69; *ṬbI1,* p. 274: no. 22-f.32/64; *AcṬ4,* p. 4: f.7/64, See the chapter "Dower," p. 46.
272. See, e.g., *JfQ1*, p. 161: no. 267-f.2/55; *JfQ2,* p. 570: no. 585-f.1/63; *JfQ4*, p. 97: no. 104-f.60/68; *ṬbḤ1*, p. 174: no. 31; *NzḤ15,* p. 127: no. 5/181; *AcI1*, p. 37: no. 31-f.21/49; *AcṬ2*, p. 19; *AcṬ3,* p. 196: f.39/60, p. 267: f.36/63.
273. *AcṬ2*, p. 96; *AcṬ1,* p. 15; and *JfQ1,* p. 77: no. 120-f.90/52, respectively.
274. See, e.g., *NzḤ24*, p. 114: no. 3/3-f.4/68; *AcṬ3*, p. 111: f.9/59; *JfQ3*, p. 210: no. 347-f.34/66.
275. For a more extensive discussion see the chapter "Custody," pp. 247 *seq.*
276. See, e.g., *JfQ2,* p. 569: no. 582-f.132; 162; *JfQ4*, p. 60: no. 102-f.211/69; *AcI1;* p. 54: no. 48-f.36/49; *AcṬ2,* p. 129; *AcṬ3*, p. 38: f.28/57; *NzḤ18*, p. 1: no. 27/57; *ṬbḤ1*, p. 141: no. 41.
277. See, e.g., *JfQ1*, p. 275: no. 424-f.29/57; *JfQ3*, p. 210: no. 347-f.34/66, p. 351: no. 493-f.15/67 (it was agreed to close a file relating to the divorce and the wife declared that she consented to it); *NzḤ21*, p. 2: no. 4/19; *NzḤ24,* p. 190: no. 9/103-f.187/68; *AcṬ3*, p. 111: f.9/59.
278. In several cases, it was said that the wife "had redeemed herself" (*fadat nafsahā)* with a certain sum of money. See e.g., *AcṬ2,* pp. 151, 152-4, 161. See also *ṬbḤ2,* p. 255: no. 37.
279. Cf. Qadrī, art. 277.
280. *JfQ3,* p. 357: no. 499-f.70/67; *JfQ4,* p. 17: no. 17-f.67/67.
281. See, e.g., *AcṬ2*, p. 19; *ṬbḤ4*, p. 243: no. 12.
282. See, e.g., *ṬbḤ1*, p. 175: no. 32; *ṬbḤ2*, p. 14: no. 33, p. 177: no. 61; *NzḤ23*, p. 163: no. 2/22-f.32/66; *NzḤ24,* p. 6: no. 6/51-f.58/66; *AcṬ3*, p. 12: f.7/57; *AcṬ4,* p. 6: f.12/64. Cf. Granqvist, vol. 2, p. 285-7; see Anderson, *Africa,* pp. 54, 111, 140, 209, 292, 296; Coulson, *History,* pp. 137-8.
283. See, e.g., *ṬbḤ1*, p. 175: no. 32; *AcṬ3*, p. 48: f.36/57, p. 49: f.37/57; *AcṬ4*; p. 103: f.41/67; *NzḤ23*, p. 163: no. 2/22-f.32/66; *NzḤ24,* p. 202: no. 4/11-f.29/69.
284. Cf. Granqvist, vols. 2, p. 282.
285. *NzI4,* p. 234: no. 2/30-f.65/63 and p. 249: no. 2/26-f.127/64 (the man appeared in court a year after divorcing his wife, claiming

that she had remarried and demanding the consideration for the *ṭalāq*); *NzḤ22*, p. 95: no. 10/89-f.147/63; *NzI4*, p. 291: no. 1/18-f.128/65; *JfQ4*, p. 41: no. 40-f.137/67.

286. *JfQ3*, p. 6: no. 11-f.129/62.

287. Interview with Shaykh Muḥammad Ḥubayshī.

288. Shaykh Tawfīq 'Asaliyya's letter to the author dated December 13, 1970. Cf. *al-'Arif*, pp. 133-4; Anderson, *Africa*, pp. 320-1; Coulson, *History*, p. 136.

289. See, e.g., *JfQ1*, p. 275: no. 424-f.29/57; *JfQ4*, p. 102: no. 114-f.70/68; *NzI4*, p. 71: no. 1/20-f.51/50; *NzḤ14*, p. 85: no. 14/30; *NzḤ18*, p. 29: no. 11/96; *NzḤ24*, p. 29: no. 7/77-f.134/66; *AcṬ3*, p. 28: f.19/57.

290. *AcṬ2*, pp. 36, 120.

291. See, e.g., *JfQ1*, p. 121: no. 267-f.2/55; *JfQ4*, p. 101: no. 112-f.66/68; *ṬbḤ2*, p. 57: no. 22; *ṬbI1*, p. 112: no. 421/57; *NzḤ23*, p. 37: no. 4/18-f.39/65; *NzḤ24*, p. 187: no. 6/100-f.184/68; *AcṬ2*, p. 147; *AcṬ3*, p. 56: f.44/57; *AcṬ4*, p. 83: f.22/67.

292. A usual formula of renunciation divorce is ". . .I renounce every one of my matrimonial rights, both prior and subsequent to the *ṭ alāq*, in your favour . . . in return for my divorce from you. . ."; the husband then replies at once at the session of the court: "And I, in return for this, divorce you." See, e.g., *ṬbḤ1*, p. 1: no. 1/2.

293. See, e.g., *AcI1*, p. 31: no. 25-f.14/49; *AcṬ3*, p. 172: f.15/60 and p. 173: f.16/60, p. 236: f.13/62.

294. See, e.g., *NzḤ19*, p. 135: no. 9/28; *NzḤ20*, p. 5: no. 8/99; *NzḤ23*, p. 110: no. 9/87-f.138/65.

295. See, e.g., *JfQ3*, p. 357: no. 499-f.70/67; *NzḤ21*, p. 49: no. 11/18-f.23/60; *AcṬ4*, p. 15: f.29/64.

296. See, e.g., *NzḤ19*, p. 41: no. 4/39; *AcṬ4*, p. 40: f.5/66, p. 43: f.10/66, p. 52: f.20/66.

297. See, e.g., *NzḤ17*, p. 80: no. 35/215; *AcṬ2*, pp. 152-4; *AcṬ3*, p. 126: f.23/59.

298. See, e.g., *AcṬ4*, p. 134: f.23/66.

299. See, e.g., *ṬbI1*, p. 155: no. 19-f.33/59.

300. *NzI4*, p. 162: no. 1/10-f.34/54.

301. See, e.g., *JfQ4*, p. 130: no. 153-f.132/68; *JfQ5*, p. 59: no. 100-f.207/69. p. 105: no. 176-f.296/69.

302. Cf. Rosenfeld, *Peasants*, p. 129; Granqvist, vol. 2, pp. 266-7; Dirks, p. 89; Anderson, *Africa*, p. 209.

303. See, e.g., *JfQ3*, p. 192: no. 316-f.103/65 (the wife said that her relations with the husband had worsened to an intolerable degree). Cf. Anderson, *Islamic Law*, pp. 52-3.

304. See, e.g., *JfQ4*, p. 165: no. 203-f.49/69 and p. 166: no. 204-f.50/69, p. 184: no. 237-f.87/69 and p. 184: no. 238-f.88/69;

ṬbḤ1, p. 103: no. 2/70 and p. 103: no. 3/71, p. 164: no. 15 and p. 165: no. 16.

305. *SAI,* 1969, No. 20, p. 64.

306. See, e.g., *ṬbḤ3,* p. 103: no. 11; *ṬbḤ4,* p. 53: no. 12, p. 135: no. 114: *NzḤ20,* p. 128: no. 2/56; *NzḤ22,* p. 21: no. 4/4-f.9/63; *NzḤ24,* p. 2: no. 5/45-f.70/66, p. 15: no. 10/60-f.95/66, p. 35: no. 4/84-f.147/66.

307. See Anderson, *Dissolution*, pp. 271, 273; Coulson, *Succession,* p. 19.

308. Qadrī, arts. 44-50; Anderson, *Islamic Law,* pp. 44, 47; Schacht, pp. 161-2; Goitein and Ben-Shemesh, pp. 131-2.

309. *ṬbI1*, p. 46: no. 6-f.5/53 and p. 68: no. 5-f.28/54 (her application was dismissed on a formal ground).

310. *JfQ2,* p. 528: no. 510-f.93/61; *JfQ3,* p. 137: no. 215-f.10/64; *NzḤ20*, p. 149: no. 11/88.

311. See the chapter "Age of Marriage," Table II, p. 22.

312. Qadrī, arts. 344-40. See Goitein and Ben-Shemesh, p. 139; Fyzee, pp. 159-60; Schacht, p. 165; Levy, pp. 120, 136.

313. *JfQ1,* p. 275: no. 424-f.29/57; *JfQ2,* p. 383: no. 537-f.58/58; *NzI4*, p. 109: no. 1/21-f.86/51 and p. 118: no. 1/14-f.50/52.

314. But cf. Anderson, *Africa,* p. 168.

315. *JfQ2*, p. 434: no. 421-f.27/55.

316. Qadrī, arts. 298-302. See Anderson, *Dissolution,* pp. 277-9; Fyzee, pp. 165-6.

317. See, e.g., *ṬbI1*, p. 58: no. 10-f.14/54, p. 145: no. 7-f.9/59; *NzI4,* p. 362: no. 3/26-f.70/68.

318. *ṬbI1*, p. 145: no. 7-f.9/59, p. 58: no. 10-f.14/54; *NzI4,* p. 222: no. 3/8-f.88/62; *AcI1*, p. 75: f.43/50.

319. *NzI4,* p. 257: no. 9/38-f.42/64, p. 362: no. 3/26-f.70/68; *AcI2,* p. 36 [46]: f.110/52.

320. *ṬbI1*, p. 145: f.7/59. See also *ṬbI1*, p. 66: no. 4-f.14/54; *NzI4,* p. 47: no. 2/4-f.6/49.

321. Qadrī, arts. 190, 575-8; *ENFRL*; Anderson, *Dissolution,* pp. 279-83; Coulson, *Succession,* pp. 19-20, 196-8; Goitein and Ben-Shemesh, pp. 229-30.

322. *JfQ2*, p. 333: no. 525-f.3/59, p. 378: no. 530-f.14/59; *NzI4,* p. 276: no. 3/34-f.99/65, p. 344: no. 9/46-f.123/67, p. 347: no. 3/3-f.150/67, p. 361: no. 1/24-f.36/68; *AcD7,* p. 62: f.22/67.

323. See, e.g., *JfQ5,* p. 52: no. 86-f.161/69 (wife asked for dissolution of the marriage 21 years after the husband's disappearance); *AcD6,* p. 27: no. 27-f.60/64 (16 years); *NzI4*, p. 282: no. 3/3-f.156/65 (18 years).

324. See, e.g., *JfQ1*, p. 148: no. 250-f.9/54, *Ṭb11*, p. 46: no. 6-f.5/53, p. 71: no. 10-f.13/55; *Nz14*, p. 282: no. 4/4-f.177/65; *AcQ5*: p. 12-f.13/62.
325. *Nz14*, p. 347: no. 3/3-f.150/67; *Ac13*, p. 78: no. 10/58-f.60/57.
326. See, e.g., *JfQ1*, p. 43: no. 71-f.38/51, p. 44: no. 72-f.46/51.
327. *Nz14*, p. 344: no. 9/46-f.123/67, p. 185: no. 1/3-f.12/58, p. 276: no. 3/34-f.99/56, p. 184: no. 1/14-f.32/57; *Ṭb11*, p. 98: no. 6-f.10/57; *AcD7*, p. 62: f.22/67.
328. *JfQ1*, p. 189: no. 308-f.10/54, and p. 46: no. 74-f.32/52, respectively.
329. This is a ground for dissolution under the Sudanese Judicial Circular No. 17 of 1916. See Anderson, *Dissolution*, p. 285.
330. *Ṭb11*, p. 46: no. 6-f.5/53, p. 71: no. 10-f.13/55, p. 98: no. 6-f.10/57.
331. See, e.g., *Nz14*, p. 244: no. 5/15-f.50/64, p. 282: no. 3/3-f.156/65.
332. *Nz14*, p. 344: no. 9/46-f.123/67, p. 351: no. 7/10-f.123/67 and p. 361: no. 1/24-f.36/68.
333. See Anderson, *Dissolution*, pp. 284-5. For a more extensive discussion see below, sec. VI. "The *Qāḍīs* and Divorce," pp. 180 *seq*.
334. See, e.g., *JfQ1*, p. 117: no. 199-f.21/52.
335. A three days' journey on camelback. Qadrī, art. 208.
336. *JfQ1*, p. 44: no. 72-f.46/51, p. 106: no. 170-f.86/52, p. 111: no. 178-f.41/53.
337. *Ṭb11*, p. 98: no. 6-f.10/57.

7

Paradox of Progress: Women's Rights in Three Islamic States

I. EGYPT

Introduction

The stirrings of reformism and feminism in Egypt were linked both to the attempts by successive rulers to modernise the country's educational, cultural and administrative structures in the years after 1830 and the growth of nationalism and anti-imperialist feeling in the country in the period of British occupation after 1882.

Egypt was a part of the Ottoman Empire, but was in effect separately governed. Important changes took place during the rule of the General Mohamed Ali (1805-1848), when efforts were deliberately made to modernise Egypt, to bring the country into contact with European thought and to introduce educational, military and economic reforms and promote state run industries. Further advances were made during the rule of the Khedive Ismail (1863-1882), who also followed strategies of modernisation, diffusion of technology and scientific knowledge and changes in education, administration, irrigation and public works policies. Modernisation was considered to be the panacea for Egypt's 'backwardness' in general and to be necessary for the country's greater prosperity and power. (Vatikiotis '80: 117-18) Some Egyptians began to study abroad—especially in France—but these intellectuals, who were from the higher echelons of Egyptian society, on their return to Egypt, worked within the framework of an authoritarian state structure and the monarchical system, which they did not challenge.

During the last decades of the 19th century, a period of aggressive imperialism and competition between European powers, British control was established over Egypt. The financial problems of Khedive Ismail's government in the 1870's led to several political changes. In order to avoid bankruptcy new un-popular taxes were devised which further burdened the peasantry; the Khedive's shares in the Suez Canal were sold to Britain, and British and French officials were allowed to overseer the economy. The succeeding crisis resulted in the overthrow of the Khedive, the unsuccessful revolt of Arabi Pasha against the British presence in Egypt and the occupation of Egypt by the British in 1882. During the first two decades of British occupation, the Egyptians were allowed administrative power while effective political and military control was retained by the British.

Growth of Reformism

The transformation of Egypt into a semi-colony of the British on the one hand and the influence of liberal thought, the movement for reform and the growth of nationalist consciousness on the other, forms the background to the intellectual debates that took place. One of the key influences on the intellectuals of the period was *Sayyed Jamal ad-din al Afghani* (1839-1897) who was born in Iran, educated in the rationalist tradition of Avicenna and became the best known radical agitator and pan-Islamist of the Muslim world. He lived in India, Afghanistan, Turkey, Egypt, Russia and Europe. In Paris, he edited an anti-British, pan-Islamic paper in Arabic, which was influential among the Arab intelligentsia; returning to Iran, he was involved in grouping Iranian reformists and in conspiring to overthrow the Shah. Afghani advocated the reform of traditional structures; he promoted alliances of religious and radical forces in society, opposed feudal oppression and corrupt governments and launched the idea of Islamic unity. His consistent anti-imperialist, nationalist stand, as well as his inclination to Socialism, made him the most spiring of the Muslim reformers of the 19th century. His influence in Egypt, where he lived in the 1870's was considerable and his "appeals to unity around Islam to fend off the West had a multiclass appeal" in the Muslim world. (Keddie '81: 189, 65).

It is not surprising that during a period of intellectual discussion and reformist activity in the second half of the 19th century, the debate on women's rights also arose in Egypt, the first advocates being from among the male reformers. These included *Ahmed Fares El Shidyak* who, in 1855, had published 'One Leg Crossed Over the Other', one of the first books to support women's emancipation. Others like *Rifa'a Rafi'i El-Tahtawi* (1801-1871) wrote on the need for women's education and the redress of injustices to which women were subject. Tahtawi, a high government official, had studied in Paris from 1826 to 1831 and was a leading Egyptian intellectual and reformer of the 19th century. In France he had been influenced by the writings of Voltaire, Rousseau and Montesquieu. On his return to Egypt he was part of the campaign to modernise education, helping establish the School of Languages in 1835 which trained translators, jurists and administrators. In his own writings, Tahtawi popularised concepts of secularism both in politics and law, as well as ideas of liberty and political rights. "He was the first Egyptian to report fairly systematically and intelligently to his campatriots on the general outlines of European political institutions, the ideas of the enlightenment and the French Revolution. . . . Above all he advanced the idea of the rule of law and a stable order as the most important manifestations of a civilised society." (Vatikiotis '80: 115). Tahtawi was also a pioneer of women's education in Egypt, putting forward his views on the need for female education in 'A Guide to the Education of Girls and Boys' which he published in 1872. It was a period when the debate on women was in full swing "Every shade of opinion regarding the emancipation of women was represented and nationalists were far from agreeing on the matter. The issue was an essential one, directly touching the life of everyone. An increasing flow of books and articles about the topic gives evidence of its importance" (Philipp '80: 278).

As in Asian countries, the Egyptian reformers tried to show that it was not the tenets of religion that subordinated women, but an incorrect interpretation of the religion and later corrupt practices and additions that went against the purity of the original faith. A debate therefore started among the Muslim reformists on religion and the status of women in Islam. One of the pioneers of this trend was *Sheik Mohammed Abdou* (1849-1905), who had studied in Cairo and came under the influence of al Afghani. After being exiled by the British, Abdou lived in Europe and on his return became a leading reformer. He influenced a generation of intellectual nationalists and reformers, but like many others of this period, he was essentially a moderate rather than a revolutionary reformer. "His ideology aimed at a gradual transformation of Egyptian society by means of an education programme geared to slowly changing the people it reached, through free universities, benevolent societies and organs of the Egyptian state, still controlled by the British." (Rodinson '79: 24). However Abdou denounced polygamy as being against Islam and condemned the prevalent practices of concubinage and women slaves. Citing the Koran in favour of women's education, he claimed that the backwardness of Arab women was detrimental to the future of the Arab peoples. (Philipp '80. 278). On the theme of education Abdou stated "we wish that our daughters should be educated. For Allah the Almightly has explained 'To them are due the same good deeds that we expect from them'. There are many sacred verses that . . . clarify that both man and woman share in fulfilling the same duties towards life and towards religion. To leave our girls a prey to ignorance, and taken up with stupid pursuits, is indeed a great crime" (El Saadawi, '80: 171).

It was however his disciple *Kasim Amin* (1865-1908), educated in France, and a judge by profession, who created a furor, in 1899, with his book 'Tahrir al Mara' (Women's Emancipation). Using religious texts he argued that female seclusion, the veil, arranged marriages and prevalent divorce practices were un-Islamic. He advocated the right to work for women as well as legal reforms to improve their status, claiming that there could be "no improvement of the state of the nation without improving the position of women" (Philipp '80: 279) He stressed the importance of women's education not only in children's up-bringing, but also in creating a better relationship between husband and wife, based on mutual respect. (Abdel Kader '73: 11). Not unexpectedly, his book was denounced in orthodox Muslim circles and many refutations of his views were published. The opposition also came from those nationalists who held that in the campaign against foreign domination, issues of women's emancipation weakened and diverted the struggle. Kasim Amin answered his critics in a second book 'Al-Mara Al Jadida' (The New Woman), basing his arguments less on religion, as he had done earlier, but on the doctrine of natural rights and the concept of progress. (Philipp '80: 279). The debate was further carried on by male reformers such as *Ahmed Lofti El Sayed* and a group of intellectuals who expressed their liberal views on women's rights in the paper El Gareeda, while other newspapers of this period also carried articles on the question. (El Saadawi: '80: 172).

Female education became an issue of importance and some advances in this sphere were made in the 19th century. In rich families, girls had been educated at home and poor girls could attend the 'kutabs' where the Koran was memorized and some writing and reading taught. In 1832, the Khedive Mohammed Ali had built a school where girls (mainly slaves and orphans) were trained to the midwives. The missionaries were also active from the mid-19th century onwards, opening the school, 'Dame de Bon Pasteur', in 1846, followed by an American Mission School in 1859. In 1873, the third wife of the Khedive Ismail, *Jashem Afet Hanum* started the Suyfiyya Girls School which soon had 400 pupils and gave instruction in arithmetic, geography, history and religion as well as sewing and domestic skills, and in 1875, the government began another such school, giving a Western-style primary education to girls. But the purpose of female education was restricted to preparing girls to be efficient mothers and good wives, and it was mainly the girls of urban bourgeois, families who benefitted from education. (Abdel Kader' 73: 18-19)

Women and Nationalism

The turn of the century was an era of a growing national consciousness and saw the emergence of a group of politicians led by *Saad Zaghlul* who demanded self-determination for Egypt. These demands were intensified after the First World War when the victory of the allies raised the issues of Egypt's political future. Zaghlul and his group of Egyptian lawyers, officials and land-owners and those with interests in commerce and the cotton industry, formed a delegation (Wafd) to present Egypt's case to the British. This group, which emerged as the Wafd party, was supported by intellectuals, teachers, students, peasants and women. The refusal by the British to negotiate with the Wafd and the exile of the Wafd leaders by the British, led to demonstrations, strikes and assasinations. In 1922 the British recognised Egypt as an independent state, but the British retained absolute control of the Sudan and over Egyptian defence, imperial communications and the protection of foreign interests. Fuad I was proclaimed King, and after a period of difficulties, the elections in 1924, under a new Constitution, gave the Wafd 90 per cent of the seats with Zaghlul forming the government.

This was the political background for the rise of a wave of feminist activity in Egypt in the pre-First World War and post-war period. Saad Zaghlul and his group who were secularists, had been earlier identified with promoting women's education, and many influential women writers used their talents in writing extensively on feminist issues in the first decades of the 20th century. Among them was *Malak Hifni Nassif* (1886-1918), the most forceful woman writer of her time, who under the pen name Bahissat El Badla (Searcher in the Desert), wrote in the contemporary press on marriage, divorce, veiled seclusion and women's education. Her father, a university lecturer in Arab studies, had been a disciple of Mohammed Abdou, and she was one of the first to qualify as a teacher in 1900. After marriage, she had lived away from Cairo near the desert and began to critically examine the seclusion the patriarchal subjection under which women lived. Being a victim of her husband's polygamy, she was particularly articulate on the evils of the system. Her fame was such that in 1911 she spoke in the Egyptian Legislative Assembly putting forward a programme for the amelioration of the situation of Egyptian women which included demands for universal elementary education for girls, with emphasis on religious education, hygiene, first aid and child rearing and the training of women as doctors and teachers to fulfil the medical and educational needs of women.

Another woman writer of the period was *May Ziada,* who had a literary salon in Cairo in 1915-16 and led the life of an independent woman. "She was able to impose her personality on literary circles in Egypt, to mix and talk freely with men, and to correspond regularly with them at a time when the veil still hung heavily over the faces of many Egyptian women in the same sector of society." (El Saadawi '80: 122). The proliferation of women's journals and the numbers of women who wrote on various issues was striking—there being 15 Arabic women's magazines in the per-1914 period, a large number being edited by Syrian Christian women. (Philipp '80: 280).

The other area of activity for middle-class women was philanthrophy. For example, *Hidiya Afifi* (1898-1969), (daughter of a high official) educated at a French convent, and related by marriage to the nationalist leader, Saad Zaghlul, is best known for her work in charities connected with health, forming the Mabarat Mohammad Ali in 1909 (along with other wealthy women), which ran a network of clinics for women. The same group of women also formed the Société de la Femme Nouvelle in 1919, concerned with girl's schools, orphanages and child care centres. (Al Sayyid Marsot '80: 272).

However, open political agitation and action by women began with the participation of women in the nationalist movement against the British, after the First World War. The repression by the British and the exile of Zaghlul and other Wafd leaders in 1919 led to violent demonstrations which marked the beginning of militant nationalist agitation by the Egyptian people; the disatisfaction was not only political but also economic. "Discontent had been accumulated during the war. In the cities inflation had hit the lower classes, and in the villages the peasants had suffered from such measures as mobilization of draft animals, forced labour, and confiscation of products. The tax burden had increased. The frustration and disaffection of the various classes found an outlet in the general demonstrations of 1919". (Philipp '80: 288). It was during this nationalist upsurge in which all classes participated, that political demonstrations by women occurred on four occasions in 1919. Many of the wives of the Wafd founders organised the women in this agitation and for the first time middle-class women were seen protesting in public. Active in this protest was *Huda Sharawi* (1882-1947), who was of a wealthy family—educated at home in French, Turkish and Arabic and widely read. In 1910 she opened a school for girls which gave a general education. Her husband was a founder member of the Wafd and she moved in Egyptian nationalist circles; she organised women to demonstrate during the agitation of 1919, and collected signatures of women to a petition to the British High Commissioner, condemning the shootings of demonstrators and the exiling of the Egyptian leaders; "We the women of Egypt, mothers, sisters and wives of those who have been the victims of British greed and exploitation . . . deplore the brutal, barbarous actions that have fallen upon . . . the Egyptian nation. Egypt has committed no crime except to express her desire for freedom and independence." (Fernea & Bezirgan '78: 193-196).

There are many contemporary accounts of women's participation in demonstrations in 1919. Sir Valentine Chirol, (to whom there were only two categories of women "good" and "bad") wrote in the *London Times*, "In the stormy days of 1919, (the women) descended in large bodies into the streets, those of the more respectable classes still in veil and shrouded in their loose black coats, whilst the courtesans from the lowest quarters of the city, who had also caught the contagion (of political unrest) disported themselves unveiled and arrayed in less discreet garments. In every turbulent demonstration women were well to the front. They marched in procession—some on foot, some in carriages shouting "independence" and "down with the English" and waving national banners (Philipp '80: 288-9). The presence of both women of the bourgeoisie and poor women has been noted by many writers. "The veiled gentlewomen of Cairo paraded in the streets shouting slogans for independence and freedom from foreign occupation. They organised strikes and demonstrations . . . boycotts of British goods and wrote petitions . . . . protesting British actions in Egypt" (Al Sayyid Marsot '80: 269). But it was not only the 'veiled gentlewomen' who participated in the upsurge. "Toiling women in the industrial areas and rural villages constituted the female force that participated vigorously and effectively in the national revolution of 1919. They went on to the rural roads, side by side with the men, cut the telephone wires and disrupted the railway lines in order to paralyse the movement of British troops. Some of them participated in storming the improvised camps and jails in which many of those who had led the uprisings or participated in them had been imprisoned. Women were killed or injured when British troops fired on them. Some of them are known such as Shafika Mohamed, Hamida Khalil, Sayeda Hassan, Fahima Riad and Aisha Omar. But hundreds of poor women lost their lives without anybody being able to trace their names". (El Saadawi '80: 1176).

But the militancy of this phase soon died out. *Huda Sharawi* and other middle-class women formed the Egyptian Feminist Union in 1923, which became the main women's association concerned with education, social welfare and changes in personal law. The same year, Huda Sharawi made a gesture against tradition by throwing her veil into the sea on her return from Rome where she had attended the International Conference of Women. "This naturally caused a scandal, particularly as Huda was an eminent pasha's wife. Undaunted, other prominent women cast off their veils, one after another." (Minai '81: 69).

But in the new constitution of 1924, the Egyptian politicians chose to ignore women's political rights only making minor changes—raising the age of marriage for girls to 16, but not giving voting rights or rights of divorce to women. There was a protest demonstration in March 1924 at the opening of parliament when some feminists demanded the right to vote, but this seems to have been the last spark of revolt on this issue. (Philipp '80: 289). In 1925 Huda Sharawi started a journal in French, L'Egyptienne, edited by *Ceza Nabarawi,* who had also been at the conference in Rome. The elitist nature of the venture is seen in that it only catered to the French-speaking women of the Egyptian bourgeoisie. Nevertheless, the issues discussed included the Turkish reforms regarding women, which had influenced Egyptian women, and the issue of Islam—the journal's editor, stating in 1927 that "In wanting to see it practiced in its true spirit . . . we are doing more for it than those who submit themselves blindly to the customs that have deformed (Islam)." (Minai '81: 72). The issue of polygamy also evoked little response from the legislators. In 1928 a new law limited polygamy to those who could look after "the family they already have charge of", which was hardly a restriction on existing practices. Egypt, although the intellectual leader of the Muslim world, remained very conservative with regard to the reform of personal law, and on the question of polygamy did not reach the level of progress achieved in Turkey. In 1935 when *Huda Sharawi* gave a lecture at the American University of Cairo on the status of women and called for the abolition of polygamy, two sheiks from El Azhar university demonstrated their protest; but it was perhaps a sign that educated opinion was changing, that the audience sided with Sharawi. Her speech on this occasion was "received with enthusiasm in the university gathering, . . . was printed in full in a leading newspaper and thus widely circulated through the Arabic—speaking world". (Woodsmall '36: 121-2).

But the climate of political opinion and the class bias of the women's movement in Egypt of this period, stunted the rise of feminism. As El Saadawi has written of the reformist women's activities, "The movement was not representative of the overwhelming majority of toiling women, and its leadership ended, just as the political leadership did, by seeking accommodations with the British, the Palace and the reactionary forces in the country. The women's movement . . . kept away from an active involvement in the national and political life of the country and limited its activities to charitable and social welfare work." (Saadawi '80: 176).

The feminism of the earlier phase thus petered out. The entry of a few women to the University of Cairo in 1928 caused an outcry in orthodox circles and a crisis within the government. Nevertheless, new generations of educated Egyptian women arose, making inroads into some professions; in 1934, *Lutfiya El Nadi,* a graduate of the American Girls' College of Cairo, was the first woman pilot to make a solo flight. (Woodsmall '36: 81). But the majority of women remained unschooled, the numbers of girls in school, in 1975, being 27 per cent as opposed to 49 per cent of boys. Religious interests and male opposition remained strong in Egypt and it was only in 1956, that women obtained the right to vote; in 1979, parliament reserved 30 out of 392 seats for women, and the same year, marriage and divorce laws were liberalized to benefit women. (Minai '81: 74 and 78).

In conclusion, one can say that the earlier democratic and nationalist struggles in Egypt gave rise to an intellectual debate on the status of women, to moves to give women access to education and to the rise of a feminist consciousness which expressed itself in a feminist press, in women's organisations, in demands for the suffrage and other rights and the appearance of women of all classes in agitation and street demonstrations against the British. However, the expectations of the early years were not fulfilled and feminism did not survive into the 1930's.

II. TURKEY

External defeats and the conditions of the Sèvres treaty led to protests and armed uprisings against the capitulation by Sultan Mohamed VI to foreign pressure. The Turkish nationalists were led by *Mustapha Kemal* (1881-1938), an army captain who had fought in the Turkish army during the First World War, but opposed the Sultan's defeatist policies, and had set up a revolutionary government in Ankara in 1920. Kemal's forces made the French, Italians, Greeks and British withdraw their occupation of parts of Turkey and a peace treaty was signed with the British in 1922. Soon after, the Sultanate was abolished and the Turkish republic set up in 1923 with Kemal, the leader of the Republican Peoples Party—becoming the President of the Republic and remaining in this office until his death in 1938. Mustapha Kemal (referred to subsequently as Atatürk, the father of the Turks) began a deliberate process of Europeanisation which meant not only economic development on capitalist lines, but also attempts to secularise and modernise the state by separating politics from religion, attacking tradition, latinising the alphabet, promoting European dress, adopting the Western calendar, introducing civil marriage and divorce, and banning polygamy.

To be European was equated with being "civilised', and Turkish 'backwardness' was contrasted with Western 'progress'. The fetish of Europeanisation was to become the new ideology. The country's leading thinker *Zia Gokalp* urged the Turks to "Belong to the Turkish nation, the Muslim religion and European civilisation" and in similar voice, *Sadri Etem* asserted "we are Europeans, to be European is our ideal" (Rodinson '74: 127). To be European also meant following the capitalist path of development, but in the absence of entrepreneurs, the state assumed the task of developing industry in order to pave the way for capitalist growth. As Gokalp wrote in 1923, "If the new Turkey is to be a modern state it must above all develop a national industry. Jut as we have done in the field of military technique, so in industry we must reach European levels by an effort undertaken on the national scale" (Rodinson '74: 126). Politically, under Kemal's rule, experiments in democracy were tried but soon given up and a dictatorship was established where dissent was not tolerated. The Kurdish revolt of 1925 was crushed and liberal opinion and the surviving strands of the Young Turk movement were suppressed, with virtually all powers finally being vested in Kemal.

Advent of Reforms

The question of women's emancipation was first highlighted through the issue of women's education, which had already been debated in the 19th century under the Ottoman Empire. The Sultan, Abdul Aziz had opened middle-level schools and a teachers training college for girls in 1863, but the education given to girls was a very basic one, mainly religious in orientation with the aim of creating good Muslim wives and mothers. However, some upper-class girls were given a cosmopolitan education at home by foreign governesses, or attended foreign schools in Turkey. For example, in 1871 the American College for Girls—was started, but for two decades only Christians attended, the first Muslim girl to complete her studies there being *Halide Edip*, a future women's leader. Thus in the 19th century with the emergence of a Western-educated Turkish aristocracy and bourgeoisie, the issue of educated wives had already arisen. "Though Turkish fathers . . . had their women wear the best Paris fashions . . . and took them to the most elegant capitals of Europe, they expected the governesses to give their daughters much more than charm-school training. They wanted their daughters to have serious Occidental and Oriental education, *as befitted the future spouses of important men.*" (Minai '81: 49 emphasis added).

Many women educated in this manner were to make their mark as novelists and writers on women's emancipation. "Unlike their mothers, who expressed themselves through the nightingales and roses of formal Turkish poetry, the daughters wrote letters, memoirs, newspaper articles and novels." The first woman novelist of this epoch was *Fatima Aliye* (born in 1862), daughter of a historian and politician; she was educated at home in French, and first achieved success as the translator of a novel in 1890. In 1892, she wrote a novel, 'Womanhood' (Muhadarat), a story of a gifted woman stunted by traditional society, followed by 'Islamic Women', which denounced the misinterpretation of Islam and urged the participation of women in society. In 1895, she published and wrote extensively in 'A Newspaper for Ladies', "one of Turkey's first and longest lived newspapers for women by women", which produced a spate of feminist writers and journalists. Another woman writer *Zeyneb Hanoum* who had travelled in France and Britain, wrote on the contradictions faced by those Turkish women who had received a European style education, but still remained confined by tradition. The details of harem life she gave Pierre Loti, the French writer, led to his novel 'Les Desenchantées' (published in 1906) which 'describes the malaise of a Turkish woman whose brain had leaped to the twentieth century while her body remained imprisoned by medieval customs'. (Minai '81: 50-52).

During the years after the Young Turk revolt of 1908, high schools, teacher's colleges, and in 1915, the first university for women were begun and the status of women became an issue discussed in literature, drama and in journals. Moreover, the general discussion on democratic rights led to concern about the role of women and many of the country's leading male intellectuals were involved in the debate. In 1910, *Halil Hamit* published 'Feminism in Islam', supporting women's suffrage; in 1915, *Celal Nuri* wrote 'Our Women', in which he urged that polygamy be banned. Another leading politician and intellectual of the period *Ahmet Agaoglu,* who had studied in Paris argued in favour of women's rights and encouraged his daughter Sureyya, to become the first woman lawyer in Turkey. Like many other intellectuals in Muslim countries, Agaoglu associated the denial of rights for women with backwardness and claimed that 'these rights were in accordance with the tenets of pure Islam cleansed of misinterpretations'. (Minai '81: 48).

In addition, the country's best known writer and sociologist, *Zia Gokalp,* often referred to as the theoretician of Turkish nationalism, writing around 1915, advocated equal marriage, divorce and succession rights for women (Abadan-Unat '81: 9). He further argued that women's emancipation was part of an early Turkish tradition of the free nomads of Central Asia (Minai '81: 48). Expressing himself in poetry Gokalp wrote.

> All must be equal, marriage divorce, wealth
> No nation can ever bloom if its daughters
> Are not given the weight they deserve.
> We have fought for and won all our other rights
> Only the family is still in its dark age.
> Why do we still turn our backs or women.
> Tell me, have they not a part in our struggles?

In this period, when the role of women was being eagerly debated in intellectual and reformist circles, there was also a flourishing feminist press; between 1908 and 1919, there were nine womens papers, some in both French and Turkish. They catered to educated women and highlighted the freedom women were said to have had in the days of the prophet; in their advocacy of women's emancipation in Turkey, they were influenced by their Western education and had knowledge of European feminist movements. These papers not only "interpreted Western ideas for Turkish women's consumption, they also became a forum to unite the readers, each of whom had thought that she was alone in her frustration and confusion. The women enthusiastically took up the chance to communicate with one another. 'For the first time I feel proud to be a woman "wrote one of them.'" (Minai '81: 48 & 54-61).

While education for upper-class women had existed earlier, advances were made in university education for other women in the early 1920's, with co-educational university education being allowed in 1921; but there was also opposition to women's education from orthodox opinion. For example, in 1921, the Minister of Education resigned after being criticised in the National Assembly for holding a Teachers Congress attended by men and women teachers. (Sayari '81: 286-7).

Mustapha Kemal supported the movement for a secularised, modern education for women, especially since he was keen that the Westernised Turks should have wives who were equally 'civilised' and modern in outlook and appearance. His wife, *Latife Hanem* (whom he married and divorced in the early 1920's) was educated in Britain and France and appeared unveiled with him on public occasions. One of Kemal's main arguments was that society could not function efficiently if women remained uneducated, "if only some of the members of a social body are active while the others remain inert, the social body is thereby paralysed" he declared in 1923, urging that a scientific and technical education be given to both men and women. He claimed that if Turkey was to become a strong nation, the education of women was necessary since children receive their first lessons from their mothers; "Hence our women have the obligation to be more enlightened, more civilised and wiser even than the men". (UNESCO '63: 48-50). In 1924, an Education Bill secularised education, brought religious schools under government control and made provision for equal educational opportunities for both sexes, but women's education never became universal and remained constrained by class.

The first woman doctor in Turkey, *Safiye Ali,* opened a clinic in Istanbul in 1922 and by the 1930's there were women in many of the well-paid professions. But women's education in Turkey remained and still remains very uneven. [In the 1970's, while Turkish women formed 20 per cent of the legal profession and 17 per cent of the medical profession—a figure higher than the USA, France and many other countries of Europe, the illiteracy rate for women was as high as 52 per cent. (Oncü '81: 181)].

Apart from the field of education, Turkish women from the early years of the century onwards began to be active in the social, political and economic life of the country. The 'Young Turk' movement of the beginning of the century aimed at ousting the autocratic monarchy and introducing democratic, constitutional government. With the deposition of the Sultan in 1908, activity among women was given an impetus. In that year, the first women's club was formed in Salonika, named 'Red & White'—the Young Turks' colour; other women's organizations of the period included 'The Association for the Betterment of Women' led by *Kadriya Ihsan,* and the more radical Ottoman Association for the Defence of Women's Rights led by *Nuriye Ulviye Mevlan* who in 1913 began a journal 'Women's World'. (Abadan—Unat. '81: 7).

The involvement of Turkey in the Balkan wars and the First World War brought Turkish women into new avenues of public employment, as nurses on the war fronts and in amunition, food and textile factories as well as in banks, hospitals, and in the administrative services. Political events led to women's involvement in militant activities. The occupation of various parts of Turkey by European troops in 1919 aroused protests in which women joined, and women in Anatolia participated in Mustapha Kemal's forces, which had launched a war against the invaders. In 1919 the 'Anatolian Women's Association for Patriotic Defence' was formed with many branches. "They became the female counterpart of the core group of Mustapha Kemal's bureaucrats, soldiers and merchants. The major aim of these associations was to show the European public that the whole Turkish nation was united and determined to fight for its independence". (Abadan—Unat. '81: 10).

Saga of Halide Edip

The best-known woman nationalist in Kemal's forces was *Halide Edip* (1883-1964), who came from an influential family, her father being the Sultan's secretary. She had received a European education at home and school and wrote for the liberal papers in literary subjects and women's emancipation. Her greatest successes were as a novelist and political agitator. In her novels, which are mainly concerned with women's rights (the best known being 'Sinekli Bakkal'), she tries to synthesise the two prevailing ideologies of the time, Turkish nationalism and the westernisation ideal.

> 'As she began writing in the pre-republican period and continued to do so during the period of Ataturk's reforms, the problems she approached and the images of women she created show great variety . . . images of nationalistic women, modernized women, women with a strong personality, women rising up against oppression and idealistic women striving to educate the masses.' (Altiok, '81: 226).

Halide Edip was active in the nationalist movement of the years 1910 to 1912, and was the only women member of the council of Ojak, the nationalist organisation which had branches all over Turkey. During the World War she organised schools and orphanages in Syria and Lebanon. With her second husband, she became one of the leading writers and public speakers in Mustapha Kemal's forces and was a corporal of the army. She became nationally renowned and was one of several nationalists sentenced to death by the Sultan's government. That the daughter of a former palace official was challenging the system made her a target for attack and praise. "As an eloquent public speaker and an adviser to Kemal, she was the most visible woman of the revolution" (Minai, '81: 62). Her writing and activism had an important impact at the time and in future years as well.

> During Halide Edip's life time her influence was great; it continues to be today. Her novels are still

> read in Turkey. Her life spanned one of the most dramatic periods in Turkish history, from the crumbling of the old Ottoman Empire to the emergence of an independent nation. Her example helped prepare the way for the appearance of a new kind of Turkish woman" (Fernea and Bezirgan '78: 167-8).

Mustapha Kemal who had been impressed by the militancy of the women in the struggle had promised that "Turkish women shall be free, enjoy education and occupy a position equal to that of men as they are entitled to it", but the first Turkish National Assembly had been against such changes. In the early twenties, the entrenched orthodox groups opposed moves to extend women's rights. Supporters of such rights like *Emin Bey* and *Tunali Hilmi Bey* were insulted in the Assembly and not allowed to speak. But the issue was kept alive by Mustapha Kemal who consistently spoke for women's rights. In 1923, he claimed that the fact that Turkish women had been able "to march along with men, sometimes even ahead of them is clearcut proof of their equality and their outstanding ability" (Abadan-Unat. '81: 11).

In his many public pronouncements on women's status, Kemal took a clear stand and paved the way for reforms.

> "The weakness of our society lies in our indifference toward the status of women . . . we must have Turkish women as partners in everything, to share our lives with them, and to value them as friends, helpers and colleagues in our scientific, spiritual, social and economic life" (Abadan-Unat. '81: v).

In 1923 he made the claim that "domestic work constitutes only the smallest and the least important of the tasks of women". (UNESCO '63: 49).

The Kemalist Reforms

One of the most important reforms of the Kemal Atatürk government was the Civil Code of 1926, based on the Swiss

Civil Code. Under the new law, polygamy and marriage by proxy were declared illegal, women were given equal divorce rights, equal custody of children, equal inheritance rights, and the minimum ages for marriage were raised to 18 for men and 17 for women; the courts also accorded equality to women in respect of testimony (to replace the earlier practice where the testimonies of two women equalled that of one man), as well as the separation of property and goods and the right of the woman to freely dispose of her property (Abadan—Unat. '81: 13-14). The reforms caused a sensation at the time, and Turkey became the first Muslim country to adopt a civil code in place of the Sharia, or Muslim legal code. Kemal in his speeches had referred to the need for 'reaching a level of contemporary civilisation' and this was to be the keynote of the discussion justifying the changes. In introducing the Code, Mahmud Esad, the Minister of Justice stated 'the Turkish nation has decided to accept modern civilisation and its living principles without any condition or reservation' (Rodinson '74: 127) and another speaker stated 'The new law incorporates such principles as monogamy and the right to divorce—principles, which are required for a civilised world' (Oncü '81: 181).

However, these reforms were in the context of continued patriarchy. For example, the husband remained the head of the family, alone entitled to choose domicile, while the wife had to obey the husband and needed his consent to work outside the house. What is more, inspite of the laws, it was not possible through legislation to change the force of tradition which ruled in the countryside. Inspite of these limitations, Turkish women intellectuals claim that the reform 'was a great step forward as far as women's status was concerned' (Tekeli '81: 297). The Code was certainly a step forward as was the subsequent enfranchisement of women in local elections in 1930 and in the national elections in 1935. In the elections of 1935, 18 women (4.5 per cent of the Assembly) were elected, constituting the highest number of women deputies in Europe at that time, a period when many European countries, including France and Italy, did not even have female franchise (Tekeli '81: 299).

The imposition of dress reform was another integral part of Mustapha Kemal's policy of 'westernising' and thereby 'civilising' the country by challenging traditional customs. The issue of the red fez hat and Turkish dress became a political one, and in enforcing the wearing of Western clothes and banning traditional dress, Kemal was not only hitting at symbols of the old Ottoman society, but was also enforcing a 'secular' dress which did not proclaim religion or ethnicity. Kemal led the way—himself wearing a European hat and clothes and giving orders that the Turks, including religious leaders, should discard the fez and wear European style hats, on the grounds that "we have to resemble the civilised world in our costume" (Bisbee: '51: 23). In a defiant mood he stated that the dress of the 'civilised' world was suitable for Turkey and declared:

> 'We will wear boots and shoes, trousers, shirts, waistcoats, collars, ties . . . we will dress in morning coats and lounge suits, in smoking jackets and tail coats. And if there are persons who hesitate and draw back, I will tell them that they are fools' (Wortham, '31: 193).

Similarly, women's dress became a controversial issue. Turkish women were requested, but not compelled by the government to abandon the veil and to wear Western clothes. Appealing to the people's national pride he said.

> 'I see women covering their faces . . . or turning their backs when a man approaches. Do you really think that the mothers and daughters of a civilised nation would behave so oddly or be so backward? . . . I firmly believe that the women of our country are by no means inferior to European women' (Minai, '81: 65).

The women of the bourgeoisie also believed so and did not hesitate to adopt the latest European fashions, but the dress reform hardly affected the women of the countryside. Moreover this view of 'civilised' behaviour included discarding old forms of salutation (the salaam), encouraging Muslim women of good families to become actresses, discouraging Turkish music and propagating Western music and popularising European social etiquette, including ball-room dancing; Kemal himself gave regular dances and ordered his officers and their wives to dance, resulting in a craze for ball-room dancing in the large cities of Turkey, which outraged the traditionalists. In his personal life too Kemal challenged Muslim orthodoxy, by marrying in a ceremony where no imam was present and the bride herself was unveiled, and encouraging his adopted daughter to become a pilot. It is interesting to note that Kemal is supposed to have considered his wife to have ideal feminine virtues such as the ability "to talk, dance, and drink cocktails" (Wortham '31: 167).

However such a forcible imposition from above of Western dress and social graces on a population with its own strong culture, resulted only in superficial change. It was not easy to revolutionalise social customs by decree, especially customs involving challenges to religious orthodoxy, although a powerful cultural organisation (the Turk-Ojak) was used to make propaganda in favour of the new changes through schools, books, dramas and films; in addition, an inquisitional committee was formed, called the Tribunal of Independence, to go from village to village punishing those who were not conforming to the new dress regulations, "the rumour of its approach might cause the veils to disappear and the baggy Turkish trousers . . . to vanish until these dreaded gentry left the neighbourhood. Things could then return to their comfortable ways" (Wortham '31: 203). The Kemalist reforms which have so often been cited all over the world as a successful attempt at women's emancipation by decree from above, have been analysed by Turkish women political scientists, who themselves, were the products of these reforms. Dr. Nermin Abadan—Unat, a Professor of Political Science, claims that though Kemal "focussed his attention mainly on the elimination of polygamy, sex-differentiated legislation and traditional Islamic ethical norms", an assessment of these changes "indicates that revolutionary efforts through law have only resulted in partial changes both in the status and role of women in Turkish society". She adds that the main progressive changes were not fought for, but were given in order to prove that in granting equal rights to women the new Turkey was "reaching a level of contemporary civilization", and was "a symbol to the world". She concludes that "the major rights conferred on Turkish women were much more the result of unrelenting efforts of a small revolutionary elite, rather than the product of large scale demands by Turkey's female population" (Abadan-Unat '81: 5, 12-13).

Another woman academic, Dr. Sirin Tekeli, a political scientist analysing Kemal's reforms, has shown that the model followed was one based on capitalist ideology. She writes:

> "The objective of the revolutionaries was to create a modern Turkey, and 'modernity' was defined as the social organisation prevalent in the West *i.e.* capitalist social formation. The forces of production that the new state inherited from the Ottoman Empire were not developed enough to be historically determining; therefore one had to start with modernising the super-structures. The new 'civil code' adopted in 1926 reorganised civil and property relations on the basis of the model relationships dominant in capitalist states'. (Tekeli '81: 297).

Inspite of the undoubted breakthrough in Turkey, the reforms remained class-bound, barely affecting the masses of Turkish women. As Dr. Fatma Mansur Cosar has written, "The sudden changes . . . thrust upon Turkish society in the early 1920's were made bearable and did not dislocate the social structure because, in the final analysis, only a very small number of women were able to use the rights granted to them by Atatürk.

III. IRAN

In economic terms in the preceding century, Iran was reduced to a semi-colonial status, being forced to give concessions to foreign entrepreneurs and being unable to protect its own markets from foreign competition. For example, after a defeat in war, Iran was forced in 1828 by Russia to establish customs duties which were advantageous to Russia and in effect, prevented the development of local industry. This policy was followed by concessions to other powers and between 1885 and 1900, fifteen countries extracted capitulations from Iran. "The effect of foreign competition was greatly increased by the concessions that were granted to foreigners by virtue of their political predominance while, in turn, the country's state of economic under-development caused it to be politically helpless in relation to the West." (Rodinson '74: 125).

Moreover in the late 19th and early 20th centuries, a bourgeoisie had arisen in Iran involved in importing foreign goods, exporting domestic produce, and investing in mining and a few industrial activities. Sections of this bourgeoisie thus developed contradictions not only with foreign capital over the home markets but with the feudal interests that ruled the country. Some regard the agitation between 1906 and 1909 as 'bourgeois democratic' in character while others disagree. "The weakness of the bourgeoisie in tackling the bases of feudalism and its lack of decisiveness in facing colonialism, the absence of a properly formed working-class movement as well as the absence of peasants in the Revolution, do not exclude it from being regarded as a bourgeois democratic revolution, albeit in its elementary form—as was the case with the Turkish Revolution of 1908 and the Chinese Revolution of 1911" (Jazani. '80: 6). In class terms the Constitutionalists were led by the bourgeoisie (including the clergy and urban intellectuals) and backed by British interests in Teheran, who gave their support only because the agitation was also against the Shah's pro-Russian policies. The movement was also inspired by the Russian Revolution of 1905 against the Czar.

In 1906, there were popular demonstrations organised by the Constitutionalists all over Iran and in the face of popular uprising, the Shah arrested a large number of the leaders of the movement, but was compelled to acceed to some of their demands, including a national assembly (majlis), which met in October 1906 and drew up a constitution. The Shah died during this period and his son Mohamed Ali attempted a coup against the nationalists, who retaliated. It was at this point that Britain and Russia, faced with new nationalists forces in Iran, came together in a horse deal, the Anglo-Russian Convention of 1907. This pact allegedly defended the independence and integrity of Iran, but in reality it was an excuse for keeping the threatened monarch on the throne, and for dividing the country into two spheres of influence—Rusian in North Iran and British in the South-West.

Using this opportunity, the Shah, with the support of the Russians, attacked the parliament; this lead to an armed struggle with the nationalists, who succeeded in re-capturing Tehran and replacing the Shah by his son. But the Russians invaded again and served a further ultimatum on the Constitutionalists who were forced to acquiese in the Russian domination of North Iran. In the South, the British position was strengthened by the discovery of oil.

During the First World War (after 1914) Iran became a battleground between Turkish, British and Russian forces and after the 1917 Russian Revolution, White Russian and Bolshevik forces fought each other on Iranian soil. At the 1919 Peace Conference, Iran sent a delegation to demand the country's political and economic independence and the abrogation of the 1907 Convention, but it did not even get a hearing. In 1919, the British imposed the Anglo-Persian Treaty on the country, which was in a state of economic collapse, thereby making Iran into a British protectorate. The Soviet government renounced all Czarist claims on Iran, and in the meantime, Iranian rebels led by Kuchik Khan, formed a Soviet Republic of Gilan in the North, and in 1920, the Communist Party of Iran was formed.

It was at this point that an army officer, Reza Khan of the Iranian Cossack Brigade, dismissed its Russian Commander and led the successful march on Teheran in 1921; he reorganised the armed forces, crushed the Soviet in Gilan, suppressed tribal revolts and established his rule over the country. In 1925, the Qajar dynasty of monarchs was ended by parliament; after some hesitation about whether, like Turkey, to declare a republic, the decision was made to preserve the monarchy and to crown Reza Khan as Shah of Iran, thus founding the Pahlavi dynasty (which was overthrown in 1979).

As in many other parts of Asia and the Arab world, the 19th century and early decades of the 20th century saw the emergence of women activists in Iran during a period of increased national awareness which had culminated in the constitutional agitation of 1905-1911. However, in an earlier period there had been queens, women warriors and militant women who challenged the existing norms of society. In fact the early religion of Iran, Zoroastrianism, which flourished over 2500 years ago, had given certain rights to women over property, the performance of religious ceremonies and equal status in law. In the Sassanian period of Iranian history, there had been two famous queens (*Pourandokut* and *Azarmidokht*) and the national epic of the country deals with the bravery of *Cordafarid,* a woman warrior who led the Iranians against a Turkish invasion (Sanghvi *et. al.,* 67: 10). In the 12th century, there seems to have been a discussion on the status of women during which the Iranian scholar *Ibn Rushd* (Averroes), criticised the confining of women to child-bearing on the grounds that this denied the country half its labour power and the potential of a better standard of life; he remarked that "because women are not being fitted for any of the human virtues, it often happens that they ressemble plants". (Fischer '78: 190).

Women's participation in religious heresies has been observed in many countries and in Iran too, in the 1840's, a heretic movement, Babism, (later known as Bahaism) advocated reforms, including greater social justice, freedom of trade and rights of personal property, reduction of unjust taxes, a higher status for women, limits on polygamy, a prohibition of violence against women and measures for their education. (Keddie '81: 50). The best-known woman of this movement, *Qurrat Ul Ayn* (1815-1851), who was from a family of mullahs, was a poet, well-versed in religious questions, participating in intellectual debates with religious leaders. She joined the Babi movement, leaving husband and relatives, and was active in the cause, preaching in public, fighting on the battle field and dying a martyr. She evidently attracted much attention, the French diplomat Gobineau stating that "she turned against not only polygamy but also the veil, and she appeared face unveiled in public places, causing much fright and scandal amongst her kind and amongst pious Muslims." (Bayat-Philipp '78: 296).

Several male intellectuals and radical reformers of the 1880's and 1890's (many of them associates of the famous scholar Al Afghani) also took up the cause of women's rights and wrote on the subject. They included *Mirza Malkom Khan* (1833-1908), an anti-clerical Armenian Iranian who had received a Western education and had been exiled from Iran for forming a society based on freemasonry. In London he edited 'Qanun' a journal to which Al Afghani contributed, which was opposed to the arbitrary rule of the Shah and was smuggled into Iran where it was widely read among dissenting groups. Another important writer of the period was *Mirza Aqua Khan Kermani,* a Babi who had become a radical freethinker. As editor of the newspaper Akhtar and collaborator of Al Afghani he was forceful in his critique of conditions in Iran; he glorified the pre-Islamic past, criticised orthodox Islam and was representative of the current of anti-religious nationalism which existed at the time. Linked with similar activities was *Shaikh Ahmad Ruhi* (also a Babi), a writer, teacher and freethinker who, along with Kermani, formed a group of Iranian reformists (in 1891), centered around Al Afghani who was in Istanbul. Another influential writer was *Fath Ali Akhundzadeh,* an Iranian of Azerbaijan origin who lived in Russian Transcaucasia. In the late 19th century he wrote a series of letters denouncing conditions in Iran, which formed part of the considerable output of critical writings by Iranian radicals in exile. (Keddie '81: 68, 71, 191). These four writers were for women's emancipation, supporting women's right to education and opposing polygamy. "Their primary concern seems to have been the necessity to breed a new generation of Iranian patriots, and they felt that only with a proper "healthy" family environment where the mother is educated and given a prominent role as the first educator of the child, could this be achieved." (Bayat-Philipp '80: 296-7).

The intellectuals of the early 20th century—many of whom had studied in Europe—were at the forefront of the nationalist and democratic agitation, establishing secret societies to debate political issues. "They were used as platforms to sound the alarm and to call for revolt against the corrupt Qajar government, as well as for the dissemination of new concepts and ideas: . . . The new mood of rebellion caught and met a corresponding and equally legitimate desire for change among a small but then growing number of Iranian women". (Bayat-Philipp '80: 296).

It was in such a climate of opinion that education for women expanded. In 1874, an American Presbyterial Missionary School had been started in Teheran, and was attended by non-Muslims, but two Muslim girls attended the school in 1891, the number rising to 120 in 1909. In 1907, the first Iranian girls school and in 1908 a French girls' school were also founded in Teheran. By 1910 there were 50 girls schools in Teheran and increasing numbers of women teachers, journalists and activists in women's organisations. (Bayat-Philipp '80: 300). One such pioneer was *Khanum Asamodeh* whose husband had liberal views and believed in women's education. Around the early 20th century she started a school in her home for 20 girls which grew into a large middle school for girls with 400 pupils, (Namus School), a venture that in spired the creation of many more private girls' schools in Iran. (Woodsmall '36: 145-6).

As in other countries, women in palace circles and the royal harem in Iran were also involved in political intrigue and protest, harems being "rarely the dens of idleness and iniquity imagined by Westerners". (Keddie '81: 34). It is claimed that *Anis Ud Daula,* Shah Nasir Ud Din's third wife conspired to secure the downfall of the prime minister whom she held responsible for her recall from Europe in 1872, where she had been on a visit with the Shah. Since the prime minister was also under attack for selling the country to British interests, the incident was politically important. "Thus . . . a member of the Qajar harem became involved in one of the first important nationalist political movements." (Bayat-Philipp '80: 297). The harem was also involved in the first expressions of Iranian opposition to foreign economic domination which occurred in 1890 when the entire tobacco monopoly including the production, sale and export of the country's tobacco crop was given to G.F. Talbot, a British capitalist. (Rodinson '74: 126). The protests included a boycott of tobacco launched by the women of the royal harem. "The successful boycott was to be a prelude to the constitutional revolution in 1905". (Bayat-Philipp '80: 298).

During the constitutional agitation that erupted in 1905, women joined the protests on the streets, and in this form of agitation they were very effective. Women also participated in the agitation against the Shah in 1906, when they demonstrated in the streets, surrounded the Shah's carriage and handed a petition with their demands, one woman giving him a letter saying "Fear the time when we shall finally take away the crown off your head and the royal cane off your hand". It is not surprising that this new phenomenon of women protesting caused hostile reactions and that when Iranian women marched unveiled in Teheran shouting "long live the Constitution, long live freedom. We must free ourselves from the religious obligations to live the way we want!", they were denounced as prostitutes hired by reactionaries to dis-credit the 1906 revolution. (Bayat-Philipp '80: 298 and 302).

The new constitution of 1906 did not grant women's suffrage, article 10 stating that "Those deprived of the right to vote shall consist of all females, minors . . . fraudulent bankrupts, beggars, murderers, thieves and other criminals punishable under Islamic law." (Sanghvi '68: 300). During this period however, a number of women's secret societies, arose. Some of the prominent members of these societies were *Malikiya-yi Iran, Safia Yazdi, Sadiqa Daulatabadi* and *Badri Tundari,* wives or relatives of constitutionalist leaders. One of the women's societies published a weekly paper, *Danish* (Knowledge), edited by the wife of a doctor, and said to be "the only newspaper written exclusively for women and discussing topics of special interest to women." One of the main activities of the women's groups was propaganda on the need for education for girls, and the opening of girls' schools. The nationalist and feminist nature of the women's agitation can also be seen in the appeal of the Persian Women's Society, in 1911, to British suffragettes against Russian threats to Iranian independence. "The ears of the men of Europe are deaf to our cries; could you women not come to our help?"—to which the British women not replied "Unhappily, we cannot make the British government give political freedom even to us, their country women. We are equally powerless to influence their action towards Persia". (Bayat-Philipp '80:299 and 307).

However, when the conservative forces did attempt to destroy the constitutional government, women joined in the resistance, demonstrating on the streets and joining in battle. In the second attempt against the Majlis, women's participation in mass protests was noted by the *London Times*. "The patriotic demonstrations continue. A curious feature is the prominent part taken in them by women. At a large meeting of women . . . addresses were delivered by female orators. One lady announced that, although the law of Islam forbade it, the women would . . . take part in a holy war." (Bayat-Philipp '80: 30).

The participation of women in the 1911 demonstrations after the invasion of North Iran by Russia, is of interest, since the women staged separate demonstrations of their own. The revolutionary zeal of the women during this period of crisis, though hidden from official history, has been documented by eye-witnesses. For example, Morgan Shuster, an American financier (whose employment by the Constitutionalists had led to a Russian ultimatum for his removal, thus providing a pretext for Russian, invasion) witnessed the women's action. In his book 'The Strangling of Persia' he recounts that when rumours spread that the deputies of the national assembly had capitulated to Russian demands, the question arose as to what could be done to prevent this humiliation.

"The Persian women supplied the answer. Out from their walled courtyards and harems marched three hundred women . . . many held pistols under their skirts or in the folds of their sleeves. Straight to the majlis they went and gathered there, demanding of the President that he admit them all . . . they confronted him . . . exposed threateningly their revolvers, tore aside their veils and confessed their decision to kill their own husbands and sons and leave behind their own dead bodies, if the deputies wavered in their duty to uphold the liberty and dignity of the Persian people and nation." (Sanghvi *et al.*, '67: 15-16).

Of the women activists of the period, one can highlight *Sadiqa Daulatabadi* who was one of the early pioneers of women's education. Her father, a leading mujahid of Isfahan was said to have 'advanced' ideas and she attended her brother's school dressed as a boy. In the early years of the 20th century, she opened the first girls' school in Isfahan and in later years became a government inspector of girls' schools. Sadiqa

Daulatabadi was also active in women's journalism, publishing a bi-monthly 'The Tongue of Women' (Zabaun-i-Zanan) in Isfahan, which took a strong nationalist stance on political issues, protesting very strongly against the Treaty with Britain in 1919 which "stirred up such strong opposition that the magazine was finally closed". (Wood-small '36: 145 and 365).

It is interesting to record that as early as 1911, when the constitution was being discussed, a deputy of the Majlis, *Hadji Vakil el Roaya* proposed in Parliament that women be allowed to vote. According to a report of the *London Times,* he asked why women were deprived of the vote, "are they not human beings, and are they not entitled to have the same rights as we have? I beg the ulama for a reply". The religious leader Sheikh Assadollah replied, "we must not discuss this question, for it is contrary to the etiquette of Islamic Parliament. But the reason for excluding women is that God has not given them the capacity needed for taking part in politics". (Bayat-Philipp '80: 301).

The activities of Iranian women during this period were noted by foreign correspondents. "The movement is in its infancy, but the fact that last April for the first time Persian women held a large meeting in Teheran to discuss problems of education seems to suggest that the education of women will play an important part in the future evolution of Persia". (*London Times*, quoted in Bayat-Philipp '80: 300) and an American writer commented on the role of the "veiled women who overnight became teachers, newspaper writers, founders of women's clubs" rapidly absorbing "absolutely new ideas . . . with the elan of the crusader who has a vision". (Shuster quoted in Bayat-Philipp '80: 300).

The defeat in 1912 of the Majlis led to a period of reaction, but the lessons of women's participation in the agitation of the period, though ignored by historians, was not forgotten. An Iranian woman scholar Dr. Mangol Bayat-Philipp, has commented "In most of the historical accounts of the revolution subsequently published, the women's role is either severely under-estimated or overlooked altogether. Their participation in the 1905-1911 political events seems to have been a spontaneous, free move on their part . . . the role of women clearly reveals not only a new nationalist feeling that suddenly overwhelmed them and spurred them to action, but also a nascent though strong desire for official recognition. . . . The revolution therefore turned out to be a fertile ground for their experimental struggle for emancipation. It did not immediate fruit, but the seeds were planted." (Bayat-Philipp '78: 305-6).

Liberation Under Reza Khan

In the next historical phase, Reza Khan, the soldier who became the Shah in 1924, ruled despotically, crushing dissent, preserving the existing class structures internally, and externally taking the country towards Fascist Germany in his effort to steer clear of the traditional enemies, Britain and Russia. Reza Khan had, in his career, been influenced by the Turkish experiment in secularising and modernising the country. In his sixteen years of autocratic rule, Reza Khan's policies were to strengthen his hold on the country by modernising the state apparatus, especially through army reforms—introducing conscription and establishing military academies, medical corps, military police and other services ancillary to the army. Through the army and police, rebellions were crushed and nomadic tribes were disarmed and forcibly settled. The Shah's dictatorial policies included the repression of political opponents. In 1931 the Communist party was outlawed. In 1932, Taqi Arani and some students who had been influenced by Marxism while abroad, formed a study group of 53 intellectuals while writers; they were arrested and imprisoned, some of them later joining Communist activists to form the Tudeh Party.

A rigid bureaucracy was also established to keep the people under control and financial and tax reforms as well as judicial reforms were undertaken. In addition, a programme of major roads and the Trans-Iranian railway were built during Reza Khan's regime. The policies of industrialising and modernising the country took place through imposing new structures on the traditional economic and society. "Interaction with the West influenced the direction of change. In addition to pressures from the small middle class, 'modernisation from above' was seen by Reza Shah and those around him as the only way to make Iran a strong, self-respecting nation that could hold its own in the modern world". (Keddie '81: 93).

The Shah's policies of crushing all opposition were paradoxically carried out at the same time as his efforts to 'free' women and bring them out of seclusion into society and into the work force. Inspired by Mustapha Kemal in Turkey, Reza Khan who had visited Turkey in 1934, made efforts at modernisation included the delinking of religion from politics, law and education and the attempt by a few reforms from above to 'emancipate' the women of Iran, through the encouragement of women's education, and measures of dress reform including the ban on the veil. Twelve women were permitted to enter the university for the first time in 1935. Delivering an address to the students of the first Women's College the Shah said "The women of this country, because of their being aloof from society, could not show their abilities and personal qualities. They could not play their role in the building of their beloved country and as a result they could not perform their duties towards their country." (Sanghvi *et al.*, '67: 25).

Not surprisingly, the issue that created hostility among religious interests was the Shah's efforts to compel women to give up wearing the chador. There was an apocryphal story that the Queen Mother appeared at a shrine in Qom in 1928, with a light veil in place of the orthodox black chador; the religious ulama reprimanded her, leading to Reza Shah beating the ulama, after striding into the Mosque with his boots on. In 1934, women teachers and students were ordered to appear unveiled; in February 1936 the wearing of the chador was prohibited, making Iran the first Muslim country to legally outlaw the veiling of women. "As of that date any officials of the Ministry of Finance whose wives were found to be wearing the chador were not allowed in cinema houses or into public baths, and taxi and bus drivers were liable to fines if they accepted veiled women as passengers." (Savory '78: 98).

It was in 1936 that a concerted attempt was made to highlight the issue and the initiative came from the Palace. In January 1936, the Shah attended the presentation of awards at the

Normal School in Teheran and the Queen and princesses appeared in public unveiled and in European dress—a function that was publicised as an important milestone in women's emancipation. The Shah spoke to an audience of five hundred women and declared, "we must never forget that one-half of the population of our country has not been taken into account, that is to say, one half of the country's working force has been idle." However he stressed the familiar theme of the need for women's education in order to benefit the next generation. "The happiness of the future is in your hands. You are the educators of the coming generation, you have the possibility to become good teachers and to bring up good citizens". (Elwell-Sutton '78: 34).

A contemporary account of the event states that all the women present on this occasion were unveiled and that the streets were linked with crowds of unveiled women who had come to see the royal procession.

> "The repercussion of this event was felt all over Iran. Emulating the Shah's example, in many places the Governor with the Chief of Police and School Superintendent held meetings in girls' schools to promote the progress of women . . . and pupil threw off their veils. The Iran Press after the eventful day of emancipation (January 8, 1936), was filled for days with news articles and pictures on women's advance. Photographs of school girls' athletics, Girl Scouts, Women's Club activities, held the front page. The forward movement was also promoted through the theatre by a special play depicting social advance with two Iranian girls in the contrasting roles of the old and new women of Iran." (Woodsmall '36: 44).

In the following years an active campaign to encourage women to discard their traditional clothes in favour of European styles was begun. There was such a demand for women's coats, dresses and hats that rules against profiteering by Teheran tailor shops had to be introduced. In addition newspapers kept women informed of 'correct' social etiquette linked to the new fashions. "Ladies in public meetings should not remove their hats; they may or may not take off their coats and gloves. . . . Those who have always put their handkerchiefs, cigarette cases and other articles up their sleeves must now use their hand-bags for such things. . . . To take fruit or sweets with gloves on is forbidden". (Woodsmall '36: 45).

While legally abolishing the veil was a super-structural change, which did not reflect any basic change in society, nevertheless for certain women, it presented a welcome reform. The country's leading woman poet *Parvin-i I'tisami* (1907-1941), wrote a poem on this occasion called 'Woman in Iran' (Zan dar Iran).

> "It is as if the woman in Iran was not an Iranian before.
> She had no pursuit other than misfortune and distraction.
> She lived and died in a solitary corner.
> What else was a woman in those days if not a prisoner?
> No one like a woman dwelt in darkness for centuries.
> No one like a woman was sacrificed in the temple of hypocrisy."
>
> (Bayat-Philipp '80: 306)

However measures from above affecting social customs can have negative long-term results. Writing of the outlawing of the veil, an Iranian woman scholar comments "The brutal enforcement of this law until 1941 was one reason for a later pro-veil backlash, and many now doubt that legislation is a useful approach to veiling." She adds that the measures taken during Reza Shah's regime did nevertheless make for some changes. "There was a de facto decline in upper-class polygamy and in inequality in marriage and divorced in the modernized classes, and a rise in paid work for women. These trends affected primarily middle and upper-class women, who nevertheless did not obtain political rights or complete economic and social equality, though their advance in a decade was considerable." (Keddie '81: 108-9). Under the Pahlavi dynasty, women's emancipation remained a purely bourgeois urban phenomenon; unfortunately the militancy of the early 20th century—when the 'woman question' was keenly debated and when women formed organisations, started newspapeers and came out in public demonstrations, gave way to a period of reaction under Shah Reza Khan and his son Shah Mohamed Reza Pahlavi. Some gestures were however made; in 1963, the Shah gave Iranian women franchise rights and The Family Protection Law of 1967, merely made polygamy a possible reason for divorce and gave women more opportunities to initiate divorce. But even the right to vote in a situation where women had few other rights meant little to the majority of Iranian women. Their first experiences of feminist activity in the years before 1920 were short-lived, the reforms of the following period were class-based and the association of measures of 'women's emancipation' with the Shah's unpopular, repressive regime has led to the further deterioration in women's position under the new rulers.

8

Women and Social Uplift in Islamic Society

Shari'ā Court

With the end of the British Mandate and the outbreak of the 1948 War, the communal organization of Muslims in Israel collapsed completely. The members of the Supreme Muslim Council and the *shar'i* élite *(muftīs, qāḍīs* and *'ulamā'*—religious scholars of Islam) left the country; the religious judicial system, the *waqf* (religious endowment) administration and communal educational and welfare institutions crumbled and ceased to exist. The Israel Government set about rehabilitating the organization of the Muslim community[1]: the judicial system was re-constituted; the management of endowment for public purposes (*waqf khayrī*), consisting of holy places (mosques and cemeteries) with their secular appurtenances, was in part entrusted to Muslim boards of trustees, while at the same time far-reaching reforms in the institution of the *waqf* itself were introduced by the Knesset (Israeli Parliament), most of the restrictions on the transfer of property and the use of its income were lifted with regard to *waqf khayri* and the family *waqf* was abolished altogether with a view to handing over the property to the beneficiaries as full owners.[2]

The Government-administered Muslim religious services, paid the salaries of the religious functionaries—*imāms* (prayer leaders), *khaṭibs* (preachers at Friday prayer in the mosque), etc.—and assisted in the establishment of mosques and communal educational, welfare and health institutions. At the same time, the Muslims had no autonomous communal organization or religious-political leadership such as they had enjoyed in Mandate days.

Thus, the *shar'ī* judicial system was integrated into the general judicial system of Israel.[3] The *qāḍīs* were appointed by the President of the State and had to pledge allegiance to the State and dispense justice in accordance with its laws. There were four *shari'ā* courts of first instance in the State; in Nazareth (since 1948; area of jurisdiction: Nazareth and Eastern and Upper Galilee); in Acre (since 1948; area of jurisdiction: Acre, Ḥaifa and Western Galilee); in Jaffa (since 1950; area of jurisdiction: Lod, Ramla, Jerusalem and its countryside, the Southern Region and the Negev); and in Ṭayyiba (since 1950; area of jurisdiction: the Little Triangle—Hadera, Sharon and Petah Tikva subdistricts). A *sharī'ā* court of the first instance consisted of a single *qāḍī*. In 1953 a *Shari'a* Court of Appeal was established with a bench of two or three *qāḍīs* its permanent seat being Jerusalem. The Appeal Court was formed by *qāḍīs* of the courts of first instance, excluding the one whose judgment was appealed against. Seven *qāḍīs* served in the *shari'ā* courts in the period under review. Shaykh Ṭāhir al-Ṭabarī served in Nazareth and as President of the Court of Appeal. He died in 1959 and was succeeded in Nazareth in 1963 by Shaykh Ḥusnī al-Zu'bī. Shaykh Mūsā al-Ṭabari served in Acre until his death in 1962, and his successor, after 1963, was Shaykh Amīn Qāsim Mudlij. Shaykh Ṭāhir Ḥamād served in Jaffa, and as President of the Court of Appeal in succession to Shaykh Ṭāhir al-Tabari; he retired on pension in 1963 and was succeeded in Jaffa in 1965 by Shaykh Tawfiq Maḥmūd 'Asaliyya. Shaykh Ḥasan Amīn al-Ḥabash has served in Ṭayyiba since the establishment of the local *shari'ā* court and was the successor of Shaykh Ṭāhir Ḥamād as President of the Court of Appeal. Most of the *qāḍīs* received *a shar'ī* training at Cairo's al-Azhar, the central institution of higher religious learning in the Muslim Middle East. Shaykh Ḥusnī al-Zuʿbī was a *sharʿī* advocate by profession.

Despite the *shariʿā* court's integration into Israel's legal system, the Muslim religious community enjoyed the widest judicial autonomy of any religious community in the country. Article 51 of the Palestine Order in Council, the principal enactment defining the powers of the *shariʿā* courts, granted them exclusive jurisdiction in all matters of personal status and *waqf* of Muslims, both nationals and foreigners, the latter on condition that under their own national law they were amenable to the jurisdiction of Muslim religious courts. In Israel, the competence of the *sharīʿā* court was restricted in some matters. The Age of Marriage Law, 5710-1950, empowered the district court to permit under certain circumstances—but not to perform—the marriage of a girl under 17, and a welfare officer was empowered to request the dissolution of such a marriage—but the power to dissolve it remained with the religious court.[4] The Succession Law, 5725-1965, downgraded the jurisdiction of the *shariʿā* court in matters of succession and wills from exclusive to concurrent, *i.e.*, jurisdiction in these matters was transferred to the district court except where all the parties had consented in writing to the jurisdiction of the religious court.[5] In Israel, the Beduin, too, were amenable to the *sharʿīa* court in matters of personal status.

The legal status of women is a function of the various sources of material law and of the judicial authority interpreting it, in this case the *sharʿī qāḍī*. The material law applicable to personal status in *shariʿā* courts in Israel is a mixture of religious and secular sources. Its basis is the theoretically immutable *shariʿā,* which reflects the structure of the pre-Islamic Arab family with all its typical features, with variations resulting from Muḥammad's reforms. The religious norms imposed on the family on its absorption into Islam did not essentially alter the concept underlying patrilineal and patriarchal society of the superiority of men to women and precedence of agnatic (*ʿaṣabāt*) over cognatic relatives.[6] The Ottoman legal heritage in the country includes important legal reforms concerning marriage, divorce and succession. The Family Rights Law of 1917 did not disrupt the *sharʿī* legal system: reforms were mainly carried out by means of the *talfīq* principle, *i.e.,* by combining various elements of different schools of religious law. The Succession Law of 1913, framed on the basis of a European source, maintains complete equality of the sexes.[7] Israeli *qāḍīs* frequently relied in their decisions on the well-known collection of laws of personal status and succession by an Egyptian, Qadrī Pasha, which has no statutory standing locally; they sometimes even gave it preference over provisions of the Ottoman Family Rights Law not based on the Ḥanafī school.[8] The Ḥanafī school is dominant in the *shari'ā* courts although most of the population, especially in the villages, belongs to the *Shāfi'ī* school and even some followers of the Ḥanbalī school can be found in the villages of the Little Triangle. This, too, is a legacy of Ottoman rule.[9] The Mandatory legislator gave effect to the recent Ottoman reforms and scrupulously preserved the *status quo* as to the material law relating to Muslims; when introducing reforms by means of criminal legislation, such as the ban on the marriage of minor girls and on polygamy, he provided a good defense to Muslims and exempted them from penal sanctions.[10]

The Knesset intervened in many matters of personal status, going extremely far in some. The purpose of its legislation was to improve the legal status of women in Israel and to adapt it to present-day conditions. It abolished some of the provisions of religious law discriminating against women and granted them social and political rights. Section 1 of the Women's Equal Rights Law, 5711-1951, which is the keystone of its legislation in this matter, provides: "A man and a woman shall have equal status with regard to any legal act; any provision of law which discriminates, with regard to any legal act, against women as women, shall be of no effect." The Israeli legislator, for obvious reasons, could hardly adopt the legislative technique of the *talfīq* customary in Arab countries, intended to give the reforms the character of an internal refurbishing of religious law.[11] Out of regard for the legal systems of the various religious communities, the Knesset subjected its legislation to two severe restrictions: abstention from interfering with any religious prohibition or permission as to marriage and divorce and adoption of procedural provisions and penal sanctions as deterrents in preference to substantive provisions which would have invalidated the relevant religious law; and, in matters for which provisions superceding religious law were enacted, the parties were usually given an option in litigate in accordance with religious law.[12]

In sum, the position of Muslim women in Israel in matters of personal status was thus determined by two legal systems, a religious one and a secular one, based on different social philosophies. Only in matters of succession has there been since 1965 a clear demarcation between the religious judicial authority, which applies religious law, and the civil judicial authority, which applies secular law. In other matters of personal status, the *shari'ā* court must, in the absence of consent of the parties, apply Knesset legislation specifically addressed to it.[13] Disregard of this legislation is excess of authority and a ground for intervention by the High Court of Justice. Disregard of other secular legislation or of the religious law of the community does not constitute excess of authority but is at most a mistake of law.[14]

Social, Economic and Cultural Pressures for Change

The position of Muslim women, as of the general population in Israel, has been determined not only by progressive Knesset legislation but also by demographic, economic, cultural and social factors.

In 1968 the Muslim population of Israel formed about three-quarters of the total non-Jewish population. From 112,000[15] in 1949 it had increased to 301,000. Sources of this increase were the approximately 40,000 refugees, mostly Muslims, who had entered Israel under the family reunion scheme, and especially, infiltrators whose residence had been approved *ex post facto* in the first years after the establishment of the State, as well as the 69,000 inhabitants of East Jerusalem (over 80 per cent Muslims), added on the reunification of the city following the Six-Day War. But about half the additional population stemmed from natural increase, which was one of the largest in the world (43 per mille in 1968, as against 23 per mille among the Arab Christians).

The equilibrium, characteristic of traditional society, between a high birth rate and a high death rate had been drastically upset. The death rate had dropped to one-third of what it had been at the end of the Mandate period and had become equal to that of the Jewish population (six per mille). This was due to an improvement of the health services. On the other hand, the birth rate remained high, as is usual in traditional society (about 50 per mille). The overall fertility of the Muslim woman was nine children (as against four for the Christian woman). Early marriage lengthens the period of fertility; the average age of marriage of the Muslim woman in 1968 was almost 21 years, the median age of marriage almost 20 years (as against 23 years and more than 22 years, respectively, for the Christian woman). The fertility of the urban woman, especially in the mixed towns, was considerably lower than that of the village woman, and the higher a woman's education, the lower her fertility; of course, besides the type of settlement account should also be taken of religious affiliation. Until recent years, the birth rate was steadily rising, which was probably due to the youthful age structure of Muslim society (average age 21 years, median age 16 years[16] in 1961, as against 25 years and 21 years, respectively, among the Christians) and to the improvement of women's state of health. A decline has recently been noticeable in this rate, and hence also in the natural increase, but it is too early to say whether this tendency will be of any lasting significance.[17]

The Muslim population was a definitely rural one. In 1961, only about one-sixth was concentrated in towns (as against 60 per cent of the Christians): in Nazareth (half of the population), Shafā 'Amr (one-third) and mixed towns (Acre, Haifa, Tel Aviv-Jaffa, Lod and Ramla). About two-thirds or, together with the Beduin (an additional sixth), over four-fifths of the Muslims lived in rural areas (as against some two-fifths of the Christians). About half of the Muslim population was concentrated in Galilee (Northern District) and about 30 per cent in the Little Triangle. The rural population in these two areas was almost equal (over 50,000 in 1961). About two-thirds of the Beduin lived in the surroudings of Beersheba and south of it and about one-third in different places in Galilee.[18]

Distribution according to type of settlement had lost its significance in many respects. The Beduin, especially those in

Galilee, were at an advanced stage of sedentarization; some of them even skipped the rural stage and became town dwellers in every respect (for example, the inhabitants of the Beduin settlement at Bosmat Tiv'on). The gap between the rural and the urban population had narrowed considerably. The village had undergone radical changes: the irrigated area had been enlarged, a variety of market crops had been introduced, cultivation methods had been improved (mechanization); the agrarian system had been completely transformed; large-scale basic investments had been made in approach roads, drinking water, electricity, educational institutions, health services and the like.

As a result of all these and other circumstances, Israeli Arab labourers commuting from home localities to centers of employment in Israel amounted to half of the Israeli Arab labour force in 1961, and in some villages the proportion of commuters reached two-thirds or more.[19] The Arab town, on the other hand, dwindled owing to the exodus of the elite strata to Arab countries in the 1948 War. Urban settlement did not increase significantly after the establishment of the State despite increasing numbers of commuters. Social, economic, cultural and political factors militated against urbanization. In fact, A. Cohen has found that not only did the urbanization process cease in the Little Triangle villages, but villagers who had settled in towns during the Mandate returned to their villages in the first years of the State, and the balance of migration was also negative in Nazareth between 1954 and 1964.[20] As a result of these developments the differences in standard of living, level of education, occupational structure and social stratification between towns and villages were blurred considerably.[21] This applied especially to the villages of the Little Triangle, which had known economic prosperity since the late 1950s, and to villages near large, well-established urban centers. Several large villages, such as Ṭayyiba and Umm al-Faḥm[22] in the Little Triangle, outstripped towns such as Jaffa, Lod and Ramla (especially as to the Muslim population of these towns). In many respects Shafā 'Amr had a definitely rural character.

The rate of participation of Muslim women in the civil labour force in 1961 was 11 per cent of the total number of

Muslim women from the age of 14 upward (the corresponding figure for Christian women was 17 per cent and for Jewish women 29 per cent).[23] The causes of this low rate were the youthful age structure of the Muslim population, the early age of marriage of women, the high rate of fertility, the low level of education, but above all, the severe restrictions imposed by traditional society on women's work, especially as regards married women and work outside the localities where they lived.[24] Cohen, who studied Little Triangle villages in the late 1950s, notes that most women who worked in agriculture ceased to do so after marrying and veiling their faces.[25] The rate of participation of women in the labour force was higher in the towns, especially the mixed towns, than in the villages, because of a higher standard of education, religious affiliation, and the greater opportunities of non-agricultural employment, in the towns.[26]

About two-thirds of the women employed in the Arab sector worked in agriculture (double the percentage of the men). Agriculture afforded solutions to some of the limitations on women's work in traditional society. Owing to the increase of commuting, the demand for female workers had grown; Cohen and H. Rosenfeld found that for this reason many women preferred to marry landless men or were not willing to marry peasants at all. On the other hand, there were also relatively more women than men in the professions, especially in teaching.[27] Several dozen women worked in the civil service as welfare and health officials. An isolated few worked in journalism. Muslim women were not represented in medicine or advocacy. Women's share in handicrafts and industries was small owing to the organization of the work (shifts, work together with men).[28] The Arab section of the Working Women's Council has in recent years made great efforts to train Arab women as nurses and thus to enable them to earn a living in permanent employment outside their homes.[29]

Forty-four per cent of the female Arab labour force worked outside their home localities, most of them young and single. They usually did seasonal work in agriculture. The fact that women worked outside their own locality does not mean that they enjoyed freedom of movement. Their outside work was organized by a middleman (*ra'īs*), who kept their movements under strict supervision. This arrangement was an old-style solution to a modern problem which had evolved following changes in the rural employment structure.[30] The rate of women's participation in the upkeep of the family was low. A sample taken in Nazareth in 1964-65 showed that the average annual income of the wife of the family head from wages was about 4 per cent of the gross income of the family from all sources. The woman's contribution to the family income was the greater the higher the family head's level of education, and the smaller the more children there were; it was also affected by the rural nature of the Muslim population.[31] The relative share of women in the labour force had been steadily increasing since the late 1950s, and it was estimated that with the spread of education, the rise of the age of mariage, the progress of family planning, the improvement in economic opportunities, the growth of the demand for labour and the loosening of family and clanship ties, its future increase would be greater than that of the relative share of men.[32]

About 14 per cent of Muslim women could read and write at the time of the 1961 census (as against 66 per cent of Christian women and 61 per cent of Muslim men). The level of education was the lower the older the age. About one-quarter of Muslim women of the 14-29 age group could read and write (as against 84 per cent of Christian women and 76 per cent of Muslim men), but only 2 per cent of the 65-and-over age group could do so (as against 41 per cent of Christian women and 22 per cent of Muslim men). The relatively high percentage among the young was chiefly due to the implementation of the Compulsory Education Law. Moreover, those under 14 years of age, the overwhelming majority of whom received an elementary education, were about one-half of the population in that year. The number of Muslim female pupils in the State educational system rose from 6,400 in 1951-52 to 28,000 in 1969-70. Hundreds of girl students attended secondary schools and dozens teachers' colleges. Some trailblazers appeared in the institutions of higher learning.[33]

The patriarchal extended family in Israel was rapidly disintegrating and was being superseded by the nuclear family.[34]

Rosenfeld found that the number of married sons in Ṭur'ān village leaving their father's house before his death increased from 50 per cent in 1954 to two-thirds in 1966,[35] and that the proportion of nuclear families in that village increased from 75 per cent to 88 per cent during the same period. Cohen found that the proportion of nuclear families in Bint al-Ḥudūd village reached 84 per cent in the late 1950s,[36] and an economic survey carried out in Nazareth in 1965 revealed that 80 per cent of the local Muslim families were nuclear ones.[37] Rosenfeld notes a tendency in recent years of sons to leave their father's house even before their marriages. In mixed towns, the extended family was probably still rarer. The causes of this development were the large-scale commuting of manpower to centers of employment in the Jewish sector, which ended the economic, dependence of the sons on the head of the family[38]; the fragmentation of landed property by inheritance,[39] and its curtailment by large-scale nationalization[40]; the lessening importance of extensive farming as a source of income, resulting in large areas being left uncultivated; disputes within the extended family arising from disharmony between the division of labour on the family farm and the complex of property relations in which the women played a major role; the spread of education and the adoption of modern standards (such as heightened economic expectations on the part of young couples, and improved housing). Most of these factors were not new,[41] but their intensity and extent in Israel were unique. The transition from the extended to the nuclear family largely liberated women from dependence on the husband's family, with all that this implies in terms of kinship and property relations, self-sufficiency and freedom of movement.

Paradoxically, however, despite the disintegration of the extended family, endogamous marriages in Israeli Muslim society were on the increase compared with earlier periods, mainly as a result of the numerical growth of families and clans. In the Galilean village of Ṭur'ān, studied by Rosenfeld, the rate of intra-clan and cousin marriages was 80 per cent in the years 1954-63, and in the Little Triangle village of Bint al-Ḥudūd, studied by Cohen. 57 per cent in the years 1953-59. A high percentage was observed by E. Marx in a sample taken among peasant Beduin in the Negev.[42]

The findings with regard to women's social status are meagre and do not convey a comprehensive picture. Rosenfeld says that village women were restricted in their movements and required the permission of men even for the purposes of supplementary vocational training, the sexes were separated in entertainment and in what little other social activity there was in rural areas.[43] As against this, Yūsūf Dasūqi, Secretary of the *Shari'a* Court of Ṭayyiba, found instances of women's freedom of movement: they travelled alone, unveiled, visited places of entertainment and maintained social contact with men.[44] The choice of the mate was still a family matter, and a woman's modesty was still judged by traditional standards, although deviations from these norms did occur here and there; expectations as to the marriage partner's education were rising[45]: a woman might refuse to marry the man chosen for her by her father and might complain to the *qāḍī* that she was being pressed to marry someone she did not want.[46] Cohen lengthily describes the case of a woman who married the man of her choice in open defiance of her father's wishes.[47] Although no research has been conducted as to the townswomen in Israel, it may be assumed that, especially in the mixed towns, they enjoyed a greater measure of freedom of movement and other benefits of social liberation than their sisters in the countryside.

Notes and References

1. The remarks concerning communal organization are mainly based on Layish, *Communal Organization*.
2. See Layish, *Waqf.*
3. See Layish, *Communal Organization,* pp. 51-61.
4. See Layish, *Jurisdiction,* pp. 50-60; *idem, Waqf,* pp. 43-7.
5. Succession Law, 5725-1965, secs. 151(a), 155(a). See Yadin, *Reflections,* p. 133.
6. See Gibb, pp. 233-45; Goitein and Ben-Shemesh, pp. 83-4, 124-6, 134-5; Levy, pp. 91-5, 121; Anderson, *Patriarchal Family,* pp. 221-2; Lecerf, p. 306; Schacht, p. 161; for pre-Islamic marriage customs in Arabia see Robertson Smith, ch. 3.
7. See Anderson, *Islamic Law,* pp. 26-7, 54, 91-3. For an Arabic text of the Family Rights Law, in use in *shari'ā* courts, see Goitein and Ben-Shemesh, pp. 290-311.

8. For the title of the collection see Qadrī. See Schacht, p. 100; Layish, *Qāḍīs*, pp. 241, 249; Maḥmūd al-Māḍī, *AI,* vol. 11(1968), Nos. 1-2, p. 15.
9. See Baer, p. 77.
10. Criminal Code Ordinance, 1936, secs. 181(c), 182, 183. See Eisenman, pp. 155-83, 258-63, 307-12; Dykan, p. 437.
11. To the extent that he did so, he was guided by the norms of Jewish law. See Layish, *Qāḍīs*, p. 239; Eisenman, p. 386.
12. Cf. the remarks of the Minister of Justice in the Knesset on presenting *IFB, KP*, vol. 20, p. 1929, col. 1.
13. See Layish, *Jurisdiction,* pp. 60-79; *idem*, *Qāḍīs*, pp. 238-9, 255. Some uncertainty exists as to the applicability of the Capacity and Guardianship Law in the religious courts. For a detailed discussion of the reforms made by the Knesset in the various fields of personal status see the introductions to the relevant chapters.
14. M. Silberg, pp. 172-7, 421-3; High Court of Justice No. 187/54, Ḥalīma Sulaymān Barriyya vs. *Qāḍī* of the *Shari'a* Court of Acre, *PD,* vol. 9, p. 1193. Parts of the said judgment are quoted by Goitein and Ben-Shemesh, pp. 242-5; cf. Vitta, pp. 123-4, 129-30.
15. This figure includes the 31,000 inhabitants of the Little Triangle, which was incorporated into Israel by the Rhodes Armistice Agreement in 1949.
16. In other words, nearly half of the Muslims were born in the State of Israel.
17. The data are based on the following sources: *Census Publication No. 17,* pp. XXIX, XL, 3, 6, 43-5; *DCPI,* p. 58; *Vital Stats. 1965; 1966*, p. 18; *Vital Stats. 1967; 1968*, pp. 6, 36, 105; *SAI*, 1970, No. 21, pp. 63, 69, 85; *SAP 1944-45*; *GMBCS*, 1948; Layish, *Changes,* pp. 2-6; Ben-Amram; Stendel; Shidlovsky, pp. 1-14; Ben-Porath, p. 13 *seq.*
18. *Census Publication No. 17,* pp. 11-12, 18-19. The rural population in Galilee includes also Beduin.
19. *Ibid.*, pp. LVI, LVII, 74 *seq.*; Ben-Porath, p. 59 *seq.; NzDS,* p. 13; Cohen, pp. 30, 34, 38; Rosenfeld, *Peasants,* p. 47; Shidlovsky, pp. 15-27; Stendel, pp. 57-9. The proportion of commuters declined in 1967 to 40 per cent; *Labour Force, 1963-1967*, p. 23.
20. Cohen, pp. 21, 24. Only one resident of the Little Triangle village of Bint al-Ḥudūd, studied by Cohen, migrated to town in the ten years last preceding the study *(ibid.*, p. 52). See *NzDS*, pp. 14-15; Ben-Porath, p. 67; Layish, *Changes*, pp. 4-5; Stendel, pp. 59-62.

21. See Rosenfeld, *Change and Conversation,* pp. 208-9.
22. In recent publications of the Central Bureau of Statistics, these two villages are treated as urban settlements, the criterion being size of population.
23. Ben-Amram, p. 22.
24. See Ben-Porath, pp. 20-4; *NzDS,* pp. 40, 57.
25. Cohen, p. 35. See also *ibid.*, pp. 41, 47.
26. Ben-Porath, p. 24. This rate of participation of Arab women in the labour force in 1967 ranged from 7 per cent for those with 0-4 years' schooling to 40 per cent for those with nine years' schooling. See *Labour Force, 1963-1967*, pp. 16-17.
27. See Ben-Porath, pp. 28-9, 33; Cohen, pp. 34-6, 50: Rosenfeld. *Peasants*, pp. 67, 192-4; *NzDS,* pp. 54, 57, 69.
28. Women of Baqa al-Gharbiyya in the Little Triangle were unwilling to work in the local canning factory (together with men), preferring to work in agriculture or take jobs outside the village. Only five Arab women worked in a factory in Upper Nazareth in 1965 (none of them married); *NzDS*, pp. 57, 69, 70.
29. In the years 1960-65 630 vocational courses were held, attended by some 9,000 women, and a women's dressmaking co-operative was set up in Nazareth. See Katsab. See also Rosenfeld, *Peasants*, pp. 198-9, 209-10.
30. See Ben-Porath, pp. 56-7, 66-8; Cohen, pp. 39, 49; Rosenfeld, *Peasants,* pp. 167-8.
31. The share of the wife of the Muslim family head was greater than that of her Christian counterpart: 5.6 per cent as against 2.4 per cent; but the contribution of Christian girls to the family income was considerably greater than that of Muslim girls owing to different attitudes of the two communities to the gainful employment of girls, the high proportion of Christian women teachers and the different age structures of the two communities. *NzDS,* pp. 164-70.
32. Ben-Porath, pp. 24-6; Ben-Amram, p. 22; *NzDS,* pp. 39, 40, 57, 143, 165-6, 170.
33. *Census Publication No. 17,* pp. XLIII-XLV, 50; *SAI,* 1970, No. 21, p. 561; Ben-Porath, pp. 18-19; Stendel, pp. 69-71. Interviewee Su'ād Qaramān said that the liberation of woman would be achieved by education and the acquisition of voational skills, which would make her economically independent.
34. Unless otherwise indicated, the data on the fragmentation of the extended family and the analysis of its causes are based on Rosenfeld, *Peasants,* pp. 21-45, 74-92, 142-54; *idem, Recent Changes*, pp. 21-30; *idem, Change and Conservation,* pp. 208-17; Cohen, pp. 50-9, 108; *NzDS,* pp. 146-8.

35. In one of the villages studied in 1944 in a survey of five Muslim villages, only one-third of the sons left their father's houses after their marriages. Rosenfeld, *Peasants*, p. 78, quotes that survey.
36. Cohen apparently includes among the nuclear families those independent families which maintain separate households but continue for a time to live under roof. The proportion of such families was 9 per cent; Cohen, pp. 58-9. In the five Muslim villages studied in 1944, nuclear families were 56 per cent of the total number of families; Cohen, p. 51, Table 6.
37. This includes 8 per cent of married couples without children and 3 per cent of unmarried persons living alone, *NzDS*, p. 148.
38. If commuting eventually led to urbanization, this undoubtedly accelerated the passage from the extended to the nuclear family.
39. Granott, pp. 205-6.
40. Layish, *Absentees*, pp. 191-2. Cohen found that all the landless families at Bint al-Ḥudūd were nuclear families; see Cohen, pp. 50, 53.
41. See Baer, pp. 59-61.
42. See Rosenfeld, *Peasants*, pp. 116, 137; Cohen, p. 93; Marx, *Bedouin*, pp. 111-13; *idem, Marriage Patterns*, pp. 397-8.
43. Rosenfeld, *Peasants*, pp. 209-11.
44. *AI*, vol. 8(1962), Nos. 1-2, p. 4.
45. See Rosenfeld, *Peasants*, pp. 67-8; Cohen, pp. 126, 135.
46. The author was present on such an occasion at the *Shari'ā* Court of Ṭayyiba on May 21, 1971. The girl, who was not yet 17, said that her parents, and especially her mother, were putting pressure on her to marry her maternal uncle, and *qāḍī* ordered them to desist. See *JfQ2*, p. 310: no. 480-f.23/58 (the daughter, aged 13, had been married against her will and had run away from home). Su'ād Qaramān knew of several cases of girls committing suicide because they were told to marry someone they did not want. Shaykh Mūsā al-Ṭabarī instructed that it first be ascertained that the bride indeed agreed to marry the groom. *AI*, vol. 8(1962), Nos. 1-2, p. 13.
47. Cohen, pp. 78-88. In one case, a woman committed suicide because she was not allowed to marry the man of her choice, a member of another clan; *ibid.*, p. 123. See also *NzI4*, p. 231: no. 2/28-f.94/67 (the couple had married without the permission of the parents; a month later, the fathers gave their consent).

9

Muslim Women and Developing Societies

In an organically developing society, law reflects the social conditions under which it grows and crystallizes.[1] In traditional Muslim society, an equilibrium exists between the social and the legal status of women because Muslim family law is adapted to the structure of the patrilineal and patriarchal family. The salient features of the extended family, *viz.*, the supremacy of men, patrilineal relationships, patrilocal residence and endogamous customs, find exact legal expression in Muslim matrimonial law, with a few deviations induced by Muḥammad's legal norms, which were designed to protect women. The basic cause of women's inferiority is thus social custom, in part legitimized by the *shari'ā*: women's low legal status is chiefly attributable to the factors shaping the Arab extended family. In order to maintain a dynamic balance between social and legal status, the family law should be capable of constant adaptation to changing social conditions. Late Ottoman legislation was the first modern attempt to maintain such a balance. The objects of the Ottoman Family Rights Law were limited and relatively moderate because the changes in the structure of the family and the status of women were only in their beginnings, and reforms in the status of women could be introduced within the existing legal system.[2] Any attempt to assign to women artificially, from above, a legal status not consonant with their social status disturbs the equilibrium between the two spheres, creates tensions and usually does not stand the test of reality, for social custom is stronger than law, even *shar'ī* law. Muḥammad's reforms, intended to improve the legal status of women, were circumvented or ridiculed because they did not reflect women's social status at that period. Thus, for example, the regulation that a woman inherits, which originated in urban society, does not fit a tribal society in which only male agnates (*'aṣ abāt*) inherit.[3]

In a non-Islamic state, such as, Israel, the balance between the legal and the social status of Muslim women has been drastically upset because developments on the two planes, the social and the legal, have not come about through internal growth, but are mainly the reuslt of direct contact with a Western society in all its aspects. Owing to the dual, religious-secular, legal system obtaining in Israel, that imbalance, too, has two-fold dimensions: on the one hand, the social status of women today is generally better than their status under religious law, but on the other hand—and this is the crux of the problem—it is still far from catching up with their legal status under secular law. An anomaly has thus been created in that social conditions, which normally change slowly and over a long period, are required to adapt instantly to a legal framework shaped in accordance with the needs of a modern society and imposed on Muslim society from above.

Muslim women in Israel are at a transitional stage. On the one hand, there are the usual manifestations of female inferiority in traditional society: marriages of minor girls and polygamy; deprivation of the right to dower, succession and custody of the children; residence at the home of the husband's family; obedience to the husband, confinement to the house and restriction of freedom of movement and social contacts; unilateral divorce, and so forth. These phenomena are contrary not only to secular law but in part also to express provisions of the Qur'ān. The causes of the deprivation of women's rights are social inferiority, owing to which they are ignorant of their rights or incapable of exercising them, and social custom, which in day-to-day reality still takes precedence over religious percepts[4]; this custom is mainly operative in the domain of kinship and property relations within the extended family.

But beside these phenomena there are significant indications of a change in the status of women: the age of marriage of the bride has risen, marriages of minor girls have become considerably less frequent and polygamy has become rate; women are now paid the whole or part of the dower into their own hands; the dower is changing its function, and becoming a means to prevent divorce or to assure the economic position of divorced women, and there is even the emergent phenomenon of marriages without dower (which may be to the advantage of women); women strive for a dwelling separate from the residence of the husband's family and sometimes in their home locality, availing themselves of the device of the stipulation inserted in the marriage contract; they frequently leave the house against the will of the husband, work away from home, earn money and support themselves, and their children; they renounce their right to maintenance and are not afraid of being declared rebellious; they exercise their right of succession and enjoy great freedom in disposing of property; they enjoy their *shar'ī* right to custody and their secular-legal right to guardianship of their children; most divorces are by mutual agreement of the parties; the practice is spreading of compensating the wife or paying her maintenance beyond the waiting-period (*'idda*) in return for her consent to the divorce; in many cases, the wife is the active party in the dissolution of the marriage, using various devices to obtain her freedom. The change cannot always be appraised in quantitative terms, but there can be no doubt that it is on a significant scale. Some of the phenomena are not new, but it seems that they were not so frequent and marked in the past as they are today. The change is more pronounced and comprehensive in towns than in villages and more in mixed than in Arab towns, and more in the villages of the Little Triangle than in those of other regions. Incipient changes are noticeable also in the status of Beduin women, especially in Galilee.

The intervention of the Knesset has undoubtedly made an important contribution to the improvement of the social status of women. Its impact is mainly due to the penal sanction attached to several enactments. Clear indications of a deterrent effect are applications to the court for permission to divorce one's wife without her consent and in a few cases for the marriage of a girl under 17 or for polygamy; the payment of compensation to a divorced woman in return for her consent to the divorce; and the conversion of traditional grounds for polygamy—as far as an inclination for this type of marriage still exists—into frequent grounds for divorce (especially in the Little Triangle villages). The fact that men resort to various devices in order to circumvent Israeli legislation is also significant in this connection. The impact of substantive legislation is especially noticeable in the matter of guardianship and of the agreement of the parties to the jurisdiction of the *sharī'ā* court under the Israeli Succession Law.

At the same time, it is doubtful that secular legislation is the main cause of the improvement in the position of women in matters of personal status, since there are numerous instances of circumvention of that legislation by various means. This is mainly true for marriages of minor girls, divorces against the wife's will and the application of the Ottoman Law of Succession to *mulk* and movables under the Women's Equal Rights Law. Secular legislation is circumvented in those social strata which cannot live up to the norms prescribed by the Knesset, just as it is usual to circumvent the *shar'ī* norms; but whereas Muḥammad's reforms are supported by toothless ethical sanctions, the Knesset's reforms are bound up with legal and penal sanctions, which is why more sophisticated devices are required to circumvent them.[5]

Moreover, the Knesset, in its eagerness to impose on the Muslim public progressive norms, tailored to Israeli society, has sometimes harmed more than helped Muslim women. The ban on polygamy has caused an increase in the divorce rate and reduced the opportunities for levirate marriages (by which the dead man's brother marries his widow), which are the structural solution for widows wishing to remain united with their children at the house of the husband's family[6]; and the intervention of the welfare officer, who is guided by the principle of the best interest of the child, may impair the status of a woman as a natural guardian of her children when that principle is translated into traditional terms. The sporadic character of the secular legislation has led in many cases to a disturbance of delicate balances in the Muslim family. The accidental, unsystematic mixture of elements of two legal systems, religious and secular, based on completely different social norms, has created distortions and anomalies which have sometimes shaken the legal frame of that family. Thus, for example, the restriction of the husband's freedom of *ṭalāq* without his being given grounds for judicial dissolution or a good defense to the charge of divorce against the wife's will in special circumstances, such as when she is rebellious, has created a practically intolerable situation because the husband cannot divorce the wife without her consent whereas the wife has a long series of definite grounds for judicial dissolution without need of the husband's consent. The husband cannot protect himself against such a predicament by taking a second wife because polygamy is forbidden, too. As a result, the traditional equilibrium in the sphere of divorce is disturbed (as indeed the Knesset had intended it to be), but a new equilibrium has not been created, even on the basis of equality of the sexes.[7] Compensation to the wife for her consent to the divorce is one of the manifestations of this new situation.[8] The two prohibitions have also disturbed the traditional equilibrium between the mutual rights and obligations of the spouses, for *ṭalāq* and polygamy were means to enforce the wife's obedience, and in this case also a new balance, based on progressive social norms, has not taken the place of the old. In sum, the importance of the secular legislation lies mainly in increasing the wife's legal security by the creation of a mechanism enabling her to realize her rights through the threat of penal or other legal sanctions. The mere existence of such a mechanism, even if it is not frequently resorted to, may to a certain extent deter potential offenders.

It seems that the changes in the social position of women in matters of personal status are mainly attributable to economic, cultural, social and other factors: their joining the labour force, especially their penetration into occupations requiring education and specialized skills; the spread of education among girls; the social, vocational and cultural activities of State and public bodies among women; the development of the villages and the raising of the standard of living; the transition from the extended to the nuclear family; the absorption, of modern concepts of the institution of marriage, and so on. In this connection, Israeli legislation is important as a medium for imparting the normative values of Israeli society to Muslim society. The impact of these factors is particularly noticeable in the mixed towns because of the direct contact with Israeli society.[9] The educational factor is operative in the comparatively young age-groups of women who have acquired their education in the State of Israel. This is clearly reflected in marriage contracts drawn up in recent years, *viz.*, in dower practices and stipulations. On the other hand, this factor has so far not been noticeable in other matters of personal status, such as succession and divorce, which by the nature of things relate to older women. The exogamous type of marriage no doubt makes it easier for women to exercise their rights in various matrimonial matters because it leaves them free from pressures arising out of blood-relationship and family loyalty. It seems, on the other hand, that endogamy does not present very serious obstacles to women who are aware of their rights and not prepared to forgo them.

Muslim women do not tend to settle matrimonial matters before a civil court although their legal position is incomparably better there than before a *shari'ā* court both as regards the substantive law and the rules of evidence and procedure. As stated, in 1965 the jurisdiction of *shari'ā* courts in matters of succession was reduced from exclusive to concurrent. Women and the Muslim public in general, prefer the more intimate atmosphere of the *shari'ā* court (the proceedings of which are conducted in Arabic) and the *qāḍī*, who is close to them in his religious and social outlook and firmly rooted in the day-to-day life of his community, to an alien, impersonal civil court, which is identified with the government authority, and a judge remote from the Muslim environment.[10]

Thus, there exist in Israel, side by side, women deprived of their rights by both secular and religious law and women who enjoy their rights to a greater or lesser degree. This is, as stated, a transitional phase, and there can be no doubt that, as the factors of change become more powerful, the gap between women's social status and their legal status under secular law will narrow. Paradoxically, many of Muḥammad's reforms and ethical commands, as in the matter of polygamy and divorce and of women's right to dower and succession, are for the first time given significant effect at a time when the *shari'ā* is in retreat and has lost much of its power in society and state, particularly in Israel. The reason for this is that the religious norms Muḥammad sought to impose on his believers were unsuitable for the patrilineal and patriarchal family and society and are more in keeping with the nuclear family and the modern concept of the social status of women.[11] Thus, for example, it is only within the framework of the nuclear family that the *shar'ī* principles, basic to modern Israeli legislation, of the separation of property, and of women's capacity to own and dispose of property, can be realized.

The creation of a new equilibrium between the social and the legal status of women depends largely on the *qāḍīs*, who are competent to interpret both religious and secular law. As far as can be judged by declared attitudes, most *qāḍīs* acknowledge the need to adapt the law of personal status to the changes in the structure of the family and in the position of women, and some even challenge the inflexible *shari'ā*. They are guided by humanitarian motives, the most typical manifestation of which is the doctrine of *maṣlaḥa*, the public interest, and by the principle that innovations are permissible to the extent that—as, for example, in the matter of compensation to a divorced woman for her consent to the divorce, they are not opposed by express prohibitions in, the textual sources of religious law. Although the *qāḍīs* denounce arbitrary divorces and one of them even suggested negating their validity, they are not prepared to go far in this matter because the *ṭalāq* is rooted in the Qur'ān. Their attitude is generally liberal and favourable to the woman: it is marked by pragmatism. On the other hand, they find themselves in a conscientious conflict where religious and secular law clash.[12]

The most important and meaningful measure of the *qāḍīs* attitude regarding the status of women is found in their judgments, which, indeed, sometimes reveal a gap between the declared positions of some of them and their day-to-day practice.[13] Ambivalence is the most characteristic trait of their approach to religious and secular law. They usually interpret religious law in strict adherence to the *taqlīd* ("imitation," the unquestioning acceptance of the Sunnite orthodox schools of law), regardless of the consequences for the woman involved. This formal approach is to her advantage where there is a question of realizing her *shar'ī* rights, such as dower, maintenance or the custody of the children, but to her detriment where there is a question of a man's rights, such as obedience, guardianship or *ṭalāq*, where she renounces any right (such as her share in an inheritance) or where she is to be deprived of a right on *shar'ī* grounds based on traditional norms (as by her disqualification from custody on account of her marriage to a stranger). By their formal approach, the *qāḍīs* assist in depriving women of their right to dower in exchange marriages; they make no normative distinction between types of divorce with their various legal effects: in matters of custody and guardianship, they are guided by religious-legal norms, which are not always consistent with the best interest of the child. Moreover, some *qāḍīs* adhere so staunchly to the Ḥanafi school as to deliberately refrain from applying provisions of the Ottoman Family Rights Law because they deviate from the teachings of that school, such as, for instance, provisions permitting dissolution on the grounds of a defect or illness of the husband, non-payment of maintenance to the wife of an absent husband or discord between the spouses. Some uphold the rigorous classification of irregular and void marriages, consciously or unconsciously disregarding reforms introduced by the Ottoman legislator.

But beside the aforesaid approach, there are many instances of decisions other than in accordance with the rigid *shar'ī* norm. The *qāḍīs* most customary method of reaching a desirable solution without conflicting with religious law is by using their personal authority (sometimes through middlemen) in order to reconcile the parties and give the compromise arrived at the force of a judgment; this method does not involve the application of religious law. This practice is most noticeable in matters of maintenance, obedience and divorce, and it seems that the principal concern of *qāḍīs* is the preservation of the marriage. The institutionalized organ of arbitration in reaching judicial decisions is the family council within the meaning of article 130 of the Family Rights Law. But there are also express deviations from the teachings of the Ḥanafī school. Thus, some *qāḍīs* add to the grounds for judicial dissolution the non-payment of maintenance, injury, cruelty and the husband's imprisonment, which are recognized by schools other than the Ḥanafī (and provide legitimation for modern legislation in Arab countries), and most *qāḍīs* confirm stipulations inserted in the marriage contract even if they mean a change in the matrimonial rights or obligations of one of the parties, such as the establishment of the marital dwelling in the wife's home locality; in fact, it is through the active assistance of the *qāḍīs* that the stipulation in the marriage contract has become an efficient instrument for improving the status of women.

There are *qāḍīs* who award the *radd* to the widow or hold that the dissolution of the marriage of the wife of an absent husband is a revocable divorce, again in deviation from the teachings of the Ḥanafī school. The flexibility of the *qāḍīs* as regards the different schools of law has probably something to do with the fact that most Israeli Muslims belong to the Shāfi'ī school (the Ḥanbalī school is also represented—in the Little Triangle villages); at any rate, there is evidence that *sharī'ā* courts were already giving judgments in accordance with Shāfi'ī teachings in the Mandate period.[14] By using the mechanism of the *talfīq* (selective combination of legal doctrines) in their decisions, the *qāḍīs* have scored impressive achievements, some not inferior, perhaps even superior, to those attained in Arab countries by means of secular legislation.

The sanctifying role of the *qāḍīs* is crucial in the process of Islamization of social custom, both traditional (among the Beduin) and modern (in the cities), which still continues in Muslim society. This is so, for instance, in the matter of token dower, marriages without dower, compensation to the divorced wife, and compensation to the ex-husband on the remarriage of his former wife. The process occurs through a compromise between the customary and the *shar'ī* norms, and is aided by the mechanism of arbitration.[15] There is, of course, a close connection between custom and the social motivation underlying the principle of the *maṣlaḥa* (public interest).

Ambivalence is also conspicuous in the *qāḍīs* attitude toward Israeli legislation. On the one hand, there are those who ignore the Knesset's intervention in matters such as age of marriage offenses, polygamy and divorce against the wife's will, most of them do not use the wide discretion given them by the Knesset as to permission for divorce against the wife's will and polygamous marriages (in so far as the court is resorted to in these matters), and consider themselves bound by the accepted *shar'ī* norms as to marriage and divorce; permission is granted almost automatically or the divorce, marriage of a girl under age or polygamous marriage is registered *ex post facto* without any reference to the question of criminality. The *qāḍīs*, contrary to the expectations of the Knesset, do not recognize the bride's being under the age of 17 as a ground for dissolution.[16] Some misinterpret and misapply substantive provisions, as in the matter of guardianship or succession. Lastly, there are those who, consciously or unconsciously, assist in circumventing secular legislation, as by using the mechanism of suspended repudiation for the purposes of divorce against the wife's will.

On the other hand, there are many indications that secular legislation has made an impact on the *qāḍīs*. Some rely on it explicitly in their decisions, adopting its principles even when these conflict with the *shar'ī* view, as in the matter of the recognition of a woman as a natural guardian of her children or the appointment of a guardian with reference to the best interest of the child. Some frequently have recourse to the welfare officer in this connection. Some display a keen awareness of the ban on divorce against the wife's will and the ban on polygamy, warn the husband against committing an offense and when it has been committed, although confirming the divorce or marriage *ex post facto*, call the wife's attention to her right to bring a criminal charge against the husband.

The *qāḍīs* perplexity and vacillation between religious and secular law is sometimes expressed in simultaneous application of substantive elements of both legal systems, despite material contradictions between them. Thus, there are those who recognize the status of a woman as a natural guardian of her children by virtue of secular legislation and at the same time appoint the grandfather guardian over them on the ground that he is the natural guardian according to religious law. There are those who harn the husband against divorcing the wife against her will and at the same time recognize his *shar'ī* right to divorce her unilaterally. This ambivalent attitude has an ideological basis in the declared positions of the *qāḍīs*. They are not opposed to the Knesset's intervention in matters of personal status so long as no encroachment on the *sharī'ā* is involved. Some of them would even welcome further reforms of a procedural or penal nature, such as additional defenses to the charge of divorce against the wife's will or of polygamy in the case of a rebellious, sick or barren wife, with a view to creating a new equilibrium between the social and the legal status of women. There are even those who believe that a secular penal sanction can be used in matters of marriage and divorce to reinforce a *shar'ī* norm supported by ethical sanction lacking deterrent effect. But there are also *qāḍīs* who do not shrink from calling for secular legislation of an expressly substantive character—for example, in order to ensure the subsistence of a divorced woman—as a matter of *siyāsa* (policy), a governmental regulation designed to supplement the *sharī'ā*.[17]

In conclusion, it would seem that, considering the theoretically immutable character of religious law and the difficulty of imposing secular legislation on religious courts, the *qāḍīs* have, nonetheless, made an important contribution to the improvement of the position of women in matters of personal status.[18]

Notes and References

1. See Smith, p. 25.
2. See Anderson, *Islamic Law,* p. 26.
3. See Goitein and Ben-Shemesh, pp. 142-3; Fyzee, pp. 380 *seq.*, 411, 416-17.
4. See Baer, p. 34 *seq.*
5. Cf. Dirks, pp. 146, 176 *seq.*; *MH.*, vol. 21 (1971), p. 459.
6. See Rosenfeld, *Peasants,* pp. 40-2. Cf. Goitein and Ben-Shemesh, pp. 136-7.
7. The ban on polygamy without radically tackling divorce might, in Anderson's opinion, harm women more than help them. See

Anderson, *Patriarchal Family,* p. 231.

8. The husband's stipulation in the marriage contract that he shall be permitted to divorce the wife against her will or that their dwelling shall be in his home locality is likewise significant in this connection.
9. Cf. Woodsmall, p. 86.
10. A Muslim District Judge has recently been appointed in Nazareth, but it is too early to assess the significance of this fact in relation to the matter under reference.
11. Cf. Coulson, *History,* pp. 219-20; *idem, Conflicts,* pp. 97-8; *idem, Succession,* pp. 135-6.
12. For a more detailed discussion see Layish, *Qāḍīs*, pp. 240-51, 255-72.
13. Cf. Anderson, *Africa*, pp. 69, 321.
14. Shaykh Ṭāhir Ḥamād, *AI,* vol. 4 (1956), No. 1, p. 8. Most of the *qāḍīs*, at a conference in 1966, adopted the position of the Shafi'ī school concerning relationship by suckling as an impediment to marriage (*AI*, vol. 10(1966), Nos. 1-2, p. 83) and Shaykh Ḥusnī al-Zu'bī relied on a collection of *fatwās* of a Shafi'ī *muftī* in support of his attitude with regard to birth control (*AI*, vol. 9(1964), Nos. 3-4, p. 11). Cf. Anderson, *Dissolution*, p. 271; *idem, Africa*, pp. 30, 55-6, 79, 110, 146, 280.
15. For a more detailed discussion see Layish, *Custom,* pp. 402-9. Cf. Anderson, *Africa,* pp. 211-12, 218.
16. Cf. Coulson, *Conflicts,* pp. 115-16; el-Naqeb, pp. 202-3.
17. See Layish, *Qāḍīs*, pp. 255-8; Schacht, p. 54; Coulson, *Succession*, p. 137. The *qāḍīs* practice of relying on the welfare services of the State in judgments for maintenance contributes, indirectly and unintentionally, to the disruption of the balanced system of rights and obligations underlying the traditional family.
18. Cf. Tedeschi, p. 229.

10

Women's Role and Status in Different Communities

It might be assumed that in traditional societies the status of women as seen by their communities and the way in which they view themselves largely coincide. One does not expect the degree of conflict between society's expectations of women and young women's own aspirations, which is fairly common in modern society. It must be admitted, however, that while a good deal is known about the status of women in Asia, very little is known of the ambitions or frustrations of women themselves. An anthropologist in Bangladesh had the utmost difficulty in eliciting opinions from women, so unaccustomed were they to being asked for their views.

Definition of Status

The term *status* has been discarded by some analysts as being too general; it is used here to convey its customary meaning both of standing and of ascribed respect, essentially abstract concepts understood in all communities. *Role,* by contrast, implies concrete activities. Status is also held to signify the degree to which women have authority or power in the domestic and/or public domain (Sanday, 1974). Authority usually implies the right to control the use of joint resources and the lives of others, while power is defined as the ability to influence decisions made by those with authority. The status of women in Asia is more closely linked to their exercise of power than to their much rarer exercise of authority. Stoler (1977) prefers the more specific terms *female autonomy* and *social power* to status. She defines *female autonomy* as the extent to which women exercise control over their own lives and returns from their labour *vis-a-vis* men. *Social power* signifies the extent to which women exercise control over the lives of others outside the domestic sphere.

In considering status in its broadest sense, one has to beware of the discrepancy between the elite model for behaviour and custom which tradition holds the actual behaviour which, especially for lower socio-economic groups, may diverge considerably from the ideal, usually for economic reasons. In northern Taiwan, for example, in the traditional and most valued form of marriage a mature girl comes to the home of her affines as a bride. In the minor and formerly more common form of marriage, a young girl is brought up with her future spouse by her affines and married at maturity (Wolf, A., 1975).

It is not always easy for an outsider to discern the real, as opposed to the traditional and formal, status of a woman in her own family and community. A woman may and often does have a prominent position within her own family but a very minor one in her community. In Korea, women are officially and formally denigrated, but are in fact often self-assertive and highly valued (Brandt, 1971). Formal indicators point to complete male dominance. It is unseemly, bordering on indecent, for open affection to be shown by husband to wife in public; to support one's wife in a dispute with one's mother is impious. Men are supposed to, and usually do, control finances, make important decisions and represent the family in all official contexts. Women have no formal role in administrative or political matters and do not attend village meetings, even as spectators. In reality, however, an atmosphere of harmony is discernible in many homes, and male superiority is asserted in proportion to the formality of the occasion. In one village studied, several women are more competent than their husbands. Village women do not have subservient personalities (Brandt, *loc. cit.*). It is easy for the casual observer to be deceived by stereotyped behaviour. A husband known as a cuckold throughout the village was none the less followed at a respectful distance by his errant wife on the way to their field, and she carried the heavier load.

Even an anthropologist thoroughly versed in the culture of the group he is studying, well acquainted with individuals over a number of years, may still find it difficult to ascertain correctly whether a given form of behaviour is determined by cultural norms or by individual personality (Jacobson, 1978). In the Mysore village studied by Srinivas (1976), dominance of one spouse over the other varied according to the strength of personality of the partners, a finding with which most anthropologists would agree.

Economic Contribution and Status

Many studies have drawn correlations between the function or role of women in production and their status in society. In China, "forced seclusion, imposed ignorance, lack of educational opportunities, discrimination against working women and repressive marriage customs inevitably resulted in women's economic dependence in traditional society" (Yang, 1959). Economic dependence implied inferior status. Now the rural New Territories of Hong Kong show consistently rising status for young women, based on the availability of jobs, especially in city factories, and an independent income (Baker, 1968).

In a pioneer study on women in development, Boserup (1970) concludes that where population is sparse and swidden (shifting cultivation) the basis of the economy, women perform most of the work; with greater density of population and plough agriculture, men do more work than women, and where land is irrigated and intensively farmed, both put in a great deal of hard work. Boserup associates the first and last categories with higher status for women than the second. How far can these conclusions be applied to Asia? On the whole they can. In tribal societies, women are esteemed members of their hunting/collecting or swidden communities. In the former, the roots and other forest produce gathered by women provide the regular staple food of the community, but the supply of meat from the hunting of men is sporadic. In family decisions, women have an equal say with their husbands, and often a considerable role in community affairs, especially in those groups where men are customarily absent for weeks or even months, formerly headhunting, more recently on expeditions for collecting jungle produce for sale. In both such groups, women's contribution to subsistence is essential.

Women in early India supervised agriculture, animal husbandry and vegetable gardens. In modern Asia, however, women do not generally enjoy high status in regions of settled, dryland cultivation, thus conforming to Boserup's second category where men do more work than women.

Women enjoyed relatively high status in early China when it has been assumed that they were food-gatherers (Lang, 1968) and in the early stages of agriculture and pottery-making before the invention of the plough and the potter's wheel gave these tasks to men. Indeed, burial patterns during the Neolithic Ch'ing-lian-kiang culture (the earliest in the lower Yangtze in Kiangsu, Anhwei and (Chekiang) seem to indicate that society was organized in clans, was possibly matriarchal and there was no sexual division of labour (Shih, 1974). To the north the slightly later Liu-lin culture of southern Shantung and north Kiangsu, however, appeared to be patriarchal and family-based. The *Biographies of Women,* ranging from peasant women to the wives of emperors and covering the legendary period to the late Han in the first century B.C., indicate that women had greater freedom of movement and participated more in work outside the home in the earlier period than subsequently (O'Hara, 1971).

The position of women deteriorated under the feudalism of Chou times among the nobility, but peasant women were still comparatively free. As feudal structure came to be replaced by centralized bureaucracy under the empire and family structure increasingly followed the upper-class patriarchal model which was enshrined in the teachings of Confucius, the poor and middle classes observed as best they could the manners of the upper classes; women became wholly subservient to their fathers, their husbands and subsequently in theory to their sons.* Since

* Women were not wholly without sympathy in their circumscribed Lives. Li Ju-chen's traveller, Lin Chih-yang, reached the *Land of Women,* where traditional sex roles were reversed. He had to undergo the agony of ear-piercing and foot-binding, and was meticulously prepared to await the pleasure of the female ruler of the country (from the *Ching-hua Yuan,* written in the mid-Ch'ing dynasty). (Quoted by Brandauer, 1977).

the poor were unable to afford the cost of divorce and a second marriage, their wives received more considerate treatment than those of the wealthier. Women achieved more freedom in Kwangtung, Kwangsi and Fukien than in the north and participated more regularly in field work (Lang, 1968).

In the rice-dominated economy of Japan, rural women have enjoyed greater freedom in the past, particularly in the southwest where village structure was of a more egalitarian type, ruled by consensus. The position of the bride was more secure and the status of women in general higher than in the northeast, where the vertically oriented *dozoku* structure predominated (Johnson, 1967). A more egalitarian marital relationship characterized the southwest, particularly the fishing villages where men were absent at sea and women assumed day-to-day authority; they maintained relations with their own parents, resulting in a greater tendency towards bilateral kinship structure. With the onset of modernization at the beginning of the Meiji period (1868) the status of women in rural areas became progressively lower since samurai (Confucian) norms spread to other groups. This was reinforced by the new uniformity of behaviour which resulted from service in the army and from compulsory education which stressed traditional values. None the less, fishing villages were too poor to attempt to improve their status by the adoption of upper-class ways (de Vos and Wagatsuma, 1973b).

Women have always played an important role in production on Japanese farms. The difference in status between farming and fishing villages relates not so much to function as to the authority which fishermen's wives must exercise during the increasingly long absences of their husbands. The farmer's wife can communicate with her husband in the city, but the fisherman's wife cannot reach her husband at sea.

When one comes to consider Boserup's third category, that of irrigated land where women are as much involved as men and where their status should be correspondingly high, the immense variety of custom in Asia conflicts with her scheme. In southest Asia women work in padi cultivation as intensively as men, but not, if they can afford it, in Bangladesh or Bengal. In lower socio-economic groups in north India women must work in the fields; they predominate among landless labourers in some areas of the south. Nowhere do they enjoy the equality of women padi workers in southeast Asia. Women perform 70 per cent of all farm work in Japan, but nominally, at least, they seek the decisions of their husbands, even when they are working in distant cities. It has been cautiously concluded that female production is a *necessary* but not *sufficient* condition for the development of female status (Sanday, 1973); these are no universals in society and culture (Needham, 1973).

A study comparing pastoral and agricultural societies in the Balkans reveals that pastoralism requires solidarity among male members of a co-operative kin group, while women have low status (Denich, 1974). It would be interesting to compare the status of women among nomadic and migratory groups in south Asia. In nomadic groups, the whole family moves together; in migratory groups only the men move. The health and levels of education of family members left in the village must be higher than among nomads. How does the necessity of making decisions during the six-month absence of men affect the position of women? Is there any difference today in the position of women among China's pastoralists of minority groups and among neighbouring Han practising settled agriculture?

Murdock (1949) believed that ownership of land enhanced female status, but even where land is inherited matrilineally, actual power may reside with men—with a woman's uncle or brother, rather than with her husband or herself. As matrilineal Nayar households in Kerala, India, which shared the proceeds from land owned and worked jointly, came to be divided and eventually replaced by nuclear households, there were changes in the status of women (Fuller, 1976). Women still have important rights over property, but men bequeath property to their own children, no longer to their sisters' children. "Today husbands dominate their wives in a way which was intrinsically impossible when they did not live together, but men also seem to have greater power over women than they used to" (Fuller, *loc. cit.*). Tambiah (1973) considers ownership of land by owmen conducive to bilateral kinship structure and ambilocality, both of which appear associated with higher status for women. Murdock's theory appears to hold for Asia. While women rarely held land in traditional China or today in Korea ("daughters inherit nothing but personal memories"—Brandt, 1971) or the south Asian subcontinent, women often hold land in southeast Asia, where society is more egalitarian.

Access to opportunities for production has been shown to have bearing on the standing of women in society. In north India, many agricultural tasks are male preserves, while in Islamic communities in India and Bangladesh women do not generally work in the fields. In south India, however, female agricultural labour is common and indeed, dominant in the rice-producing region of Tanjore. Greater value is attributed to women in the south than in the north (Leonard and Leonard, 1981).

It has been suggested that women have lower status than men because their tasks are mainly subsistence-oriented, while men work on cash crops (Boserup, 1970). This appears to apply more to Africa than to Asia, where women have been associated with men in work on cash crops. Others believe that it is not so much subsistence tasks as lack of ownership of the means of production which brings lower status (Castillo, 1976a).

In Java, women gain autonomy and economic independence through the flexibility of the sources of income available to them. Here it is not just the type of production, but the productive relations involved which are important for social power (Stoler, 1977). Female autonomy and social power are functions of their access to strategic resources within the domestic and social sphere, but economic independence of the poor does not mean social power. It may be asked whether these aspects of status will not become increasingly important as size of plots become smaller and less able to meet the subsistence needs of families. However, access to these strategic resources is independent of sexual distinctions, despite the clear division of labour between the sexes in rural Java (Stoler, *loc. cit.*).

The relation between earning capacity, status and autonomy within the family in India depends to a great extention the status of a woman's earning activity (Indian Council of Social Science Research [ICSSR], 1975). Women employed as wage labourers or unskilled and menial workers do not enjoy higher status, but women in high prestige jobs may. The value which society places on different tasks is important; many observers have noted that the agricultural tasks performed by women are invariably of lower status than those performed by men. Men usually plough and control draft animals, whereas women more often carry out operations by hand (Boserup, 1970).

In southeast Asia, women commonly participate in petty marketing, but enterprises involving the accumulation of capital, both financial and in equipment, are in the hands of men and their activities are more highly regarded. Middlewomen operating between a central Javanese village and Yogyakarta have considerable economic independence, but not economic power (Stoler, 1977). Among poor households, a woman's earnings provide her with an important position within the household economy; among wealthier households such earnings provide her with the material basis for social power (Stoler, *loc. cit.*). Similar conclusions could be reached in Malaysia, particularly in the northeast.

Some believe that women's role in production is less significant in determining her status than is kinship organization. Patrilineal, patriarchal groups invariably confer low actual (though, as in south Asia, sometimes high ideal) status on women, while in matrilineal, matriarchal groups, women are dominant. Bilateral societies range between these extremes. Tribal women in India, for example, are equally productive irrespective of the prevailing kinship pattern, but have authority only in matriarchal groups (Sachchidananda, 1978). Comparison of polyandrous groups in the Himalaya leads to the same conclusion (Nandi, 1977). However, it still seems possible to demonstrate that women in control of the economic returns from their production invariably have higher status than those who are not, irrespective of kinship mode.

Purdah System

Purdah has long been viewed as implying a much inferior status for women. This may perhaps represent a simplistic, western bias. It is true that seclusion automatically reduces a woman's freedom of movement and above all her opportunities for economic independence by means of paid work. In this sense, purdah has an effect similar to footbinding in traditional China. Undoubtedly, the social status of women is low in communities practising purdah. But can it also be concluded that a woman's status in her own home is any lower than that of unveiled women at either socio-economic extreme in her own society, or of women in a comparable socio-economic position in the societies where seclusion is not the norm?

Opportunities for employment are severely restricted in Bangladesh, even at higher levels of education (Martius von Harder, 1977), and in Pakistan, by inadequate provision of separate facilities for women at their place of work. Opportunities for work for rural women in Bangladesh are limited by their inability to move beyond their *baris* (Martius von Harder, *loc. cit.*) although the availability of "portable seclusion" in the form of the *burqa* has offset these restrictions in Pakistan and Bangladesh (Papanek, 1971). The acquisition of knowledge of improved crop processing and household techniques is limited by the fact that the information has to come from men, with whom a village woman cannot have contact (Martius von Harder, 1977). Yet a rural women in seclusion is as fully and usefully occupied as is a woman working in the fields (Khatun and Rani, 1977; Martius von Harder, 1977).

In a broad sense, the purdah system is related to status, since the poor cannot afford to forego income or pay for the extra service required. It is related also to social distance and the maintenance of moral standards, expressed as "separate worlds" and "symbolic shelter" (Papanek, 1971). "In a culture where male pride is a very significant—and very fragile—element of identity and status, the seclusion of women is an important aspect of male control" (Papanek, *loc. cit.*). Muslim purdah does not apply within the immediate kin group, only outside; Punjabi women do not wear the veil in their villages, but only when they go to town. Hindu purdah is based on a set of avoidance rules between a woman and her male affines. However, in an Indian Muslim village women observe purdah before their father-in-law and older brothers-in-law exactly as does a Hindu woman* (Vreede de Stuers, 1968). Seclusion of women arose in Islamic society because of men's distrust of other men, while the Hindu woman was secluded because of men's distrust of her purportedly licentious nature. The *Laws of Manu* state: "If she be chaste, it is because she has not found a proper man, place or opportunity" (Kapadia, 1966).

The "separate worlds" denote the district division of labour, yet a high degree of interdependence in purdah society. "Symbolic shelter" is provided as protection against sexual desire and a potentially hostile world outside the home; dominance and dependency are integral to its operation. Women so sheltered are important demonstrators of status and their behaviour is important in terms of honour and family pride, underlining the male ability to control his environment. Emphasis on female purity stresses the role of procreation (Papanek, 1973).

Hindu avoidance patterns, represented by veiling the face, reduce friction between members of extended families, since a junior bride is invisible to her husband's older brothers, father and uncles and is thus theoretically not sexually competitive with their wives. Equally, since the veil further prevents easy interaction between spouses before a woman's mother-in-law, this most frequent source of conflict is somewhat reduced (Sharma, 1978). All male members of a village in the hill tracts of northern India are considered courtesy kin by women, who must veil themselves and behave circumspectly before all senior to her husband. The low status of a young bride is thus compounded by her inability to approach any senior member of her affinal village—for example a *panchayat* leader—who might be able to redress her wrongs (Sharma, *loc. cit.*).

---

* Hindu avoidance patterns may apply even to the young. When Nirad Chaudhuri was taken to his ancestral village in former East Bengal, "we could never find a house or place where there was not at least one uncle, nephew or cousin. Furthermore at five years old I was the uncle of half a dozen grown-ups. . . . Nothing disappointed me more in 1907 at the age of nine than not to have been permitted to go near a bride, in fact to have been turned out after having sneaked into the room, because her status in relation, to mine was that of daughter-in-law" (Chaudhuri, 1951).

There was no purdah in pre-Muslim times in India, although the defenceless (daughters and widows) might remain within the confines of the home. The ruling classes preferred to veil their women from common sight. Only after the advent of the Muslims, however, was purdah adopted, in imitation of the conquerors, and only in the north and in the Muslim community of Hyderabad, Andhra Pradesh (Altekar, 1959).

It is a matter for speculation why those who adopted Islam in south Asia imposed seclusion on women, while in southeast Asia this did not occur. Dube (1978a) has suggested that seclusion was less likely to be enforced in matrilineal or bilateral societies than in patrilineal groups which subscribed to the notion that women belonged to men. It cannot be said, however, that the purdah ethic was absent in southeast Asia in the past. Isabella Bird (1883), who travelled in the Malay peninsula 100 years ago, wrote, "They seclude their women to a great extent, and under ordinary circumstances the slightest courtesy shown by a European man to a Malay woman would be a deadly insult, and at the sight of a man in the distance the women hastily cover their faces."

Emily Innes (1885), who lived in Malaya where her husband was a government servant from 1876 until 1882, also wrote, "Another sarong is then thrown over the head and shoulders by the common women as a veil, and when in the presence of men, this is drawn up over the face till only a narrow slit is left open for the eyes. Women of a superior class generally wear veils of cambric, muslin or figured net." Women veiled their faces before strangers until comparatively recent decades (Datuk Haji Mohammed Yusof Bangs, personal communication, 1979). Should one assume that lower socio-economic groups had greater liberty, since Sir Frank Swettenham noted the predominance of women in the markets of Kelantan? Or was this due rather to the pronounced independence of women in northeast Malaya, an area which remained relatively isolated from the western coast until after the Second World War? At the time Isabella Bird and Emily Innes were writing, knowledge of Malay custom was confined to western and southern Malaya; few Europeans had visited the east coast. The (British) Adviser from the Kingdom of Siam to the Raja of Kelantan during the first decade of the twentieth century noted that women wore a shawl (*kelumbong*) over head and shoulders which was intended to cover the face, but which was rarely so used. Kelantan women followed the customs of Siamese, Burmese and Cambodians, moving about "with perfect freedom, buying and selling in the markets and in the shops, visiting their friends and assisting their husbands in their agricultural pursuits" (Graham, 1908). Seclusion of women is unknown in aboriginal communities in Malaysia.

The segregation of girls before marriage is more strict in Islamic southeast Asia than in Thailand or the Philippines, and is thus in keeping with the norms of seclusion. It seems likely that the secularization of education following the independence of Malaya in 1957 somewhat mitigated the seclusion of young teenage girls and contributed to the discarding of the head shawl. This is used extensively by girls attending religious schools. Women who belong to Islamic revivalist movements, which have gained support in the late 1970's, wear a head scarf which leaves the face visible only between eyebrows and chin.

In modern India, a study of purdah revealed a whole range of attitudes, from women who retain the *burqa* as an article of faith, despite modernizing pressures from their husbands, to the poor who are unable to afford its protection, but observe all the tenets of purdah behaviour as best they can and look forward to the day when their husbands or their sons will be able to afford to keep them secluded in their homes. There are also young women who study unveiled at college, but who wear their *burqas* when they return home, to avoid hurting family feelings. Mothers living a life of seclusion said they did not want their daughters to follow their example. Purdah, whether maintained from religious conviction, a desire to purify Islamic practices, or as a form of social propriety, is thus described as being a state of mind (Vreede de Stuers, 1968). Those who work in the fields unveiled, but take care to avoid men to whom theoretically they could be married, are observing "unmanifested" purdah.

Baluchi women are able to remain secluded in their homes because of the availability of labour from pastoral nomads.

Purdah here is seen as a highly ritualized expression of explicit values, usually referred to as "honour" and "shame", which are directly concerned with the status of women. Male honour is dependent upon the unsullied honour of women who, having more inherent shame than men, must be protected and secluded (Pastner, 1974).

The ending of purdah restrictions is seen as a prerequisite to improving the position of women in those Islamic societies which impose seclusion. Attempts at abolishing purdah in Pakistan, chiefly in the cities, led initially to social ostracism (Alvi, 1977). The wife of Abdul Wali Khan, the Pathan leader, has emerged as a politician in her own right; she believes that a more favourable position can be attained in society without challenging some of its norms. "It is the tradition, even if we try we can not go without purdah. It does not harm a woman to cover her head or her arms, so I won't oppose it" (Begum Nasim Wali Khan to Richard Wigg, *The Times,* August 25, 1977). After a detailed study of the role of women in Comilla District, Bangladesh, an anthropologist concluded that overcoming seclusion was a precondition for the integration of women in the economic life of the country, but any improvements must take local values into account (Martius von Harder, 1977).

One direct consequence of the norms of decency imposed by purdah has been the stigma attached to nursing as a profession in south Asia. Greater respect for this calling has been growing in India and nurses and other medical and health technicians are now 72.2 per cent female (Rao, 1978). In Pakistan, however, there are only 6,725 registered nurses, 95 per cent of whom are female (Shah, 1978). Before the separation of Bangladesh, in 1965 there was one nurse per 32,000 of population and one doctor per 7,000 (Papanek, 1971). In East Pakistan in 1947 there were only 50 nurses. In Bangladesh today, while 1,000 out of 8,000 doctors (of whom 5,047 are graduates) are female, there are only 1,350 nurses, of whom 1,180 are female. This signifies one doctor per 10,000 of population, and one nurse per 80,000 (Sattar, 1978). Middle-class males look on nursing with a disfavour only exceeded by that accorded to acting as a profession for women. Nursing is considered both a threat to morals and in conflict with purdah requirements (Jahan, 1975). Nurses are therefore more than usually overworked and under-rewarded in Bangladesh. Some suggestions have been made to improve their prospects (Alam, 1975).

Influence of Major Religions on Status

We have considered the bearing which economic factors have on women's status, since they are seen by most observers to be crucial. There is, however, a fundamental influence exerted by tradition but with relations to economics which are not always clear. The effect of the major religions seems at first sight to be equally important, particularly that of Hinduism. This has influenced Indian society so fundamentally that its traditions have not been eliminated even among those practising the other religions subsequently adopted.

The oldest sacred text in Hinduism, the *Rigveda* (middle of the second millennium B.C.) calls upon the wife to rule supreme, and the *Mahabharata* (400-200 B.C.) considers women worthy to worship; it further claims that if women are unhappy in a society, that society cannot be successful in any field. Sons at this time were required to respect their mothers even more than their fathers. The *Upanishads* (about 800 B.C.) tell of many women taking a leading role in highly learned discussions. It was only later in the time of the lawgivers that woman's position deteriorated (Sen, 1961).

In Vedic times, daughters could undertake studies of the scriptures and sacrifice to the gods, but when ancestor worship increased in importance, only sons could sacrifice (Altekar, 1959). As pre-puberty marriage gained wide acceptance from the beginning of the modern era and sub-caste complexity made the choice of a partner increasingly difficult, so the anxiety caused by daughters made them progressively less welcome (Altekar, *loc. cit.*). Many Indian scholars have associated women's low status with the mingling of Aryan invaders with the .original population, whose women they took as wives. Automatically wives were of low caste status. By about 500 B.C. women had come to hold inferior status, were considered dangerously polluting, scheming temptresses who must be kept within carefully circumscribed limits to protect the ritual purity and wellbeing of men (Dube, 1963). The sexual appetites of women were believed to be greater than those of men. Yet at the same time, the goddesses of the Hindu pantheon are models of exemplary behaviour compared with their male counterparts. The education of girls received low priority from medieval to modern times, yet the deity of learning, Saraswati, is a goddess.

The raising of the status of women in Islam faces the special problem of the immutability of Koranic injunctions, received by the Prophet from Allah. Sura 4:31 of the Koran says: "Men have authority over women because God has made the one superior to the other and because they spend their wealth (to maintain them). So good women are obedient, guarding the unseen (parts) because God has guarded (them). As for those from whom you fear disobedience, admonish them and banish them to beds apart and beat them; then if they obey you seek not ocasion against them" (Guillaume, 1954). Injunctions and advice by later followers of Mohammed are susceptible to modification, the Koran is not. This led the modern Indian poet and philosopher, Iqbal, to write:

> I, too, am most sorrowful at the oppression of women;
> But the problem is intricate; no solution do I find possible.

The adoption of Confucian ideals came to restrict the hitherto comparatively free life of women, first of the upper classes, and progressively of society in general, in those countries which adopted Chinese culture—Korea, Japan, and, to a lesser extent, Vietnam. The rigorously circumscribed lives and the leisure thus imposed led to a remarkable flowering of literary talent among the women of the Heian Court in tenth-century Japan; Lady Murasaki and Sei Shonagon are the best-known writers.

In Buddhism, women have been vilified thus: "Women are soon angered, Ananda, women are full of passion, Ananda, women are envious, Ananda, women are stupid. That is the reason, Ananda, that is the cause, why women have no place in public assemblies, do not carry on business, and do not earn their living by any professions" (*Sullavaga* X.1.6, quoted by Rudra, 1975).

Yet, in Thailand, no greater value is given to men than to women, as it is deemed that all will be reborn many times as either men or women (Hanks and Hanks, 1963). This equality is underlined in the marriage ceremonial: "Let the wife know how to please her husband, saying sweet words to him and admonishing him only in private, not before others. Let the husband perform his duty of loving and protecting his wife and never use harsh words to her." A less egalitarian relationship is, however, discerned in a study of a north Thai village, where male dominance is clearly accepted. Property is inherited in the matriline, but authority passes from father-in-law to son-in-law. A proverb states that men are superior to women as the front legs of an elephant are superior to the hind (Potter, 1977).

In Burma, men are universally acknowledged as superior to women spiritually and also widely considered as intellectually and morally superior (Spiro, 1977). There is none the less social and legal equality. If men manipulate the symbols and control the tokens of power (religion and politics), men are manipulated and controlled by women in the domain of real power (the family and household). They play an important role in production, the provision of family income and in family decisions, and their status is high, even though outwardly they are deferential. A common saying is: "Having a husband in the house is like having a nat around"—the nats being powerful spirits requiring deference and devotion (Nash, 1965).

Thus, there is a conflict between the scriptural stereotype and the actuality, for if women hold low symbolic positions in the Buddhist hierarchy, Burmese and Thai society is as egalitarian as is the predominantly Catholic Philippines or largely Islamic Indonesia. The great religions, particularly the newer reforming religions of Buddhism, Islam and Christianity, are not after all useful guides for predicting social structure and the status of women. They have been grafted on to older belief systems which had a profound influence on the ordering of society long before they were adopted. The contrast between the dominating Kelantanese market woman, overseeing her stall, telling her husband (if he is visible at all) what to do, driving a shrewd bargain while cracking jokes with all comers with complete self-possession, and the Bangladeshi woman who retires from view the moment a stranger appears at the entry to her compound, never goes to market and is reluctant to express an opinion, even to another woman when her confidence has been gained, is overwhelming. Yet both are followers of Islam.*

Status and Performance of Religious Duties

A devout woman is respected by her family and community, but this does not imply that she will be regarded as competent in secular matters or will be accorded high status in village affairs. There is, in the more primitive religions of the region, a division of labour in ritual which reflects daily life, where women play an important part. The great religions often severely limit the role of women. The effect that this may have on women's public role was shown in the 1978 elections to the State Legislature of Kelantan, Malaysia, where no woman candidate was put forward by any party; each knew the opposition would call on the populace to vote against her, as "a woman could not lead prayers or recite the *khutbah* and neither could they enter a mosque during their periods" (*New Straits Times*, February 25, 1978).

In India, festivals without "great tradition tries" are women's festivals; women participate and even dominate life cycle rites. Men's rites focus on a good crop, or ridding the village of disease. Women are active practitioners but have little religious authority in orthodox Hinduism (Wadley, 1977). Thus, the religious duties of women are accorded a lower status than those of men. However, the cook is crucial in maintaining the orthodoxy of the family (Khare, 1976); except where families are able to employ a Brahmin the cook is invariably one of the women, under the instruction of her mother-in-law. Women

---

* It is not claimed that all Kelantanese or Bangladeshi women conform to this picture, but these stereotypes are acknowledged as such by their societies.

ensure the ritual wellbeing of the family and derive a sense of importance therefrom (Jacobson, 1977; Srinivas, 1976).

Production of food for the temple in a northern Thai village gathers women together and gives some authority. Ancestral spirits inhabit the oldest house in the family compound, which will be inherited by the family's youngest daughter (Potter, 1977).

In traditional China, the ancestral hall was the locus of an agnatic community, where women had no public place. This was in sharp contrast with domestic ancestor worship, which was the sphere of women and in which they played a crucial part (Freedman, 1970b). This still applies in Taiwan and to overseas communities of Chinese.

In Korea, while the most valued form of worship is the male rite of ancestor worship, women may consult shamans (who are mostly female) to counteract the inauspicious influence of restless ghosts and ancestors. Male rites acknowledge only those "ancestors" who produce sons and die within the patrilineal family. Women's rituals acknowledge a broad bilateral kindred, including sisters and daughters who marry out of the family and the wife's own natal kin (Kendall, 1979).

Islam also appears to confer lower status on women's sacral duties. In the Prophet's time women attended public prayers in the mosques, standing behind the men, "but there is a tradition that he said it was better for women to pray at home and . . . they do not attend public prayers" (Guillaume, 1954). In Malaysia it has been said that "women do not go to mosque for worship on any occasion" (Zainal Abidin, 1949). Women are, however, permitted to attend Friday prayers, separated from the men by a curtain.

It seems that historic, probably prehistoric, societal norms must be sought to explain the differences which prevail between the patrilineal societies of south Asia and east Asia and the less rigidly structured societies of southeast Asia where, no matter what the major religion or form of economic production, women enjoy a fairly egalitarian position *vis-a-vis* their husbands and in society.

Status and the Life Cycle

Female status does not remain unchanged throughout the life

cycle. Inferiority is acknowledged at the moment of birth, when mid-wives commonly receive better payment, in cash or kind, for a boy than for a girl; in a Pakistani village Rs. 10 are paid for a boy, and Rs. 5 for a girl (Khan and Bilquees, 1976).

Preference has traditionally been expressed for male children. In Pakistan, when asked how many daughters they had, men would answer "God has been merciful" or just "thank God" to indicate they had none (Saghir Ahmed, 1974). In the People's Republic of China, economic considerations make parents as anxious to have sons today as in the past (Parish, 1975). In the rural New Territories of Hong Kong, sons are preferred, daughters "goods on which one loses" (Potter, 1969). Another stricture in traditional China is: "A boy is born facing in, a girl is born facing out" (Freedman, 1958). In Taiwan, sons are crucial to the identity of a woman in the family and village into which she has married and much affection is lavished on them; close emotional bonds unite mothers and daughters, but a female child has lower status than her brothers (Wolf, 1970).

Poverty at one end of the social scale in India and at the other the practice of hypergamy, which automatically meant that there were not enough high-status men for high-status girls to marry, have in the past caused harsh treatment of girls. Even today poverty and the reservation of scarce resources for boys means, that girls are less well treated. The Harvard School of Public Health, in collaboration with the Governments of India and the State of Punjab, found during the 1950's and 1960's that girls of less than 2 years of age had a substantially smaller chance of survival than boys of the same age, who were given better medical care and probably more supplementary food (Wyon and Gordon, 1971). Mortality is higher in Bangladesh among female infants, being 38 per cent for parities 0, 1 and 2, and is similar for the 1 to 4 years age group (Mosley, 1979). The mortality rate for girls under the age of 5 years is 30 to 50 per cent higher than for boys (Jahan, 1975).

In modern Asia, infants of both sexes are generally the centre of family affection, though discrimination starts early and girls are soon made aware of their responsibilities in the care of younger siblings and household tasks. Thailand seems to be an exception, without a clear division of roles, even between adults. It is felt, there that women contribute more to the continuity of generations than do men (Hanks and Hanks, 1963). Westernization has introduced sharper distinctions between boys' and girls' dress, behaviour and roles than was traditional.

In the traditional east Asian and south Asian worlds, a girl learns quite early to keep what is today called a low profile; her brother has greater freedom until he is of an age to assist in agricultural activities. Excellence in studies is no excuse for the incompetence of an Indian girl in household affairs (ICSSR, 1975). Girls learn early in life the need to be flexible and submissive; they hesitate to develop strong opinions and commitments which they may not be allowed to pursue after marriage. Among poorer people, the education of girls is sacrificed in favour of boys, and there is a lurking fear that education may alienate girls from their roles and submissive behaviour (ICSSR, *loc. cit.* Attitudes Towards Education). In the People's Republic of China, girls are withdrawn from school more readily than boys to help in household tasks (Parish, 1975; Orleans, 1978). The same is true of Hong Kong (Field and Baber, 1973). An adolescent boy in southeast Asia has considerable independence and may work for a wage rather than help on the family plot. A close link unites women with their parents for life in this sub-region.

Girls, on reaching puberty have their freedom greatly curtailed and are often withdrawn from school to work within the home until a suitable match is arranged. At this time in most settled communities, girls experience the ritual impurity associated with menstruation, an impurity which also occurs later at the birth of their children. Males, by observing rules of distance from potentially polluting women, need never experience this sense of inferiority.

In many Asian communities young women, like their husbands, achieve adult status only with marriage, often only after the birth of their first child. In Malay *kampongs,* children mix freely until about the age of 13, when girls are segregated, supervised and trained for marriage. In the past if married before puberty, a girl stayed at home or with her affines but did not cohabit with her husband. If a child was born immediately after marriage at 13 or 14, a girl was considered too young to look after it and her parents would take charge, giving her extra training in the process (Hashimah Roose, 1963). The young couple would be allowed to set up home only when considered sufficiently mature and experienced. Even then they were still under parental influence, especially regarding family life and social obligations. Similarly, a Pakistani bride did not have the right to bring up her children, who were under the jurisdiction of her mother-in-law (Gani, 1963). A Bangladeshi daughter-in-law is responsible for work, her mother-in-law having authority, even over the young bride's husband, whom she instructs about marketing (Abdulla, 1976). An educated Bengali wife in Calcutta finds her relations with her husband improve only after she has borne a child; he shows her more overt attention and affection as his child's mother. Before then such attention was more properly directed to his mother, sisters and the wives of his older brothers (Roy, 1975).

In Java, it is impressed upon a young couple that they should provide for themselves (Jay, 1969); they are considered minors, unable to contract social and economic debts, until they are economically independent. This can be achieved by the control of an independently earned food store and maintenance of separate cooking hearth, even though still within the home of one of their parents.

A Thai girl is considered an adult at the birth of her first child, but her husband attains adult status only when his father-in-law retires, if it is a joint family, or when he himself farms his own land. Only then can he take part in village affairs (de Young, 1966).

In traditional China, the subservience of a woman's lineage to her husband's was underlined by the fact that her family took no part in the ceremonies of the marriage; the groom's lineage ancestors were worshipped and homage paid to his parents, on whom the bride's economic dependence was absolute (Yang, 1959). At each stage of her life, a woman was in an inferior position to male members of her family of the same generation in vital matters, and to those of the next generation in all matters (Yang, *loc. cit.*).

If it is only in the criteria for achieving adulthood that there is no discrimination between male and female, the female in south and east Asia and traditionally holds a position of complete inferiority to all family members older than herself and a fairly remote relation with her husband. The southeast Asian bride is far more secure.

Some have suggested that teknonymy, the practice of addressing a married woman as "mother of . . ." or "auntie of . . . ," leads to a weakened sense of individuality in the adult woman, implying that her status in achieved only in relation to some other, usually a male. However, in societies where this is the norm, such as in south Asia, it would be necessary to apply psychological tests and to compare the results with societies where the practice was not prevalent. No such investigations have been seen by the authors. Some evidence suggests that, on the contrary, those excluded from the practice where it is current suffer accordingly. Men who never have children in Bali and who continue throughout their lives with their childhood name, while their peers progressively become "father of . . ." and "grandfather of . . .," feel the shame deeply (Geertz and Geertz, 1975).

For both men and women age, particularly experience and success in agricultural and domestic and childrearing undertakings, brings greater respect from their society. Older women often exercise considerable authority and, even in patriarchal societies, have an important role in arranging their children's marriages. An older woman may control the income of a number of daughters-in-law in India (Dube, 1978a).

The effect of widowhood on status varies greatly throughout Asia. In south Asia, widows often have to shave their heads, perform menial work and observe enforced ritual and physical distance from family and community events, so polluting and dangerous to others are they. Remarriage remains almost totally unacceptable among castes and communities which prohibited remarriage in the past, despite higher levels of education and legislation (Leonard and Leonard, 1981). A traditional Chinese widow left in charge of family land would leave its management to her sons, but would still enjoy considerable power within the family. Remarriage was not sanctioned, however, and entailed loss of children and property. A Korean woman can succeed temporarily to the household headship until her son (or adopted son) is of age, but after the early Yi dynasty, she could not become the ritual heir (Deuchler, 1977). A Vietnamese widow traditionally supervised land, but this was merely a continuation of the high status she enjoyed throughout life. A southeast Asian widow has traditionally held property and been free to remarry. The change in Japan from the extended patrilocal to nuclear neolocal family pattern has robbed the Japanese widow of the respect and security which she formerly enjoyed.

Divorce has traditionally entailed little stigma in southeast Asia, although this is changing among the more educated. In east and south Asia, divorce has always been unacceptable, even among Islamic communities in south Asia. The Shariat Act of 1936 safeguarded the right of Muslim women to divorce, but social convention makes this difficult even today (ICSSR, 1975).

Marriage Negotiations and Status

It has been claimed that the status of women in any society can be gauged by the form of negotiation involved in her marriage. The institution of bride price, with its assumption of the value of the girl and of her labour, reflects a higher conception of her position than does that of dowry, with its undertone of "buying" a husband. The prevalence of ruinous dowry payments makes the arrival of several daughters a family disaster and soon makes a girl aware of her burdensomeness. It follows that the different systems are a function of the division of labour—perhaps at some time in the past—in any region.

Bride price is often common where women take an active part in production, particularly in shifting forms of cultivation. In mainland and insular southeast Asia, bride price has, with few exceptions, been the custom in all societies, both settled and swidden. If a groom was unable to obtain the bride price, he worked for a varying number of years for his father-in-law until the sum was considered paid (Lebar, Hickey and Musgrave, 1964; Lebar, 1972; Lebar, 1975). Dowry is more commonly the norm where the role of women is confined to "unproductive" household tasks and child-raising. In south Asia dowry is associated with the transmission of property through both males and females, as enshrined in classical treatises such as the *Dharmashastras*, even if in India women's rights are confined to movables (Tambiah, 1973).

There is often confusion regarding the significance of dowry, dower and bridewealth. Dowry is always given by the bride's parents, and dower by the groom's; both form part of the conjugal estate. Bridewealth, however, is given by the groom's family to the bride's, and clearly represents compensation for the loss of the girl. Controversy regarding the function of bride price goes back some decades (Gluckman, 1953; Leach, 1953; Schneider, 1953) and continues today. Some argue that bridewealth discourages the bride from seeking divorce, since her parents would be obliged to return the sum. Under Islam, however, bride price payment restrains the groom, since his family pays only part of the sum at marriage, the remainder at divorce. The Islamic dower given by the bridegroom is intended for the bride herself and thus is not bride price. Canon law fixes the amount of dower according to that received by the Prophet for his daughter, Fatimah. In north India, however, a customary dower of unrealistic amount is fixed in the marriage contract as a symbol of status of the bride's family. Canon law dower was intended to protect the women against capricious divorce, but customary dower is so high that it could never be paid, and is in any case usually renounced by the wife. This is in her interest, for it enhances the responsibility of her affines towards her if her husband dies (Vreede de Stuers, 1968). A recent study of a Bedouin community sought to show that bride price was above all a status symbol (Kressel, 1977), but this aroused considerable disagreement; there is still no consensus on the true function of bride price (*Current Anthropology,* 18: 450-458).

In rural Burma, dower is an essential component of marriage and protects the girl against the insecurity of philandering, improvident husbands, particularly since divorced women find it difficult to remarry (Spiro, 1975). Dower is actually the groom's inheritance and helps the couple to become established. It is argued that bridewealth in Thailand is actually dower, since residence is matrilocal and girls expect to inherit, whereas conventional bridewealth stays with the bride's parents.

Status and family honour are also factors; a poor Burmese bride commands a lower dower, and a poor Thai girl a lower bridewealth, than the wealthy. Dowry may occur along with dower in rural Burma, but dowry alone is paid among certain élite urban Burmese associated with hypergamous marriages between wealthy, low-status women and impoverished, high-status men. As in India, dowry is a recent innovation, following the introduction of western education and the availability to men of high-status jobs in the civil service.

It is suggested that when neither side gains status or wealth from a marriage there is no payment, but if the cost-benefit ratio is unbalanced, marriage payment repairs the balance (Spiro, *loc. cit.*). It is difficult to find a theory to meet all Asia's variations, for the status of a Chinese girl for whom bridewealth had been paid was comparable with an Indian girl who brings dowry.

Bride price was common in south China and dowry, varying greatly in amount, in the north (Smith, 1899/1970). In Taiwan, however, the father of the bride gains face by the payment of dowry (Wolf, 1972). Domestic services and fertility were the chief ritual attachments transferred to a girl's agnatic family in marriage; this was validated by the payment of bride price (Freedman, 1958). Chinese bride price was in fact indirect dowry, since cash payment by the groom's family was used dower the bride with furnishings and other necessities (Goody and Tambiah, 1973). The bride's family in Taiwan is expected to contribute as much again as the bride price in the form of dowry (Diamond, 1969). The diminution or disappearance in the People's Republic of China of dowry payments reflects the increased economic value of women (Whyte, 1977; Parish and Whyte, 1978), while bride price remains common. Today, however, only part of this is used to dower the bride, most being saved and used later to marry off a brother of the bride (Parish and Whyte, *loc. cit.*). These improvements in the status of women are still closely related to economic sufficiency. The Chairwoman of the National Women's Union, K'ang K'e-ch'ing (*People's Daily,* November 27, 1978), discussing the economic deterioration of the previous decade, stated "social morality (was) also greatly corrupted to such an extent that there was restoration of buying and selling of brides. (There are) great differences between well-to-do villages and relatively poor villages. In places where production levels and living standards are low, the buying and selling of brides . . . are not easy to eliminate completely" (London and London, 1979).

Korean women receive dowry on marriage and have no further economic claims on their natal lineage (Deuchler, 1977). Dowry does not often come in the form of money or jewellery which gives a woman security, but as household costs and clothing (Soon, 1977a).

A dowerless girl's lack of face in her new home may be aggravated by many reproaches; the custom is proving extremely difficult to eradicate in modern India, despite much propaganda. Indeed, the ensuring of good treatment for their daughters is one of the major reasons fathers give for high dowry payments.

In early times bride price was the norm in India, and frequent protests at the system are recorded throughout history; it increased with child marriage (Altekar, 1959). The dowry system was connected with the idea of marriage as a gift of a daughter, when a religious gift in kind was normally accompanied by a small gift in cash or ornaments. In mediaeval times it was only among the Rajputs, where competition for high status grooms was intense, that the dowry system assumed serious proportions. It became widespread only in the nineteenth century, assuming excessive proportions during the past 50 to 60 years with the advent of higher education for men (Altekar, *loc. cit.*). Since the beginning of this century, men from higher castes sought English education to obtain jobs in the bureaucracy and to enter the professions. Such men were in great demand as grooms, and over a period of time this stimulated the spread of the institution of dowry. Previously in Bengal and throughout south India (with the exception of Kerala) cash was paid to obtain a bride. Dowry began among the upper levels of society and has now reached even the sweepers of Calcutta (Srinivas, 1977). In Bangladesh bride price was formerly provided by the groom's family, but today the family of an educated groom will require dowry (Abdulla, 1976). The bride's position may be improving slowly, however. Much of the dowry of a new wife in a Rajput community, studied over a period of 20 years, was formerly taken by her mother-in-law and placed in the dower of her own daughter; today this is left in the control of the bride herself (Minturn, 1976).

An exchange between the parents of the bride and groom, such as that described above for traditional China, is in fact common. Marriage expenses paid by the Malay groom's father are often supplemented by the bride's father and the total often exceeded by the sum the groom's family traditionally gives the bride as her own property (Swift, 1963). Among the tribal Gonds of central India, marriage by negotiation involving heavy expenditure by the groom's family is most prized, but the alternatives, whereby a poor youth works for his father-in-law for a stipulated number of years to earn his bride, or capture (prearranged or otherwise), are more common (von Fürer-Haimendorf, 1974). These practices are found among many tribal peoples in southeast Asia.

Status and Personality

The effect of status on the development of personality is undoubtedly of great importance, but little work has been done in this field in Asia.

An explanation of differences in male and female personality which are considered almost universal has been based on psychoanalytic theory (Chodorow, 1974). Most traditional accounts of socialization stress early role training, but Chodorow considered unconscious features of personality. After the age of 3, male and female development is radically different: a boy's gender development is based on identification with the father who, Chodorow assumes, is generally relatively inaccessible to his son. Identification with him is thus more abstract, and conception of the masculine role based on fantasy rather than observation. Gender identification for boys is also achieved at the expense of devaluing what is feminine in the world around him. A girl's relation with her mother, on the other hand, is unbroken, her identification with her personal, and she is likely to participate in an intergenerational female world, while her brother will associate chiefly with his peers.

Current patterns of socialization lead Chodorow to conclude that while men feel "sociocultural superiority", they are also "psychologically defensive and insecure. Women by contrast, although always of secondary social and cultural status, may in favourable circumstances gain psychological security and a firm sense of worth and importance, in spite of this."

As Chodorow admits, psychoanalytical theory is based largely on western culture. Asia would seem to provide a promising testing ground for theories of the effect of patterns of socialization upon the development of personality. Fathers tend to become more remote to sons at the age generally associated with the development of "reason," around the age of 6 to 8, when discipline becomes more strict (Nydegger and Nydegger, 1966; Jocano, 1969; Minturn and Hitchcock, 1966; Wolf, 1972). Asian boys around the age of 3 are not cut off from their father or other adult males, and small children of both sexes grow up in close interaction with a number of relatives and children of different ages. In the extended family an aged grandparent or a young uncle may be a regular companion. Fairly close participation of men in the socialization of boys seems to be characteristic of much of rural Asia, with the exception of Japan, and girls rarely grow up in close interaction only with their mother. Chodorow considers these characteristics make for the development of strong individuality and are a means of bringing about greater equality between adult men and women.

A study of childhood in India, however, shows that while the father is present, his son is unable to identify with him as is required for the development of autonomy, since tradition requires the father to remain distant, treating all children in an extended family with impartiality. A boy is separated from his mother abruptly at the fourth or fifth year, when absolute obedience and conformity to familial standards may be imposed upon him. "The slow detachment from the mother considered essential to the development of a strong independent ego is not a feature of early Indian childhood;" consequently "the mental processes characteristic of the symbiosis of infancy play a relatively greater role in adult personality" (Kakar, 1978). This prepares the individual for participation in a world requiring strict observance of a traditionally elaborated hierarchical social order and the subordination of individual preferences and ambitions to the welfare of the extended family and *jati* communities.

This pattern of child-raising has fundamental consequences for the future relationship between husband and wife. The extreme dependence of the son on his mother is allied to fear (Kakar, *loc. cit.*). "Underlying the conscious ideals of womanly purity, innocence and fidelity and interwoven with the unconscious belief in a safeguarding maternal beneficence is a secret conviction among many Hindu men that the feminine principle is really the opposite—treacherous, lustful and rampant with an insatiable, contaminating sexuality." This leads to "avoidance behaviour in sexual relations, which in turn causes women to extend a provocative sexual presence towards their sons, which eventually produces adult men who fear the sexuality of mature women . . . Taken into the child's ego, the good mother's maternal tolerance, emotional vitality, protectiveness and nurturing become the core of every Indian's positive identity. Alongside this positive identity, however, and normally repressed, is its counterpart; the negative identity that originates in experiences with the demanding, sometimes stifling, all too present mother."

A further contributory factor to this pattern is derived from the early age of marriage. The process of adolescent development is normally incomplete at the time of marriage when a girl is transplanted into an unfamiliar, possibly hostile environment, a "traumatic transition which an Indian girl undergoes at precisely the most sensitive and vulnerable period of her development." Her position becomes tolerable when she bears a child. It is thus comprehensible that the great emotional investment she places in her infant, especially if it is a son, prolongs and intensifies the mother-son relationship.

Socialization in Asia usually shows favouritism to boys and stresses that girls must defer to their brothers. What effect does this have on personality development? Psychoanalytic theory would lead to the expectation that the cultural devaluation of girls would heighten female hostility and envy towards males, producing strong antagonism between the sexes. Kakar (*loc. cit.*) finds little evidence of this in India. There is, however, evidence that women turn aggression against themselves, transforming cultural devaluation into feelings of worthlessness and inferiority. This may be offset by the strength of wellbeing and self-esteem generated by a strong mother-daughter bond which sustains a girl through the realization during late childhood of her cultural inferiority; she comes to accept that submission and docility are inseparable from her role. Conformity to expectation is reinforced by the Hindu concept of *dharma* (roughly translated as right-living), which implies that behaviour is good if it conforms to the traditional pattern of kinship and caste groups. This leads to suspicion of innovation and unconscious avoidance of unconventional activities by both men and women. The fact that older women gain power to make vital decisions affecting the family further contributes towards conservatism, since older women wish to be able to control their daughters-in-law as they themselves were controlled.

In Japan, girls learn that men and boys have fragile egos which women and girls must build up and protect. A girl must develop an amiable, flexible, nurturant personality, but the emotional support she later gives her husband is overwhelmingly one-sided. Women may gain their own support from mothers or sisters, but increasingly these live too far away for frequent contact. Inevitably such comfort comes from her children, in the past chiefly from her sons, but in modern times more from her daughters (Vogel, 1978).

In the Philippines, despite the widespread acceptance of woman's role in economic activities, whether it be as a professional in the cities or tending a small rural sundry store, the primary role remains that of mother, and children are her greatest emotional satisfaction. "A person grows up in the Filipino culture with one paramount assumption; that he belongs to someone" (Lapuz, 1973). He belongs to the family as a whole as well as to its members, especially to his parents and principally to his mother, "partly because of biological circumstances, but also because of the intense emotional nurturing received from her." Women remain very close to their mothers, even after marriage (Lapuz, *loc. cit.*). The successful carrying out of the role of mother is more important than individual achievement as a woman.

It has been suggested that patterns of socialization in Thailand, whereby the affection showered on the youngest is withdrawn when the child is supplanted by another infant, leaves a boy without a real role until adolescence, whereas a girl is soon given tasks around the home. This may account for female dominance in Thailand and to the weak ego of men (Piker, 1975), or—since similar patterns occur in Java—to "the most henpecked men on earth" (Jay, 1969). Daughters in Thailand are reared as mothers, wives and caretakers of the elderly; men's roles are far more diffuse. Moreover, emotional support is gained more from mothers than from husbands (Mecke, 1974), further strengthening female solidarity. Thai boys are traditionally taught to receive things and attention in the home. They are treated with greater consideration, made to feel that they are of first importance and can have what they want, while girls give in to them and please them. This differential pattern is the basis for an evaluation of Thai men as immature and narcissistic, while girls have stronger characters. But women are less secure and self-confident than men as a result of this training (Boonsanong, 1971).

It is believed that the need of Burmese men for dependence on their wives, despite the formal role of female subservience, results from their early relationships with their mothers in which they are "spoiled" and strongly dependent on them. Thus the domination by women of their husbands may be viewed rather as the dependence of the men (Spiro, 1977).

A clear understanding of cultural values is as essential for understanding adult personality in Asia as is knowledge of child socialization. Western stress on economic and occupational achievement, and derogation of the maternal role, overlooks the fact that in many cultures achievement motivation is towards the maternal role, seen as a specialized counterpart to that of men. The relative lack of discord in Japanese marriages is partly due to the degree to which women derive personal satisfaction from being competent in their roles, rather than from having a mate who meets their personal needs (de Vos and Wagatsuma, 1973a). It should not be supposed that the acceptance of the maternal, home-making, nurturant role signifies a more submissive character. Overt behaviour masks the frequent operation of actual control of the family by women; no significant differences are found between men and women in the incidence or distribution of structural traits of personality—basic active or passive attitudes, dominant or submissive needs. The personal self has been de-emphasized in Japanese culture, and traditional self-awareness is fused with some conception of expected role behaviour; the Japanese person is uncomfortable thinking of the self as separable from the role (de Vos and Wagatsuma, *loc. cit.*).

An attempt to assess personality is central Thailand was based on a number of questionnaires, one such relating to aspirations. It was found that 40 per cent of all replies were related to status (Phillips, 1966). A woman respondent wished to be the mother of a doctor, district officer or governor, showing perhaps a realization that higher status was more likely to be achieved by reflected glory from a close-related male than by her own achievements. Twenty per cent of replies from both sexes showed that individuals wished to be good, respected and non-trouble-making. The "most important thing in life" for the majority, however, was earning a living, or food and money (Phillips, *loc. cit.*). The same emphasis on economic preoccupations and status is revealed in more recent studies of ten villages in north and ten in central Thailand. Thirty-six per cent of women wanted their daughters to be teachers and 23 per cent either nurse or doctor; 15 per cent hoped their daughters would take up dressmaking and only 11 per cent wanted them to work in agriculture, as did the mothers. Ninety-nine per cent of these women worried "a lot" about economic factors and, knowing the importance of woman's financial contribution to the family budget, only 3 per cent wanted their daughters to confine themselves to household activities (Nantanee *et al.*, 1977).

A survey of major life concerns of Filipino women stresses two basic Filipino values: economic security (house and home; social benefits and family health and the good provider factor); and social acceptance (education, childrearing and marital relationship, housekeeping and social participation, status and esteem). "Being a woman in Filipino society means that her prestige lies mainly in her credible performance as a mother, wife and home manager. Although she might be a success in her profession or career, her 'failure' as mother or wife is given greater weight" (Illo, 1979).

An anthropologist working on the life history of an elderly woman in central India, whom she had known intimately for some years, was struck by the clarity with which she remembered trivial details from her early youth, compared with the confusion which appeared to cloud her memory of the birth order of the 8 of her 12 children who had died during childhood; this was recognized as a form of defence mechanism against distress (Jacobson, 1978). May it be asked what is the effect upon a woman's personality of the awareness of a constant threat to disease to her family, of economic hardship of one kind or another, of the difficulty of attaining education for her children and concern at their future employment and marriage prospects? All these preoccupations are more acute at lower socio-economic levels throughout Asia.

An apparent lack of introspection has been noted among lower socio-economic groups in the Indian subcontinent by various workers (Jacobson, *loc. cit.*). This echoes the findings of Lewis in a Mexican community (1951), who wrote:

> Like many peasant peoples, Tepoxtecans are not introspective. They have little insight in understanding their own character and even less of others. There is little interest in or need for self-revelation, mutual confidences, confession, or lengthy conversation; imaginativeness, fantasy life, originality, initiative, and individuality are either undeveloped or suppressed. Always, the emphasis is upon conformity to traditional ways.

The science of psychological anthropology is still at its beginnings in Asia. What do we know of the effect on personality and development of an abrupt break from an affectionate family life to a hostile environment in which a young bride's status is low? Surely the confidence of young bride, and consequently her self-esteem and ability to assert herself and her ideas, must be far greater if she can turn to her mother for support, advice and companionship, as in southeast Asia, than in the isolation, the "psychological aloneness" (Wolf, 1975) of east and south Asia. The psychological isolation must have made for greater submissiveness and malleability, and perhaps difficulty in raising her status in her husband's eyes—especially when he probably preferred a peaceful life wholly undisturbed by difference of opinion among the women of his family.

Under the joint family system which prevails among higher status Bengalis in India, considerable frustration is engendered by the gulf between the romantic view of marriage envisioned by educated young women, and the more prosaic actuality of their limited role:

> Personality needs are generated, and then in part frustrated; but to achieve any level of gratification, the full array of joint-family roles is required. A system such as this must sacrifice the whole satisfaction of one individual, either on the structural or psychological level, so that other members in different roles may be at least partly satisfied (Roy, 1975).

Marriage for a young man does not involve separation from his mother, sisters and sisters-in-law, from all of whom he receives affection; he does not expect his wife to fulfil romantic needs, and sexual enjoyment is connected not with her, who will become another respected mother, but with women not to be respected. It is usually his mother who looks after his needs during the day (Roy, *loc. cit.*). The effect of this upon a young woman expecting love and fulfilment can be imagined. Emotional satisfaction with her own children is not permanent, since they too will evnetually grow away from her. Many women in middle life find the emotional satisfaction and support they have missed in devotions to a guru (Roy, *loc. cit.*).

But we are dealing here with patterns which Roy has shown to be in part confined to Bengal and, moreover, to a highly favoured minority. Of the frustrations and satisfactions of the majority of poor Indian women, as of Asian women in general, we know remarkably little. More studies within the different cultures, preferably by specialists from the same culture, are needed before any clear conclusions can be drawn on the effect of acculturation on personality development and on the status of Asian women. In particular, it needs to be demonstrated that there are differences in child-raising, not apparent from the literature, which explain the differences in public-self confidence between women in southeast Asia and those in west and east Asia. If no crucial differences are found, then different female experiences at other stages in the life cycle must be isolated. It seems to us that marriage is the most promising variable.

11

Striving Beyond Religion: Women Mystics in Islam

Right from the early years of Islam, sainthood was open to men and women without discrimination. By women saints I mean both holy owmen and women mystics, otherwise known as Sufis. To the category of holy women belong such women as the Prophet's mother, Amina; the Prophet's daughter, Fātima; Umm Harām, a warrior-woman who took part in the first holy war which stretched across the sea to Cyprus; and Fizza, a simple peasant woman with husband and children whose sheep gave milk mixed with honey. To the category of women mystics belong women who came to feel the force of divine love. Their mode of life inspired respect and the miracles which were attributed to them certified this respsect; these women had an exceptional claim to recognition. Society acknowledged them.

In the case of women mystics—to which this study is devoted—the terms of reference extend to a rather special field: that of mysticism. It is, therefore, necessary to judge and evaluate the position of the woman mystic first, within the philosophical framework of mysticism, and secondly, in relation to the institutions to which mysticism has given rise.

The goal of the mystic quest is union with the Divine. The mystic renounces this world and its attractions, and proceeds along the various stages and states of mystical experience.

Some of these stages and states are attained by self-discipline and some are the gift of God. The final stage and state of mystical attainment is the experience of divine knowledge, and vision in which the mystic becomes one with the Beloved, the abides in the Beloved forever. In such a relationship between the mystic and the Beloved there is no room for the distinction of sex. 'Attār, the thirteenth-century poet and mystic, who wrote a biography of saints, has these words to say about women and mysticism:

> The holy prophets have laid it down that 'God does not look upon your outward forms'. It is not the outward form that matters but the inner purpose of the heart, as the Prophet said, 'The people are assembled (on the Day of Judgment) according to the purposes of their hearts'. . . . So also 'Abbās of Tūs said that when on the Day of Resurrection the summons goes forth, 'O men', the first person to set foot in that class of men (*i.e.,* those who are to enter Paradise) will be Mary, upon whom be peace. . . . The true explanation of this fact (that women count for as much as men among the saints) is that wherever these people, the Sufis, are, they have no separate existence in the Unity of God. In the Unity, what remains of the existence of 'I' or 'thou'? So how can 'man' or 'woman' continue to be? So too, Abū 'Ali Fārmadhī said, 'Prophecy is the essence, the very being, of power and sublimity. Superiority and inferiority do not exist in it. Undoubtedly saintship is of the same type.'

According to the theoretical hierarchy of sainthood, a *qutb* would be the highest spiritual head of the Sufi fellowship at any one moment. Some theologians consider Fātima, the daughter of the Prophet, as the first *qutb*. Below the *qutb* were the four *awtād,* from whose ranks the succeeding *qutb* would be chosen, and below the *awtād* were forty *abdāl* who are described as being the pivot of the world and the foundation and support of the affairs of men. Jāmī, the author of a sixteenth-century biography of saints, relates how someone was asked, 'How many are the 'Abdāl?' and he answered, 'Forty souls,' and when asked why he did not say 'Forty men', his reply was, 'There have been women among them.'

A further point of consideration *vis-a-vis* eligibility for sainthood is that at a certain stage of the mystical path the mystic cannot proceed by his will or determination alone, nor by the guidance of the sheikh or *pir,* the spiritual leader. Divine sanction, a kindly glance from the Beloved, is necessary. According to Jāmī, Abu Hafs regarded the traditions (*hadīth*) handed down by women as improper until he saw Umm 'Alī, a mystic and wife of Ahmad ibn Hazrawiyya. Then he understood that God almighty bestows His knowledge and acquaintance on whomever he pleases. So, if there is any question of élitism in mysticism it is the prerogative of God, the Beloved, to elect His lovers. Otherwise sainthood was in principle open to men and women alike, and in practice, there were no conditions attached regarding the social status or background of a mystic. Women mystics could be married and have children or could be single. Margaret Smith, a modern scholar, points out that it was easier for slave-women to remain single—once they had obtained their freedom—than it was for free women.

Views on celibacy were mixed; Hujwīrī, an eleventh-century author on Sufism sums up the paradox neatly: the Sufis must consider in his mind the respective evils of celibacy and marriage in order to choose the lesser evil for himself. The evils of celibacy consist in neglecting the ordinance of the Prophet and in the danger of falling into unlawful ways, while marriage involves the evils of the distraction of the mind with other than God and the concern of the body with sensual pleasures. Marriage, therefore, is best for the sociable and celibacy for the solitary. But Hujwīrī personally preferred celibacy.

Closely connected with the idea of celibacy is the desire for retirement and solitude which gave rise to the institution of retreats. There were women recluses from an early date. Influential women were the founders of these institutions. Apart from providing for the needs of the resident women mystics and wandering dervish women, these retreats were known to provide shelter to divorced or deserted women until their circumstances improved.

As already mentioned, women mystics could be married or single, slaves or free women. They could be rich or poor, noble or common, educated and skilled or illiterate and unskilled. None of these factors entered into the making of a mystic.

Initiation into the mystic path usually had to be administered by an experienced sheikh. It would be the duty of the sheikh to guide the novice through the various stages of the mystical path. The initiation ritual and the training process would depend on the particular mystical order. Of course, the evolution of the mystical orders took place long after the time of the first mystics. In the case of many women mystics we do not know who their guide was; for example, the greatest of women mystics, Rabi'a al-'Adawiyya, does not seem to have had an initiator or a guide at all. Women mystics or aspirants could be initiated into the path or order by another woman mystic who might, at the same time, be presiding over separate gatherings for women. But on this point, too, there are variations; women are also initiated and guided by men mystics and often attend mixed gatherings. Rabi'a, for example, attended the gatherings for men, and men were present at her own gatherings. It is either a case of individual preference or in accordance with the prescription of particular mystical orders.

The contribution of women mystics can, again, be reviewed from the point of view of their contribution to the theory of mysticism and then from the point of view of their contribution to the organization and rituals of mystical orders.

It seems that Rābi'a is the only woman mystic who had something original to say. Though she was not the first to realize that the way to God must be sought through love, she was perhaps the first to lay stress upon the doctrine and combine it with the doctrine of *kashf,* the unveiling of the Beloved to the lover at the end of the way.

Rābi'a was also one of the first to teach the doctrine of disinterested love of God. This was a new conception to many of her fellow mystics who, for the most part, served God in the hope of eternal reward or in fear of eternal punishment. There are a number of stories about Rābi'a on the subject. One of her prayers goes as follows: 'O God, if I worship Thee for fear of Hell, burn me in Hell, and if I worship Thee in hope of Paradise, exclude me from Paradise; but if I worship Thee for Thy own sake, grudge me not Thy everlasting beauty.'

Poetic activity, though not essentially a mystical phenomenon, is observed in many mystics. There are many mystic poetesses, for example, the Turkish poetess Sidqi of the seventeenth century. We may consider poetry a form of contribution both to the exposition and the rituals of mysticism.

Women mystics, however, have not founded any one of the main orders, nor do they feature in any of the genealogies of the orders. There are two types of genealogies, the first one shows the chain of saints who handed instructions to the founder of the order. Usually this chain goes back through 'Alī to the Prophet. This is a nominal sign of the order's respectability *vis-a-vis* Islam. The second genealogy shows the chain of sheikhs who were at the head of the order and who have transmitted the blessed influence of the original founder to later generations. It seems that no woman appears in this chain in any of the main Sufi orders.

In summary and conclusion it may be said that the mystic approach gave scope to men and women alike, whereas the ranks of orthodox Islam were closed to women. Qualitatively there is no difference between male or female mystics, both were revered alike and to both were attributed miracles. Regardless of origin, anyone could become a mystic. Women could take part in the organizational aspect of mystical life. There were retreats for women and these retreats were run by women. Quantitatively, however, there was a difference between men and women mystics. In the biographies of saints considerably fewer women saints are mentioned than men saints; for example 'Attār mentions only one woman saint as opposed to 71 men saints. In reality, too, there must have been fewer women than men who took up the Sufi path. Again from a quantitative point of view, there were fewer retreats for women than men. Women are not included in the genealogies of the main orders.

'Attār relates the anecdote concerning Rābi'a:

> A party of men once visited her to put her to the test, desiring to catch her out in an unguarded utterance.

'All the virtues have been scattered upon the heads of men,' they said. 'The crown of prophethood has been placed on men's heads. The belt of nobility has been fastened around men's waists. No woman has ever been a prophet.' 'All that is true,' Rābi'a replied. 'But egoism and self-worship and "I am your Lord, the Most High" have never sprung from a woman's breast. No woman has ever been a hermaphrodite. All these things have been the speciality of men.'

Index